Reason and Its Others:
Italy, Spain, and the New World

HISPANIC ISSUES • VOLUME 32

Reason and Its Others:
Italy, Spain, and the New World

David Castillo

AND

Massimo Lollini

EDITORS

Vanderbilt University Press
NASHVILLE, TENNESSEE
2006

© 2006 Vanderbilt University Press
All rights reserved
First Edition 2006

This book is printed on acid-free paper.

The editors gratefully acknowledge assistance from the College of Liberal Arts and the Department of Spanish and Portuguese Studies at the University of Minnesota.

The complete list of volumes in the Hispanic Issues series begins on page 357.

Library of Congress Cataloging-in-Publication Data

Reason and its others : Italy, Spain, and the New World / David Castillo and Massimo Lollini, editors.—1st ed.
p. cm.—(Hispanic issues)
Includes bibliographical references and index.
ISBN 0-8265-1544-4 (cloth : alk. paper)
ISBN 0-8265-1545-2 (pbk. : alk. paper)
1. Spanish literature—Classical period, 1500–1700—History and criticism.
2. Spain—Intellectual life—1516–1700.
3. Baroque literature—History and criticism.
4. Italian literature—16th century—History and criticism.
5. Italian literature—17th century—History and criticism.
6. Italy—Intellectual life—1559–1789.
7. Latin America—Intellectual life—16th century.
I. Castillo, David R., 1967- II. Lollini, Massimo, 1954-
PQ6064.R43 2006
809'.911—dc22
2006023520

HISPANIC ISSUES

Nicholas Spadaccini
Editor-in-Chief

Antonio Ramos-Gascón and Jenaro Talens
General Editors

Nelsy Echávez-Solano and Luis Martín-Estudillo
Associate Editors

Fernando Ordóñez and Eric Dickey
Assistant Editors

*Advisory Board/Editorial Board
Rolena Adorno (Yale University)
David Castillo (University at Buffalo)
Jaime Concha (University of California, San Diego)
Tom Conley (Harvard University)
Eduardo Forastieri-Braschi (Universidad de Puerto Rico, Río Piedras)
David W. Foster (Arizona State University)
Edward Friedman (Vanderbilt University)
Wlad Godzich (University of California, Santa Cruz)
*Carol A. Klee (University of Minnesota)
Antonio Gómez-Moriana (Université de Montréal)
Hans Ulrich Gumbrecht (Stanford University)
Javier Herrero (University of Virginia)
*René Jara (University of Minnesota)
Susan Kirkpatrick (University of California, San Diego)
Eukene Lacarra Lanz (Universidad del País Vasco)
Tom Lewis (University of Iowa)
Jorge Lozano (Universidad Complutense de Madrid)
Walter D. Mignolo (Duke University)
*Louise Mirrer (The New-York Historical Society)
Alberto Moreiras (Duke University)
Bradley Nelson (Concordia University)
Michael Nerlich (Université Blaise Pascal)
Luis A. Ramos-García (University of Minnesota)
Iris M. Zavala (UNESCO, Barcelona)
Santos Zunzunegui (Universidad del País Vasco)

Contents

Introduction: Reason and Its Others in Early Modernity
(A View from the South)
David Castillo and Massimo Lollini   ix

PART I
Of Walls and Windows:
Containment Machines and the Drive Towards the Unknown

1   The Telescope in the Baroque Imagination
      Andrea Battistini   3

2   Descartes in Naples: The Reception of *Passions de l'âme*
      Silvia Contarini   39

3   Fernando de Herrera Invented the Internet: Technologies
      of Self-Containment in the Early Modern Sonnet
      Leah Middlebrook   61

4   A Ritual Practice for Modernity:
      Baltasar Gracián's Organized Body of Taste
      Bradley Nelson   79

5   An Unreasonable Journey? The Place of Europe and
      Italy in Francesco Negri's *Viaggio settentrionale*
      Nathalie Hester   101

6   Baroque Sapphic Poetry: A Feminist Road Not Taken
      Dianne Dugaw and Amanda Powell   123

PART II
Of Houses and Cities:
Early Modern Spaces and the Aporias of Baroque Reason

7   The Foreigner and the Citizen: A Dialogue
      on Good Government in Spanish Naples
      John A. Marino   145

| 8 | The Baroque Public Sphere
William Childers | 165 |

| 9 | Reason's Baroque House (Cervantes, Master Architect)
William Egginton | 186 |

| 10 | Spanish Mannerist Detours in the Mapping of Reason: Around Cervantes' *Novelas Ejemplares*
Julio Baena | 204 |

| 11 | The Genealogy of the Sublime in the Aesthetics of the Spanish Baroque
Anthony J. Cascardi | 221 |

PART III
The West Wing: America and the Frontiers of Reason

| 12 | Sacrificial Politics in the Spanish Colonies
Fernando R. de la Flor | 243 |

| 13 | Bartolomé de las Casas on Imperial Ethics and the Use of Force
George Mariscal | 259 |

| 14 | Imperialism and Anthropophagy in Early Modern Spanish Tragedy: The Unthought Known
Margaret Greer | 279 |

| 15 | Reason and Utopia at the Imperial Borders: Modernity/Coloniality in the Jesuits' Reducciones in Paraguay
Fernando Ordoñez | 296 |

| 16 | Universal History: Vico's *New Science* between Antiquarians and Ethnographers
Giuseppe Mazzotta | 316 |

Afterword: Reasoning the Other
Luis Martín-Estudillo and Nicholas Spadaccini — 331

Contributors — 341

Index — 347

◆ Introduction:
Reason and Its Others in Early Modernity
(A View from the South)

David Castillo and Massimo Lollini

> ... denunciation of what is currently called reason
> is the greatest service reason can render.
> —Max Horkheimer, *Eclipse of Reason*

> The principle of immanence, the explanation of every event as repetition, that
> the Enlightenment upholds against mythic imagination, is the principle of
> myth itself [...] The dualization of nature as appearance and sequence, effort
> and power, which first makes possible both myth and science, originates in
> human fear, the expression of which becomes explanation.
> —Theodor Adorno and Max Horkheimer, *Dialectic of the The Enlightenment*

There is little doubt that the twentieth century will be remembered for the unprecedented display of violence caused by the rise of fascism and Nazism and the tragic events of World War II. The traumatic nature of these events was intensified by the fact that such monstrous displays of human cruelty would have originated on European soil. The old continent that had given birth to the high ideals of western reason and created a form of discourse that proudly told the story (Universal History) was now forced to confront its own monstrous face. What went wrong in the crib of modern culture at the very epicenter of Western civilization? This is a question that History and its brethren in the Humanities and Social Sciences have been mulling over for the past half century. While very different answers have been attempted, the question still looms large at the dawn of the twenty-first century.

To be sure, the assumption that fascism and Nazism are historical anomalies in no way connected to the forces of progress and reason seems to permeate much of the western political and educational establishments, as well as the news media. Yet, many intellectuals from Antonio Gramsci and Walter Benjamin, to Theodor Adorno and Max Horkheimer, to Jacques Derrida and Michel Foucault, among others, have been less willing to exonerate the legacy of the Enlightenment. In following their lead, we could say that the violent history of the twentieth century may be seen as tragic confirmation of the truth of Goya's nightmarish warning that "el sueño de la razón produce monstruos" (the dream of reason produces monsters).

The new century has brought with it new forms of terror that threaten the stability of the West from the outside. Clearly, politically and religiously inspired terrorism is not new; what may be new is its direct impact at the very heart of the Western world: New York City, September 11, 2001. Among the most notoriously controversial statements made in the immediate aftermath of the terrorist attacks, one would have to recall the widely quoted interview of Jerry Falwell conducted by Pat Robertson on the *700 Club*, in which the two religious leaders appeared to agree that the horror of September 11 was God's way of punishing the United States for its tolerance of liberals, feminists, gays, and lesbians. While most people would not consider this a serious assessment of the situation, the shocking mass killings of 9/11 left us with a renewed sense of urgency to understand the reasons behind the unreason.

To add to the complexity of the issues, widely circulated assumptions that aid in the justification of the military and political programs associated with the "war on terror," including the suggestion that "they hate us for our progress" or that "they hate us for our freedom," coexist in the current political climate with unambiguous administrative pronouncements against gay marriage and stem cell research and presidential calls to downplay or altogether exclude the theory of evolution from the school curriculum in favor of the "intelligent design theory."

Beyond the specific individual explanations of anti-U.S. or anti-western terrorism and the sectarian political agendas that sometimes inspire them, what interests us here is the fact that—as with the long-lived debates on fascism and Nazism—the forces and ideals of reason find themselves, once again, in the eye of the storm. In particular, we are thinking of the "western belief" in the liberating potential of scientific reason and technological progress, and the assumption that western capitalism is the economic system and de facto world order that most effectively safeguards the universal human rights to freedom and equality.

These beliefs have been traced back to the "age of exploration" and the philosophical, scientific, and political developments of seventeenth century Europe, more precisely Northern or Oceanic Europe. Within the corpus of western history, the 1500s and 1600s have often been painted in bright colors as the dawn of a brave new world of ever-expanding horizons. Yet, alternative fields of knowledge, from postcolonial studies to cultural materialism to eco-feminism, have uncovered fundamental flaws and contradictions in the foundational principles and beliefs of the nascent "modern episteme" (to use the term coined by Foucault).

Carolyn Merchant's highly controversial book *The Death of Nature* deserves a special place among early offerings within the emerging field of ecofeminism. Contrary to the traditional western view that instrumental reason holds the promise of human liberation, Merchant argues that the constitutive principles of modernity—beginning with scientific and instrumental reason—and the capitalist structures that have since fostered them resulted in new and more insidious modes of exploitation. The book reveals shocking similarities between the scientific terminology and analytical methodologies proposed by the "founding fathers" of modernity (Descartes, Bacon, Hobbes) and the language and methods employed in inquisitorial interrogations and witch trials.

If Merchant takes as her point of departure the early modern push towards controlling women and nature in the name of scientific reason and technological progress, others focus on the connection between modern reason and the institutional control of the imaginary (Costa Lima), and most significantly, the control of space. Thus, for José Monleón modern reason imposes exploitative and alienating center-periphery dialectics onto the urban landscape of the enlightened city. Similarly, Manuel Aguirre has focused on the increasingly fortified walls that separate the spaces of Reason from those of Unreason in western culture. He traces these dynamics back to the success of Judeo-Christian theology and dogma to the detriment of other ancient notions (including the Celtic belief system) that may have allowed for continued and more productive forms of interaction between the two realms.

Aguirre's provocative argument hinges on the paradoxical idea that, for all its outward movement toward infinity and its inspiring imagery of expansive horizons, modern western thought is fundamentally hampered by an entropic desire to realize the most dangerous dream ever conceived by Reason: the perfectly secure citadel, i.e., "the closed space." In his contribution to this volume, Andrea Battistini suggests that the modern fear of open spaces is a byproduct of the scientific revolution: "human minds were upset by the melancholic sensation that the Earth was deprived of its ancient centrality, lost in the infinite spaces that lacked secure points of reference as there no longer existed anything motionless in the universe [. . .] The new science had released an anguished fear of open spaces" (Battistini).

According to Aguirre, the more we try to protect our modern citadels of reason from the forces of Unreason, the more vulnerable we become to any potential or imagined threats from the outside world. The perfectly "closed space" is in fact the impossible ideal evoked in Cervantes' exemplary novel *El celoso extremeño*. As William Egginton points out below, Carrizales' plan is to erect the ultimate fortress in order to protect his honor and social identity against any potential outside threats. The result is a prison-house with two sets of walls that disallow direct—potentially defiling—communication between the inside space inhabited by his virgin wife and the outside world. Of course, in the novelistic world of Cervantes, the self-protecting enclosures that guarantee the stability of our social identity do not hold up well. This is clearly the case here, as the protagonist's "greatest fear is realized, and his prize possession, the virgin child he calls his wife, is spoiled" (Egginton).

While Egginton thinks of the Cervantine distrust for containers as a characteristic of what he calls the "baroque minor strategy," Julio Baena prefers to link it to Mannerism, which he defines as "a conflict of reason" in his discussion of *Don Quixote* and the *Exemplary Novels* in this volume. Baena's suggestion is that Cervantes resists the self-enclosing proposition of a narrowing conception of Reason in his search for holes and escape routes. This would be a characteristic that Cervantes would share with Mannerist poets—Góngora in particular—artists and musicians, such as El Greco and Victoria, and also with the major figures of Spanish mysticism—especially Teresa de Avila and Juan de la Cruz.

Leah Middlebrook deals with the paradoxes of containments and communication technologies in her account of the genesis and evolution of the early modern sonnet from Boscán to Herrera and into the baroque period. Middlebrook argues that the sonnet was originally conceived as a potential "citadel of reason" and model of restraint, even as it would eventually become a refuge for stylistic affect and representational excess. For his part, Anthony Cascardi discusses the "aesthetic excesses" of the Baroque, which he views as expressions of a Southern or Mediterranean sublime that would have anticipated many of the concerns and aesthetic tendencies of the Northern European sublime of the eighteenth century. He focuses on the Mediterranean fixation with astonishment as an "excess of wonder" that, in the eyes of René Descartes, would need to be restrained by reason.

Baroque culture would thus seem capable of comprehending rationalism as well as the type of "excessive wonder" contemptuously evoked by Descartes. This situation is, in fact, not new in the history of Mediterranean western culture; on the contrary, it can be traced back to the origins of Greek literature and philosophy. E. R. Dodds has shown that unwise and unaccountable behavior in Homer's *Iliad* is not typically seen as an expression of personal or individual choice, but rather as a state of mind, i.e., a partial or temporary insanity that can be ascribed to external "daemonic" agencies (2). In his apology for stealing

Achilles' mistress, for example, an act that he conceived as a form of compensation for the loss of his own, Agamemnon refuses to accept personal responsibility for actions that were inspired by the divine forces of unbound passion and madness (see Dodds).

There are indeed numerous passages in the work of Homer where erratic or "unreasonable" behavior is attributed to supernatural agencies. This is not to deny or downplay the central role of reason in Ancient Greek culture. Greek philosophy often conceives "its others" as irrational forces that resist or oppose the unifying project of reason. The following is a paradigmatic example from Plato's *Timaeus*: "And [man] would have no rest from these toilsome transformations until he had dragged that massive accretion of fire-water-air-earth into conformity with the revolution of the Same and uniform within him, and so subdued that turbulent, irrational mass by means of reason" (42c–42d). Nevertheless, one should keep in mind that the totalizing drive of reason in classical Greek philosophy was counterbalanced by an acute sense of the limits of philosophical discourse. Suffice it here to mention Socratic irony as an endless search for rational truth—something that admittedly man cannot fully possess—and the Platonic notion of *theia mania* (divine madness) as a legitimate irrational mode of knowledge, which in *Phaedrus* is said to be available to the lover, the poet, the prophet, and the mystic (242d–257b).

Rational and philosophical discourse within Greek culture was also counterbalanced by tragedy, which staged the fragility of man's knowledge and the radical vulnerability of human life, always subject to uncontrollable forces, from fate to excessive passions and death. Thus, the "irrational" side of Greek culture did not dissolve with the arrival of the classical period of the fifth century B.C., which is usually seen as the apex of Greek philosophy, i.e., the age of reason that was supposed to bring freedom from the myths of the past. Moreover, the rationality of the classical period did not endure, but was in fact succeeded in the Hellenistic period by an eruption of enthusiasm for alchemy, magical medicine, and astrology. The world of magic—as ethnographer Ernesto De Martino discovered while undertaking his research in Southern Italy—cannot be relegated to the past of human civilization. Instead it needs to be acknowledged as one of the key sources of reason.

The dialectic of reason and unreason would persist in Renaissance culture, even at the core of the humanist project. A good example is the work of Giovanni Pico della Mirandola whose view of humanity rests on a conception of man as a "creature of indeterminate image," endowed with "free will" and placed by God at the center of the world (6–7). According to this view, human beings would be capable of transforming in infinite ways insofar as God bestowed upon them the seeds of every form of life (8). Consequently, reason and unreason would not be considered separate realms in Pico della Mirandola's system; rather, they would represent different sides of our common humanity. Most fittingly, Pico's manifesto, the *Oration on the Dignity of Man* (Oratio De Hominis Dignitate), is a formidable attempt at creating a synthesis of Christianity, Platonism, Aristotelianism, and the Jewish cabbala.

In Spain, different versions of this chameleon-like humanity posited by Pico della Mirandola and other humanists would come to life in vivid colors in works such as Fernando de Rojas' *La Celestina* and especially the anonymous *Lazarillo de Tormes*. Celestina and Lazarillo inhabit a fundamentally secular world ("mundo desdivinizado," as Maravall puts it in *El mundo social de la Celestina*) where rationally measured "interests" cannot be separated from the murky waters of passion and desire. In this type of urban landscape, protean figures, such as the paradigmatic *pícaro*, deploy complex techniques of control and manipulation of appearances, emotions, and social codes in pursuit of material success. These works open up oblique views that reveal the centrality of unreason to all aspects of human and civic life.

Hence, it seems fair to say that the philosophical and literary culture of the Renaissance incorporated its own "crisis of reason." From this perspective, the relatively recent (or recently proclaimed) crisis of humanist reason may be seen as the result of an ideological construction that has run its full course. The nineteenth-century view of the work of Leon Battista Alberti would be a case in point. As one of the leading figures of Italian Humanism, Alberti is presented in Jacob Burkhardt's *The Civilization of the Renaissance in Italy* (1867) as the exemplary *uomo universale* or Renaissance man, who would master all aspects of Renaissance culture. Yet, Burkhardt silences a significant part of Alberti's work that seems to go against his own narrowly defined rationalistic views. Thus, in the Latin dialogue "Somnium" from his *Intercoenales* (1439), Alberti stages the role of folly and insanity in human life. Libripeda, the protagonist of this dialogue, narrates his journey through the world of dreams and dreamers where he would be able to find everything that human beings had lost over time—everything except insanity, which is said to have never abandoned the human world and its civil institutions.

The contrast between the image of Alberti as paradigmatic *uomo universale*, supremely confident in man's rational powers, and the skeptical and self-mocking intellectual emerging in the *Intercoenales* points in the direction of a continued interaction between reason and unreason which has to be taken into consideration as we reexamine the legacy of Humanism and Renaissance culture. Though often overlooked in traditional interpretations, the themes of folly and madness are at the core of humanist thought and were to take center stage in seminal expressions of Renaissance culture such as Erasmus' *Praise of Folly* (1509) and Ariosto's *Orlando furioso* (1532).

To be sure, before the birth of the mental hospital in the seventeenth century, folly and madness were not treated as pathological exceptions. In fact, they had become central metaphors for the representation of human weakness, ignorance, and insecurity. Moreover, the forces of madness and folly had encompassed cognitive functions that worked to counterbalance and complement those of reason. Erasmus praises folly as a necessary component of the rational process that contributes to our appreciation of the complexity of human life. According to this view, folly would help us recognize the limits and flaws of established certainties.

In *Orlando furioso*, Ariosto takes this notion a step further in his insightful discussion of the limits of human knowledge. Orlando's folly, which resulted from unsatisfied desire and jealous love, is apparent in his lack of self-restraint. Ariosto seems to suggest that folly is the result of a lack of rational control and the resulting loss of oneself (XXIV, 1–2). Yet, Orlando's folly does not signal the crisis of humanistic reason as has been suggested; rather, Orlando's "excesses" are within the realm of possibilities of human nature as conceived by Humanism. Orlando's wisdom is eventually found on the moon, in a valley where—as it happened in Alberti's *Somnium*—one could find everything that had been lost on Earth—everything but folly itself, which is fundamentally earthbound. The implication of this central episode (XXXIV) is that while human wisdom may indeed "go to the moon," folly, or foolishness, is always found on Earth as a constitutive part of human nature. Thus, in the humanistic works of Alberti and Ariosto, as in Erasmus' *Praise*, folly is tied to disillusionment (or *desengaño*, to use the telling Spanish expression), and thus, it has the power to reveal the endless contradictions of the human soul and our inability to resolve them.

The rhetoric of modern science that begins to emerge in the seventeenth century will not put an end to the dialectics of reason and its others, as Andrea Battistini effectively shows in his contribution. Galileo's telescopic observations of the moon establish a new scientific paradigm founded on instrumental science. His carefully recorded lunar exploration shatters unified and finite conceptions of the cosmos, introducing the principle of chaos in scientific research and denying long-lived hierarchies of sacred and profane spaces. Significantly, Galileo's text is marked by a fundamentally baroque tension between the scientific goal of unperturbed objectivism and the stylistic affect of its prose. These stylistic "excesses" and the anxious pathos that is revealed in Galileo's reporting may in fact be tied to the aesthetics of a "baroque or Mediterranean sublime" (as posited by Cascardi in this volume).

The coolness and detachment introduced by the principle of scientific certitude—which is based on the notion that the book of nature is written in the language of mathematics—contrasts with the pathos and ancestral anguish with which the human mind gazes at the infinite universe first announced in the speculations of Giordano Bruno. Thus, for all its groundbreaking scientific methodology, Galileo's broad philosophical investigation is not devoid of fantasy and wonder. As Battistini writes, "next to reason, fantasy (which was also rising and mobile), acquired a totally unforeseen positivity, especially when the scientist, facing the infiniteness of the universe, could at any step collide with the unexpected."

While Galileo's discoveries drastically changed the way travelers and explorers would look at the world, it is also interesting to note that the language of the scientific revolution borrows metaphors of the journey from the emerging genre of travel writing. As Norman Doiron argues—and Nathalie Hester reminds us below—Cartesian philosophy is clearly influenced by the travel narrative approach to *scientia* in privileging experience over *autoritas*, and thus, moving readers away from the authorities of Classical Antiquity and toward the direct experience of "the book of the world." Hester studies Francesco Negri's *Viaggio settentrionale*, which is exemplary of the contradictory nature of early modern approaches to scientific exploration. Standing at the crossroads of different explorative methodologies that circulated concurrently in the seventeenth century, the *Viaggio settentrionale* shows that "competing ways of categorizing knowledge could coexist in a single work without compromising the validity or credibility of its representation of reality" (Hester). The coexistence of different forms of knowledge and discourse had been a distinctive feature of geographical explorations since the time of Columbus's first voyage. One can find, for example, even as late as the *Tratado descriptivo do Brasil em 1587* by Gabriel Soares de Sousa, geographical and ethnographic accounts that attribute the Amerindians' lack of law and proper monarchical rule to the absence of the letters *L* and *R* in their language (Soares de Sousa 66).

If the geographical discoveries of the period ripped the boundaries of the finite Mediterranean world establishing a new and chaotic "Oceanic infinitude," the scientific revolution led by Galileo and Descartes shattered the ordered and finite cosmos of Antiquity replacing it with the infinite mathematical universe of modern science. The essays in this volume testify to the profound and pervasive consequences of this double spatial revolution, which is said to have created favorable conditions for the establishment of the oceanic and technological primacy of the English Empire (see Carl Schmitt), while relegating the Mediterranean world to a peripheral role. The collection suggests that the Mediterranean contexts represented here by the products of early modern Italian and Spanish culture provide ample opportunities to reexamine the legacy of modern western rationality from a "southern perspective."

Thus, Giuseppe Mazzotta shows how Vico's *New Science* reflects a theological universality that had been tested by New World ethnographers such as Acosta and Oviedo. Drawing primarily on Cicero's principles of natural law and on the metaphysical perspectives provided by Suarez's and Grotius' respective inquiries into the nature of international law, Vico explores the possibility of developing a new universal history on the basis of individual and singular realities. At the heart of Vico's view of history, theology, and poetics, one can find an inclusive conception of reason that re-incorporates the realm of imagination (*universali fantastici*). His notion of "poetic imagination" allows him to recognize the importance of the singularities out of which universality is created.

In her contribution, Silvia Contarini discusses Vico's thought in the context of the eighteenth-century debates stirred in Naples by the reception of Descartes. Contarini shows that Vico's *De ratione* contradicts the Cartesian distinction between the *sapienti*, who would operate following "subtle reasoning," and the common people, who are said to be absorbed in disorderly emotions. This view runs counter to the moralistic digressions that fill the pages of Capaccio's description of the marvels of Naples in *Il Forastiero*. John Marino notes (In this volume) that within the boundaries of Capaccio's predicated "reason of state," there is actually no place for the "unreason" of the common people. Despite the seemingly self-referential title of Capaccio's narrative, the true foreign entity here is the Neapolitan people: "the other in Spanish Naples was not so much the lying foreign historian or the curious foreign visitor out to see the world, but rather the resident commoners—the *popolo* and plebs—whose 'unfaithfulness' and 'un-reason' challenged noble governance and authority" (Marino).

By contrast, Vico's own "Neapolitan" take on the subject of reason would challenge this type of distinction between reason and unreason by insisting on the fragility and finitude of all human knowledge, regardless of its social origins. In his *Scienza nuova*, for example, Vico talks about a lost or hidden world that lurks beneath centuries of human culture. He argues that the genealogy of human reason and culture is ultimately rooted in this submerged world of myths and obscure passions. To put it plainly, the Neapolitan thinker opposes Cartesian rationalism calling into question reason's proclaimed mastery over passion and myth (see Contarini).

Vico's thought fits well within José Antonio Maravall's conceptualization of the baroque mentality. According to Maravall, baroque authors conceive the world as a succession of individual, changing phenomena, while simultaneously asserting their deep-seated belief in a universe ruled by essentially uniform and eternal laws. While this observation may provide important insights into the maddening paradoxes of well-known baroque texts such as Calderón's *La vida es sueño*, Cervantes' *Persiles,* and Gracian's *Criticón*, it could also help us interpret the work of other neglected or relatively overlooked authors such as Céspedes y Menéses, María de Zayas, and Cristóbal Lozano. They all paint providentialist landscapes where the chain of causes can be traced back to the supreme will in accordance with the logic of Christian reason. Yet, certain human actions are sometimes attributed to the intervention of unexplained dark powers and to secular notions of destiny and/or fortune.

In Zayas's *Desengaños amorosos*, for example, the cruel and cold-blooded torture, victimization and killing of women that are the trademark of the collection are invariably attributed to the malice of men, and also to a dark sense of human destiny reminiscent of the ancient tragedy, as well as to the blind arbitrariness of fortune (*la fortuna*). When all is said and done, however, Providence reappears to transform the violated bodies of the victims into beautified corpses. By virtue of this sudden turn of events, or rather, this turn of the frame, the tragic course of these women's lives and their violent destiny acquire a new spiritual significance as we readjust the lens to see things from the proper providentialist perspective. As the horridly mutilated bodies of the victims turn into beautified corpses that show the signs of saintliness and grace, the episodes acquire martyrological meaning (see Greer, *María de Zayas*). And yet, previous frames linger, especially the "militant frame" that denounces masculine and institutional violence against women. In the end, we are left with a double or multiple image of the same cadaver, not unlike the anamorphic devices evoked by Baena in his discussion of Mannerist aesthetics.

Perhaps no author or thinker represents the paradoxes of baroque culture better than the Jesuit moralist Baltasar Gracián. As Bradley Nelson explains below, Gracián has been portrayed as a spokesman for Counter Reformation ideology as well as the greatest proponent of "baroque rationalism" (Maravall 1984). Nelson devotes much of his essay to a reexamination of this apparent dichotomy of Gracián's thought in light of Catherine Bell's work on ritual theory (Catherine Bell). Nelson rightfully observes that mythical beliefs and ritual practices do not disappear with the advent of modern rationalism. Rather, myth and ritual are at the heart of the modern experience of the world. Hence, the modernity of Gracián's thought "does not emerge by disentangling it from the ritual residue of the Baroque; rather, ritualization is the only way we can approach the lessons that baroque culture holds for modernity" (Nelson).

Along the same lines, William Childers looks at Gracián as the theorist of "the baroque public sphere," which he defines as "a hybrid, compromise formation, made up of a blending of earlier and later practices, technologies, and social structures." Childers argues that Gracián's central insight into the functioning of the baroque public sphere is "always act as though you are being observed" (obrar siempre como a vista) (aphorism 297 in *Oráculo manual*), which shows that the Jesuit is aware of the fact that "there simply is no private self from which the gaze of the other is excluded" (Childers). The echoes of the Lacanian concept of the gaze here suggest that Gracián's insight may be valid to describe a dimension of the modern experience that goes well beyond the historically defined boundaries of the baroque period.

The notorious non-transparency of baroque performativity may remind us of the truth behind the illusory transparency of the bourgeois public sphere, arguably one of the most pervasive and enduring ideological constructs of the Enlightenment. As Childers puts it, "modern bourgeois culture's pretense of disinterested, rational debate was itself a performance, despite which rumors reached the metropolis that what was happening in the colonies was not altogether pretty. Unfortunately, that pretense is still with us, though the cynicism of the performance shows through more plainly than it used to."

George Mariscal draws a similar connection between past and present cultural and political pretenses in his discussion of the highly publicized debates of Valladolid concerning the Christian definition of the "just war" as a means to facilitate the conversion of the Amerindians. Against the humanist view championed by Las Casas, who vehemently denounces the illegitimacy of the Spanish military operations in America, Sepúlveda would argue that Christian nations have the moral obligation to employ all means at their disposal, including military force, in their efforts to convert and civilize the Amerindians. The implication here, as Mariscal rightfully points out, is that the authority to use force "resided in the colonizer's superior system of values and form of government." This observation allows him to draw a direct parallel between the Imperial notion that Spain was a "vehicle for God's work" and the assumptions behind the presidential speech of the 2003 State of the Union Address: "Americans are a free people, who know that freedom is the right of every person and the future of every nation. The liberty we prize is not America's gift to the world; it is God's gift to humanity" (quoted by Mariscal).

Several essays in this volume focus on the subject of colonial aggression and its impact in the context of Spanish colonialism in the New World. We could say that colonial America becomes the place where Western culture and civilization come face to face with the unreason of reason. Here, millenarian utopias and Christian dreams of universal deliverance meet traumatically with the technologies of colonization precipitating the crisis and ultimate collapse of evangelical reason. As Fernando R. de la Flor argues below, the failure of the expansionistic logic of evangelical reason will lead to attitudes of cynical dissimulation as well as mystical and eremitic escapisms. As missionary discourse turns away from the egalitarian utopias of the Christian ethos, a new nightmarish vision begins to emerge, "a type of sinister allegorical story about a 'fallen' world devoid of the possibility of redemption in which a humanity deprived of utopias and ideals [. . .] awaits the end of all suffering" (de la Flor).

By the end of the sixteenth century, we are a long way away from the utopian images of America as a new dawn for humanity. Instead, the New World invented by the dream of reason turns into a desolate landscape plagued by illness and devastation. In this context, the shining image of Spain as the messenger nation that delivers "God's gift to humanity" gives way to a far darker picture of an Empire that devours its own. This is precisely the focus of Margaret Greer's reinterpretation of Cervantes' tragedy *La destrucción de Numancia* and Tirso's *Las Amazonas* in light of their common treatment of the ancient motif of the anthropophagi, which Greer relates to Christopher Bollas's concept of the "unthought known." Her suggestion here is that whereas the *Numancia* foregrounds Spain's dual historical role, first as victim of the Roman Empire and then as Imperial victimizer, "the unthought known figured in Tirso's play is that of an imperial Spain that devours their own along with its nameless indigenous victims in Peru" (Greer).

Yet, some New World utopias seem to endure even in the midst of Imperial devastation. According to Fernando Ordoñez, the resilience of the Jesuit utopia is apparent in the writings of missionary Antonio Ruiz de Montoya. Ordoñez notes that in the colonial borderlands of Paraguay, the Jesuits established a utopian community that may be seen as an alternative project of "modernization." Despite its ultimate failure, this type of residual utopian thinking is emblematic of the "roads not taken' or abandoned in the race toward the establishment of our Atlantic or Oceanic version of modernity. Ordoñez's contention is that in the case of the Jesuit *reducciones* of Paraguay, this road not taken amounts to an "other' or alternative modernity informed by a different—more inclusive and respectful—view of otherness.

Dianne Dugaw and Amanda Powell explore a different "road not taken": a Sapphic utopia that is conceived, and to some extent realized, in the language of baroque poetry. This essentially homoerotic literature written by women would flourish in aristocratic and Catholic contexts, everywhere from Italy, Spain, France, and the Netherlands and into the heart of the British Empire, even as the nascent ideology of bourgeois protestant capitalism establishes its primacy over the new Oceanic world. Dugaw and Powell see this Sapphic poetry as an expression of a utopian feminism that predates "the heterosexual imperative" established by the bourgeois model of gender construction. They note that despite its residual aristocratism, baroque Sapphic poetry addresses important issues in our postmodern context, beginning with "its championing of women's passions and reasons together" (Dugaw and Powell).

There is a certain utopian drive in this gesture of looking back at an earlier time, which is also our time, in search of alternative ways of thinking and truncated paths. This utopian drive—which may be linked to the critic's own passions, frustrations, and hopes—is in fact germane to our collection of essays. We may think of it as a sense of what could have been and what might still be. Thus, the present volume looks at Mediterranean culture in the Age of Exploration as a reminder of the unreason of reason. This is indeed where baroque (un)reason meets the (post)enlightened sublime (Cascardi), and perhaps postmodern skepticism as well. Not surprisingly, some have come to see the Baroque as "the truth of modernity," i.e., the stain in the picture that allows us to look at high modernity from a different, more revealing angle (to use, once again, the anamorphic trope).

From this perspective, the internal conflicts that Maravall highlighted in the work of major baroque figures such as Galileo, Vico, and Gracián may be seen as symptomatic of the resilience of the western Mediterranean worldview as it confronts the infinitude of the modern Oceanic situation. Vico's appeal to the universal "light of metaphysics," for example, goes hand in hand with the recognition of the particularities of the cultures of the New World, while his search for the eternal laws of human civilization coexists complementarily with his understanding of the contingency and artificiality of human cultures. These conflicts are at heart of baroque rationalism, which is deeply marked by an irrepressible nostalgia for the old, substantive, living nature, and a longing for the immediacy of the numinous experience in a world scarred by the absence of the Absolute.

An exemplary allegory of the resilient fragility of baroque culture can be found in Vincenzo Consolo's commentary on the destruction and rebirth of southern Sicily in "The Rebirth of the Val di Noto." Consolo describes the great devastation caused by the earthquake that in January of 1693 destroyed Catania, Siracusa, Ragusa, Modica, and other villages of the Val di Noto. The level of destruction reached the magnitude of an apocalyptic event that dragged an entire civilization back to a pre-historical time. Yet, in a few years the people of the Val di Noto would rebuild their cities, turning the horror of destruction into a spectacle of architectural beauty. The result of this back-and-forth oscillation between primal nature and historical temporality is said to have given birth to the paradigmatic Sicilian Baroque. Focusing on the uniqueness of this style, Consolo interprets it as a means to give stability and order to a region that is always facing the danger of chaos and destruction. Like a beautiful monument built in a desert or a flower that grows on a Volcano, Sicilian Baroque architecture is permeated by an overwhelming sense of instability and precariousness, accompanied by an irrational superabundance of decorative elements. It represents the radical exposure of European reason to its "pathological" Mediterranean roots, where it can rediscover its "natural" finitude.

Some time ago Paul Hazard lamented that Europe had not listened more attentively to Giambattista Vico. He suggested that if we had let ourselves be guided by Vico's insights into the unreason of reason "nos ancêtres du XVIIIe siècle n'auraient pas cru que tout ce qui était clair était vrai; mais au contraire que 'la clarté est le vice de la raison humaine plutôt que sa vertue,' parce qu'une idée claire est une idée finie. Ils n'auraient pas cru que la raison était notre faculté première, mai au contraire l'imagination" (Hazard 1963 43) (our eighteenth-century ancestors would not have believed that all that was clear was true; but on the contrary that "clarity is the vice of human reason rather than its virtue," because a clear idea is a finite idea. They would not have believed that reason was our first faculty, but on the contrary that imagination was). What Hazard writes here about the work of Giambattista Vico seems equally appropriate to describe much of the literature discussed in this volume. The observation may be especially relevant at a time when ideological rigidity and self-righteousness threaten to trample open debate on matters that affect us all. We hope that the essays included in this collection will contribute to keeping the debate alive.

Works Cited

Adorno, Theodor and Max Horkheimer. *Dialectic of the Enlightenment*. New York: Continuum, 1998.
Aguirre, Manuel. *The Closed Space: Horror Literature and Western Symbolism*. Manchester: Manchester University Press, 1990.
Alberti, Leon Battista. *Intercoenales*. Bologna: Pendragon, 2003.
Ariosto, Lodovico, Carlo Muscetta, and Luca Lamberti. *Orlando furioso*. Torino: G. Einaudi, 1968.
Bell, Catherine. *Ritual Theory, Ritual Practice*. Oxford: Oxford University Press, 1992.
Benjamin, Walter. *Illuminations*. Ed. Hanna Arendt. Trans. Harry Zohn. New York: Schocken Books, 1969.
Bruno, Giordano, Giovanni Gentile, and Giovanni Aquilecchia. *Dialoghi Italiani*. Florence: Sansoni, 1972.
Burckhardt, Jacob. *The Civilization of the Renaissance in Italy*. New York: Harper, 1958.
Cacciatore, Giuseppe. *Mediterraneo e cultura europea*. Soveria Mannelli (Catanzaro): Rubbettino, 2003.
Cervantes, Miguel de. *El ingenioso hidalgo don Quixote de la Mancha*. 2 vols. Ed. John Jay Allen. Madrid: Cátedra, 1998.
———. *Novelas ejemplares*. 2 vols. Ed. Harry Sieber. Madrid: Cátedra, 1990.
———. *Los trabajos de Persiles y Sigismunda*. Ed. Carlos Romero Muñoz. Madrid: Cátedra, 1997.
Consolo, Vincenzo, and Giuseppe Leone. *Il Barocco in Sicilia: La Rinascita Del Val Di Noto*. Milan: Bompiani, 1991.
Costa Lima, Luiz. *Control of the Imaginary: Reason and Imagination in Modern Times*. Minneapolis, MN: University of Minnesota Press, 1988.
De Martino, Ernesto. *Magia e civiltà*. Milan: Garzanti, 1976.
Derrida, Jacques. *De la grammatologie*. Paris: Editions de Minuit, 1967.
Descartes, René. *The Philosophical Writings of Descartes*, I. Trans. John Cottingham, Robert Stoothoff, and Dugald Murdoch. Cambridge: Cambridge University Press, 1985.
Dodds, E. R. *The Greeks and the Irrational*. Boston: Beacon Press, 1957.
Dorion, Normand. "L'art de voyager: Pour une définition du récit de voyage à l'époque classique." *Poétique 73* (1988): 83–108.
Erasmus, Desiderius. *The Praise of Folly*. Trans. Clarence H. Miller. New Haven, CT: Yale University Press, 1979.
Foucault, Michel. *The Birth of the Clinic: An Archaeology of Medical Perception*. Trans. A.M. Sheridan Smith. New York: Vintage Books, 1973.
———. *Discipline and Punish*. Trans. Allan Sheridan. New York: Pantheon Books, 1977.
———. *The Order of Things: An Archeology of the Human Sciences*. New York: Vintage Books, 1973.
Galilei, Galileo. *Sidereus Nuncius*, a cura di Andrea Battistini. Letteratura Universale Marsilio. Venice: Marsilio, 2001.

Gracián, Baltasar. *Obras completas*. Madrid: Aguilar, 1944.
Gramsci, Antonio. *Selections from Political Writings*. Ed. and Trans. Quintin Hoare. Minneapolis: University of Minnesota Press, 1978.
Grassi, Ernesto, and Maristella De Panizza Lorch. *Folly and Insanity in Renaissance Literature*. Binghanton, NY: Medieval and Renaissance Texts and Studies, 1986.
Greer, Margaret. *María de Zayas Tells Baroque Tales of Love and the Cruelty of Men*. University Park, PA: Pennsylvania State University Press, 2000.
Hazard, Paul. *The European Mind, 1680–1715*. Trans. J. Lewis May. London: Hollis & Carter, 1953.
———. *La pensés européenne au XVIIIe siècle: De Montesquieu à Lessing*. Paris: Fayard, 1963.
Horkheimer, Max. *Eclipse of Reason*. New York: Continuum Publishing Company, 1974.
Lacan, Jacques. *The Four Fundamental Concepts of Psychoanalysis*. Ed. Jacques Alain Miller. Trans. Alan Sheridan. New York: Norton, 1981.
Maravall, José Antonio. "Antropología y política en el pensamiento de Gracián." *Estudios del pensamiento español. El siglo del Barroco*. 3a Madrid: Ediciones Cultura Hispánica, 1984. 197–222.
———. *La cultura del barroco: Análisis de una estructura histórica*. Barcelona: Ariel, 1975.
———. *El mundo social de La Celestina*. Madrid: Gredos, 1986.
Mazzotta, Giuseppe. *The New Map of the World: The Poetic Philosophy of Giambattista Vico*. Princeton, NJ: Princeton University Press, 1999.
Merchant, Carolyn. *The Death of Nature: Women, Ecology, and the Scientific Revolution*. New York: Harper & Row, 1989.
Monleón, José. *A Specter Is Haunting Europe: A Sociohistorical Approach to the Fantastic*. Princeton, NJ: Princeton University Press, 1990.
Ossola, Carlo. "Métaphore et inventaire de la folie dans la littérature italiennes du XVIe." in *Folie et Déraison à la Renaissance*. Bruxelles: L'Université de Bruxelles, 1976.
Pico della Mirandola, Giovanni. *Oratio De Hominis Dignitate*. Pordenone: Studio Tesi, 1994.
Plato. *Complete Works*. Ed. John M. Cooper. Indianapolis: Hackett Publishing Company, 1997.
Schmitt, Carl. *Land and Sea*. Washington, DC: Plutarch Press, 1997.
Soares de Sousa, Gabriel. *Tratado descriptivo do Brasil em 1587*. São Paulo: Universidade de São Paulo, 1971.
Vico, Giambattista. *Opere*. I Meridiani, a cura di Andrea Battistini. Milan: A. Mondadori, 1990.
Zayas, María de. *Desengaños amorosos*. Ed. Alicia Yllera. Madrid: Cátedra, 1983.

Part I
Of Walls and Windows: Containment Machines and the Drive Towards the Unknown

◆ 1

The Telescope in the Baroque Imagination

Andrea Battistini

(Translated by Chris Picicci)

The Celestial Messenger as *buona novella*

In the frigid winter of 1609, Galileo Galilei made up his mind to spend "la maggior parte delle notti [. . .] più al sereno et al discoperto—che in camera o al fuoco" (X, 302) (the major part of his nights [. . .] in clear and open sky, instead of being in his room or at the fireside)[1] in order to search the skies with his telescope. Galileo was by this point in his life a mature scientist pushing fifty. His experience over the course of many years as a university lecturer in Padua had assured him respected local fame as a professor and mathematician. He was recognized even more in his native Tuscany—an area in which he had continued to maintain contacts during his summer vacations—and in Rome where he still had some friends. Until this point in his life, Galileo had not published any work of great importance—those he had were not considered to be so, neither *La Bilancetta* (The Little Balance), nor the booklet on the *Operazioni del compasso geometrico e militare* (Operations of geometric and military compasses) which was invented by him, nor the subsequent *Difesa contro alle calunnie et imposture di Baldessar Capra* (Defense against false accusations and imposture of Baldestar Capra)—rather, his notoriety was limited to the group of people with which he associated (Wallace). On the other hand, at the moment of Galileo's summons, which occurred in 1592, the Venetian Republic had turned to him because, aside from his scientific capabilities, it was interested in a technician, an engineer, and a skillful constructor of scientific instruments that would contrast his hardworking pragmatism with the metaphysical abstractions of the Aristotelians, led by Cesare Cremonini from the University of Padua. Galileo had specialized in mechanical studies in Pisa and had gradually familiarized himself with the work of Archimedes; he also shared mutual interests with Guidubaldo del Monte. He conformed immediately to the needs set by the city of Venice and was commissioned to work on hydraulic machines to irrigate ground used for agriculture, calipers, projects of fortification, magnets, drills to make screws, compasses, watches, oil lamps, thermoscopes, astrolabes, and solutions to the friction of oars' galleys in water.

The same attention paid to the telescope—an instrument that was not brought to Venice from Holland by chance, but likely by opticians hoping to gain a business opportunity in a foreseeable receptive market—was born from Galileo's familiarity with artisan shops, specifically in this case, the glass-makers of Murano. In this respect, Galileo—in presenting to the Doge of Venice a telescope he had perfected to demonstrate the merit of the then-insurmountable skill with which crystal lenses were smoothed in Venice—insisted from the beginning on the "straordinario benefizio" (extraordinary benefit) and the "giovamento inestimabile" (X, 250–51) (invaluable advantage) that would have been obtainable from that "utile et segnalato trovato" (X, 250–51) (useful and renowned invention), employable on earth and at sea for military ends. Galileo immediately obtained the recognition of the Venetian senate, who within a week raised his salary to one thousand florins, a tangible sign of prestige consolidating his seventeen years of intelligent and assiduous service. Well before 1609 the brilliance, cordiality, and completely Tuscan intonation of Galileo's speech, as well as his exceptional communication skills, had opened doors to the most exclusive cultural circles of Padua and Venice. These cities were known for their high reputation of tolerance and openness, which were otherwise becoming less and less apparent in a Europe disrupted by religious conflicts (see Cozzi; see Pastore Stocchi). The trauma of an interdict imposed in 1605 by the Church to defend the papal authority in these territories, which was very protective of its sovereignty, weakened its quasi proverbial cultural vivacity in the last period of Galileo's residence there. From the dispute, Venice—which had made Paolo Sarpi its intrepid point of reference—emerged evidently proud but shaken by particularly venomous internal polemics that had erupted between the most uncompromising supporters of a protest in the name of full independence from

Rome and the most moderate group of conservatives, devoted to the Jesuits and disposed to a compromise with the Church.

Galileo managed to keep these painful disagreements aside so much so, that not even in his private letters can one find echoes of them. However, it is undeniable that his discomfort became more acute, nourished by a growing sense of narrowness, by the precariousness to which his research was increasingly reduced, and by the embarrassing choices he was obliged to make in times of cultural conflict. He was forced to choose between the supporters of the Jesuits—though expelled from the Venetian Republic they were still the most up-to-date scientific interlocutors—and Sarpi's friends who preferred the most restricted and utilitarian application of mechanics to cosmological studies.

There is no greater frustration for a scholar than that of nearing old age while feeling the need to communicate many scientific truths (Galileo already had in mind the design of the *Massimi sistemi* [Dialogue concerning the two chief world systems]). Galileo was also distracted daily, dissuaded from his most intense vocation by the endless number of small and minimal commissions that up until then had prevented him from publishing the works—which he felt potentially ready to communicate—necessary to make himself known to other scientists. He had promised the secretary of the Grand Duke of Tuscany, in preparing his reentry in Florence, "magna longeque admirabilia apud me habeo" (X, 351) (I have with me great and truly wonderful things), but the dreary daily reality to which the city of Venice obligated him was the opposite of this program that he had anticipated even in the frontispiece of the *Sidereus*. Rather than revealing "grandi e oltremodo mirabili" (great and extraordinarily admirable) spectacles, the routine of his activity consisted—to say it with Galileo's discouraging words—in "dispensare [...] a minuto alle richieste di ogn'uno il suo talento" (sharing readily his talents to everyone's demand); and in "consumar diverse hore del giorno, et bene spesso le migliori" (wasting various hours of the day, often the best ones), "a richiesta di questo e di quello" (to help this and that person) (X, 232–33).

There is no doubt that some months after having written this disheartening letter, Galileo decided to point the telescope toward the sky, driven first and foremost by his own curiosity. He was attracted to astronomy in 1577 at the age of thirteen by the appearance of a comet. This event must have left an indelible impression on his vivid imagination because in his essay *Il Saggiatore* he recounted having observed it continuously from the windows of his Florentine home (VI, 314). Another reason for his attraction to astronomy was the appearance of the new star of 1604, on which there exists fragments of lessons and studies, triggered by the anti-Aristotelian ideas implicit in that phenomenon (II, 277–305). These ideas were particularly exciting for Galileo considering that for at least seven years he had embraced the alternative of the Copernican theory. Still, one cannot deny that the gesture of pointing the telescope toward the sky, which seemed gratuitous and foreboding of consequences, should be interpreted in a polemic and liberating sense. Finally, Galileo intended to escape in this way the miserable "servizio cotidiano" (daily service) and the "servitù meretricia di dover esporre le sue fatiche al prezzo arbitrario di ogni avventore" (soliciting servitude of having to expose his own efforts to the arbitrary price of every patron). All the more so because of his capabilities, which are anything but limited to technical facts, and which encouraged him to show the world that behind the "pietre" (rocks) of little discoveries, one finds the "miniera" (mine) of his intelligence (X, 233). Under this typically baroque metaphor transpired the pride of a scientist who, after obscure and futile service to the city of Venice, hoped to gain some "lode" (praise) from the "studiosi della professione" (scholars of the profession) in virtue of the "maggiore et più universale et più diuturna utilità di quello che nel resto della vita apportar potesse" (X, 232) (greatest, most universal, and longest-lasting utility that the rest of his life could give).

With a mood analogous to that of Machiavelli, who in the evening used to take off his "veste cotidiana, piena di fango" (daily clothes full of mud), Galileo used the telescope and began to explore the mysterious surface of the moon, the immense space of the Milky Way, and the blazing, luminous dots of stars and planets. The discoveries were shocking so much so that one today could call it "choc du télescope" (see Tuzet; see Grafton-Shelford-Siraisi): the mountains and the valleys of the moon, the impressive multiplication of the number of stars,[2] and the unexpected spotting of the moons of Jupiter revealed themselves to Galileo as the definitive experimental demonstration necessary to shatter the Aristotelian-Ptolemaic paradigm. This was the much-awaited opportunity to show the world his worth and to gain revenge for all of the small commissions that for so long had held back his talent. Immediately after the discoveries, there was a rush to print a work appropriate to the "magnificenza" (magnificence) and "alla grandezza del soggetto" (X, 298) (greatness of the subject). The work, then, was published without the "maestà proporzionata alla materia" (X, 425) (majesty proportioned to the matter), as it was feverishly transcribed during the day, while in the evening Galileo continued to restlessly conduct his celestial telescopic peregrination. Considering the scarce enthusiasm of Venetian intellectuals, these celestial observations, initially the "grande impresa astronomica" (X, 302) (great astronomical undertaking), which was to be committed to pages of the *Sidereus*, did not earn in Venice the merited consideration they deserved, forcing Galileo to turn to Tommaso Baglioni to print the work. He was a typographer who at the beginning of his trade in 1610 had only a "modesto" (modest) catalogue (Cioni 249).

The plain editorial format of the book coincided with a prose aimed at professional scholars and resulted in using the international language of Latin. As much as Galileo had mastered Latin prose, he still did not produce in its scholastic and functional progression the elegance and expressiveness of his sharp-witted and inimitable Italian prose (Banfi). In fact, for some, the style of the *Sidereus* seemed even *aridus* (arid) (X, 316). To a certain extent this definition cannot be considered altogether wrong, especially because the correspondent to whom Galileo confided these severe criticisms was Kepler, a scientist gifted in powerful humanistic culture a big virtuoso of the Latin language, and a refined imitator of the harmonious Ciceronian syntax and the surprising Plautus's lexicon.[3]

Nonetheless, despite appearances, Galileo was revolutionary in his well-thought-out stylistic choices. He was very modern and truthful in his clear writing which was easy to read, as well as sober and essential, though ardent in its hidden fervor to occasionally reveal a vibratile and moving emotion. While Kepler, with his learned familiarity of humanistic texts, before the coercive model of the *Sidereus*, at first did not know how to renounce the anecdotal intrusions, autobiographical annotations, digressive jokes, and metaphysical discourses (Chevalley 173),[4] Galileo carefully avoided—even in dealing with topics that traditionally would allow this, such as those about the moon—quotes from literary texts and echoes of the popular imagination, making every statement in his scientific statute precise and employing in the description an unprecedented frugality. He immediately set aside every ornament to take notice of the essential in a description governed by a clear geometrical *dispositio* (disposition). This style allowed the first readers, starting with Kepler, to easily divide the structure of the work into many chapters. These consisted of the general index of discoveries, the constructional technique of the telescope, the results of investigations on the surface of the moon (the spots, the reason for the regular circumference, the supposed ring of vapor, the height of its mountains, its ash-colored lights), the fixed stars, the Milky Way, the moons of Jupiter with the history that relates the moment of their discovery, their positions in comparison to Jupiter, and the position of the planet itself along with the results deduced from all of these observations. The upshot was the foundation of a new literary genre that would later enjoy an uninterrupted fortune: the scientific report with which one communicated (*Nuncius* means reporting) the summary of the phenomena was until that point unknown, exposed with that incisive prose, deft in its reasoning, and essential in its argument, which was also later pleasing to Calvino in his *Lezioni americane*.

The Initial Receptions

In spite of the relaxed tone of the description, even more unusual after a title deservedly resounding but in line with the hyperbolic baroque style, and after a dedication full of ceremonious verbal genuflections praising Cosimo II de' Medici, the *Sidereus Nuncius* (Sidereal Messenger), was published March 13, 1610 with a run of 550 copies, and after less than a week was impossible to find (X, 300). As the fame of this exciting booklet began to spread in all directions, Galileo's existence changed profoundly. He went from university professor, accustomed to moving around a restricted circle of university halls, his tiny workshop at the back of his residence and some Venetian salons, to suddenly becoming a public figure, on everyone's lips; in short, he was known in every part of the world. On the same day that the booklet appeared, the English ambassador to Venice, Sir Henry Wotton, hastened to send king James I a copy, accompanying it with a letter betraying his uncontainable excitement, for he was an informer by profession and well aware of transmitting "la notizia più strana mai ricevuta da nessuna parte della Terra" (the strangest news ever received in any part of the world). Having illustrated the thrilling sensation he experienced as a result of the diffusion of the *Sidereus*, the diplomat then predicted, still incredulous of what he had read, that his author would soon become "o straordinariamente famoso o straordinariamente ridicolo"[5] (either extraordinarily famous or extraordinarily ridiculous).

The scientists were much more trusting of his credibility, even if they, too, were unable to repress their most profound emotions before the catalogue of the announced discoveries. Kepler, upon hearing the news, blushed with amazement and was unable to contain his joy; he began to laugh and ceased listening entirely to his friend, who had just informed him from the street of the incredible, new astronomical development (Kepler 17). Upon receiving the work, Benedetto Castelli, friend and disciple of Galileo, immediately began to read it right away "più di dieci volte con somma meraviglia e dolcezza grande d'animo" (X, 310) (more than ten times with a lot of wonder and with heartfelt kindness). The fame of the "libretto ammirabile et miracoloso" (X, 344) (admirable and miraculous little book) was not limited to the cognoscenti because its contents were capable of affecting the collective imagination, to the point that it diffused "prima assai il grido che l'opera" (X, 298) (first its fame then the work [in its entirety]). Only two weeks after the publication of the *Sidereus* in Florence, there was a rumor in the city of the arrival of a parcel from Galileo. The people at the market gathered around the envied receiver to discover the parcel's contents, thinking it a telescope. Their curiosity did not cease, even when it was proven to be only a book (X, 305). This incident is indirect proof of Maravall's thesis on baroque culture as mass culture, connected to urban life (Maravall 79–125; Kuznecov 141).

Given the rapidity with which Galileo's discoveries spread, there was never a work more appropriately titled than the *Sidereus Nuncius*. In 1612 the message of its discoveries arrived in Moscow (XI, 68) and in India; three years later there was a translation into Chinese; and in 1631 the telescope was celebrated in Korea as well as in 1638 in Japan. In 1640 befitting his popularity, Galileo's name was translated into Chinese, becoming Chia-Li-Lueh. (D'Elia; Gjersten). In Italy, the recently discovered moons of Jupiter had become (with the approval of their discoverer) iconographic protagonists of noble emblems,[6] represented as in a ballet, with scorn for the Peripatetics "che non potevano contenersi di ringhiare, come veternosi e nimici d'ogni cosa nuova" (XII, 29) (that could not keep from snarling and acting like traditionalists and enemies to all new things).

Indeed, not everyone accepted what had been announced. Some of the most ingenuous people presented themselves in the matter, perhaps hoping to obtain easy notoriety at Galileo's expense. But his true adversaries were neither Martino Horky, nor Francesco Sizzi, nor Giulio Cesare Lagalla; unprepared and ordinary, these men quickly lost any credibility due to inconsistency of their theses. Galileo's real opponents were, more frequently, university lecturers and astrologists whose theories crumbled in light of the discoveries in the *Sidereus*. Even the men of the Church were opposed to its contents, thinking it solely possible to explain the Bible with Aristotle's cosmology. All of these various opponents were united in a cross-party attempt to discredit Galileo in every way through devious hostility and hidden plotting. Kepler, having gathered Horky's secret thoughts, was able to speak of such plots in the Italian academic world of the time (X, 458); for another correspondent, "gli Spagnuoli stimano, per ragione di stato essere necessario che il libro di V. S. si debba supprimere, come pernicioso alla religione" (X, 418) (the Spanish believe necessary that V. S. book be suppressed as pernicious to religion). This opposition was probably due to the fact that the *Sidereus*, implicitly placing in discussion the centrality of the Earth and the order of an anthropocentric cosmos, could have placed at risk social order and stability, as well as equally closed and finite mirrors of the natural world.

Galileo was certain of his discoveries and placed aside every sign of doubt and followed his innate exuberance; still a youthful person, notwithstanding that his boyhood days were over, he plunged bravely into the arguments, doing his best to dispel doubts, clear up, explain, and deepen the theses of the *Sidereus*. He supported the worth of his manifesto as an instrument of scientific propaganda (Slawinski 89–90), to be sent to many European princes together with a model telescope, "acciò possino incontrare la verità della cosa" (X, 298) (so that they can encounter the truth of the thing).

Galileo was inexhaustible. He spent an Easter teaching the Grand Duke Cosimo II how to use the telescope and on his return stopped in Bologna to offer a demonstration of its visible resources (see Baffetti), to dispense advice by letter, and to hold three public lectures in Padua, where he was deceived of having satisfied everyone (X, 349). Additionally, he continued to multiply the celestial observations, planning a new edition enriched with new data (X, 358). The didactic passion to be displayed in the development of the treatise—in which he intended to insert all the doubts and all the difficulties that he encountered, together with their answers so that everything would remain totally unquestionable (X, 373)—accompanied him for the rest of his life. Despite the advice of his friends who wanted him to write a second *Sidereus*,[7] he renounced the idea of a new edition that would be even more documented and luxurious; he had become entranced, instead, by the excitement of the new discoveries and of the new consequential controversies. Nonetheless, Galileo never ceased to discuss it with everyone (similar, in his anxiety to conquer converts, to his theatrical portrait done by Brecht).

Certainly, the *Sidereus* was a text that marked an epoch-making event, destined to strongly reflect and affect not only the astronomers, but also the epistemologists, philosophers, and even literati and artists. Although it was truly the objective and analytic communication of some star observations, it unequivocally showed a new cosmological system, intuitable beyond its journal-like appearance. Castelli acutely noted and gathered in the *Sidereus* "la consonanza et unione meravigliosa del tutto" (X, 310) (the marvelous harmony and union of everything), to signify that the dramatic impact of the work was not born out of its single details but from its total, consistent accumulation of philosophical inferences.

At least in this case, the persevering and convergent allusions to the *Apoca-*

lypse of John (AP 21,1) roused by the *Sidereus Nuncius*—in Campanella, "tu purgasti oculos hominum, et novum ostendis caelum, et novam terram in luna" (XI, 23) (you cleared men's eyes, and showed new sky and new earth in the moon); in Marino, ". . . scoprirà novo cielo e nova terra" (X, 45, 4) (. . . will discover new sky and new earth); and in Shakespeare's foretelling intuition, "then must thou needs find out new heaven, new earth," in *Antony and Cleopatra*, (I, 1, 17)[8]—are neither abstract utopian yearnings, nor emphatic maxims of the baroque magniloquence but, rather, an observation, rippled by the shivers that the unknown and the extraordinary always produce, in the presence of a revolution of grand and unforeseeable consequences.

Aside from their mere factual discoveries, the few pages published by Galileo suddenly negated more deep-rooted and indestructible beliefs. Since immemorial times, it was sustained that the sky was unalterable, perennial, and incorruptible because it was composed of ether, a solid quintessence, crystalline, transparent, and totally different from the Earth, which was the seat of every metamorphosis, birth, and death as well as formation and destruction. Suddenly, the configuration of the lunar landscape as rough, unequal, with hills and depressions, demonstrated that there was no substantial difference between the Earth and other celestial bodies in the sense that they, too, were exposed to the corruption and phenomenal events. It was also strongly believed that the universe was vast, though finite, and enclosed by the sky and the fixed stars. The nebulae and the Milky Way through Galileo's discoveries were proven to be formed by an alarming number of stars, each equal, if not exceeding the volume of the Earth. Even though Galileo never mentioned Giordano Bruno, it was easier through his discoveries to confirm Bruno's very audacious and dangerous theses. Aristotle's authority and common sense suggested that the Earth was immovable and at the center of the universe. Now, suddenly, four moons were spotted rotating around Jupiter, creating a kind of reduced scale model of the Copernican universe, indicating the possibility that other planetary systems existed and proving the presence of other centers of rotation besides the Earth (Rossi, *Galilei* 16–17). On the whole, Galileo denied the hierarchy of spaces, distinguished in antiquity and in the Middle Ages between celestial and terrestrial, sacred and profane, prohibited and accessible (see Foucault 22–23). In order to carry out this theoretical deconsecration of space—as Koyré observes—"one did not only have to contrast the erroneous and insufficient theories, but to transform the very framework of intelligence, to turn upside-down a mental behavior, all in all very natural, replacing it with another that was not perceived as natural at all" (Études galiléennes 9).

The *Sidereus* ratified the defeat of anthropocentrism, or rather, the presumption that the entire cosmos was created in exclusive function to man, as if—the mocking Leopardi would write—"the stars and planets were, so to speak, lamps hung up there on high to give light (to the exclusive benefit of men) who had great goings on at night."[9] Moreover, the discoveries threatened the credibility of astrology, founded upon the superstition that the skies exerted their influence on matters of the Earth. Exemplary on this subject is the testimony of Giambattista Manso who in writing to Paolo Beni reveals the resonance that occurred in Naples after the Galilean discoveries. He disturbingly reported "to have received a very bitter complaint by all of the astrologists and a majority of physicians, who understood that by adding so many new planets to those already known, astrology and a major part of medicine as they knew it were necessarily ruined" (X, 295). Though they did not have to underestimate Pico della Mirandola's role and that of other humanists in combating the superstitions of the astrologists, their sensationalism, and the absence of method in their discipline (Rossi, *La scienza* 25–39), it is certain that it was this new science to give them the decisive blow on the epistemological ground; it canceled the ontological distinction between Earth and sky and in turn denied the possibility that the stars were the remote and primary cause of all events and terrestrial processes of generation, alteration, and corruption. On the one hand, the skies were deprived of their perfection, and, on the other, the Earth was no longer the fixed center of the universe. Instead, as one can deduce *a posteriori* from Galileo's activity immediately following the *Sidereus*, the extracted inferences opened anew the discussion on the reliability of the cosmology based on a kinetic view of the Earth.

Leaving aside Aristarco, too far in time for a real comparison, the hypothesis had already appeared with Copernicus. Nevertheless, his *De revolutionibus orbium caelestium* had a weak influence on the cosmic imagination because in the end, its static view of the sun conserved the idea of a system ordered around only one center, and, although alternative to the Ptolemaic system, it was no less abstract in its cold geometry than was reconstructed theoretically with a ruler and compass (Nicholson, *Science and Imagination* 1–3; Rossi, *La scienza* 160–61). On the other hand, in the *Sidereus* even the physically distant phenomena—intriguing for touching upon archetypal questions (such as the plurality of the worlds, the possible presence of other living beings, the sense of the end of one epoch and the inauguration of another, and the radical devastation of the proven mental frameworks)—could all be verified by a sensorial experience thanks to the telescope and the instructions on how to use it. The new cosmology excited the imaginary because it reconciled with a method that pursued the democratization of knowledge, which was at this point within everyone's reach. This, in turn, caused agitation, frenzy, and restlessness to procure the best models of telescopes throughout Europe. When amateurs were finally able to personally repeat the astronomical experiences of Galileo, they felt seized by the contemplative delight. This feeling was exemplarily transmitted by one of those anxious to explore the infinite skies in person:

> Io vidi poi [. . .] tutte quattro le Stelle Medicee; [. . .] del che ne sentii grandissimo contento, non perché io ne dubitassi, ma per havere una volta ottenuto la bramata satisfattione di vederle con gli occhi proprii. (XI, 300)

> (I saw then [. . .] all four of the Medicean stars; [. . .] from which I felt much happiness, not because I doubted, but for finally having obtained the longed-for satisfaction of seeing them with my own eyes.)

Scientific and Symbolic Refractions

Who knows how many others must have shared this concrete pleasure, triggered by the truth seized in its naturalness, as if to see the phenomena "con gli occhi proprii" (with ones own eyes) meant in some way to possess and dominate them! In the history of science, the *Sidereus* has further heuristic merit for having investigated the natural world by means of instruments that made the results more easily inferred by the human senses. Galileo defeated the epistemological obstacle of the Aristotelians, who were suspicious of the telescope both because it was perfected only by the empirical method (which meant it did not have any theoretical support), and because they feared its optical aberrations based on the assumption that vision, interposing itself by a refractive means, could only be compromised (Redondi 182). Moreover, coming from the world of the *meccanici* (artisans), the telescope did not enjoy any dignity with the official aristocratic science. On the contrary, employed with a methodical spirit and with scientific mentality, the instrument showed how "frivolous and puerile" the "reasons for doubt" were. Furthermore, testing it "centomila volte in centomila stelle et altri oggetti" (100,000 times on 100,000 stars and other objects), Galileo could "recognize the deceptions" that his denigrators "without ever having seen it, attributed to the telescope" (X, 357; XI, 106).

In a still unequalled essay on the *Nuova scienza e la visione degli oggetti* (New Science and Vision of the Objects), Ezio Raimondi maintains that Galileo's example infused the scientific community with "the honest certainty of the rigorous technician who knows he can trust" the optical apparatus made ready by him, to the point of conferring a essential regulating function. Since vision gained an intermediary operation of connection between the process of sensible perception and the cycle of elaboration or intellectual reconstruction, the visible experience came, from that time, to coincide with that of knowledge.[10] Not by chance, Benedetto Castelli, who was educated by Galileo on the scientific representation of the real, later exalted in his *Discorso sopra la vista*—which was written when Galileo's eyesight was nearing blindness—Galileo's

> occhio tanto privilegiato, e di tanto alte prerogative, che si può dire, e con verità, ch'egli abbia visto più egli solo che tutti gli occhi insieme degli uomini passati, ed abbia aperti quelli de' futuri, essendo toccato in gran parte a lui solo fare tutti gli scoprimenti celesti ammirandi a' secoli futuri.

> ([Galileo's] very privileged and talented eye, with many other prestigious prerogatives that one could say with truthfulness, his eyes saw more than all the eyes of men who came before him. He helped to open the eyes of the future having been largely responsible for the celestial discoveries admired by future centuries.) (21)

This praise, in which Galileo's gaze functions as "minister of his wonderful intellect, exciting to philosophize so highly about these things," and which confirms his acquired intellectual and gnosiological functions, could not but make an oblique yet recognizable reference to the "glorious archetype" of the *Sidereus Nuncius* and to its "cognitio ocularis" (visual cognition) (Raimondi, *La nuova scienza* 51). Nevertheless, paradoxically, to mark the transition from an acoustic supremacy, the title contained an allusion to the orality of the public notices and proclamations of the *avvisi* (announcements), which immediately prompted a German admirer to rename Galileo "Mercurius alter" (X, 396) (New Mercurius). The content however, was dominated from beginning to end by the semantics of sight, expressed with a homogeneous lexicon that is circumscribed within the sphere of the *apparere* (appearing), *oculis cernere* (discerning through the eyes), *conspicere* (observing), *inspectio* (inspecting), *intueri* (considering), *manifestare* (manifesting), *spectare* (examining), *visus* (sighting), representing the *refrain* of an objectivity granted by the perceptive exactitude of a scientist to whom, for Castelli, was granted the gift of "the most noble eye that ever fabricated nature" (Castelli 11–12). Filtrated by the organ of sight, "the most distinguished of the senses," as one can read in *Saggiatore* (VI, 350), the objects, although separated by sidereal distances, take on the clarity of tangible bodies, making the *Sidereus* amazingly simple to read and comprehend, also thanks to the help of the illustrations that accompany the text. On the contrary, the writing is handmaid to the figures, the exegesis of their geometric rigor and the analytical support of the *occhio della mente* (eye of the mind), that in them synoptically, through the enlargements of the telescope, gather the images of the physics of vision, the lunar topography, the constellations, and the positions of Jupiter and its satellites.

Still today, historians of science from Guglielmo Righini to Owen Gingerich, and up until Giorgio Tabarroni,[11] have discussed the exactitude of Galileo's designs. It could be true even for Galileo what Ernst Gombrich showed in *Art and Illusion*, that the figurative experience is influenced by either the meditation of prearranged crystallized forms, as those inherited by the lunar descriptions of Plutarch (Casini), or by the assumed Copernican philosophies. Certainly the illustrations of the *Sidereus* no longer offered themselves as decorative frames conditioned by ornamental appeal and by picturesque satisfaction, but as integral didactic guides of the scientific discourse, indispensable because their geometric accuracy fulfilled the clearness and the distinction of the new Cartesian space better than the writing itself, too much subject to the alphabet and to the mimesis of the acoustic oral discourse. Much more than words, however, what must have been truly impressive was the dark within the spots of the lunar surface that made the peaks of its mountains stand out, an effect that seemed to influence even the painting of the time, considering that the artist and Galileo's friend, Ludovico Cardi da Cigoli—having to paint the moon under the image of the Virgin in the dome of the Roman church Santa Maria Maggiore—wanted to represent dark and light exactly as they were portrayed in the *Sidereus*. The illustrations remained an undeniable aid to understanding this treatise.

On the other hand, it would not be imaginable to conceive the *Sidereus* without designs, since all of the work consists in the reproduction of what was seen with the telescope, inaugurating the season that Koyré called "instrumental science," in the sense that its progress from that moment on would be closely linked to that of employed instruments (Koyré, 1957 90). If the new science proceeds to a geometrization of the universe and irreversibly organizes the work of the mind according to a spatial model, the telescope occupies a first-rate role in the transformation of the human sensory from "a world of approximation to a world of precision." The telescope was improved under the impulse of a practical spirit and remained open to the technical experience of the artisans; its importance transcended the discoveries, for certain sensational aspects, that it made possible: it became the symbol of a new era and of a new method. Galileo, with his usual clairvoyance, thought right away of making it an emblem, introducing to history the model with which he carried out his first discoveries. He sent it to the Grand Duke of Tuscany with the following message:

così inornato et mal pulito quale *se* l'haveva fatto per *suo* uso; ma da poi che è stato strumento a sì grande scoprimento, desiderò che *fosse* lasciato nel suo primo stato, non convenendo che si rimuova cosa alcuna delle vecchie per onorarne delle nuove che non sono state a parte nelle vigilie et fatiche delle osservationi. (X, 297-98)

(so simple and badly cleaned, just as he had made it for his own personal use; but after it had become an instrument of great discovery, he desired it to be left in its original state, agreeing not to remove and replace any of its old parts with new ones not originally used in the difficult nightly observations.)

In representing the new *ethos* of the scientist who no longer accepted the easy reading of other books, which were now perceived with an almost intolerant claustrophobia, the telescope revealed to one who used it "a modern conscience of experimenter," becoming a figurative synonym of "scientific logic that teaches one to see clearly" (Raimondi, *Introduzione* xvi).

The telescope was promoted to a metonymy of Galileo's own figure, since he not only understood its scientific value but also perfected and used it in the best way possible, teaching how to employ it and, above all, making it a symbol of the new scientific habit. For Kepler, in the preface of *Dioptrice*, the telescope was "more precious than a scepter" because "it was an instrument of much knowledge," and Galileo, who seized it, had become "king and master of divine works." On the wake of the *Nuncius*, an adversary of Galileo, Giulio Cesare Lagalla, having compared his maker to Mercury, messenger of the gods, substituted the telescope for the caduceus (III/1, 322-23). On one hand, scientists such as Kepler and Descartes were inspired by the empirical instructions of the *Sidereus* to theoretically formulate the optical laws that presided over the enlargement and approach of the objects analyzed through its lenses.

On the other hand, both the well-read and the laity were irresistibly subject to its fascination, which was carried out in their imagination. The strengthening of human sight, as permitted by the telescope, made the instrument a tangible symbol of the enterprising resources of the human spirit to indefinitely amplify one's own horizons. The very conformation of the telescope—in Marino's essential words, "a little cannon and two crystals" (*Adone*, X, 42, 8)—bore witness to the simplicity with which nature works, being capable of producing wonder through daily objects within the reach of all, according to the Galilean thesis that "the most admirable operations derive from very weak means" (XI, 109). If the distinctiveness of the Baroque resides in the taste for contradictions[12] and oxymora, from this point of view the telescope is once again its emblem. This is because the splendor of human conquest is based on a weak and modest structure, a notably paradoxical synthesis identified by Pascal in a thinking stick.

Finally, if one would like to compete with the baroque man's wit, the telescope could seem the iconic equivalent of the *Sidereus* that defines itself in the first lines as a "brief treatise" making "big things" visible precisely in accordance with the antithesis of the apparatus that, in its smallness, shows grandiose phenomena. Its metamorphic power to magnify smaller things and, if turned upside-down, to make larger objects microscopic, led in little time to its adoption within poetics, inspired by the Aristotelian techniques of amplifying and diminishing within a game of concave and convex mirrors, which could also be applied to the word and its processes of rhetorical refractions. In short, the telescope functioned exactly like *ingenium*, the human faculty to approach and bring closer things that are far away.

Emanuele Tesauro, the most acute of baroque intellectuals, had his *Cannocchiale aristotelico* (Aristotelian Telescope) illustrated by an allegorical frontispiece where Poetry, assisted by Aristotle, observes lunar spots through the telescope, a symbol of the false enthymemes. Since the operation takes place in the presence of Painting, on whose palette are reproduced the same spots visible on the sun (Reeves 129–35), once again the iconicity of sight and the verbal illusion of poetry—in perennial equilibrium above all in the seventeenth century-between artifice and mimesis, as well as geometric rationality and theatrical spectacle—are summarized in the telescope. Perhaps for this reason the telescope, from the time it was announced to the world by the *Sidereus*, remained throughout the century a privileged protagonist of *imprese* (emblems), the symbolic representation constituted by a witticism, and a figure that complementarily reciprocated and interpreted one another. In scientific texts the writing was integrated with the illustrations and drawings. Without realizing what he was doing, the extremely authoritative intellectual Paolo Giovio supported the iconic use. For him, the emblem could "be very cheerful" if represented precisely for specific "mechanical instruments" (Giovio 37).

The telescope, after the *Nuncius* had ecumenically propagated its revelations—in an age in which curiosity fought with mysteriousness, when news of Parnassus and of the first gazette were at war with honest dissimulation, and subtle intellectuals were able to describe and decipher, just as Oedipus dialectically faced the Sphinx, the enigmatic messages and the art of signs—was assumed as an oppositional *pendant* of the mask, transferring itself directly from the more exclusive realm of science to the spacious camps of emblems, figurative arts, and poetry. Already the young Accademia dei Lincei, which had co-opted Galileo after his celestial discoveries, had immediately realized a program of highest attention, at the same time scientific and symbolic, to the instrument, which Cesi named *telescopio*. In this way, a syncretism was created between the lynx, an animal with acute sight classified among the eccentric *mirabilia* of nature, and the reproducible product of human technique, democratically at the disposition of every man.[13]

However, while the optical science and its refined geometry were cultivated by few experts, the allegorical implications were paradoxically responsible for spreading the popularity of the telescope among the common people. Synonymous with closer vision and a penetrating look, the telescope was already, to paraphrase a work by Daniello Bartoli, "trasportato al morale" (interpreted in a moral sense) by Galileo's friends. Sagredo, in some aspects distracted by the astronomical qualities of the instrument, ironically asked Galileo—following his own epicurean vein that was disenchanted before the evils of the world—

> chi sarà colui che possi inventare un occhiale per distinguere i pazzi da i savii, il buono dal cattivo consiglio, l'architetto intelligente da un proto ostinato et ignorante? (XI, 172)

> (who will be the one able to invent an eyeglass that will distinguish the crazy from the sane, the good advice from the bad, the intelligent architect from an obstinate ignorant technician?)

No one will be capable of answering this question, not even three centuries later, when Italo Calvino will attempt in vain to understand using a telescope, the "spiritual state" of a woman while reading (Calvino, *If on a Winter's Night* 169). In the seventeenth century, only mock-heroic poetry, a literary genre authorized to unlikelihoods, could agree that the telescope had visual powers capable of piercing the screen of appearances. This happens in an episode of the *Fiesole distrutta*, a poem by the Sienese author Giovan Domenico Peri published in 1619, in which a Sibyl is able, with the help of the modern instrument, to show a young gentleman the true face of pleasure, which, in reality, is much less seductive than it appears with the naked eye.

Like all objects promoted to the polysemous values of the symbol, even the telescope accumulates within itself opposite meanings, with the result of multiplying its semantic diffractions and extending its limits of use from the lyric to the epic genre, from literary criticism to the ethical-political lexicon. On one hand, Tesauro marked the maximum wit of the optical emblems, "which, for certain proportions of perspective, through strange and ingenious appearances, make you see things that you do not see." Moreover, he praised, with the pride of a modernist, the signs of human enterprise and progress, articulated by the discoveries of the *Sidereus* and the subsequent *Istoria e dimostrazioni intorno alle macchie solari* (History and Demonstrations on the Solar (Spots and their Characteristics).[14] On the other hand, Diego de Savvedra Fajardo, a Spanish writer of treatises educated at a Counter-Reformist reason of state, created an emblem in which the Galilean instrument, married to the motto "auget et minuit" (augments and diminishes) became more equalized to passion, with the warning to "recognize things as they are, without letting them grow or diminish" as a consequence of depraved appetites. He replies ideally to the anamorphic windmills of Tesauro, claiming that "sean siempre unos mismos los cristales de la razón, por donde se miren con igualdad" (Savvedra Fajardo 56) (let always be the same crystals of reason where they see with equality).

Finally, Filippo Picinelli, in his late inclusive encyclopedia on the *Symbolic World*, inventoried the many values of the telescope with much manneristic diligence. In turn, the instrument became a metaphor for Faith, particularly because it enabled one to see remote and arcane things and to believe in that which is not seen with the naked eye. It also represented the contemplative life and was a sign of how the look of God penetrates the recesses of the soul, "le macchie dei peccati" (the stains of sin), just as the optical instrument discovers solar spots. Moreover, after much apprehension, it was conceived as an expression of the celestial consolations, analogous to the happiness that Galileo finally experienced after many tiring explorations. Finally, the telescope became a sign of both prudence, which scrutinizes vastly and deeply, and of prophecies that draw the future to the present. At the same time, however, the capacity to transform a small piece of land into a mountain degraded it to the derogatory uniform of a braggart, while the individualization of the spots on the sun and the imperfections of the moon recalled as much malevolence that finds defects in another as sadness that blurs happiness. The symbol of the telescope was so pervasive that it even came to connote the cooperative community of Jesuits, particularly because the lenses and the tube had to be combined to permit vision.[15] In the syncretic culture of the Baroque, in which everything is linked, the instrument that made Galileo famous was even capable of representing the religious order that had contributed most to condemning his discoveries. Not by chance a scientist among the most distinguished of the Society of Jesus, Giambattista Riccioli, did not hesitate to illustrate the frontispiece of his *Almagestum novum* with an Argus that, dissatisfied with its proverbial one hundred eyes, held a telescope in hand.

After the telescope's visible virtues had been recorded by the *Sidereus*, it crossed specialistic boundaries, behind which scientific apparatuses are usually kept, to use the common language, favored in this by the baroque man's more general attraction to the discovery of technique, sung perhaps for the first time in poetry.[16] The moralist could refer to the telescope to distinguish good from evil; it could be used to evoke the religious idea of searching for God; or the erotic poets could praise it for capturing (with the eye of a *voyeur*) the most secret signs of female beauty,[17] particularly after the lunar explorations had revitalized the myth of Endymion. Finally, the telescope could be appropriated by a masterful narrator of fairy tales, such as Giambattista Basile, to remark with "l'acchiaro de lo Galileo" (Basile 686) (Galileo's eyeglass) on the playful excesses of the hyperbole. Contrary to the norm, holding that between literature and science osmosis either does not take place or occurs very slowly, it took less than a generation for the Galilean instrument to not only influence the imagination of poets, but to change it from the very foundation, notwithstanding that many continued to believe in the immobility of the Earth and to follow the ideas of Aristotle.

Shivers of the Starry Night and of Infinite Spaces

Moving by metonymy from cause to effect, namely from the polymorphous symbolism of the telescope to its discoveries enunciated in the *Sidereus*, the story of ideas increased—to quote Lovejoy—its "metaphysical pathos" (13) because it no longer dealt only with a human art craft, though wonderful in its controlled simplicity, but also with sensations that involved human emotions precisely because they are impalpable, dark, and archetypal. The truth is that Galileo concerned himself with expunging from his rigorous text every neo-Pythagorean or neo-Platonic temptation, because they were too inclined toward hermeism and esotericism. Nevertheless, while diligently avoiding speaking about the infinity of the universe, his keen sight had nonetheless transfused the awareness of the immensity of space, never being so expanded, and ideally confirming the ideas of his contemporary Shakespeare, who considered the universe to be much more extensive than man could imagine. In spite of the epistemological incompatibility existing between Galileo and the most enthusiastic advocate of the infinite universe, Giordano Bruno, it was natural for many to connect their names. This had also been the case with Kepler—himself no less hostile toward the idea of eliminating the order of the cosmos—who had rebuked the *Sidereus* for not having mentioned, in addition to his own name, those of Copernicus and Bruno. Bruno was the anti-conformist Nolan philosopher, who had among other things, "given him the suggestion and the occasion to investigate that which Galileo had now found" (X, 315).

The Galilean reports are not in themselves magical, particularly because the procedure of visual investigation is rational and turns to the neutral phenomena that the telescope divides in an almost surgical manner (Contardi 39; Cavaillé 23–24). The writing transposes all of this to the page, imparting a clear lesson of method in enunciating the discovery, in researching its causes and constants, in verifying and measuring it, and in extracting its epistemological inferences. Yet, from the anatomy of things, human wonder emerges equally for suggestions that are provoked either by a pure night or by the twinkling of the stars. In the desire to apply to the *Sidereus* and in part turn upside-down the absorbed meditations of Valéry on a memorable *pensée* by Pascal, one cannot help but be struck by the contrast between the "slowness caused by critical spirit and hope" (with which the scientist describes, defines, and measures, lingering with a patient hesitation of the mind on the mountains of the moon and on the daily positions of Jupiter's stars that form the constellations), and "the readiness, the impatience, the restlessness of the heart" in commotion for feeling engulfed, ignored by the infinite spaces that he wants to understand. The Ptolemaic and theological skies of the Bible "enarrant gloriam Dei" (tell God's glory) because the majority of religions place the "seat of the omnipotent" on high, finding "the sign and proof of its existence in that sidereal order." For Pascal, on the contrary, from the "espaces infinis" comes only "le silence Éternel" that dismays him.[18]

In the *Sidereus*, as in modern science, the two ideas to a certain extent coexist; even if one is able to scientifically express the greatness of the skies, adapting them to human reason and rendering them familiar to the senses, nonetheless, one can't ever separate the skies from the ancestral shivers instilled in those who contemplate them, an idea best expressed by Kant when he writes "the starry sky above us." For Massimo Bontempelli, a theorist of Italian magical realism and of a narrative delegated to derive mythical perspectives from the reality of the modern world, "the stars, no matter how science has established the skies and measured their organization, have remained the most fabulous aspect that man has at his own disposition."[19] On one hand, this emotion provoked in Galileo by the mysterious "monstrum of space and irradiation,"[20] was held back and filtered by notions full of discretion, though still unequivocal in the emergence of "admiration" for the "most beautiful," "most joyful," and "marvelous" spectacle, contemplated with "incredible joy." On the other hand, among men of letters, the moderation yielded a more frank and explicit pathos, awakened by the mystery of the starry night, or, to use the words of poets singing the Galilean glory, of the "nocturnal horror,"[21] further illuminated by the transparency of the optic crystals of the telescope.

While the *Sidereus* launched the development of spatial physics, the most receptive poets, leaning on the guidance of its revelations, began to construct a new aesthetic and a new ethics, which transformed the canon of beauty and virtue from symmetry and moderation to profusion and superabundance. Marjorie Nicolson visualized this turning point in the "breaking of the circle," the geometrical figure that at one time designed a finite universe and developed the idea of perfection as based on the harmony of each part. Her inquiries, although relative to such English writers as Milton, Donne, and various other metaphysical poets, could for the most part also be applied within the Italian *milieu*, provided there was a critic sensitive to the history of ideas. Gleaning the impressions of early readers of the *Sidereus* from the secret of their correspondence, one realizes that many people, knowing them, would have shared the unforgettable verses of Donne's *Anatomy of the World,* in which were ratified the "end of a world," the denial of "every consistency," from when the "new philosophy" of the infinite "placed everything in doubt" and his apostles "began searching for many new things in the planets and the heavens."[22]

Tasso's biographer, Manso (we already reported how he made himself the interpreter of the cosmological concerns of astrologists), confessed that the majority of friends and acquaintances was "frightened by the newness and difficulty of things" (X, 292). Obscurely, without the restless tremors of Donne, there were still many who felt that the Galilean *Nuncius* reported the end of the old order of the world and the consequent establishment of a "disorder" that threatened to "strike moral and religious values."[23] The confusion spread in all directions, marking both desperation for a fading nature that manifested its imperfection in the skies, and the decadence of a world that, almost at once, the new science had revealed to be the rancid prey of inconstancy and disproportion, replacing the order and unity of the past. In other words, the small lights of Jupiter's four stars had the effect of rendering ever more disastrous and terrible the surrounding darkness.

Human minds were upset by the melancholic sensation that the Earth was deprived of its ancient centrality, lost in the infinite spaces that lacked secure points of reference as there no longer existed anything motionless in the universe.[24] To describe this design in the words of the twentieth century author Pirandello—by this time familiar with an Einsteinian ambivalence—it is the syndrome of one who finds himself living "on an invisible spinning-top, whipped by a thread of sunlight, on a grain of crazed sand which turns and turns without ever knowing why, without ever reaching a destination" (Pirandello, *Late Mattia Pascal* 18)." In this way, man lost his "dignity" and was humbled to consider himself "less than nothing in the universe." In Pirandello's *Il Fu Mattia Pascal*, the blame for this was attributed to Copernicus who, realizing that the Earth was spinning, said that it "was the ruin of mankind, quite irremediably."[25] If one were to examine Pirandello's contiguous essay on *Umorismo* (On Humor), s/he would realize that the invective against Copernicus was born from the removal of Galileo's name, implied in the memory of the "discovery of the telescope," the "infernal little mechanism" capable of becoming a "terrible instrument, which sinks the earth and man and all our glories and greatness." They are words explained only with a Leopardian intertextuality and within the category of humor, in which the telescope would be the objective correlative to have disassembled "not the machine of the universe, but the haughty image that we had formed of it" (Pirandello, *On Humor* 141). Nonetheless, the image of the Earth reduced to the dimension of a grain of sand is identical to that of a metaphysical poet of the seventeenth century.[26]

The novelties of the *Sidereus*, when lived on the emotional plain, could not produce uniform and consistent reactions. On one hand, they induced pessimism because they cancelled the tranquil cosmological certainties and marked the end of an epoch, while on the other hand they optimistically announced new times. In fact, opposite moods usually existed dialectically, frustrating the easy schematizations. Bewilderment at the "breaking of the circle" emerged with the gratification and exultation of the absence of boundaries and the magnificence of the infinite universe, from then on lauded, together with nature, with the same words that had long been reserved for God. By creating doubt, the new science liberated man from the narrowness of a finite world; in this way what was lost in security and familiarity was regained in greatness. To the peripatetics that accused the *Sidereus* of having degraded the stars to the same low rank of the Earth (since the publication had recognized them as consisting of the same material), the Galileans replied that, in reality, it had raised the Earth to the dignity of other celestial bodies inasmuch as it had discovered similar attributes of luminosity and motion. Our planet was no longer the privileged center of every astral influence, but neither was it, as one reads in the *Sidereus*, the "sink of filthiness and ugliness."[27] As a result, the "terror" reported by Manso could easily be combined with "great delight" (X, 292).

Galileo's undertaking made a good impression, particularly the idea of the "boldness" of man that, as Kepler observed with satisfaction, "manifests itself above all" in the seventeenth century when consistent progress was made in our knowledge of nature (Kepler 62). The widening of space, therefore, was equivalent to the increased capacity of the mind to both explore the unknown and to possess the confidence to dominate it. From the same perspective, man's soul, in perceiving the infinite, discovered itself boundless, and with the revival of Pythagorean motives, there developed an aesthetic of limitless space that assumed the configuration of the sublime. It is precisely this that Edmund Burke realized when theorizing (in the modern sense) this category of aesthetics, which was launched in the seventeenth century and codified in the following century. He observed with great competence that "the starry sky, though it falls frequently under our gaze, always provokes an idea of greatness" (Burke 78). In fact, the sense of space that permeates Milton's *Paradise Lost* is no longer equivalent to that in *Genesis* because, notwithstanding that the latter has remained the paradigm of every cosmological poem, the thrill and ecstasy instilled by the telescope changed the meaning of perspective, intensified the perception of verticality (accompanied by a movement of amazement and fascination), and increased the sensitivity for distances (converting geography into cosmography), while the Earth underwent a process of reduction in size.[28] Because of the viscosity of literary conventions, the ordered paradigm of a closed and monocentric world continued to exist for a long period of time. It is certain, however, that after the appearance of the *Sidereus,* the unified and arranged description of the cosmos, which was unanimously accepted from Aristotle to Dante, was shattered and henceforth forced to undergo the alternative of infinite spaces and of the accidental disposition of the stars. Although discussed and opposed, the discoveries announced by the *Sidereus* remained indelible.

The loss of the center of the universe did not only signify an affirmation of ideas based on the chaos principle but also the triumph of a kinetic dimension of phenomena.[29] The universe is comprised of many systems—as the stars of Jupiter were there to assert—that the human mind, no less protean, can know in their variety. For this reason, the static hypotheses on the solid spheres of crystal, which enveloped the planets or the traditional barriers of the sky, were replaced by more dynamic images, connected to a rising and metaphorical nature, mobile and in line with the new baroque love for aerial forms that were light, volatile and fascinating. This period was appropriately described by Pascal, who wisely wrote that "our nature is in movement."

Alternatively, the same concept of experiment, in the antithesis to the inert *ipse dixit*, implies a dynamic of intellect that interrogates and dialectically modifies its assumptions according to the answers of the phenomena, almost as if the description of a scientific experience—and those of the *Sidereus* are in this sense exemplary—had the dramatic turn of events and *agnizione* (recognition) of a fantastic account of adventure. As a result, next to reason, fantasy (which was also rising and mobile) acquired a totally unforeseen positivity, especially when the scientist, facing the infiniteness of the universe, could at any step collide with the unexpected.

A New Golden Age?

The frightening expansion of the boundaries of the cosmos increased the problems of confrontation, upsetting, in their novelty, the peaceful certainties of those that passively trusted the *auctoritates* (authorities). The given indolent reaffirmation of truth was replaced by an ethos marked by hard work, dedication, restlessness, and the insatiable interrogation of the unknown. Brecht's Galileo was truly correct in his assertion that a new science implied a new ethics,[30] an idea already established by Galileo's contemporary Francesco Stelluti (VI, 209, vv.13–19).

Behind the apparent neutrality of the *Sidereus* diary, which registered uninterrupted celestial observations for fifty-five consecutive nights—best perceived "when the skies were serene and uncovered"—exists a zeal, a relentless fervor that was, from that moment on, an unavoidable feature for the entire Galilean school. Galileo, proud and combative as always, proclaimed the revolutionary coming of the modern scientific deontology, pointing out the necessity of such personal efforts as "vigils, studies and sweat" (XI, 113). Individual effort, however, was not enough for the vast task of sounding the "very deep abyss" of nature, and thus, solidarity became the other ethical imperative of the new science. This meant communicating personal discoveries to colleagues, an interpretative cooperation practiced by those who operated within an ideal cultural community. Because research is never-ending, progress consists of a sort of relay race, something to which even the *Nuncius* was witness, treating itself as an *Avviso* (Announcement) subject to the "judgment and criticism" of "philosophers and astronomers" so that they could verify its credibility and improve its results.

Not only did Galileo approve of free discussion, but he also made explicit requests in advance for possible criticisms of his theses, offering assurance that they would be acknowledged. It is no wonder, then, that for the prestige acquired from his fertile explorations and for the authoritativeness of his age, the Tuscan scientist was acclaimed as a modern Socrates by Castelli, Peiresc, Diodati, and many others of his contemporaries. Indeed, he was a teacher, and with his dialogue he guided the young and opened doors to the secrets of the universe. For many, the *Nuncius* marked the advent of a new era and was therefore literally a gospel speaking in biblical tones appropriate to its prophetic role. After the appearance of the *Sidereus*, one writer even went as far as to say that this little book "was able to wake me up from a very deep lethargy to which I was subjected for five continuous years" (X, 317).

The early seventeenth century seemed perfectly suited to paligenetic expectations, a human reaction to a reality that was characterized by tensions, poverty, and suffering, a time when men were easily tempted by aspirations, hopes, and comforting utopias. One group of intellectuals, the Oggidiani, were united in their anguish for the decline of customs and in their grief for a wilted and degraded nature, dark omens of world decay that assumed the guise of war, famine, plague, and such natural disasters as earthquakes and volcanic eruptions. In their pessimistic view, Galileo himself had confirmed the decrepit aging of the entire universe. Before his theories, it was accepted that the Earth was the "sink of all bads," but consolation had been found in the thought that beyond this sphere of fire there existed something unchangeable and permanent. The wrinkles on the shriveled face of the moon as well as the disfiguring spots on the sun had confirmed a general corruption. However, as Alberto Tenenti demonstrates, a sense of death stimulates love for life, and the cathartic myths of the Golden Age draw the lymph from the epochs of dark crisis, justifying Shelley's romantically rhetorical question: "If winter comes, can spring be far behind?" The first auspices of regeneration had come, from the sky as usual, in the form of a new star discovered by Tycho Brahe in 1572 near the constellation of Cassiopea, and in an even more impressive example of 1604, studied by Kepler in Serpentarium.

Galileo's announcement rejuvenated even knowledge, being finally emancipated from a sclerosis due to the geostatic paradigm, which the old establishment was defending. While the *novatori* (innovators) understood the reasons for such obstinate protection of well-established ideas, the certainty of their collapse entered their minds on the wings of a strong yearning for reform. With the *Sidereus*, Galileo, though already greatly esteemed, rose from a simple university professor to an emblem of modernity. Having put an end to secular beliefs, he became a representative personality for a new epoch. Not by chance, in the early signs of the *querelle des anciens et des modernes* (quarrel of the ancients and of the moderns), his telescope would become, for Tassoni, an argumentative weapon with which to overcome "as many Latin and Greek inventions as were found so famous over the course of the years."[31] When announced to the world, the shock of these new wonders reintroduced the *topos* of indefinite progress, gathered the newest vital energies and galvanized enthusiasm that today, accustomed as we are to everything, is impossible to understand. "In the extreme old age of this world in ruin—as a seventeenth century man excitedly exclaimed—if ever something so marvelous could occur in the arts and letters, beyond all hopes and expectations, it was certainly the content of your booklet entitled *Sidereus Nuncius*, oh world-famous Galileo" (X, 394).[32]

The structure of the *libello* (booklet) is itself essential and austere, invoking confirmation and in-depth analyses at every step, prior to the conclusion, where the deferment to a work of more ample breath was unconventional. The future *Dialogue concerning the two chief world systems* was, by this time, already an advanced project, as can be gathered philologically by the many arguments of the *Sidereus* that are reconsidered, nearly to the letter, in the following *opus maius*. Thus, Galileo introduced the *Sidereus* as a kind of presentiment, a program for the future that was inevitably suggested by the excited tone of the preliminary essay, which opened unlimited perspectives even if the rational method and the consciousness of the difficulty inherent in the research anticipated a long course of implementation.

Some though, more impatient, took shortcuts, imagining in the infinite universe a plurality of inhabited worlds, to be reached through utopian journeys and confronted with not only a novelistic view, but also—especially for libertine thought—with a theological and philosophical one. In this sense, the *Sidereus* provided an unintentional incentive for science fiction, a genre based on the desire to reach, in one bound, the same far away destinations discovered by the telescope. It mattered little that in the modern scientist's *reportage*, the existence of "innumerable cavities and prominences" on the moon had been proven to exist "no longer solely in the imagination, but also in sensorial experience, and as a necessary demonstration"—"filosoficamente" (philosophically), therefore, and not "favolosamente" (XI, 142) (fantastically), as had happened to Plutarch. In reality, nothing at that moment was impossible, nothing incredible for those that, yearning for a freer and vaster world, were released from the laws of verisimilitude and able to reason in utopian terms. Our moon continued to exercise its mythical and anthropological suggestions, acting as a protagonist of legends, with magic and superstition explained by the ancient animistic and metaphysical paradigm (Casini 400; Camporesi, *La terra e la luna* 282–323).

Though Galileo never supported the idea of lunar inhabitation, the insistence with which the *Sidereus* made the moon resemble the Earth was interpreted by some as proof of life on the moon.[33] As there is no doubt that Galileo was fascinated by the moon, we may choose to apply the sympathetic emphasis of Italo Calvino: "whoever really loves the moon is not happy contemplating it as a conventional image, (s)he wants to enter in a closer relationship with it." The author of *Palomar*, a postmodern enthusiast of the telescope, explains that as soon as Galileo began to speak of the moon his prose rose "to a level of precision and evidence," that for the first time made it "a real object," described "minutely as a tangible thing." This does not exclude, however, the "prodigious lyrical rarefaction," that "rises in the enchanted suspension of a dream":[34] a statement that is certainly worthy of the unconditional admirer of Ariosto, cosmic and lunar poet, annotated with much of care.

Besides the precise assertions, the high literary and expressive consciousness that will later serve as a model even to Leopardi, had also allowed a science fiction reading of the *Sidereus*, inculcating an unprecedented realism in the chroniclers of spatial flights at the precise moment in which the relationship between the Earth and moon, for long time imagined in terms of alterity, was now considered in terms of identity.[35] In an attempt to not stray too far from Galileo, it is enough to mention the *Somnium de astronomia lunari* (The Dream of Lunar Astronomy) by Kepler—an allegorical, dream-like work with an appendix established by the *De facie in orbe Lunae* (Face which appears on the orb of the moon) by Plutarch—in which, when the topography of the moon is described, fantasy is displaced to illustrate the real landscape as investigated with the telescope. After the *Sidereus*, science imposed new limits even on the liberty of science fiction books. The cosmic journey, in the past completed with such prodigious means as flying wagons or on the wings of Icarus or the hippogriff, little by little was forced to confront problems of mechanical physics and to devise technology capable of mastering friction and the force of gravity (Bailey 13–14). In Kepler's *Somnium* at the moment of the preparations, one has to confront, among other things, the difficulties produced by the very low temperature of interstellar space, and by the hard impact with the lunar ground, by the necessity to avoid the solar rays during the stay on the moon (Rossi, *Il sogno* 379).

Even with the increased verisimilitude caused by technology, the men of the seventeenth century never renounced the utopian hope that the solid conquests of new science were carriers of peace and well-being, so that the realism acquired with the tangible instrument of the telescope did not harm dreams and chimeras. As shall be made clear in the next section of this essay, the bloody military expeditions conducted by Spain during the colonization of the Americas prevented Christopher Columbus from becoming the founder of a new golden age, while the new worlds of the *Sidereus* seemed to herald a period of newfound harmony. It is clear, in hindsight, that these hopes were soon to be frustrated, for in one of the many ironies of destiny, the telescope, which at first was an omen of peace (because of the painless way in which Galileo had realized his discoveries), in little time would be the cause of a strong dispute between Galileo and the Church. At that point Galileo once again returned to his sharp rhetorical weapons to defend the cosmological theory, founded on what his optical *cannone* (cannon) had shown him.

Toward More Restless Times

Perhaps it is inevitable that every researcher hoping to penetrate the mysterious territories of the unknown will sooner or later encounter, to paraphrase Marino in the *Adone* (X, 45, 7), "risks" in the form of envy, the subversive force of new ideas, threats to the status quo, and even as a consequence of achieved success, since popularity inevitably limits one's time for continued study. Columbus makes a fundamental comparison to Galileo, for he celebrated the very interplanetary journeys documented in the diary of the *Sidereus*, navigating the large waves of the Atlantic. In transferring to Florence, Galileo, like Columbus, was immediately forced to weather his own storms, which were no less insidious. These were shrewdly predicted to him with expert diplomacy by Sagredo, who warned his friend "the stormy sea of the Court," where "furious winds of competition" would "torment and worry him" (XI, 171). This prediction proved true, as the most malevolent attacks against Galileo came right from Florence, initially by Francesco Sizzi, who was well known in the Medicean court, and then by Lodovico delle Colombe, both of whom dedicated their anti-Galilean works to Giovanni de' Medici. Additionally, the first accusation against the so-called Copernican letter to Castelli was forwarded to the Holy Office not from Rome but by the Dominicans in Florence. before these facts, though not quite a storm, there was, nonetheless, a slight breeze that arose in the Florentine court regarding defamation and suspicion: that is, if it is true that the Grand Duke, before imprinting the emblem of the Medicean planets on the medal that was to be a gift to Galileo, thought it better to verify its existence (X, 368), seeking—according to the plausible opinion of Giorgio Tabarroni[36]—the verdict of Kepler, who replied with the *Dissertatio*.

Galileo could no longer stay in Padua. He had already decided to leave before the unexpected revelations of the telescope, which, rather than holding him back, actually hurried his departure. The *Sidereus*, dedicated to Cosimo de' Medici, was the best card Galileo could play in the negotiations for his transfer. The advantageous conditions that Galileo obtained were certainly influenced by the secret negotiations with the grand-ducal diplomacy on which names would be assigned to the recently identified moons of Jupiter. In Venice, these discoveries were not as valuable, neither for encomiastic reasons (as there was not a sole prince or dynasty that stood to gain by self-glorification) nor epistemologically speaking, because for Sarpi and for the entire scientific *entourage* of the Veneto, the consequences drawn in favor of the Copernican theory remained anchored to an abstract level of mathematical hypothesis, while for Galileo they implied a new conception of the universe (Cozzi 129; Sosio 269–311). After all, for Venice, the telescope had already been exhausted of its practical advantages during times of war. Although divided by an irreducible hostility toward Aristotle, even the intellectuals that referred to Sarpi agreed with the peripatetic Cremonini, who regarded Galileo's most recent astronomical studies as nothing more than "girandole" (XI, 165) (windmills), as scarce profit with respect to mechanics.

For its author, the *Sidereus* was a first manifesto, a *cartello di sfida* (written challenge), as defined in a modern way, that urgently expected its systematic completion, resulting in a new cosmic order. After many fruitless attempts, did it still make sense for Galileo to hope that the senate of the Veneto would free him of the tedious obligations connected to his office as university professor, so that he could place his energy entirely into his program? His work was not peaceful: from the beginning traditionalists had opposed resistance, and for his success he required political protection that was lacking in Venice, where, paradoxically, the ecumenical fame of the *Sidereus* resulted in a never-before experienced isolation for its fortunate author. Moreover, Galileo looked beyond a simple astronomical reform because, with greater and greater clarity, he aspired to pursue a cultural politics in which the Copernican theory would be forced to reconcile with Christian faith in order to regenerate its spirituality, so that the new science would be accepted by the Church, and, in turn, overcome the obsolete limits of scholastic and Counter-Reformistic thought, to which all still officially conformed. Hence, in 1610 an attempt to obtain Jesuit consent was inconceivable in the progressive environment of Venice, which had recently received the Interdict. Also for this reason, the discoveries of the *Sidereus*, supported by the high degree of technical perfection of the Venetian arsenal, could only effect its epistemological consequences in Florence, near an influential family, whose scientist would be granted at court both comfort to speculate and diplomacy, authoritatively represented in the Church of Rome by the considerable number of cardinals and the close proximity of the Pope.

To conclude a design that was to move from the contemplation of the skies to palaces of power and mundane initiatives, Galileo chose to abandon the service of the Venetian Republic and to place himself in the charge of an "absolute prince" (X, 233), leaving the academic world (that as a whole proved immune to the novelty of his discoveries) to become a man of the court (Guaragnella 105). Unfortunately, the "comfort" he had hoped for proved a chimera, because, though he was no longer tormented by the procession of clients, he now had to defend himself from adversaries, ever refining his talents as a polemicist rather than a theoretical scientist. By this point, the *Sidereus* had radically transformed his life, and not always for the better. On one hand, he was free from the labor of teaching, having attained fame both on a personal level, and, in scientific progress, having made confirmations of a new system of the world. On the other hand (leaving aside inferences on the presumed moons of Saturn), his astronomical research on the sunspots (observed while still in Padua) and the phases of Venus (discovered during his first days in Florence) had been halted, due to continuous distractions, caused by the constant obligation to reply to skeptical objections on the floats, sunspots, comets, and the relationship between the Copernican theory and the Bible.

Galileo later transferred to Florence to write *De sistemate seu constitutione universi* (On the System or Constitution of the Universe), a work that was "immense and full of philosophy, astronomy and geometry" (X, 351) that he conceived following the impulse of the *Sidereus*, in which an announcement for the work had already appeared. Instead, in the twenty years following the wonderful celestial events of 1609–1610, he no longer conceived his writings as autonomous scientific texts, not provoked by outside involvement. His Copernican crusade forced him to take a continuous and immediate stand, which was, as a result, neither organic nor calm, committed as he was, not to the systematic nature of a treatise, but to the more rhetorical genres of discourse, letters, and dialogue (Wallace 281–82). He was never able to complete a more sumptuous edition of the *Sidereus*, to which his exhibitionism, some vanity, and the affectionately pressing requests of his friends inspired him. The enthusiastic cultural politics that intended to drag the ecclesiastical authorities from supporting heliocentrism prevented him from publishing the new version that was to include elegant copper incisions, a text that this time would abandon Latin in favor of "Tuscan" (as curiosity had tainted even the common people), and an abundant laudation with "many poems" celebrating the wonders of the new firmament, gathered in an anthological preface (X, 299).

Galileo's failure to realize this project, which he had firmly supported during his last months in Padua, added to other problems, caused in large part by envy, triggered by his dazzling astronomical success. The opposition to his pro-Copernican propaganda was more tenacious than expected, producing in him covert bad moods and perhaps even some feelings of regret. In Padua, just one year after his departure, there were rumors of his returning "to the former tranquility and liberty" (XI, 230). Regardless, the separation from the Veneto was irreversible, not only because the proud and stubborn Galileo could not go back on the decisions he had made, but also because his behavior had given the Venetian patricians the feeling of "having been scorned by him" (XI, 246). It would no longer have been possible to retrace his steps, even had he been inclined to do it. His sudden departure, prepared in absolute secrecy, and his silence regarding help received by Venetian technicians in preparing the telescope, had made Galileo appear ungrateful. In the moment in which all were avidly seeking the *Sidereus*, ready to devour its contents, Paolo Sarpi remained indifferent, confessing to not having yet read the work, since its contents had already been discussed in person with the author.[37] When the popular Galileo sought to say a good word for everyone, Paolo Gualdo warned him "to save an eyeglass to see us, your servants" (X, 477), doubling the extant accusation of ingratitude by asking him "where does so much silence come from? How is it possible that V. S. has completely forgotten these regions?" (X, 230). Giovan Francesco Sagredo furthered the accusation by writing in his letters about the bitterness one feels at a friendship betrayed.

In truth, Galileo, though not exempt from baseness, was of a fundamentally generous nature, and if, after his return to Tuscany, he had ceased his relationship with the old group, it had not been out of ingratitude. He knew that the Sarpian circle could not understand the extent of his projects, because, due to its intellectual formation, it was devoted to the study of mechanical physics and of problems of motion. In his missionary zeal, Galileo realized that in the Veneto region the Pentecostal revelation of a new sky and Earth was not equally received in other circles, which were more sensitive to the spiritual values implicit in its message. Galileo became ever more passionate and pugnacious after his first successful results. Thus, he could not retrospectively reflect on the period that, after his conviction and abjuration, would seem the happiest of his life. His program oriented him toward noble youths gathered around Cesi to form the Academy of Lincei, toward the Society of Jesus that enumerated scientists among the best in the field of geometric optics and astronomy, and finally, toward the more open and influential cultural circles that hoped for a profound renewal in the heart of the Church. Inspired by Mercury and his unfailing vigor as messenger of the gods, the "short treatise" that announced great epiphanies dragged him irresistibly toward Rome, the ambassador of more modern truths.

Notes

1. All quotations from Galileo and his correspondents are taken from the national edition of *Opere* edited by A. Favaro (1890–1909; repr., Florence: Barbèra, 1968). The Roman numeral in the text indicates the volume, and the Arabic numeral indicates the page.
2. The originality of this numerical expansion in respect to the past is noted by Francesco Stelluti in the poem placed in the 1623 *Princeps* in the opening of the *Saggiatore* (VI, 210).
3. See E. Pasoli, "Caratteri letterari e umani della "Dissertatio" e sua attualità," in *Dissertatio* by J. Kepler, xxxii–xxxiv.
4. Kepler himself will make an essential explanation of the *Sidereus* in the following *Dioptrice*.
5. Wotton's letter, absent in the Ed. naz. of the *Opere* by Galileo, can be read in M. H. Nicolson, *Science and Imagination*, 35–36.
6. "A prominent man pushes me to create an emblem of celestial things; and I thought to gain credit using the new Medicean or Galilean stars as a figure that places before me a nice concept suitable to the author's grave sentence." This intention of the Bolognese Giambattista Agucchi is expressed in one of his letters to Galileo (XI, 205), where it earned the consensus of the scientist (Ibid., XI, 264).
7. See the anxious suggestions of Giovanni Roffeni (X, 392) and of Federico Cesi (XI, 175). Instead, as known, the reprint of the *Sidereus* published in Frankfurt did not contain anything more than what already appeared in the *princeps*.
8. One could accept the very personal but plausible interpretation of G. Sacerdoti, *Nuovo cielo, nuova terra: La rivelazione copernicana di "Antonio e Cleopatra" di Shakespeare*, Bologna: Il Mulino, 1990.
9. G. Leopardi, "Dialogue of an Imp and a Gnome," in *The Moral Essays*, 61. The same image of a world without people can be found in the sketch of "Dialogue between a Horse and an Ox."
10. E. Raimondi, "Lettere italiane," *La nuova scienza e la visione degli oggetti*, 21 (1969): 280, 269, 267. The essay was gathered with the less incisive title "Verso il realismo," *Il romanzo senza idillio*. (Torino: Einaudi, 1974), 3–56, where the quotes correspond to the pages 22, 9, and 6. From now on, the pages will refer to the more accessible volume instead of the magazine.
11. The dispute was inaugurated by a paper by G. Righini, *New Light on Galileo's Lunar Observations,* which had the replica by O. Gingerich, *Dissertatio cum Professore Righini et "Sidereo Nuncio"* included in the same miscellaneous volume *Reason, Experiment, and Mysticism in the Scientific Revolution* 77–88. More recently, G. Tabarroni praised, referring to the manuscripts that were printed, the "immagini pittoriche di rara efficacia impressionistica" (pictorial images of rare impressionistic efficacy (51).

12. See the conclusions tinged to the multiple collected requests in *L'uomo barocco*, edited by R. Villari.
13. The blending of magical motives and curiosities in the emerging rationality is underlined by E. Garin, 19.
14. Read E. Tesauro, *Il cannocchiale aristotelico*. (Torino: Zavatta, 1670), 89–90, keeping in mind Raimondi, *Introduzione*, xvi–xviii.
15. F. Picinelli, *Del mondo simbolico ampliato, formato d'imprese scelte, spiegate et illustrate con sentenze et erudizioni sacre e profane* (1653) (Milano: F. Vigone, 1669), 751, col. 1–752, col. 2.
16. See F. Pevere, 119–148. Besides the telescope it includes poems dedicated to spinning wheels, wool winders, organs, clocks, compasses, zoomorphic robots, and mills.
17. See the recovery of Piero Camporesi, discoverer of a forgotten satire *Contro la lussuria* by Lorenzo Azzolino, according to which "... per civettar fin da l' altane / ha ritrovato il modo il Galileo" (*I balsami di Venere* 103). Moreover, Bartolomeo Dotti is an author of a sonnet whose theme is *Mirando con cannocchiale una bellissima dama*, *Rime*, (Venice: 1689), 238. On this poet see W. Binni, "La rassegna della letteratura italiana," *Tre lirici dell' ultimo barocco, III. Bartolomeo Dotti*, 67 (1963): 1, 3–49; and V. Boggione, *"Poi che tutto corre al nulla:" le rime di Bartolomeo Dotti* (Torino: Università degli studi di Torino, 1997).
18. P. Valéry, *Variazioni su una "Pensee," Varietà*, 107, 104, and 102.
19. M. Bontempelli, *Galileo poeta* (1943), in *Introduzioni e discorsi*, 230.
20. P. Valéry, *Variazioni su una "Pensee,"* in *Varietà*, 107.
21. The syntagm is common for Francesco Stelluti as much as for Iacopo Cicognini. See N. Vaccalluzzo, *Galileo Galilei nella poesia del suo secolo* (Palermo: Sandron, 1910), 49 and 33.
22. J. Donne, vv. 205, 213, 210–11, "An Anatomy of the World: The First Anniversary", *The Complete English Poems*, 276.
23. Rossi, "La pluralità dei mondi," La scienza e la filosofia dai moderni, 1989: 159.
24. The new science had released an anguished fear of open spaces. See E. Bellone 24–26.
25. Ibid.
26. "How small the biggest parts of Earth's proud title show! / [...] And seems a grain of sand." These verses are from Abraham Cowley's poem "The Exstasy." Cf. M. H. Nicolson, *The Breaking of the Circle*, 195.
27. On this crucial chapter of the history of ideas, see the pioneering works of Nicolson and H. Blumenberg, "Cosmologia metaforizzata," *Paradigmi per una metaforologia* (Bologna: Il Mulino, 1969), in particular 148–54.
28. See the chapter "Milton and the Telescope" in Nicolson, *Science and Imagination*, 80–109.
29. According to Kuznecov, "the *ratio* of the universe did not consist in a static outline of natural places, but in a kinetic pattern of motion" (42).

30. B. Brecht, *Vita di Galileo*, in *I capolavori*, a cura di C. Cases (Torino: Einaudi, 1963), 113.
31. A. Tassoni, *Pensieri*, X, XXVI, in *Pensieri e scritti preparatori*, 931–32.
32. "Si quid praeter spem et exspectationem [. . .] hac ultima et corruentis mundi senecta, in artibus et scientiis accidere potuit admirabilius [. . .], hoc certe est tui, Galilaee celeberrime, libelli, cui nomen fecisti Nuncii Siderei, material" (Letter written by Bartolomeo Schroeter to Galileo on July 8, 1610: X, 394).
33. It is what Pierre Borel supported in 1657 in his *Discourse nouveau prouvat la pluralité des modes*. Cf. Rossi, *La pluralità dei mondi*, La scienza e la filosofia dai moderni, 1989: 179.
34. I. Calvino, *Una pietra sopra* (Torino: Einaudi, 1980), 183, 186.
35. Cf. G. Piazza 13–34. Later in science and imagination there was a new separation between the two celestial bodies.
36. Introduction to Kepler, *Dissertatio*, xxiv–xxv.
37. CF. Letter by Paolo Sarpi to Jacques Leschassier on April 27, 1610 in P. Sarpi, *Lettere ai Gallicani*, ed. B. Ulianich. (Wiesbaden: F. Steiner, 1961), 79.

Works Cited

Baffetti, Giovanni. *Il* "Sidereus Nuncius a Bologna." *Intersezioni*, XI (1991): 3, 477–500.
Bailey, James Osler. *Pilgrims Through Space and Time: Trends and Patterns in Scientific and Utopian Fiction*. New York: Angus Books, 1947.
Banfi, Antonio. *Vita di Galileo Galilei*. Milan: Feltrinelli, 1962.
Basile, Giambattista. *Lo cunto de li cunti*. Ed. M. Rak. Milan: Garzanti, 1986.
Bellone, Enrico. *Il sogno di Galileo: Oggetti e immagini della ragione*. Bologna: Il Mulino, 1980.
Blumenberg. Hans. *Paradigmi per una metaforologia*. Bologna: Il Mulino, 1969.
Bontempelli, Massimo. *Introduzioni e discorsi*. Milan: Bompiani, 1964.
Brecht, Bertolt. *Vita di Galileo*. In *I capolavori*. a cura di C. Torino: Einaudi, 1963.
Burke, Edmund. *A Philosophy Enquiry into the Origin of our Ideas of the Sublime and Beautiful*. New York: Columbia University Press, 1958.
Calvino, Italo. *If on a Winter's Night a Traveler*. Trans. William Weaver. New York: Alfred A. Knopf, 1993.
_____. *Una pietra sopra*. Torino: Einaudi, 1980.
Camporesi, Piero. *I balsami di venere*. Milan: Garzanti, 1989.
_____. *La terra e la Luna. Alimentazione, folklore società*. Milan: Il Saggiatore, 1989.
Casini, Paolo. "Plutarco: Galileo e la faccia della luna." *Intersezioni* 4 (1984): 2, 397–404.
Castelli, Benedetto. *Lettera a Monsignor Giovanni Ciampoli con un discorso sopra la vista, in alcuni opuscoli filosofici*. Bologna: Giacomo Monti, 1669.

Cavaillé, Jean Pierre. *Descartes. La fable du monde*. Paris: Vrin, 1991.
Chevalley, Catherine. *Kepler et Galilée dans la bataille du "Sidereus Nuncius" (1610–1611)*. In *Novità celesti e crisi del sapere*, Atti del Convegno internazionale di studi galileiani. a cura di P. Galluzzi. Florence: Giunti-Barbèra, 1984.
Cioni, Alfredo. *Tommaso Baglioni. Dizionario Biografico degli Italiani*. Rome: Istituto della Enciclopedia Italiana, 1963.
Contardi, Bruno. *La retorica e l'architettura del barocco*. Rome: Bulzoni, 1978.
Cozzi, Gaetano. *Paolo Sarpi tra Venezia e l'Europa*. Torino: Einaudi, 1979.
D'Elia, Pasquale. *Echi delle scoperte galileiane in Cina vivente ancora Galileo (1612–1640)*, "Rendiconti della Accademia Nazionale dei Lincei." Classe di scienze morali, storiche e filologiche. s. VIII 1 (1946): 125–93.
Donne, John. *The Complete English Poems*. Ed. A. J. Smith. Harmondsworth, England: Penguin, 1973.
Foucault, Michel. "Of Other Spaces." *Diacritics* XVI 1 (1986): 22–23.
Galilei, Galileo. *Opere. 20 vols*. Ed. A. Favaro. Florence: Barbèra, 1968. First published 1890–1909.
Garin, Eugenio. *Fra '500 e '600: Scienze nuove, metodi nuovi, nuove accademie, L'Accademia dei Lincei e la cultura europea nel XVII secolo*. Rome: Accademia Nazionale dei Lincei, 1991. Published in conjuction with the historical exhibition in Paris, December 13, 1991–January 8, 1992.
Gingerich, Owen. "*Dissertatio cum professore righini et sidereo nuncio*," in *Reason, Experiment, and Mysticism in the Scientific Revlution*. Eds. Maria Luisa Righini Bonelli and William R. Shea. New York: Sciente History Publications, 1975: 77–88.
Giovio, Paolo. *Dialogo dell'imprese militari e amorose*. a cura di M.L. Doglio. Rome: Bulzoni, 1978.
Gjertsen, Derek. *The Classics of Science*. New York: Lilian Barber Press, 1984.
Guaragnella, Pasquale. *"Avvisi" del moderno in Sarpi: Galileo e la nuova scienza*. Bari: Adriatica, 1998.
Grafton, Anthony, April Shelford, and Nancy G. Siraisi. New Worlds, *Ancient Texts: The Power of Tradition and the Shock of Discovery*. Cambridge, Mass.: Belknap Press of Harvard University Press, 1992.
Kepler, Johannes. *Dissertatio cum Nuncio Sidereo*. a cura di E. Pasoli e G. Tabarroni. Torino: Bottega d'Erasmo, 1972.
Koyré, Alexandre. *From the Closed World to the Infinite Universe*. Baltimore: Johns Hopkins Press, 1957.
———. *Études galiléennes*, Paris: Hermann, 1939.
Kuznecov, Boris G. *Galileo*. Bari: Dedalo, 1979.
Leopardi, Giacomo. *The Moral Essays: Operette Morali*. Vol. 1. Trans. Patrick Creagh. New York: Columbia University Press, 1983.
Lovejoy, Arthur Oncken. *The Great Chain of Being*. Cambridge, MA: Harvard University Press, 1936.

Maravall, José Antonio. *Culture of the Baroque: Analysis of a Historical Structure*. Trans. Terry Cochran. Minneapolis: University of Minnesota Press, 1986.
Marino, Giambattista. *L'Adone*. Milano: A. Mondadori, 1976.
Nicolson, Marjorie Hope. *The Breaking of the Circle*. New York: Columbia University Press, 1960.
_____. *Science and Imagination*. Ithaca, NY: Cornell University Press, 1962.
Pastore Stocchi, Manlio. *Il periodo Veneto di Galileo Galilei*, in *Storia della cultura veneta*, a cura de G. Arnaldi e M. Pastore Stocchi, Neri Pozza, Venezia 1984, vol. IV, t. II, pp. 37–66.
Piazza, Gianguido. "La Luna nella Luna: Metafore, congetture e scoperte della moderna astronomia planetaria." *La Luna allo specchio*. a cura di N. Minerva. Bologna: Pàtron, 1990.
Picinelli, Filippo. *Del mondo simbolico ampliato, formato d'imprese scelte, spiegate et illustrate con sentenze et erudizioni sacre e profane* (1653). Milan: F. Vigone, 1669.
Pirandello, Luigi. *Late Mattia Pascal*. Trans. Nicoletta Simborowski. London: Dedalus Ltd., 1987.
_____. *On Humor*. Trans. Antonio Illiano and Daniel P. Testa. Chapel Hill, NC: University of North Carolina Press, 1974.
Quint, David. "La barca dell'avventura nell'epica rinascimentale." *Intersezioni* v. 3, (1985): 467–88.
Raimondi, Ezio. *Introduzione* 1981 a *Letteratura barocca. Studi sul Seicento italiano*. Florence: Olschki, 1982.
_____. *La nuova scienza e la visione degli oggetti: Il romanzo senza idillio*. Torino: Einaudi, 1974. 3–56.
Redondi, Pietro. *La luce messaggio celeste*. In *Novità celesti e crisi del sapere*, Atti del Convegno internazionale di studi galileiani. a cura di P. Galluzzi, Florence: Giunti-Barbèra, 1984.
Reeves, Eileen. "The Rhetoric of Optics: Perspectives on Galileo and Tesauro." *Stanford Italian Review* VII 1–2 (1987): 129–45.
Righini, Bonelli, M. L. Shea, William R. *Reason, Experiment, and Mysticism in the Scientific Revolution*. New York: Science History Publications, 1975.
Rossi, Paolo. *Galilei*. Rome and Milan: Compagnia Edizioni Internazionali, 1966.
_____. "Il sogno di Keplero." *Intersezioni* 5 (1985): 2, 379.
_____. *La scienza e la filosofia dai moderni. Aspetti della rivoluzione scientifica*. Torino: Bollati Boringhieri, 1989.
Sacerdoti, Gilberto. *Nuovo cielo, nuova terra: La rivelazione copernicana di "Antonio e Cleopatra" di Shakespeare*. Bologna: Il Mulino, 1990.
Sarpi, Paolo. *Lettere ai Gallicani*. Ed. B. Ulianich. Wiesbaden: F. Steiner, 1961.
Savvedra Fajardo, D. *Empressas políticas*. Ed. F.J. Díez de Revenga. Madrid: Planeta, 1988.
Shakespeare, William. *The Tragedy of Anthony and Cleopatra*. Ed. Michael Neil. Oxford: Clarendon Press, 1994.

Slawinski, Maurice. "Rhetoric and Science/Rhetoric of Science/Rhetoric as Science." *Science, Culture and Popular Belief in Renaissance Europe*. Ed. Stephen. Pumfrey, et al. Manchester: Manchester University Press, 1991.
Sosio, Libero. "Galileo Galilei e Paolo Sarpi." *Galileo Galilei e la cultura veneta*. Venice: Venetian Institute of Sciences, Letters and Arts, 1995. 269–311.
Tassoni, A. *Pensieri e scritti preparatori*. Ed. P. Pulitati. Modena: Panini, 1986.
Tesauro, E. *Il cannocchiale aristotelico*. Torino: Zavatta, 1670.
Tuzet, Hélène. *Le Cosmos et l'imagination*. Paris: J. Corti, 1965.
Vaccalluzzo, N. *Galileo Galilei nella poesia del suo secolo*, Palermo: Sandron, 1910.
Valéry, P. *Varietà*. Ed. S. Agosti. Milan: Rizzoli, 1971.
Villari, R. *L'uomo barocco*. Rome and Bari: Laterza, 1991.
Wallace, William A. *Galileo and His Sources: The Heritage of the Collegio Romano in Galileo's Science*. Princeton, NJ: Princeton University Press, 1984.

◆ 2

Descartes in Naples: The Reception of the *Passions de l'âme*

Silvia Contarini

(Translated by Stephen P. McCormick)

In perhaps the most representative text of the philosophical and scientific revival of the *Accademia napoletana degli Investiganti* (Neapolitan Academy of the Investigators), *Parere sull'origine e i progressi della medicina* (Opinion on the Origin and Progress of Medicine) by Leonardo Di Capua (1681), the open and unexplored space of the research takes on before the eyes of the *novatores* (innovators) the worrisome yet seductive forms of a "stormy sea" and of a "dense and unknown forest" (Di Capua 485). This is a "confused labyrinth" in which the followers of Galileo and of Descartes—who are compared by the author to the helmsman who goes to sea in a "small and poorly supplied ship" or to the "little experienced wayfarer" surprised in the forest of "obscure night"—renounce from the very beginning the certitudes of ancient and scholastic knowledge in order to achieve the wonders of the universe supplied only by the tools of natural philosophy, geometry, and ethics. If recalling the importance of experience and the knowledge of mathematical characters is—after Galileo—essential to decode the "obscure labyrinth" of nature, the choice of ethics reveals, on the other hand, the strongly perceived necessity to investigate the less-known knowledge of man, that interior and mysterious part from which depend the causes and effects of illnesses and the very well-being of the organism.

Still with regard to the principle role taken by ethics inside the new paradigm of knowledge, the author of *Parere* clarifies:

> Come potrà il medico, adoperando il suo mestiere, con valenti medicamenti sanar gli ammalati del corpo se in prima le malattie dell'animo loro non toglie? Cioè a dire, se non sa di filosofia morale? Imperciocché i mali tutti del corpo, come da prima e principal cagione, da alcuna passione dell'animo sovente nascer sogliono, la qual certamente né conoscere né rimuover potrà il medico giamai se dalla moral filosofia non sia scorto.

> (How can the physician, with his/her professional expertise and valid medications heal the people sick in the body without first eliminating the illness of the soul? This is to say, without having some knowledge of moral philosophy? In fact, every bodily illness quite often finds its first and principal cause in some passions of the soul that the physician would certainly neither be able to recognize nor remove without being illuminated by moral philosophy.) (493)

The close relationship between the passions and the dysfunctions of the *organismo* (organism) returns to a functional and not ontological concept of illness present in all of classic tradition, according to which diseases are in fact a result of a physiological alteration of the balance of the body's humors (Verbeek 45–61). As noticed, the Cartesian epistemology of the human machine provides medicine—in particular Italian medicine at the end of the seventeenth century—not only with an anatomical and physiological theoretical model, but also with a clinical-therapeutic frame of reference that authorizes the split from Galenic medicine (Di Giandomenico 651–58). Nonetheless, the perspective delineated in *Parere* and the tie that unites medicine and ethics seem to allude not only to the physics developed in *De l'homme* (On Man), but rather to the more problematic and far-reaching indications of the *Passions de l'âme* (On the Passions of the Soul)—a text that begins to take hold in the culture of Naples only several years later—in which Descartes had declared to examine the nature of affections and their manifestations in the realm of medicine, putting into practice the affirmation of what he wrote in the letter to Chanut of June 15, 1646 concerning the dependence of ethics on notions of physics and mechanics (Descartes 82–83).

Not by chance, in the very same year as *Parere*, the treatise on passions was read and utilized in the Latin version that circulated from 1650 in the collection *Opera* (Works) by another doctor close to the circle of the Investiganti, Luca Tozzi, who illustrates in Cartesian terms the mechanical concept of passions and the origin of affections from the modification of blood in the chapter "*De motibus cum animi tum corporis"* (On the motions both of the body and the soul), from his *Medicinae pars prior* (Medicine part one), published in 1781 (Serrapica; Lojacono 58–59).

In this text Tozzi quotes from the medical scheme of the *Passions de l'âme*, but he misses the notion of *dressage* (training) and of *maîtrise* (mastery) of the affections that constitute the new principle of the Cartesian treatise, upon which, several years later, the more mature insight of the Accademia di Medinacoeli would be based (Tozzi 44). At closer inspection, the orthodox division between the *passions élargissantes* (invigorating passions), which contribute to the orderly functioning of the organism, and the *passions déprimantes* (depressing passions), which obstruct this order, appears in Tozzi's work split by the fleeting mobility of the affections that continuously intersect one another, changing physiognomy and characteristics, in a sort of perennial metamorphosis, emblematic of their intrinsic and, in the end, ungovernable instability.

The binary and changing nature of the passions, and the relative trust in the diagnostic power of medicine, that aims to correct impulses and motions damaging the economy of the organism, returns in the 1721 addition entitled *De recto usu sex rerum nonnaturalium* (The Right Use of Six Unnatural Things). Here Tozzi, perhaps influenced by the most recent reading of Gregorio Caloprese, confronts once again the problem of the origin of the affections—in conjunction with the Cartesian duality and with the role of imagination as mediator between the body and the soul—including the passions as the neutral causes that may indifferently benefit or damage human beings, and whose good use is necessary for the conservation of life (207). Like Descartes, Tozzi believes that the passions are at the same time the cause and the principal remedy for illness. Also, he suggests as therapy the universally understood method of balancing the various affections: a sort of "allotropy" by which the pernicious consequences of a passion are tempered or contrasted by means of its opposite.

If the Cartesian explanation concerning nature and the origins of the passions appears to be accepted within the Academy of the Investiganti, the most general and innovative theory of the use of passions seems to remain confined to the physiological realm, as an external practice exerted on the body, establishing anew the correct flow of the vital spirits and the organism's machine. This is without doubt the position of doctor Nicola Cirillo—a friend not only of Tozzi, but also of Vico and Caloprese—who participates actively in the battle of the *novatores (innovators)* on the side of Cartesianism as an emblem of the revived *libertas philosophandi* (freedom of philosophizing). In the collection of the *Consulti medici* (Medical Consultations) published posthumously in 1738 in Naples and reprinted afterward in Venice, the rise of the hysteric and convulsive affection is diagnosed considering the Cartesian theory of the vital spirits, composed of unequal particles, or "of different form." These particles, when "agitated in exceeding measure," move irregularly causing convulsive motions, the insurgence of "extremely different ideas" and of an "agitated imagination" (Cirillo 2).[1]

When Leonardo Di Capua reconsidered the question of ethics in light of medicine, the experience of the Investiganti appeared already concluded, and the plan outlined with such clear awareness in the *Parere* could therefore be deemed finished only in part. The ingenious syncretism, the probabilism, and the philosophy based on experiments started in 1663 by Tommaso Cornelio, Lucantonio Porzio, and Di Capua—in the name of the renovation of the sciences that succeeded in uniting the discoveries of the modern world on the motion and the circulation of blood with the natural philosophy of Telesio and Campanella, weaving relations with the heirs of Galileo through the Accademia del Cimento and Giovanni Alfonso Borelli—had to cede in the end in front of the offensive of the Galenic doctors. In 1770 they led to the dissolution of the Accademia and to the temporary diaspora of its most illustrious representatives (De Maio; Torrini, *La discussione dello statuto* 357–383). Basically unknown in its substance by its closest neighbors—who had focused most heavily on physical works, from *De Homine* to *Dioptrice* and *Principia*, in which the rupture from the scholastic culture was most evident and present—Di Capua's wish for the establishment of a modern ethics from the *Passions de l'âme* had to come true only in the second phase of the reception of Cartesian philosophy in Naples. This happened when the long and belabored events of the trial of the atheists—with the violent condemnation of the "moderni filosofanti," (modern philosophers) proclaimed in the *Lettere Apologetiche* by the Jesuit De Benedictis—had mobilized the most active and consistent forces of the Neapolitan civil class who were against the inquisitive procedures of the Church (Osbat; De Liguori 330–35).

But the strategies developed by the modernists united in the circle of Giuseppe Valletta—who together with D'Andrea and Costantino Grimaldi took on the task of defending the position of the *novatores* from the attacks of the traditionalists—contributed to outline an image essentially different from the French philosopher. In the Investiganti culture Descartes almost came to signify the *double* of Galileo, and the necessary complement to his philosophy in the battle to affirm scientific freedom. A different view of Descartes was presented in the apologetic writings at the end of the century, when the Accademia of Medinacoeli had already entered the picture (Rak *Le Lezioni dell'Accademia de Medinacoeli. La tradizione manoscritta*, 659–689; Recuperati); in this context he is still the metaphysical philosopher who demonstrates the existence of God and the immortality of the soul. His ideas are most often matched with and superseded by the recovery of Plato, Augustine, and Aristotle's moral philosophy in a political and civic interpretation (Lojacono 87–114), while the pages of Malebranche's *De inquirenda veritate* (On the Necessity of Looking for Truth) become an important point of reference especially for the power attributed to the will over the disordered and blind impulses of the body. The new philosophical interpretation of Descartes set forth by Grimaldi calls the attention toward the *cognitione d'Iddio* (recognition of God) as "supreme Maker," without which "the all Cartesian system's machine would fall and be reduced to nothing" (Grimaldi 188). On the other hand, this interpretation meets the more diffuse interest in history and the problem of the foundation of the states at the center of the experience of Medinacoeli, which, without forgetting the still vital experience of the Investiganti, turns naturally to the internal analysis of the passions as the base of the social life.

If it is probably excessive to discuss crisis of the scientific Cartesian system and of "triumph of the sterile and purely mental metaphysical cartesianism" (Agrimi; Suppa),[2] it is certain that the lessons of Gregorio Caloprese at the Accademia Palatina (Nuzzo,Verso la "Vita civile") and his Cartesian teaching neglect the intersection of medicine and ethics and the problem of symptomology of the passions, in order to concentrate instead on the binary nature of man as a revealing fragment of the more expansive system that constitutes the social life. From this comes the discovery that the political code of society cannot overlook the internal ethic code that regulates impulses and passions in the complex rapport between instinct and will, intellect and education.

As Caloprese writes: "Our reasoning should not begin but from the investigation of the nature of man" (Caloprese, *Dell'origine* 177). For him the science of civic living "based by Pythagoras, Socrates, Plato and many other very wise philosophers on the laws of honesty," unmasks "the wickedness of some authors," who "imagined the idea of man as a tremendous monster formed by nature to the only purpose of damaging others" (178).

The transparent polemic against Hobbes and the more underlying one against Machiavelli certainly allude to the close critical examination of *Il Principe* (The Prince) found in the letters of Descartes to Elizabeth of Bohemia, confirming that within Medinacoeli the *Passions de l'âme* was read together with the exchange of letters that constituted its origin. On the other hand, precisely in those letters conceived as a daily exercise to contrast melancholy, a sort of moral therapy started in time, centered on the attentive auscultation of oneself as a substitute to the stoic hypothesis, concerning the detachment from the passions, suggested at first by Descartes. This hypothesis appeared inadequate to guide man in the difficult journey toward that "spiritual happiness," solid and lasting, that can be secured only by a "firm and constant will" (Descartes 289).

In comparison to the inimitable examples of ancient wisdom, recalled for contrast, it is indeed the method that represents the greater novelty of the Cartesian epistolary with Elisabetta (Elisabeth). Along with the most famous *Passions de l'âme*, these letters tend to appear as a sort of compendium of secular and pre-enlightenment ethics, even when the mystery of the relations between the soul and the body becomes more intricate and the faith in the control of the passions collides with the complex reality of the dualism. The emblematic image proposed with so much conviction by Descartes is that of a *maîtrise,* a domineering will that acts in light of passions as the audience of a theatre, who "witnessing the representaion of a pitiful and deadly action" takes part in the general emotion provoked by the tragedy, without having the process of identification with the hero cancel its identity as spectator of the drama.

But at the same time the effort to decipher the frequently obscure mechanism of the affections and of the primary impulses through the principles of physics and the incertitude of the new ethical science is visible more often through the text of the letters, especially when the author denounces a widespread error in regards to the understanding of the relationship between the soul and the body. This mistake consists in using "the notions of extension, of shapes and movements, much more familiar than the others" in order to "explain the things to which they do not belong, like when one wants to use imagination to conceive the nature of the soul or when one wants to conceive the way by which the soul moves the body through that by which a body is moved by another body" (290–91). Pushed to the limits of physical experience, the imagination—as a faculty dependent on the senses—may not in fact perceive the nature of the soul, even if the bodily nature of man is such that imagination is the most likely medium between things and their abstract representations. The only recognizable notion of the relation between the soul and the body is indeed the mysterious but certain and intuitive notion of their union, from which in its turn depends on "the force of the soul to move the body, and the body to influence the soul, causing its sentiments and passions" (291).

The attempt to understand wholly the nature and the ways of such a relation represents one of most difficult inheritances of Neapolitan cartesianism, as one can gather from the enlightening example of Lucantonio Porzio. At the beginning of the new century he reconsiders the problem of the passions under the incentive of the debate opened by Medinacoeli, without forgetting the medical point of view of the Investiganti, of whom he had been part since the period of the foundation of the Accademia. Reflecting on the pernicious effects of the "affections of the soul" on the health of the body—a central theme in the correspondence between Descartes and Elisabetta (Elisabeth)—Porzio asks himself how it is possible that "if thinking is proper to the soul, the thought can influence the body so powerfully that it changes" (Porzio 28). In order to solve what appears to be a paradox, the author returns to a brief but significant digression that leads once again to the codified system of *De l'Homme*, revealing at the same time the imperfect analogy between the human organism and the machine already clarified by the Investiganti. They had alluded numerous times to the difficulty of completely superimposing the mechanical model over the wonderful and complex equilibrium of the vital functions. Porzio writes that the body "necessarily has to die because of its own nature" (28–29).

The perishable nature of the material that forms the human existence as subject to continual transformations and perpetual modifications, embraces therefore in itself, in its corporeal part, the internal reasons of an uncertain and fragile destiny, including the "accidents" of the passions beyond sickness and death. The doctor holds that even though thinking is proper to the mind, nonetheless almost in every man's thought one needs the images of corporeal things (Porzio 29). In the mind's illusory labyrinth, following the disoriented flux of the senses, the images of corporeal things corrupts the operations of the intellect, creating semblances and ghosts which take the place of true judgments, to the point that "the corporeal images of what one can imagine are true and real images: namely bodies with the typical character of corporeal nature; they are motions of motions and forms of forms" (34). Transferring the language of geometry to the mechanics of the metaphoric and obscure universe of passions, Porzio reveals the negative role of the imagination and the destructive dynamic of the "most strong and continous affections in the soul" which "can seriously offend man in his health to the point of killing him" (36). Closer to the doubtful tone of the letters to Elisabetta than to the trusting directions of the *Passions de l'âme*—according to which "there is no soul so weak that cannot gain an absolute power over the passions"—the argumentation of Porzio ends by giving voice to the intimate discord between the soul and the body, between the intellect and the imagination, indicating the incontrollable vortex of the "melancholic occasions" (36).

The hypothesis of the control and management of the passions is also put into doubt in the same years by Giambattista Vico—an author in many respects distant from Descartes—a friend of Porzio and a regular attendant of the Accademia di Medinacoeli, even though he was closer to the developments of the civil science of Paolo Mattia Doria than to the orthodox Cartesianism of

Caloprese (Mazzola 131–139). Vico's reflection—openly opposing both the "the morals based on pleasure, good for men who must live in solitude" as Epicurus and his modern followers, and the insufficient indications of Malebranche, Pascal, and Descartes himself, whose treatise "is more useful to medicine than to ethics" (*The Autobiography of Giambattista Vico* 130)—proposes a vaster wisdom which "treats human character, its dispositions, its passions, and the manner of adjusting these factors to public life and eloquence" and introduces "a noble and important branch of studies, i.e., the science of politics" (*On the Study Methods of Our Time*, 33). Vico's *De ratione* (On the study method of our time)—as shortly after Doria's *Vita civile* (Civil life)—contradicts the ecumenical intention of the Cartesian treatise which addresses all men, and distinguishes clearly the practical virtue of the *sapienti (wise people)*, who operate following the "subtle reasoning," and the disorderly motions of the common people, because they "are overpowered and carried along by their appetite, which is tumultuous and turbulent; their soul is tainted, having contracted a contagion from the body, so that it follows the nature of the body, and is not moved except by bodily things" (38).

Not by chance Vico opposes to the Cartesian confident technique of *dressage* two opposing remedies that have nevertheless the same aim of turning "to good use the agitations of the soul." On the one hand, philosophy "which acts to mitigate passions in the soul of the sage, so that those passions are transformed into virtues" on the other hand eloquence, "which kindles these passions in the common sort, so that they perform the duty of virtue" (38–39; Battistini, 1989; Contarini; Cottingham). Moreover, to further restrain the Cartesian assumption, the admonition of the *De antiquissima* (On the Most Ancient Wisdom of the Italians) that was suggested anew in the allegorical *dipintura* of the *Scienza nuova* (New Science), explains the finitude of human knowledge compared to the divine that only can act outside of the corrupted senses (Riccio). Here the author insists once again upon the overwhelming difference between the certainties of physics—dealing with the internal motions of bodies "by nature certain"—and the uncertainty of morality, examining "the motions of minds which are most deeply hidden, and arise mostly from desire, which is infinite" (*On the Most Ancient Wisdom of the Italians* 52). After the objections advanced with some doubt by Di Capua and especially by Porzio, it is therefore Vico's duty in the *De antiquissima* to reject firmly the equivalency between the physical world and the ethical world theorized in the *Passions de l'âme*, proclaiming at the same time the irreducibility of the living, including the affections, to the laws of geometry and of mechanics. In the wider view of an ethical reflection that intends to recuperate the wisdom of the ancients (see Nuzzo, "Vico e 'l'

Aristotele pratico" and "Il congedo"), the means used by Descartes, and before him by Epicurus in order to "explain natural things," namely "shapes and mechanisms," reveal themselves to be so inadequate to elucidate not only priciples and powers, but also the obscure and fleeting motions of the passions (*On the Most Ancient Wisdom of Italians* 72). These motions are "shapeless" and "limitless" in their nature, or in any case always ready to take on new forms and semblances; "they do not have any shape" and cannot move with any mechanism. To make use again of Vico's lexicon, it is necessary at this point to superimpose "the light of metaphysics"—which order and interpret the sensible reality gathered in the *topica* (topic) and employ on its part to persuade the people with the help of "more sensuous and materialistic means"—to Galileo's and Descartes's "eye of great geometrician" (*On the Study Methods* 38).[3] In this perspective one understands how Vico in his major work will conceive the design of the "ideal eternal history" like the following

> "la geometria che, mentre sopra i suoi elementi il costruisce o "l contempla, essa stessa si *fa* il mondo delle grandezze," ma nello stesso tempo "con tanto più di realità quanta più ne hanno gli ordini d'intorno alle faccende degli uomini, che non ne hanno punti, linee, superficie e figure." (349)

> (geometry, when it constructs the world of quantity out of its elements, or "contemplates that world, is creating it for itself" but at the same time "with a reality greater, by just so much as the institutions having to do with human affairs are more real than points, lines, surfaces, and figures.)

Before considering the consequences of Vico's thought in the *Scienza nuova*, it is necessary to return for a moment to what in the last decade of the seventeenth century seems the principle direction of Italian Cartesianism, the orthodox interpretation of Medinacoeli, which reconsiders from the *Passions de l'âme* the invitation to the *maîtrise* and the *dressage* of the affections insisting—with the help of Malebranche—upon the active role of will as a rational power on the obscure realm of the senses. It is not by chance that the *Lezione quarta* (Fourth Lesson) on the *Origine dell'Imperij* (Origin of the Empires) by Caloprese takes on the problem of the complex relationship between the body and the soul and the problem of the passions, retrieving Descartes's idea on the judgment which precedes the action, and Augustine's idea concerning free will understood as "firm and consistent will of living and working according to the dictates of reason."[4] By distinguishing between desire, "as motion of our soul through which we try to possess something convenient to our nature," and inclination, or "impetus by which we are drawn to join some object or to do something convenient to us," the author suggests the influence of the "bodily things" which "have great efficacy in corrupting and obscuring the ideas of immaterial and incorporeal things."[5] Both Vico and Porzio in different terms will comment in negative terms on this suggestion, pointing to the necessity of paying great attention to the "truth" influenced by corporeal passions, in order to avoid it and to judge things as they are in themselves after the excitement inspired by the body has finished.[6]

Thus, Caloprese holds that—however imperfect or faulty—the provisional and at times illusory knowledge of the senses does not turn out to be independent from the whole, nor alienated from the "the goods of the soul" which "serve to increase and preserve the perfection of the spirit." On the contrary, "because of the link between the soul and the body, in a certain way the goods of the body, become the goods of the soul as well."[7]

In Caloprese we encounter the idea of pain as instinctive sign of the body devoted to the preservation of the organism. This idea will become widespread in the eighteenth century, from Locke to the medical observation of Montpellier vitalism (Rey). It is important to highlight, however, the attempt to recompose the separation of the soul from the body, which was impending on Cartesian dualism since its origins. After recognizing the importance of sensitive experience for the conservation of organism and the "propagation of the species,"[8] the reflection of Medinacoeli establishes a precise hierarchy in which—as Doria will later note insisting on the good use of the passions necessary to civil life—the analysis of the affections and of their manifestations is a sign of the control of the intellect, "just as the pilot directs the course of a ship" (Doria 75).

It is perhaps natural at this point that the exploration of the human soul in its multiple and diverse forms takes the analysis of the passions back to the limitless universe of poetry, already mentioned by Descartes as an art of knowledge which precedes philosophy, providing anthropological models which, in a certain sense, are universal. As Vico confirms several years later in a well-known letter to Francesco Saverio Estevan, "the best poetic fables are truths closer to the eternal divine truth; they are without comparison more certain than the truths of the historians (. . .)." In this perspective for Vico, Tasso's Goffredo is the captain of all ages and nations because as a poet he depicted in him the "eternal features of human souls."[9]

From the psychologically complex characters of Tasso's poetry, divided between light and darkness, instinct and duty, reason and passion, begins the first autonomous attempt to investigate the human soul developed by Caloprese in the *Lettura sopra la Concione di Marfisa a Carlo Magno* (Reading on Marfisa's Address to Charlemagne) read at the Accademia degli Infuriati (Academy of the Infuriated) in 1690. In this text the techniques of eloquence employed in *Orlando Furioso* are compared to Armida's prayer to Goffredo in the fourth book of *Gerusalemme Liberata* (Jerusalem Liberated). As the critic philosopher notes right away, in the haughty and sublime oration of Marfisa to the French king, the positive passions of veneration and of devotion are present, while envy, which is responsible for the initial *inimicitia* (hostility) of the heroine toward Carlo, becomes at the end a positive motion thanks to the desire of emulation which places the heroine among the magnanimous. Perceived in this way, envy is in fact "indivisible companion of virtue and Glory," and "in generous souls such as that of Marfisa this affection is not used to arise if not for something great beyond measure, and difficult to obtain" (Caloprese 28–29). In this passage we find the ethic conversion of the affections from the egoistic impulse to beneficent civic passion that will meet vaster developments in the works of Paolo Mattia Doria and in the Cartesian letters by the less-known Niccolò Giovo. In fact, Caloprese wants to clarify at once that "envy or emulation of fame and honor is proper only to those souls formed by nature to great and glorious actions, as one reads in Plutarch that Miltiades' glory made sleepless Themistocles" (33).

On the one hand, the manifest intention of Ariosto's heroine, consistent with her character, is that of arousing esteem "of herself and of his unique virtue" (32) in his interlocutor; on the other hand, the hidden goal of Armida, who appeared unexpectedly in the Christian realm, is to establish the force of persuasion not as much in the magnitude of the offering, as "in Goffredo's just cause and piety" (46). As the critic says, in order for the prayer to have effect, it must first take into consideration the person to whom it turns, because "in the hearts governed by justice and piety the honest prayers are more effective than useful offerings," while "those who have only usefulness as unique goal are touched more easily by offerings" (49–50). In the notable example of rhetorical art based on the affections conceived by Tasso, "the strongest power of persuasion was devoted to raise the spirit of mercy and compassion in the heart of that magnanimous and pious Captain and of those generous warriors." It is not by chance that the cunning recitation of Armida the "deceiver" takes advantage of a particular aspect of Goffredo's personality, the *pietas (piety)* that "encompasses within itself justice, loyalty, piety and magnanimity." Nevertheless, it also aims at provoking in the soul of the captain disdain "against the impiety of the unfair persecutor," a complex sentiment in which, as Descartes instructs, the emotions of "cruelty, unhappiness, astuteness, ambition, suspect and ambition" are mixed (58).

The Cartesian discovery of mixed affections, which the poetic science of Tasso seems to anticipate, appears particularly suitable to describe what occurs in the soul of a character such as Eustazio, the more fragile alter-ego of Goffredo. He is seduced by Armida's enchanting arts and is ready to make himself her knight, forgetting that the success of the crusade demands the unity of the forces headed to Gerusalemme. But, as Caloprese notes, the strategy put into action by Eustazio to realize his ambitions appears nullified by instinctive passion and irrepressible jealousy, which reflects in the irrational language of the affections the secret intent inspiring the character, when he shows "in his face that love that he strove to hide in his words." In the tumultuous accumulation of the affections, which betray the passionate desires of the young Eustazio despite his refined rhetorical orchestration, the critic reads the struggle between the various vices, which are tempered neither by reason nor by virtue, and the final victory of arrogance over astuteness. It is the very mixing of the affections and their uncertain contention that represents, however, a definite proof of the superficial analysis of human nature conducted by authors such as Machiavelli and, most of all, Hobbes. Caloprese adds immediately that they base their thought on the "empious maxim . . . that all men are evil and wicked and only devoted to deceipt and fraud." For Caloprese this maxim is far away from the true concept of humanity and "contrary to the experience of reason" (63–64).

Men, in fact, as much as they are composed "of body and soul," are used to incline to vice or to virtue when the former or the latter prevails. More importantly, as Descartes reveals, they "change in their actions as those who cultivate the spiritual side—sometimes even for little time—turn away from the right path of virtue, in the same manner as those who follow the guide of the senses cannot always lose the light of reason, and sometimes are moved to act rightly" (67–68).

Returning then to the central problem of compassion that dominates the verse of Tasso, it is necessary at this point to illustrate the true nature of this affection considered traditionally as an indication of weakness or of cowardice of the soul, and therefore irreconcilable with the moral stature of the character of Goffredo. Also on this point, the lesson of the moderns seems if not to exceed that of the ancients, at least to correct or complete it. The pondered reading of the Cartesian treatise allows in fact to eliminate the apparent obstacle, demonstrating once again that the moral hypothesis of Descartes is closer to the truths of the Christian faith, according to which "compassion is not only the result of self-love, as Aristotle appears to think, but can also spring from charity that one should show toward those belonging to the same species" (76). Despite the intentions of the author—who intends most likely to give his contribution to the rehabilitation of Descartes as a Christian philosopher, inaugurated by Grimaldi—a modern form of piety shines already in this passage. This piety is understood as universal sentiment of man toward the members of his own species, and will constitute one of the essential elements of the secular and social ethics of the second half of the eighteenth century (Nussbaum VI–VIII). Surely the change appears here just at the beginning, but the difference from the stoic ethic of the seventeenth century is perceived in the evident passage from an abstract theory of virtue to the practice of free will understood as medium of compassion. Caloprese with regard to the Aristotelian *impasse* reminds us of the famous Cartesian metaphor of the theatre as symbol of the distance essential to reaffirm the necessity of a measured participation in the sufferings of others. This form of participation—based on the idea of the implicit difference between the still and balanced soul of the prince and the agitation of the common people—was abandoned during the eighteenth century in favor of the absolute physical and spiritual identification between the one who suffers and the one who feels compassion (Caloprese 76). The conclusion of the critic is therefore that three types of compassion exist: "two born from self-love and one from virtue and generosity," and that only the last as a product of an intellectual appetite operating according to virtue and justice is appropriate to Goffredo, "strong and fair man" (76–77). But in this way the Cartesian doctrine explained in all its breadth and complexity comes to coincide perfectly with the joint authority of Augustine and Thomas, confirming the worth of a modern thought which celebrates the virtue of the Christian hero as a universal model. Drawing on the authority of these "Doctors of the church," Caloprese writes: "the compassion adequate to the highest virtue of a perfect prince and Captain, such as Goffredo created by Tasso, must be a motion of the intellective appetite directed to help those fallen in misery, and regulated by justice" (77).

Finally these ideas are confirmed by poetry. Following Caloprese's advice, in Tasso "one can notice two beautiful different forms of compassion" (81), both contained in the "very gentle and tender answer" (Tasso IV, 67 v. 8) of Goffredo to the plea of Armida. In the first—expressed in the verse *And to find help and piety* (which recalls the Petrarch verse *I hope to find piety, and pardon* from the initial sonnet of the *Canzoniere*)—the poet limits himself to oppose the non-active piety of the senses with the active piety of the intellectual appetite. However, in the second form of compassion—condensed in the two verses "Now piety would make me less pious / if in front of its right I would not thank God" (IV, 69 v. 7–8)—the poet distinguishes to the benefit of readers between "the virtuous and prudent piety governed by justice and the one that is lacking both virtue and prudence. The latter blindly obeys both to the intellective and sensual appetites" (Caloprese 81). But at this point the difference between Eustazio and Goffredo, between instinctive desire and virtue according to reason, appears forever indicated in the inner language of the affections. The dark shadow of the passions which surrounds Eustazio seems almost a prefiguration of wthat will happen in a little time to Rinaldo—a similar character in many aspects—who in the end, in the narrative fiction, has to play both the sought-after role of Armida's paladin and that of the prisoner in the illusory garden of the senses.

After the *Concione*, the exploration of the inner universe initiated by Caloprese inside Tasso's world, deepened in the *Sposizioni* (Commentary on Casa's *Poems*) (Rak *Condizione critica e fantasia poetica,* 27–70; Contarini 79–81; Gronda 11–52). This analysis of Della Casa's poems—interwoven with allusions to *Liberata*—presents the origin of the affections and the theory of the interconnection of human passions to illustrate the tortuous and almost physical progression of passion. Even here the return to the ancient philosophers, such as Cicero, must be supplemented by the reading of Descartes in order to explain thoroughly the complex mechanisms staged by Casa—especially the "amorous sorrow" which "moving all the resources of thought and overcoming through its bitterness the power of the heart, is used to cause first languor and then furor."[10] The nature of these passions would remain incomprehensible if it were defined solely through the general reference of the *zelotypia* of Cicero's *Tusculanae*. The *cordolium* (mourning) is summarized in the inner formula of the sorrow that encompasses the desolate sentiment of loss, aggravated by the insidious melancholy of memory. Also it is described in sixteenth-century lyric and finds its poetic correspondance in the rage of Orlando and in the "desperate lament of Tancredi for Clorinda's death (ibid.)."

In the *Sposizioni* more than in the *Concione*, emerges the declared attempt at eliminating the dynamics of the affections from the physical dominion of senses and imagination in order to redirect them to the clear light of truth and to distill them of their negative effects. This happens in the case of celestial love, in which "both the intellect and the will find their fulfillment" (ibid., 133), and in the case of the fully intellectual passion of wonder. Following the indications of Descartes and of Malebranche, Caloprese perceives these passions in antithesis to desire and to cupidity, as a power "instituted by nature to contemplate things," whose "custom is to draw the spirits to the intellect" (ibid., 269).

Wonder no longer refers to the investigation of the natural world, as in Bacon and in the Investiganti,[11] and becomes in Caloprese's interpretation the prime example of the motions of the soul sustained by reason and will, establishing the true awareness of the self, different from the illusory visions of imagination which is born contaminated with the "material of the body" (ibid., 70). Not by chance and not too long after, Gianvincenzo Gravina, a critic close to Caloprese, will celebrate in his *Discorso sopra l'Endimione* (Discourse on Endymion) the sublime power of a poetic invention in which novelty and wonder "exciting the attention and removing the mind from earthly things, uplift it above itself so that it sees itself more ready and free from those ties through which our corporeal nature encompassing us delays our flight toward the contemplation of what is pure and eternal" (Gravina 55).

Although transferred into the space of interiority illuminated by the poetry of Della Casa, the hermeneutic technique set forth in Caloprese's *Sposizioni* does not ever forget the civil function of psychological knowledge turned especially to the formation of individuals in the wider perspective of states. Thus, the rereading of Cartesian ethics in a political light—already authorized by the author in a close examination of *Il Principe* appearing in the letters to Elizabeth—ties the textual exercise of *La Concione* and *Sposizioni* to the philosophical and pedagogical reflection of Doria's *La Vita civile* (Civil Life)[12] and to the later *Lettere cartesiane* of the abbot Niccolò Giovo. As Caloprese had already done, Doria distinguishes "will" as a conscious and rational motion, from the immediate outburst of "imagination," that is seduced by the images of the exterior world, the "immense theater of the world" (Doria 46). Doria also proposes a pedagogy directed to overturn since infancy the "false judgments" (50), provoked by natural impulses, without negating the vitalizing force of the affections, because "human happiness will not consist in anything else but the mixture of cognitions and senses" (60). At the beginning of the eighteenth century, the philosophical and political manifesto of *La vita civile* reconsiders with new confidence the antistoic polemic already present in Descartes, stating explicitly that passions are necessary to man to make him active and not obtuse, and that "reflection and philosophy come to moderate and well direct passions, and not to extinguish them" (80).[13] But to theorize the "good use" of the interior motions in which "human happiness consists," means firstly to distinguish between the immoral passions, dominated by instinct and excess, and the virtuous passions, regulated by reason and "very useful to civic life" (Doria 85). Among the latter are "the love for truth and human morals" or the desire for glory. These passions fashion the hero and "the perfect politician." Finally, in Doria's list of civic affections are even included those "of the conservation of the homeland, of oneself and of one's own house that form the 'good citizen'" and the "excellent artist" (ibid.).

The same positive consideration of human affections returns, together with the continous criticism of Machiavelli's political system, in the twenty-four *Lettere Cartesiane* (Cartesian Letters) by Giovo, that propose to illustrate to the noble woman and receiver of the text the "good use" of passions "so much necessary and useful to civic life."[14] Giovo's letters are already very distant from the worried and pragmatic inspection of the human soul found in Descartes's letters to Elizabeth; nevertheless, they still provide a model. They already reflect the popular spirit of the new century, inspecting the *topoi* of Cartesian doctrine in a series of fixed and constant formula, in which reappear the ideas of *maîtrise* and of *dressage* as the theory of the balancing the affections.

But the detailed analysis of the affections—which develops the theory of mixed passions, describing the nature of compound sentiments such as remorse and scorn—is concentrated especially on the meaning of compassion. Also it recuperated the Cartesian metaphor of theater and Caloprese's thesis concerning a passion that does not suit only the miserable, but strikes also the noble, "sensitive to compassion," although the "compassion of the people"[15] appears somewhat different from the compassion of the "great soul" not experiencing themselves fear and weakness, but living them as reflected, so to speak, on the stage of the world. Thus, the definition of the affections and of their manifestation leads naturally to the theory of conversion, elaborated by Doria: as Giovo observes, the ambivalent passion of jealousy, "especially of fear" in which acts "the desire to preserve some good,"[16] is deplorable in the avaricious man willing to accumulate wealth and in the suspicious and deceived husband of the novelistic tradition. On the other hand, it converts itself into an "honest and just" sentiment in the case of the "astute captain" employed in defending the city.

The confutation of Machiavelli that appears in Giovo's August 9 letter constitutes a sort of short essay on *Il principe* through a perspective of the political philosophy of Medinacoeli. The letter opens with the refutation "of the rules of chapter nineteen and twenty," a subject that was already considered by Descartes in the epistolary to Elizabeth from September of 1646. This letter focused on the prince's virtue that alone is able to persuade the people of the necessity of its measures (Descartes 167); above all the letter questions Machiavelli's idea that the people may hate the sovereign both for his good and evil actions. More in general Giovo considers the fact that Machiavelli "did not distinguish between the prince that conquered the principality through right reasons, and the one who practicing not legitimate arts, occupied it through shameful usurpation." In this way Machiavelli ended up advising in confusion to all "those precepts that are useful only to the tyrant, founding their power on murders."[17]

Vice versa, "the discerning prince" possesses one single way to escape "the hate and disdain of people," namely the clemency and love of justice. The search for virtue, practiced since infancy, makes this unique way preferred to any other form of authority.

To sustain the value of a pedagogical teaching based on the self-knowledge and in the inner regulation of instincts and desires, the author must first refute the maxim from chapter fifteen of Prince according to which men being unhappily corrupted, it is not yet possible that the one who always wants to be good would not rapidly fall in ruin. This maxim authorizes the prince "to use evil and pernicious advice, when the occasion would lead him to do so." [18] In Giovo's political vision, on the contrary, the "well-known virtue" of the sovereign becomes the essential condition of good governing for the enlightened prince who places the "public sphere before the private interest,"[19] founding his consensus on the opinion of his subjects. Here, the "Christian virtue and compassion, united to the tranquillity of the soul"[20]—indicated by Caloprese as the essential quality of the "perfect captain"—allow a confident consideration of human nature in the complex rapport between power, justice and law. This point will become one of the central arguments in eighteenth-century political treatises on the origins and statute of despotism. For instance, Locke clarifies in his *Second Treatise of Civil Government* (1690) that the intrinsic law of reason teaches to all men the equality of their original nature and also the prohibition to harm his equals in their life, happiness, and liberty.

Even though its reflection has many elements in common with the experience of Medinacoeli, Vico's *Scienza nuova* (New Science) does not share wholeheartedly the possibility of autoregulation of the affections in support of moral and civil life. In the reconstruction of the origins of civilization which opens the fourth section of the text, dedicated to method, Vico admits after all the existence of a "conatus" proper to "human will" in order to "restrain the impulses that the body urges on the mind. By means of this effort, such impulses can be completely suppressed by the sage, and can be directed to better ends by the good citizen." However, he adds immediately afterward:

> But men, because of their corrupted nature are under the tyranny of self-love, which compels them to make private utility their chief guide. Seeking everything useful for themselves and nothing for their companions, they cannot bring their passions under control to direct them toward justice. We thereby establish the fact that man in the bestial state desires only his own welfare along with that of his family; having entered upon civil life, he desires his own welfare along with that of his city; when its rule is extended over several people, he desires his own welfare along with that

of the nation; when the nations are united by wars, treaties of peace, alliances, and commerce, he desires his own welfare along with that of the entire human race. In all these circumstances man desires principally his own utility. Therefore it is only by divine providence that he can be held within these institutions to practice justice as a member of the society of the family, of the city, and finally of the mankind. Unable to obtain all the utilities he wishes, he is constrained by these institutions to seek those which are his due; and this is called just. That which regulates all human justice is therefore divine justice, which is administred by divine providence to preserve human society. In one of its principal aspects, this Science must therefore be a rational civil theology of divine providence. (*The New Science* 341)

However, another perhaps more important difference separates Vico from the political reflection of his closest contemporaries; this is the value he attributes to the imagination. The Augustinianism, Platonism and Cartesianism of Medinacoeli limit imagination as part of the obscure impulses of the body, insisting on its illusory and deceitful nature in respect to the clear knowledge of an intellect guided by reason and will. On the contrary, the allegorical and fragmentary construction of Vico's *Scienza nuova* recognizes the autonomous role of imagination, outside of Caloprese's and Doria's moral and political vision of affections. In Vico's major work the "vulgar metaphysic" of the passions gives form to the theology of the poets and to the "sublime poetry" born out of "deficiency of human reasoning" (Vico, 384) in the Homeric myths (Lollini 73–79). For the first time, in the pages of Vico the abstract nature of philosophy and the rational nature of human minds—too much divorced from the senses and too much intellectualized and spiritualized through the use of numbers—become a limit to the knowledge of the "vast imagination of those first men whose minds were not in the least abstract, refined or spiritualized, because they were entirely immersed in the senses, buffeted by the passions, buried in their bodies" (Vico 378). Indeed, from the "great fragments of antiquity—hitherto useless to science because they were squalid, mutilated and dispersed" (Vico 357), recomposed in a sort of inner map, emerge the hidden and insisting indication of a lost world from which will take form the psychological and anthropological investigation of the affections in the second half of eighteenth century. These investigations will be based on the asserted distance which separates the hieroglyphics of passions from the instruments of analytical reason.

Notes

1. Cf. on this subject E. Garin, *Per una storia dei cartesiani in Italia. Avvertenza*, in "Giornale critico della filosofia italiana," Sesta serie, XVI, 1996, 307–11 (310).
2. More open in regards to the *investigante* culture and the new civil science is the recent reflection of S. Serrapica, Note napoletane alle 'Passioni dell'anima.' (Neapolitan notes to Passions of the Soul)
3. Vico's *First Response*, in *On the Most Ancient Wisdom of the Italians*, 131.
4. G. Caloprese, *Lezione quarta*, in Silvio Suppa, *L'Accademia di Medinacoeli*, 206.
5. Ibid., 211.
6. Ibid., 205–6.
7. Ibid., 208.
8. Ibid., 210.
9. Giambattista Vico, «A Francesco Saverio Estevan,» in *L'autobiografia, il carteggio e le poesie varie*, ed. B. Croce and F. Nicolini, (Bari: Laterza, 1929) 216.
10. *Sposizioni di Sertorio Quattromani, di Marco Aurelio Severino, di Gregorio Caloprese, di Egidio Menagio e dell'Autore anonimo*, in *Opere di Monsignor Giovanni Della Casa dopo l'edizione di Firenze del 1707 e di Venezia del 1728, molto illustrate e di cose inedite accresciute* (Naples 1733), t. I, 52–53. The first volume of the 1733 edition reproduces the 1691 edition of Bulifon of the *Rime* of Casa. The analysis in question refers to his sonnet VII (*Io mi vivea d'amore, gioia e bene*).
11. Cf. M. Torrini, *Il topos della meraviglia come origine della filosofia tra Bacon e Vico*, in *Francis Bacon: terminologia e fortuna nel XVII secolo*. (Seminario Internazionale, Rome, March 11–13, 1984), a c. M. Fattori (Rome; Ed. de l'Ateneo, 1984), 261–80.
12. On the political and civil reflection of Doria, see the volume by V. Conti, *Paolo Mattia Doria: Dalla repubblica dei togati alla repubblica dei notabili* (Florence: Olschki, 1978) and the Proceedings of the Conference on *Paolo Mattia Doria fra rinnovamento e tradizione* (Galatina: Congedo, 1985).
13. On this point see M. Torrini, *Le passioni di P.M. Doria: il problema delle passioni dell'animo nella* Vita civile, in *Paolo Mattia Doria fra rinnovamento e tradizione*, 433–54.
14. N. Giovo, *Lettere cartesiane a una signora* May 3–November 22, 1728, in *Trattati diversi: Fisici, e morali*. Ms. I.E.13, Biblioteca Nazionale di Napoli. See the letter dated May 18, 1728. See also Cantillo.
15. N. Giovo, *Lettere cartesiane*, c. 82v.
16. Ibid., c. 13r.
17. Ibid., c. 106v.
18. Ibid., c. 109r–110v.
19. Ibid., c.110v, c. 110r.
20. Ibid., c. 236r.

Works Cited

Battistini, Andrea. *Vico and the Passions*, in *Teorie delle passioni*, a c. di E. Pulcini, Dordrecht-Boston-London, Kluwer, Academic Publishers, 1989, pp. 113–128.

Battistini, Andrea. *Vico tra antichi e moderni*. Bologna: Il Mulino, 2004.

Caloprese, Gregorio. *Lettura sopra la concione di Marfisa a Carlo Magno, contenuta nel Furioso al canto trentesim'ottavo, fatta da Gregorio Caloprese nell'Accademia degli Infuriati di Napoli nell'anno anno 1690: Nella quale, oltre l'artificio adoperato dall'Ariosto in detta concione, si spone ancora quello che si è usato dal Tasso nell'oratione d'Armida a Goffredo*. Napoli: Antonio Bulifon, 1691.

Cantillo, Clementina. "Appunti di lettura sul cartesianesimo napoletano tra '600 e '700," *Bollettino del Centro di Studi Vichiani* XXIV–XXV (1994–95): 183–94.

Cirillo, Nicola. *Consulti medici pubblicati da Francesco Buoncore*. Naples: De Bonis Stampatore Arcivescovile, 1738.

Conference publications: *Paolo Mattia Doria fra rinnovamento e tradizione*. Atti del convegno di studi, Lecce, November 4–6, 1982. Galatina: Congedo, 1985.

_____. *Descartes: il metodo e i saggi*. Atti del convegno per il 350° anniversario della pubblicazione del *Discours de la Méthode* e degli *Essais*. Rome: Istituto della Enciclopedia Italiana, 1990.

_____. *Francis Bacon: terminologia e fortuna nel XVII secolo*. Seminario Internazionale, (Rome, March 11–13, 1984), a c. di M. Fattori. Rome: Ed. de l'Ateneo, 1984. 261–80.

_____. *Galileo e Napoli*, a c. di F. Lomonaco and M. Torrini, Maurizio. Naples: Guida, 1987.

_____. *Momenti vichiani del primo Settecento*. a c. di G. Pizzamiglio and M. Sanna. Naples: Guida, 2001. 37–74.

_____. *Pietro Giannone e il suo tempo*. a c. di R. Ajello. Vol.2 Naples: Jovene, 1980. 659–89.

_____. *Teorie delle passioni*. a c. di E. Pulcini. Dordrecht and Boston and London: Kluwer, Academic Publishers, 1989. 113–28.

Contarini, Silvia. "*Il mistero della macchina sensibile.*" *Teorie delle passioni da Descartes a Alfieri*. Pisa: Pacini, 1997.

Conti, Vittorio. *Paolo Mattia Doria. Dalla repubblica dei togati alla repubblica dei notabili*. Florence: Olschki, 1978.

Cottingham, John. "Ragione e passioni/passioni e ragione. Note su metafisica, antropologia ed etica in Descartes e Vico," *Bollettino del Centro di Studi Vichiani* XXXIII (2003): 209–31.

De Liguori, Girolamo. "La reazione a Cartesio nella Napoli del Seicento: Giovambattista de Benedictis." *Giornale critico della filosofia italiana* LXXV (1996): 330–55.

De Maio, Romeo. *Società e vita religiosa a Napoli nell'età moderna*. Naples: Edizioni Scientifiche Italiane, 1971.

Della Casa, Giovanni. *Opere*. Naples, 1733.

Descartes, Réné. *Correspondance*. Vol.7. Edited by Ch. Adam et G. Milhaud. Paris: P.U.F., 1960.
Di Capua, Leonardo. *Parere divisato in otto ragionamenti ne'quali partitamente narrandosi l'origine e 'l progresso della medicina, chiaramente l'incertezza della medesima si fa manifesta.* Naples: Antonio Bulifon, 1681.
Di Giandomenico, Matteo, *Cartesianesimo e iatromeccanica*, in *Descartes: il metodo e i saggi*, ed. G. Belgioioso, Roma, Instituto dell'Enciclopedia italiana, 1990, 651–658.
Dini, Alessandro. *Filosofia della natura, medicina, religione: Lucantonio Porzio (1639–1724).* Milan: Franco Angeli, 1985.
Doria, Paolo Mattia. *Della vita civile: Con un trattato sull'educazione del Principe.* Torino: Pomba, 1852.
Fish, Max H. "L'Accademia degli Investiganti." *De Homine* 27–28 (1968): 17–75.
Gebhardt, Jürgen. "Sensus communis: Vico e la tradizione europea antica." *Bollettino del Centro di Studi Vichiani.* XXII–XXIII (1992–93): 43–64.
Giovo, Niccolò. *Degli avvertimenti intorno alle passioni dell'animo.* Naples: Felice Mosca, 1732.
_____. *Trattati diversi: Fisici, e morali.* Biblioteca Nazionale di Napoli.
Gravina Gian Vincenzo. *Scritti critici e teorici*, a c. di A. Quondam. Bari: Laterza, 1973.
Grimaldi, Costantino. *Risposta alla terza lettera apologetica contra il Cartesio creduto da più d'Aristotele di Benedetto Aletino: Opera in cui dimostrasi quanto salda e pia sia la Filosofia di Renato delle Carte: e perché questo si debba più d'Aristotele.* Colonia: S. Hect, 1703.
Gronda, Giovanna. *Le passioni della ragione.* Pisa: Pacini, 1984.
Guerrini, Luigi. "Note su traduzioni manoscritte delle opere cartesiane." *Giornale critico della filosofia italiana.* XVI (1996): 500–507.
Lachterman, David. "Vico, Doria e la geometria sintetica." *Bollettino del Centro di Studi Vichiani* X (1980): 10–35.
Lojacono, Ettore. *Immagini di René Descartes nella cultura napoletana dal 1644 al 1755.* Lecce: Conte, 2003.
Lollini, Massimo. *Le muse, le maschere e il sublime: G.B. Vico e la poesia nell'età della "ragione spiegata."* Naples: Guida, 1994.
Mazzola, Roberto. "Vico all'Accademia del Medinacoeli." *Bollettino del Centro di Studi Vichiani.* XX (1990): 131–39.
Nussbaum, Martha C. *Upheavals of Thought: The Intelligence of the Emotions.* Cambridge: Cambridge University Press, 2001.
Nuzzo, Enrico. "Il congedo dalla 'saggezza moderna' nella cultura napoletana tra '600 e '700: Vico e la tradizione dei 'moralisti.'" *Bollettino del Centro di Studi Vichiani*, XVII–XVIII (1987–88): 25–114.
_____. *Verso la "Vita civile": Antropologia e politica nelle lezioni accademiche di Gregorio Caloprese e Paolo Mattia Doria.* Naples: Guida, 1984.
_____. "Vico e l' 'Aristotele pratico': la meditazione sulle forme 'civili' nelle 'pratiche'

della Scienza nuova prima." *Bollettino del Centro di Studi Vichiani* XIV–XV (1984–85) : 61–129.
Osbat, Luciano. *L'Inquisizione a Napoli: Il processo agli ateisti, 1688–1697.* Rome: Edizioni di Storia e Letteratura, 1974.
Porzio, Lucantonio. *Lettere e discorsi accademici.* Naples: Nella Stamperia di Michele Luigi Muzio, 1711.
Rak, Michele. "Condizione, critica e fantasia poetica: Un trattato della storia delle idee letterarie del sec. XVII," *La Rassegna della letteratura italiana* LXXV (1971): 27–70.
———. *Lezioni dell'Accademia di palazzo del duca di Medinacoeli: Napoli 1698–1701.* Naples: Istituto Italiano per gli Studi Filosofici, 2000.
Recuperati, Giuseppe. "A proposito dell'Accademia di Medina Coeli." *Rivista Storica Italiana* LXXXIV (1972): 57–79.
Rey, Roselyne. *Histoire de la douleur.* Paris: Ed. de la Découverte, 1993.
Riccio, Monica. "Opacità della riflessione del sé e azione prudente: un excursus nei testi vichiani." *Bollettino del Centro di Studi Vichiani* XXVIII–XXIX (1998–99): 153–60.
Serrapica, Salvatore. "Note napoletane alle 'Passioni dell'anima.'" *Giornale critico della filosofia italiana* XVI (1996): 476–94.
Suppa, Silvio. *L'Accademia di Medinacoeli fra tradizione investigante e nuova scienza civile.* Naples: Nella sede dell'Istituto, 1971.
Tasso, Torquato. *Gerusalemme Liberata.* a c. di F. Chiappelli. Milan: Rusconi, 1982.
Torrini, Maurizio. "L'Accademia degli Investiganti: Napoli 1663–1670," *Quaderni storici* 48 (1981): 845–83.
———. "La discussione dello statuto delle scienze tra la fine del '600 e l'inizio del '700" in *Galileo e Napoli*, Edited by F. Lomonaco e M. Torrini, Napoli, Guida, 1987. 357–83.
———. *Tommaso Cornelio e la ricostruzione della scienza.* Naples: Guida, 1977.
Tozzi, Luca. *Opera omnia medicinae.* Venice: Pezzana, 1747.
Verbeek, Théo. "Les passions et la fièvre: L'idée de la maladie chez Descartes et quelques cartésiens néerlandais." *Tractatrix* 1 (1989): 45–61.
Vico, Giambattista. *L'autobiografia, il carteggio e le poesie varie*, seconda. Ed. B. Croce and F. Nicolini. Bari: Laterza, 1929.
———. *The Autobiography of Giambattista Vico.* Ithaca, NY: Cornell University Press, 1944.
———. *The New Science of Giambattista Vico.* Trans. Thomas Goddard Bergin and Max Harold Fisch. Ithaca, NY: Cornell University Press, 1948.
———. *On the Most Ancient Wisdom of the Italians: Unearthed from the Origins of the Latin Language: Including the Disputation with the Giornale De' Letterati D'Italia.* Ithaca, NJ: Cornell University Press, 1988.
———. *On the Study Methods of Our Time.* Ithaca, NJ: Cornell University Press, 1990.
———. *Opere.* a c. di A. Battistini. Milan: Mondadori, 1990.
———. *Opere.* a c. di R. Parenti. Vol.1. Naples: Casa Editrice Fulvio Rossi, 1972.

◆ 3

Fernando de Herrera Invented the Internet: Technologies of Self-Containment in the Early Modern Sonnet

Leah Middlebrook

> a Western Enlightenment dream—no boundaries for the mind of the subject
> —Caren Kaplan, "Transporting the Subject"

What do we privilege when we talk about how modern technologies got started? The invention of the machines, or the adoption of the metaphors? One favorable outcome of recent movements in cultural studies is the erosion of the totalizing notion of a static "modern era" that is a matter of dates, and its replacement by the tracking of various modern dispositions within a given cultural scene. Among these is the experience of selfhood in terms of the subject, that is, in terms of a contained entity, objectively perceived, constituted by fantasy and exclusion, and the product of a changing but insistent experience of interpellations into a variety of configurations of a body-mind split. Caren Kaplan, in a recent meditation on communications technology and the shifting paradigm of the subject, has suggested that the history of modernity can be thought of as a "history of concepts and metaphors of displacement" (35).

But if modernity is marked by the subject, in this essay it is specifically the "light," or "ludic" subject, which I will argue links the Internet age and the self-consciously "new" and "efficient" form of self-representation that was the sonnet in sixteenth-century Spain.[1] As Kaplan notes, "how subjects move or do not move tells us much about what counts as human, as culture" (34). The question she goes on to pose about that mobility—". . . how do globalized information technologies, with their incumbent machinery and heavily freighted divisions of labor, come to be characterized as transitory and light, as playful practices of subjectivity that enable users to slip the moorings of location and materiality?" (34)—highlights an ideology that is shared between sixteenth-century writers and thinkers, and their late twentieth-century heirs: that "subjecthood" and its necessary, constant reiteration are somehow light, the activities of *otium*.[2] From the time of the publication of *The Book of the Courtier*, subjection is fashionable, the self-policing of the courtier an amiable matter. For this reason, we can consider the early modern court as a primal scene of the ludic subject, and the sonnet, as the principal lyric form of the "modern" sixteenth-century courtier, a significant force in the conditioning of subjection-lite.

My aim here is not to conflate the early modern and the postmodern in some ahistorical, boundless poetic vision. But when our concern is with the subject, and with changes in how he or she is constituted over and against the figure of the human person, an "understanding of the history of concepts and metaphors of displacement in modernity brings these diverse mobilities . . ."—and, I would add, leavenings—". . . into relation with one another. They cannot be reduced to the same thing, but they can be linked through representational legacies and political pasts and futures" (Kaplan 35). Moreover, if we accept that metaphors give rise to technology, "and not the other way around" (35), the sonnet can be taken as one example of a "technology" that enables the imaginary displacements that allow us to identify with the compressed avatars of ourselves which pop up on cell phones and computer monitors.[3] Hence in this essay, my focus is on the desire shared by some sixteenth-century writers that poetry *be* a technology, in the Heideggerian sense of that which separates, organizes, subjects, and delivers forth.[4] I will be arguing that in Spain in particular, the sixteenth-century sonnet is imagined as a means of packaging and transmitting the self as it is represented by, and encapsulated in, the intellect, in a practical, efficient way. My starting points are the prose descriptions by Juan Boscán and Fernando de Herrera of the sonnet as the perfect poetic "container" for a new kind of self based in the mind. My endpoint is the chimeric nature of disembodied poetics. Early humanist dreams for the sonnet foundered on the nature of poetry, as well as on the intellectual and material convolutions of seventeenth-century Spanish thought. A closer examination of these dreams opens onto some interesting observations about early modern poetry and reason.

Subject-lite

In framing this argument, I should clarify that I am talking about the sonnet *form*, and not about the related, and intertwined issue, of Petrarchism. The nature of the latter as the "broadly-scaled, self-oriented poetry for present circumstances" (Greene, *Post-Petrarchism* 3) is well established within criticism; but the forms in which Petrarchan discourse is framed receive somewhat less specific consideration. Therefore, it may bear reminding that while the sonnet has for a long time occupied a central place in the Western canon of lyric forms, where it has become an icon of high-culture poetry, there was a time when the form was viewed as new, and when its status as poetry was a matter of debate. Thus a standard move in the sixteenth-century poetic defense was to claim the value, not only of the adoption of Italian words and themes, but also of Italian *forms* into Castilian, French, and English. This was necessary because these forms appeared strangely prosy, and—in the case of the sonnet—*short*, when compared to the prestigious lyrics of vernacular tradition. For this reason, the entry on the sonnet with which Fernando de Herrera initiates his critical "Annotations" to the poetry of Garcilaso de la Vega in 1580 marks a significant point in modern Spanish poetics; the passage formalizes the figure-ground shift that has taken place over the course of the century in views about what constitutes poetry:

> Es el Soneto la más hermosa composición, y de mayor artificio y gracia de cuantas tiene la poesía italiana y española. Sirve en lugar de los epigramas y odas griegas y latinas, y responde a las elegías antiguas en algún modo, pero es tan extendida y capaz de todo argumento, que recoge en sí sola todo lo que pueden abrazar estas partes de poesía, sin hacer violencia alguna a los preceptos y religión de la arte, porque resplandecen en ella con maravillosa claridad y lumbre de figuras y exornaciones poéticas la cultura y propiedad, la festividad y agudeza, la magnificencia y espíritu, la dulzura y jocundidad, la aspereza y vehemencia, la conmiseración y afectos, y la eficacia y representación de todas. (308)

> (The Sonnet is the most beautiful composition, and of the greatest artifice and grace of all of those in Italian and Spanish poetry. It serves in place of the Greek and Latin epigrams and odes, and corresponds to the ancient elegies in a certain manner, but it is so extensive and capable of any argument, that it gathers into itself all that these other kinds of poetry can embrace, without doing a single violence to the precepts and the doctrine of the art, because in it shine forth with marvelous clarity and light of figures and poetic adornments culture and propriety, festivity and wit, magnificence and spirit, sweetness and humor, bitterness and vehemence, commiseration and the affects, and the efficiency and representation of them all.)

If we are looking for the language of modernity, these lines provide it. Herrera presents the sonnet as "new and improved" lyric discourse, as not only the most beautiful, but also the most efficient means of representation to be found. Moreover, when he asserts that the sonnet can assimilate "all that these other kinds of poetry can embrace," with no perceptible loss of quality—no violence—to the format of the original material, the optimism and the hyperbole of his language can be compared to similar effusions over the technology of the digital transfer, in which the continuous waves of analog recording are chopped into intervals and measured into zeros and ones on disk, with no perceptible change in quality beyond a general sense of improvement in the clarity of phrasing and tone. Isn't this a version of the technique worked by Petrarch, when he transferred his multiple "worlds" into the alternating sonnets and songs through which his life could be stored for access by the reading public?[5]

But arguably, for everyone *except* Petrarch, the reconstitution is radical. In its own way, Herrera's language betrays this. The terms of his description glance against our current critical buzzwords, but less proleptically, they also inscribe the sonnet within the discourse of *sprezzatura*: the sonnet is the figure of "grace," "artifice," "festivity," "wit," "spirit," and "affect." It is thus set up as the analogue of the courtier, whose labor-intensive postures of "artful artlessness" require constant policing. On the one hand this formulation is nothing new. To draw the "new poetry" together with the "new man" is a standard convention of the humanist poetic defense. However, the attention Kaplan has focused on the rhetoric of "light" suggests that we consider their articulation from a new angle. Kaplan allows us to observe the parallels between Herrera's formulation of the sonnet and the late twentieth-century language of communications technology and subjectivity: given the radical psychological and physical interventions that it takes to produce the sixteenth-century courtier, how does he, with his attendant body and heavily freighted divisions of the self, come to be characterized as transitory and light?

Herrera's words suggest that one of the ways this happens is via the sonnet, whose spoken and unspoken rules engage its writers and recipients in the constant rehearsal of festive *asujetissement*.[6] The sonnet is comprised of an octet and a sestet, organized in terms of a "turn" (the *volta*) which guides utterance toward self-reflexivity: most often, the sestet comments on what has been said or depicted in the octet. In addition, as a short, closed form, the sonnet conditions poetic utterance to brevity (fourteen, eleven-syllable lines). Finally, convention encourages the voicing of the "I" and the mimesis of feeling, thinking, and confessing. Given all of these features, it is possible to see how the sonnet conditions readers and writers working with the form to a notion of the self as abbreviated and self-reflexive, to the reification of a constitutional disposition toward subjectivity-lite. The sonnet form extends an invitation to its writers and readers to identify their human selves with brief, mobile fragments, keyed to the operations of the mind. And from this perspective, the proliferation of sonneteering within early modern court culture can be taken as one avenue through which the frenetic, compulsory repetition of subjection is taken on voluntarily and playfully by the men and women upon whom it is imposed.

I@sonnet

I will return to Herrera's discussion of the sonnet slightly later, but before doing so it might be helpful to make a detour into a preliminary version of his words as they are framed in the writings of Juan Boscán. I begin by asserting that culture of modernity, generally, is a culture of displacement. However, early Spanish modernity is marked by a double enactment of that displacement: On the one hand, the fantasmatic and linguistic subject displaces other modes of experiencing the self; on the other, traditional notions of Spain as a proud and victorious Castile are overwritten by the pan-European and global Hapsburg state. Both of these phenomena are discernible in Boscán's "Letter" to the Duchess of Soma, the text in which he ceremoniously introduces Italian lyric forms to the Castilian nobility. As Anthony Cascardi has noted, the heroic era of the so-called Christian "reconquest" maintained a profound purchase on Spanish self-perception in the era of Boscán and Garcilaso (247–55). The introduction of the sonnet form was intimately and self-consciously linked with the exorcism of the figure of the noble Spanish knight from the cultural imaginary, and his replacement with the more moderate figure, the man of "arms and letters." The "Letter" is positioned within a charged moment in vernacular poiesis, as the nature and purpose of lyric is transformed from the creation of greatness (through epic and heroic ballad), to the containment of the voice within the human (and humanist) contours of the modern self; and Boscán works to fuse the two into an overt politics of form. Thus, at the start of the "Letter," he writes:

> Este segundo libro tendrá otras cosas hechas al modo italiano, las cuales serán sonetos y canciones ... La manera de estas es más grave y de más artificio y (si no me engaño) mucho mejor que la de las otras. Mas todavía, no embargante esto, cuando quise probar a hacerlas no dejé de entender que tuviera en esto muchos represores ... Cuanto más que luego en poniendo las manos en esto topé con hombres que me cansaron. Y en cosa que toda ella consiste en ingenio y en juizio, no teniendo estas dos cosas más vida de cuanto tienen gusto, pues cansándome havía de disgustarme, después de desgustado, no tenía donde pasar más adelante. (115–17)

(This second book will contain other items made in the Italian style, which are sonnets and songs . . . . The manner of these is more solemn and of greater artifice and (if I do not deceive myself) much better than that of the others. But nevertheless, despite this, when I wanted to try to make them I did not fail to understand that in this I would have many who would reprimand me . . . . All the more so as later, putting my hands to the task, I encountered some men who were tiresome. And in something in which all consists in wit and judgment, neither one of these two having more life than they have pleasure, when I became tired, I of necessity became displeased, and once displeased, I found no way to proceed . . .)

This opening announces Boscán's affiliation with Italian humanist circles, especially that of Baltassare Castiglione. Given that he had translated *The Book of the Courtier* into Castilian in 1534, it is perhaps not surprising that both the "Letter" and the lyric sequence that follows it map taste in poetry onto the contours of two modes of being.[7] Boscán employs a circumspect language and light rhetorical touch ("si no me engaño . . .") (if I do not deceive myself . . .) which portray him as a model courtier. And when he defines the new poetry as something that consists entirely in pleasure, this fits it firmly within the bounds of artlessness and concealed labor that is the hallmark of Renaissance *sprezzatura*. In contrast, the men who do not accept the new lyric are "tiresome," courtiership's cardinal sin.

We should understand this distinction, which establishes an important dichotomy for Boscán ("courtier/other"), as informing his consistent emphasis on the new poetry as the perfect container: "en este verso, dondequiera que se nos muestra . . . [vemos] una disposición muy capaz para recibir cualquier materia: o grave o sotil, o dificultosa o fácil, y assimismo para ayuntarse con cualquier estilo de los que hallamos entre los authores antiguos aprovados" (119).[8] (in this verse wherever one should look . . . [we see] a disposition quite capable of receiving any material whatsoever: grave or subtle, difficult or easy, and also to be joined with whatever style we might find among the approved ancient authors). What is at stake here is not just the poetic continence that establishes the mind as the "citadel" of reason, "protecting the self against the onslaught of experience" (Stewart 18). It is also the subjection of the traditional Castilian aristocracy in the interest of maintaining a pacified, unified state under Charles V.[9] To this end, the "Letter" imbricates poetics and the constitution of not only the rational, but also the political subject, interweaving references to poets, readers, and poems so densely that the social phenomenon of the Spanish subject's courtierization becomes inseparable from the poetic one of adopting new forms. The following passage in particular represents the new poetry as fully invested with the power of constituting the subjects who speak, write, and read it:

Los unos se quejaban que en las trovas de esta arte los consonantes no andaban tan descubiertos ni sonaban tanto como en las castellanas; otros decían que este verso no sabían si era verso, o si era prosa, otros arguían diciendo que esto principalmente había de ser para mujeres y que ellas no curaban de cosas de sustancia sino del son de las palabras y de la dulcura del consonante . . . ¿quién ha de responder a hombres que no se mueven sino al son de los consonantes? ¿Y quién se ha de poner en pláticas con gente que no sabe qué cosa es verso, sino aquél que calçado y vestido con el consonante os entra de un golpe por el un oído y os sale por el otro? . . . Si a éstos mis obras les parecieren duras y tuvieren soledad de la multitud de los consonantes, ahí tienen un cancionero, que acordó de llamarse general para que todos ellos vivan y descansen con él generalmente. (Boscán 116–17)

(Some complained that in the songs of this art the consonance did not proceed as openly, nor did it sound out as it did in the Castilian ones; others said that they did not know if this verse was verse or prose, others argued saying that this must be principally for women and that they cared nothing for matters of substance, but only for the sound of the words and the sweetness of the rhyme . . . who needs to respond to men who are not moved but by the sound of consonance? And who needs to engage in conversation with people who do not know what verse is, unless it is that which, shod and saddled with its consonantal rhyme, enters your ear with one blow, and exits with another? . . . If my works seem rough to these men, and they feel lonely for the multitude of rhymes, they have a *cancionero* which kindly called itself "general" so that all men of that sort might live and take repose with it generally.)[10]

The distinction drawn here reflects wider humanist debates about the nature of poetry as distinguished from verse; however Boscán turns these debates to his own ends by foregrounding and politicizing continence. When Boscán says that poetry should be composed in terms of judgment and taste, and not in terms of patterns of assonance and beat, he is voicing a conventional humanist distaste for the body and its senses: rhyme and meter strike on the eardrum at set intervals, inviting the body to move, anticipate, and respond.[11] A man of his time, Boscán is arguing for a poetry of the intellect to displace these base verse effects;[12] but it should also be borne in mind that traditional Castilian forms were accentual-syllabic and closely rhymed, whereas the new Italianate poetry was composed in the more flexible rhyme schemes of the sonnet and *canzone*, whose hendecasyllables did not rely on fixed rules of accent.[13] This is the key to Boscán's choice of image: As the highly regular, accentual-syllabic rhymed couplets and quatrains of the traditional ballad, *pie quebrado* and *arte mayor* forms, strike the body with blows (*golpes*), and gallop roughshod through the head, the metaphor directs humanist mistrust of melopoeia into the service of politics. Boscán's words figure the defenders of the old verse as the Castilian *caballeros*, or knights, who are made over by their meters into garrulous, loutish types who deserve to be shunned; and Boscán does so: "hanme parecido tan livianos sus argumentos, que de sólo haber parado en ellos, poco o mucho me corro; y así me correría agora si quisiese responder a sus escrúpulos" (117) (their arguments have seemed so lax to me that having paused for them, much or little, I flee; and I would flee thus now if it were required to respond to their quarrels).

In effect, then, Boscán's figure inscribes Spanish reinterpellation as a matter of form, as the substance and weight of the old Castilian is forced from the field of meaning, his place overwritten by the courtier's ever-expanding and quick mind. However, this recalibration also turns around on itself to enact a second set of effects, this time on the nature and meaning of the Spanish poem. Cascardi observes that, to substitute foreign forms for native ones called into question "the originary power of poetic speech" in Spanish (253). With little decoding, we can find an anxiety about this subtending both the "Letter" and the subsequent sequence. Consider passages such as the aside, "Vi que este verso que usan los castellanos, si un poco asentadamente queremos mirar en ello, no hay quien sepa de dónde tuvo principio. Y si él fuese tan bueno que se pudiese aprovar de suyo, como los otros que hay buenos, no havría necesidad de escudriñar quiénes fueron los inventores dél" (Boscán 118–19) (I saw that this verse that is used by the Castilians, if we wish to sit down and look at it, there is no one who knows where it had its beginnings. And if it were so good that it were approved on its own, as with others which are good, there would not be need to scrutinize who were its inventors). The roots of Castilian lyric tradition were not especially difficult to trace, but they lie in the eight hundred plus years of the so-called Christian "reconquest," the age of the knight-hero. This illustrates the delicacy of path Boscán must take as he elaborates how poetry makes the man. His words frame the ambivalent process of acknowledgment and erasure by which repressed histories are raised, aired, and subsumed into the ideologies of the new order (in this instance, the roots of Castilian lyric are from now on unspeakable, and hence, for all practical purposes, unknown).[14] Perhaps they also show a play for the recuperation of poetic power, as it is keyed to form, i.e., as it creates, as well as excludes. That is, if the context Boscán establishes as that of the new poetry is, manifestly, that of the consolidated authority of Charles V and his politically "modern," centralizing Spain, the sonnet, the Petrarchan sequence, and—to a lesser degree—the Italianate song are the forms through which members of the Spanish nobility can re-find a measure of their voice, circumscribed and translated as it may be into the forms of the new lyric.[15]

Intentionally or no, the "Letter" indicates the importance of courtierization as the "backstory" to the discourse of arms and letters. The text signals the epistemic violence that is masked by the phrase, omnipresent in Spanish poetry, "ora la spada, ora la pluma," while it simultaneously disguises that violence through the discourse of *sprezzatura*. Interestingly, Boscán protects the new poetry from any association with labor or study, for example: "Cuanto al tentar el estilo de estos sonetos y canciones y otras cosas de este género ... nunca tuve fin a escribir sino a andarme descansando con mi espíritu ..." (117) (With respect to trying the style of these sonnets and songs and other things of this kind ... I never had the aim of writing, but rather of wandering at rest with my spirit). For the courtier, which is to say for the man of the mind, as opposed to the man of the sword, the new poetry comes naturally. What remains unstated, but alive as a subtext, is the conditioning effect of this poetry on its courtly subjects.

The Internet

"Subjection," "continence," "violence," "abbreviation" ... this essay began with a series of questions about the Internet; it has headed steadily toward a narrative of containment. Isn't the Internet that boundless, ever-proliferating network of fiber-optic communication that enables limitless, self-transmission? I have devoted some time to Boscán's "Letter" because it lays the groundwork for how we can read Herrera as proto-cyberculture. Boscán imagines the *translatio* of the nobleman into the register of the virtual self, as it is effected by a poetic language invested with the power to change the very role and function of poiesis. As I have already indicated, in Boscán's ideal world poetry will no longer *be* poiesis; rather, Boscán envisions a poetry that will effect a break with worldly contexts in both tradition (epic and ballad) and history (the reconquest), and this desire informs his poetics of sententia. This is where Herrera takes him up, some thirty years later: at the description of the sonnet as the form that disencumbers poetic thought, framing it and packaging it for efficient representation and transmission. Having gained a sense of how burdened this fantasy is for Boscán, we can now better observe how the changed circumstances of Spain in the 1570s allow the consolidation of this image in Herrera's text.

In Herrera's Spain, modernity is that much more fully established. The Hapsburg dynasty is secure; the ideal of arms and letters has displaced that of the knight within the cultural imaginary, such that the "tiresome" Castilian no longer figures as a threat to society, or to poetry.[16] In terms of poetry, the sonnet's position within Spanish letters is secure. In the "Annotations," for example, each lyric form that is discussed receives a separate and specific entry; within this catalogue, the sonnet holds pride of place.[17] In sum, Herrera's culture is "sonnetized," with all of the implications I discussed earlier on: it is "subjectivized," with subjection imposed from without by threat and force, and internalized through the various performative activities that make courtiership the practice of "artless" subjection. As I have already argued, this reinforces the ease and seamlessness of the conceptualization of subjects as disembodied, via the chain of identifications: "person" as "I," "I" as the mind.[18]

It is this modern disposition that permits Herrera to move smoothly and rapidly through arguments that Boscán has represented only partially, and indirectly. Consider the speed with which Herrera shifts from his description of the sonnet as all-inclusive—"es tan extendida y capaz de todo argumento, que recoge en sí sola todo lo que pueden abrazar estas partes de poesía, sin hacer violencia" (308) (it is so extensive and capable of any argument, that it gathers into itself all that these other kinds of poetry can embrace, without doing a single violence to the precepts and the doctrine of the art) to the long list of cautions that follow:

> Y en ninguno otro género se requiere más pureza y cuidado de lengua, más templanza y decoro, donde es grande culpa cualquier error pequeño; y donde no se permite licencia alguna, ni se consiente algo, que ofenda las orejas, y por la brevedad suya no sufre, que sea ociosa, o vana una palabra sola. Y por esta causa su verdadero sujeto y materia debe ser principalmente alguna sentencia ingeniosa y aguda, o grave, y que merezca bien ocupar aquel lugar todo; descrita de suerte que parezca propia y nacida en aquella parte, huyendo de la oscuridad y dureza, mas de suerte que no descienda a tanta facilidad, que pierda los números y la dignidad conveniente. (308)

> (And in no other kind is there required more purity and caution of tongue, more moderation and decorum, where whatever small error is a great fault; and where no license whatsoever is permitted, nor is anything condoned that offends the ears, and for its brevity it does not suffer that a single word be lazy or vain. And for this reason its true subject and material should be principally an ingenious and witty sentence, or a grave one, and let it well deserve to occupy its whole space; described in a manner that appears proper and born to that place, fleeing darkness and difficulty, but in a way that it does not descend to such facility that it loses the measures and dignity suitable to it.)

The rapid "switching" that is on display here—between *everything* and *not that,* between freedom and caution, between license and threat—can be read as symptomatic of the culture of displacement in which Herrera is writing. The difference in tone between his text and Boscán's marks the distance traveled within the Spanish imaginary toward the psychological and social dispositions of modernity, in which what is recognized as present is constituted over and against a constant, unconscious stream of devaluations and exclusions.

Two features are important here. Unlike Boscán, Herrera does not find it necessary to sort the sonnet out from its contexts in the "real" of the cultural past as it has conventionally been transmitted by poetry. For the most part, these breaks have been affected over the years that separate the two critics (due in some part to the efforts of poets and humanists such as Boscán). In addition, Herrera can imagine the rupture of this tradition, and its displacement by the sonnet, in terms of the violence-free embrace we saw described in the passage quoted earlier in this essay. Both of these features place Herrera and his text firmly within the history of the "disembodied discursive practices of new information technologies" (Kaplan 34), whose suppressed bases in the material and the real are masked by rhetoric of efficiency, and supplemented by a cornucopia of hyperboles describing unlimited transmission and articulation, *la eficacia y representación de todas* (the efficiency and representation of all).

When I say that Herrera "invented" the Internet, it is with these cultural and textual homologies in mind. Herrera's opening assertions repackage Boscán's words into the articulation of a proto-Enlightenment dream, *sententia* shorn of excess and smoothed of linguistic adhesions—modern poetry for Herrera's modern age. But interestingly, it is precisely at this moment, when Herrera's language is at its most fluid and grandiose, that the orientation of his argument shifts from containment as a practice that facilitates, to containment as rough handling and contortion. The following passage shows the flow of Herrera's argument as he completes his paraphrases of Boscán's central points and then begins to write against them:

> No reprehendo la facilidad, sino la afectación de ella, porque singular virtud, es decir libre y claramente sin cansar el ánimo del que oye con dureza y oscuridad, y no se puede dejar de conceder, que regala mucho al sentido ver que ningunos vínculos y ligaduras de consonancias impiden el pensamiento para no descubrirse con delgadeza y facilidad. Mas ¿quién no condenará el poco espiritu y vigor, la humilidad y bajeza, que se adquiere con el conseguimiento della? ¿Y quién no estima por molestia y disgusto oír palabras desnudas de grandeza y autoridad cuando importa representalla? Sin duda alguna el Soneto, que tanta semajanza tiene y conformidad con el epigrama, cuanto más merece y admite sentencia más grave, tanto es más dificil, por estar encerrado en un perpetuo y pequeño espacio, y esto, que parecerá por ventura a los que no lo consideran bien, opinión apartada del común sentimiento,

puede fácilmente juzgar con la experiencia quien ha compuesto sonetos, y recogido en una sujeta y sutil materia con gran dificultad, ha esquivado la oscuridad y dureza del estilo. Porque es muy desigual diferencia escribir en modo que los versos fuercen la materia, a aquel que la materia fuerce los versos, y en esto se conoce la distancia que hay entre unos y otros escritores. (Herrera 308)

(I do not reprove ease, but rather the affectation of it, because it is a singular virtue to speak freely and clearly without tiring the spirit of he who listens with darkness and obscurity, and it cannot fail to be conceded that it is very pleasing to the sense to see that no links and ties of consonance impede thought from showing itself with delicacy and ease. For who will not condemn the lack of spirit and vigor, the humility and lowliness that is acquired with conceding it? And who does not esteem it a bother and displeasure to hear words denuded of grandeur and authority when it is important to represent it? Without a doubt the Sonnet, which has so much similarity and conformity with the epigram, for all that it deserves and admits the weightiest sentence, by just so much is difficult, for being enclosed in a perpetual and small space, and this, which will seem, perchance, to those who do not think it over well, an opinion that stands apart from the common sentiment, can be easily judged from experience by the person who has written sonnets, and, having gathered a tamed and subtle material with great difficulty, has vexed it with obscurity and roughness of style. Because the difference between writing in the mode in which the verses force the material, and that in which the material forces the verses, is great, and in this is seen the distance that there is between one writer and another.)

Herrera folds in Boscán's attacks on fixed rhyme and meter here, reorganizing and deploying them with the elegance and speed that have led me to use the metaphor of "switching"—*regala mucho al sentido ver que ningunos vínculos y ligaduras de consonancias impiden el pensamiento para no descubirse con delgadeza y facilidad*—(it cannot fail to be conceded that it is very pleasing to the sense to see that no links and ties of consonance impede thought from showing itself with delicacy and ease). But this is also the moment at which theory runs into practice and encounters a stumbling block. The poetics of disembodied mind is tantalizing marketing. However, for people who actually *write* sonnets, composing one is no light task. Despite modernity, sonneteering is still the act of making poetry, and despite the posture he takes in his opening, Herrera is too good a poet to disavow that the rhythms of poetic language as it works over and against the constraints of form are an essential part of poetic meaning. For this reason, the work of subjecting song to the service of pure *sententia* is vexed. Even in this polished gem of the intellect, expression without cadence, and discursive expression composed without attention to *los números y la dignidad conveniente* (the measures and dignity suitable to it), is not poetry.

What are we to make of this? This is a charged moment in the history of the Spanish sonnet. Rhythm—its salience in the poetry of early sonneteers of whom Herrera approved (such as Garcilaso and Cetina), and its absence in the poetry and theory of Boscán—leads him to recognize the shortcomings of a poetics whose basis is revealed to be politics, not poetry. Cued by rhythm, Herrera notices that Boscán's interest in poetics was instrumental, directed most of all toward the establishment of the appropriate form for courtiers (for subjects), and that, as a consequence, his sense of the nuances of poetic expression was limited. This yields two results: First, Herrera begins to criticize Boscán's theory, from a number of directions (Navarrete 126-51). Second, he begins to engage at a deeper level with the representational techniques available to poets interested in working in the form. In particular, from this point in the text, his remarks open a new phase of innovation in sonnet composition, as Herrera works to reestablish it as poetry. Rhythm, inscribed by means of enjambment, is paramount:

> No es vicio, sino virtud . . . como en el héroico latino, que romper el verso es grandeza del modo de decir. Refiero esto porque se persuaden algunos, que nunca dicen mejor, que cuando siempre acaban la sentencia con la rima . . . cuando quiere alguno acompañar el estilo conforme con la celsitud y belleza del pensamiento procura desatar los versos, y muestra con este deslazamiento y partición cuanta grandeza tiene el sujeto . . . mas este rompimiento no ha de ser continuo. (Herrera 309)

> (is not a vice, but rather a virtue . . . as in the heroic Latin, in which to break the line is a mode of speaking of the great. I mention this because some are persuaded that they never speak better than when they always complete the sentence with the rhyme . . . when one wishes to accompany the style with the elegance and beauty of the thought, he procures to untie the verses, and shows with this loosening and division the greatness of the subject . . . but this breaking should not be continual.)

This is a substantial turn. Both Boscán's "Letter" and the opening of the "Annotations" celebrate the free and unimpeded movement of ideas through a poetic space purged of obstacles. Now Herrera introduces the disruption of expression as the paradoxical means by which to further "free" poetic thought. But rhythm's capacities of meaning rely on bodily, not intellectual, experience. Rhythmic patterns evoke sensations of breath and percussion which, in Wimsatt's famous formulation, impose "counterpatterns of alogical implication" on sententia. Does this not disrupt the fantasy of the sonnet as the perfect form for the disembodied, rational mind? In turning his focus to rhythm and enjambment, Herrera would seem to be redirecting Castilian poetics back in the direction of the real, of the body, of history.

That is the threat, certainly. Perhaps it is the dream. As numerous critics have noted, late sixteenth-century letters are increasingly marked by nostalgia for res, or for the "real" that humanist scholars understand as lost to language understood as style (verba) in the modern, vernacular age. But as many of these same critics have also argued, the outcome of this nostalgia is an increasingly sophisticated use of rhetoric. This is especially true in Herrera's writing, as Paul Julian Smith has shown (43–46). Thus, given Herrera's finely tuned sense of both poetry and the exigencies of language, it is possible to make the case that in these passages he glimpses, however briefly, the radical, human loss entailed when being is reinterpellated in terms of the severed fragment, the abbreviated utterance, the sonneteer's "I." However, the sheer mass of the "Annotations" (some eight hundred plus entries in which Herrera argues for, evaluates, measures, and explains the rhetorical devices—present and potential—deployed in Garcilaso's fifty-poem corpus) provides ample evidence that, in the context of the verba/res split, Herrera's view of poetry falls far further on the side of verba than has that of any writer who has come before him. In this context, the return to rhythm, the prescription of enjambment, and the host of rhetorical figures and strategies that Herrera will endorse over the course of the text need to be understood as means by which to deflect attention from the definitive gap that separates language, even poetic language, from lived experience, while providing a guide to the newest and most sophisticated means by which to substitute linguistic approximation for human presence. The poet who follows Herrera's counsel will compose sonnets which are not only efficient, but efficacious, that is to say, persuasive in their mimesis of selfhood, convincing in their implication that their attenuated and delimited utterances upload "all" into a steady flow of spontaneous, witty, graceful moments of consciousness.

Looking back along the history of the early modern sonnet, we might understand Boscán and his early sixteenth-century cohort to have been victims of their own success. The poetic form that Boscán imagined would fix the image of the modern Spanish nobleman as a model of intellectual prudence and considered thoughtful restraint explodes—through the efficacy of the very fantasies of containment and ludic, playful disembodiment which he himself set in motion—into a machine for proliferating language, and for signifying vain pleasure, fugitive shadows. Consider Francisco de Quevedo's undulating feast of the senses, "En crespa tempestad de oro undoso" which begins, "En crespa tempestad de oro undoso / Nada golfos luz ardiente y pura / Mi corazón, sediento de hermosura, / Si el cabello deslazas generoso" (In a curling tempest of undulating gold / My heart, thirsty for beauty, / Swims in gulfs of burning, pure light / If you loose your generous hair). In this sonnet, and in similar works from Herrera forward, the technologies of poetic displacement do not fail the project of disembodiment; but nevertheless, sententia is undone by representational jouissance, in a poetry comprised almost entirely of stylistic effect. What an unreasonable paradox. And what a postmodern state of affairs. As Kaplan has written, "as technologies of . . . communication become more and more disembodied, more and more displaced from corporeality, and more and more a practice of mind or a simulation, the unified subject . . . is less and less a requirement" (34). Ultimately, what may link the sonnet to the Internet most fundamentally is the mad drive to elaborate structures that call into question the necessity of human being—whether embodied or "purely" mental—at all.[19]

Notes

1. "New" is in quotation marks here because the history of the sonnet stretches back to at least the fifteenth century in Spain. The form is "new" only in the sense that writers such as Boscán and Herrera chose to make it so.
2. As the flood of manuals, treatises, and instructive letters on manners produced in the sixteenth century demonstrate, Renaissance writers had a good purchase on the instability of the subject, that "what is brought into being through the performative effect of the interpellating demand is much more than a 'subject,' for the subject created is not for that reason fixed in place: it becomes the occasion for a further making . . . a subject only remains a subject through a reiteration or rearticulation of itself as a subject" (Butler 99).
3. In slightly different terms than the ones I am suggesting here, William Egginton has speculated on the links between "avatars, agents and . . . [early modern] . . . actors," with reference to Golden Age Peninsular theater. See *How the World Became a Stage*, Chapter 1.
4. In "The Question Concerning Technology," Heidegger distinguishes Platonic techne from modern technology: "modern technology does not unfold into a bringing-forth in the sense of poiesis. The revealing that rules in modern technology is a challenging [*Herausfordern*], which puts to nature the unreasonable demand that it supply energy that can be extracted and stored . . ." (15).
5. Petrarch changes "as the needs of sense making change," as Roland Greene has observed (*Post-Petrarchism* 1). John Freccero's classic essay on Petrarch's lyric self-fashioning compares the workings of the *Canzoniere* to a film strip, but that piece was written before the digital age.

6. Judith Butler defines *asujetissement*, or "subjectivation," and the question that she finds to lie at its center: "The customary model for understanding this process goes as follows: power imposes itself on us, and, weakened by its force, we come to internalize or accept its terms. What such an account fails to note, however, is that the 'we' who accept such terms are fundamentally dependent on those terms for 'our' existence. Are there not discursive conditions for the articulation of any 'we'? Subjection consists precisely on this fundamental dependency on a discourse we never chose but that, paradoxically, initiates and sustains our agency" (2).
7. Boscán's lyric sequence narrates a conversion from the suffering of medieval *fin amours*, to "pues amo blandamente, y soy amado" (loving gently, and [being] loved) (sonnet 115).
8. Interestingly, Boscán is diverging somewhat from his sources in this passage. The language of the container that he is using derives from Dante (*De Vulgari Eloquentia*; Book 2, Chapter 3), as his words are adapted by Bembo. For both Italian writers the container is the unit: in Dante's case it is the stanza, and in Bembo's, it is the sonnet, taken on its own. Given the overall direction of Boscán's remarks, it seems likely that this slippage is intentional. The principal claim made by Renaissance writers on behalf of hendecasyllabics was their formal similarity to Greek heroic meter. Since it is heroism, more than anything else, that Boscán is interested in rooting out of Spanish poetry and poetics, it makes sense that he deflects attention from connotations of the hendecasyllable with the hero by means of a caricature of vernacular line forms and the crude knights with which he will associate them below.
9. This is the principal thrust of Boscán's investment in linguistic and literary reform. As Morreale has demonstrated, his word choice when translating *cortegiano* into Castilian in his version of *Il Cortegiano* indicates that one of his aims in the text was the sorting apart of two sets of characteristics previously joined within the character of the nobleman, those of the *gentilhombre* (the gentleman-courtier) and those of the caballero (the knight).
10. Translating this passage has posed a challenge to critics, because of differences in English and Spanish vocabularies of rhyme and meter, and also because questions of beat, rhyme, and measure were the subject of serious debate among sixteenth-century humanists. Navarrete has translated *consonantes* as rhyme, but Spanish "consonantal rhyme" is based on whole syllable. This inscribes a rule of beat that is absent from the contemporary English understanding of the word. David Darst uses the rather awkward "consonantal rhyme" in his translation. I have decided to use the terms "consonance," "rhyme," and, in one case when it is unavoidable, "consonantal rhyme," as I think they are indicated by the overall sense of Boscán's text.
11. The prejudice goes back at least to Dante, who in *De Vulgari Eloquentia* elevates the canzone over the ballad form because "*canzoni* in themselves accomplish all that they are supposed to do, which ballades do not. The latter have need of dancers to keep time, who thus bring out their form. Therefore, *canzoni* should be considered nobler than ballades" (Aligheri, 37; translator's spelling).

12. On the history of "poetry"/"verse" debates, see the excellent study by Steele.
13. Darst points out that Boscán's critics protested that the Spanish hendecasyallable had been in use long before the Valencian's arrival on the scene, and that his "new" poetry was therefore not "new," just inferior (20); however, he observes, Boscán made a point of avoiding the traditional Castilian hendecasyllable, with its more or less regular stresses on syllables four or five. This is again probably for the reasons that I have just suggested, namely, their association with heroism.
14. There is also the question of the rich tradition of Judeo-Arabic poetry which had also been excised—officially anyway—from cultural consciousness. Traditional Peninsular verse was shot through with Arabic, Hebrew, and Gallego-Portuguese influences, of course; and as Maria Menocal has written, the non-Castilian lyric "had a great beat."
15. Exaggerated Horatian that he is, Boscán remains suspicious of song, even of *canzone*, as the lyric of incontinence. This is evinced in the opening line of the first song of his sequence, where he has his speaker voice his fear of uncontained speech: "Quiero hablar un poco / mas teme el corazón de fatigarse, / porque si hablo sé que será tanto / que el seso ha de alterarse, / y a su culpa no es bien tornarse loco" (134–135) (I wish to speak a little / but my heart is afraid that it will tire itself, / because if I speak, I know that I will do so so much / that my brain will become altered, / and it is not good to go mad on its account).
16. And such that, as Cruz has pointed out, the author of a treatise on sword fighting, Jerónimo de Carranza, gained fame, honor, and an erstwhile title based on popular confusion between the skills described in his text and his actual performance as a captain (Cruz 191).
17. Since Herrera is commenting on Garcilaso, he catalogs the forms he used, namely, the sonnet, the song, the elegy, the epistle, and the eclogue.
18. Moreover, given the popularity of florilegia on both sides of the Atlantic, this "sonnetization" is global. See the discussion in Greene, (*Unrequited Conquests* 135–70).
19. Many thanks to the University of Oregon EMODS: David Castillo, Lisa Freinkel, Nathalie Hester, David Luebke, Fabienne Moore, Daniel Rosenberg, and Gordon Sayre, for their helpful comments on earlier versions of this essay.

Works Cited

Aligheri, Dante. *De Vulgari Eloquentia*. In *The Literary Criticism of Dante Aligheri*. Trans. and ed. Robert S. Haller. Lincoln, NE: University of Nebraska Press, 1973.
Boscán Almogaver, Juan. *Obras Completas*. Madrid: Cátedra, 1989.
Butler, Judith. *The Psychic Life of Power*. Stanford: Stanford University Press, 1997.
Cascardi, Anthony J. *Ideologies of History in the Spanish Golden Age*. University Park, PA: Penn State Press, 1997.

Cruz, Anne. "Arms versus Letters: The Poetics of War and the Career of the Poet in Early Modern Spain." *European Literary Careers*. Eds. Patrick Cheney and Frederick de Armas. Toronto: University of Toronto Press, 2002. 186–205.

Darst, David. *Juan Boscán*. Boston: Twayne Publishers, 1978.

Egginton, William. *How the World Became a Stage: Presence, Theatricality and the Questions of Modernity*. Buffalo, NY: SUNY Press, 2003.

Freccero, John. "The Fig Tree and the Laurel: Petrarch's Poetics." In *Literary Theory / Renaissance Texts*. Eds. Patricia Parker and David Quint. Baltimore, MD: Johns Hopkins University Press. 1986. 27–35.

Greene, Roland A. *Post-Petrarchism: Origins and Innovations of the Western Lyric Sequence*. Princeton, NJ: Princeton University Press, 1991.

———. *Unrequited Conquests*. Chicago. Chicago University Press, 2000.

Heidegger, Martin. *The Question Concerning Technology and Other Essays*. New York: Harper and Collins, 1977.

Herrera, Fernando de. "Anotaciones". *Garcilaso de la Vega y sus Comentaristas*. Ed. Antonio Gallego Morell. Madrid: Gredos, 1972. 305–504.

Kaplan, Caren. "Transporting the Subject: Technologies of Mobility and Location in an Era of Globalization." Special issue, *PMLA Special Issue, Globalized Citizens, Media States* (2002): 32–42.

Menocal, Maria. *Shards of Love: Exile and the Origins of the Lyric*. Durham: Duke University Press, 1994.

Morreale de Castro, Margherita. *Castiglione y Boscán: El ideal cortesano en el renacimiento español*. Madrid: Añejos del Boletín de la Real Academia Española, 1959.

Navarrete, Ignacio. *Orphans of Petrarch: Poetry and Theory of the Spanish Renaissance*. Berkeley: University of California Press, 1994.

Smith, Paul Julian. *Writing in the Margin: Spanish Literature of the Golden Age*. Oxford: Clarendon, 1988.

Spiller, Michael R. G. *The Development of the Sonnet: An Introduction*. London: Routledge, 1992.

Steele, Timothy. *Missing Measures: Modern Poetry and the Revolt Against Meter*. Fayetteville: University of Arkansas Press, 1990.

Stewart, Susan. *Poetry and the Fate of the Senses*. Chicago: University of Chicago Press, 2002.

4

A Ritual Practice for Modernity: Baltasar Gracián's Organized Body of Taste

Bradley J. Nelson

> ¿Qué importa que el mundo sea ancho si mi çapato es estrecho?
> —Baltasar Gracián, *El Criticón*

> — ¿De dónde vienes?
> —De la nada.
> — ¿Y dónde vas?
> —Al todo.
> —Baltasar Gracián, *El Criticón*

No writings are more emblematic of the baroque courtly subject of representation than those penned under the name Lorenzo Gracián, Baltasar Gracián's unconvincingly pseudonymous "brother." Jesuit priest, popular preacher, confessor of nobles, alternately favored and chastised by his religious order, Gracián and his aesthetic and philosophical crystallizations are the culminating moment of the baroque taste for allusive, witty, and difficult verbal gymnastics (Ayala; Pelegrin). Yet, even as he has become for many critics the ultimate embodiment of Counter-Reformation art and philosophy, an equally influential vein of criticism has recognized in his aesthetic theories the bases for the modern paradigm of artistic taste as well as an undeniable thrust toward rationalism (Gadamer; Cascardi "Gracián and the Authority of Taste"). This tension between a religiously conceived art and a rationalist gaze on the world has occupied most Gracián criticism, which constantly searches for ways to reconcile his seemingly split *personae*: on the one hand, the expression of a complex yet ultimately sincere religious faith that redeems the relationship between faith and reason (Batllori; Correa Calderón); on the other, the defiant writer of daring political, artistic, and philosophical manuals and treatises whose generally surreptitious efforts to publish his works subverted the Church's attempts to contain and control the production and flow of rationalist thought (Pelegrin).

The goal of this essay is to reconsider this apparent dichotomy through the optic of José Antonio Maravall's concept—or conceit—of "baroque rationalism" (63). In particular, I will focus on the ritualistic aspects in Gracián's discursive performance of what I will call the *organized body of taste*. The main theoretical levers in this discussion will be Catherine Bell's ideologically informed definitions of ritual theory and ritual practice, and Slavoj Žižek's subversive attempt to "rescue" the Cartesian *cogito* from the antagonistic role assigned to it by New Historicist and deconstructionist thinkers (*Cogito and the Unconscious*). As the title of my study suggests, ritual is not something that rationalism leaves behind in its move toward the secularization of knowledge and the transcendental subject. The interrelated concepts of ritual and myth are at the heart of rationalism's—and modernity's—efforts to mark an ontological and epistemological break with the past and, as such, play a preeminent role in Gracián's oeuvre. My main claim in this study is that an in-depth analysis of modernity's simultaneous dependence on and resistance to ritualization breaks the stalemate between baroque and rationalist approaches to Gracián by displaying how his texts stage the primordial, ritualistic creation and rationalization of the modern, abstract subject of representation. Put another way, Gracián's modernity does not emerge by disentangling it from the ritual residue of the Baroque; rather, ritualization is the only way we can approach the lessons that baroque culture holds for modernity.

From the Divine Palate to Individual Taste

At stake in the "evolution" from what are generally perceived as more primitive, ritualistic cultures to the modern, scientific, or *realistic* worldview is a "signifying supplement," or excess. In religious ritual, this supplement is both theorized and experienced as the transubstantiation of an *other*, more permanent and universal body into the holy host, which then penetrates and merges with the bodies of the participants in the sacred dramatization of the Eucharist (Gumbrecht; Egginton, *How the World*). In the post-Trent world, this sacrament becomes the only legitimate method for evoking and experiencing the real *presence* of an otherwise irremediably distanced God. Gracián marks his modernity by displacing the trope of taste as it relates to eucharistic transubstantiation from its religious framework, and then redirecting it toward the social performance of aesthetic taste, thus effectively deterritorializing this ritual "surplus" from the godhead to the individual subject. In Discurso XXIII in *Agudeza y arte de ingenio*, titled "On paradoxical wit," Gracián introduces a short citation from his brother Felipe which draws a curious but explicit analogy between the sacred *manjar* (delicacy) of the Eucharist and his own notions of *taste*: "It had (this ingenious priest says) this Eucharistic dish had [sic] all the flavors (*gustos*), and pleasures that could be desired; it seems, that it only lacked that great delight, which is to be stolen" (220).[1] Gracián is not suggesting that the Eucharist itself is lacking anything in its perfection but rather that the imperfect taste of man is incapable of completely enjoying this sacred dish without adding something to it. And what is added corresponds precisely to man's ontological and epistemological shortcomings, which converts a perfect morsel into something imperfect, or incomplete, yet infinitely more satisfying. In an imperfect microcosm, taste, even transubstantiated taste, must be moved by a transgressive—or pathological (Egginton, "Gracián")—void, or slip, which functions as a mysterious addition. In the move from the perfect, or full,[2] taste of God to the imperfect, or empty, taste of man, the transcendental surplus is converted into a mundane lack, which is of vital importance for understanding the subject of taste. If Gracián's notion of taste marks a turning point in the development of modern ideological structures (Gadamer), then it must also be said that ritual occupies a central role in the evolution of the transcendental subject. In essence, Gracián deflects much of the signifying supplement provided by ritual discourses, symbols, and structures from the symbolic augmentation of the universal church and the (semi-) absolutist state toward the individual criterion of success (*éxito*), an emerging phenomenon that Francisco Sánchez has similarly called "[un] añadido ontológico" ("Cultura" 377) (an ontological addition). This "pivoting of the sacred" (Van Gennep, quoted in Bell, *Ritual Perspectives* 37) activates a change in perspective which allows the author to maintain the structure and forms of Counter-Reformation social hierarchies while subverting their traditionally conceived, organicist—*embodied*—notions of "natural" superiority in favor of humanist values such as personal merit and technical difficulty (Rodríguez, *Theory*; Read, *Visions*; Cascardi, "Gracián and The Authority of Taste"; Sánchez, "Cultura"; Spadaccini and Talens, "Introduction").[3]

Gracián's projection of imperfection into the sacrifice of the mass also adds a whole new dimension to Maravall's discussion of the "technique of incompleteness," which was so popular and influential in baroque theater and art (218).[4] What better way to move the faithful toward participating in religious celebrations than to suggest that their affirmation of faith is somehow transgressive? We should also take note, however, that Gracián's fabrication of ritual transgression, an admittedly irrational phenomenon, proceeds directly from his inexorably rational analysis of the encounter between mundane and transcendental *gustos*. Likewise, this irrational element is the key to Maravall's understanding of baroque rationalism: "in the baroque the pedagogy and all modes of directing human behavior endeavored to reach the individuals' extrarational levels and from there to move them and integrate them into the supporting groups of the prevailing social system" (227). Unfortunately, Maravall's insight into this irrational element of reason either has been overlooked or contained, along with the bulk of baroque art, within the "idiosyncratic," historical and cultural framework of the Counter-Reformation (Echeverría). Indeed, the key to understanding Gracián's eucharistic wit, as well as his modern construction of the individual body and the social field of taste is the philosophy and aesthetics of *desengaño*, a concept that traditionally has been regarded as almost exclusively premodern.

Gracián's radically orthodox position on *desengaño* allows him to direct the Jesuits' foundational tenets toward their logical ends, upending organicist narratives of blood purity and social superiority by submitting all material bodies to the same process of *unbecoming*: "aquí no se mira la dignidad ni el puesto, sino la personal eminencia: no a los ditados sino a las prendas; a lo que uno se merece, que no a lo que hereda" (*El Criticón* III, 12, 803) (neither nobility nor position are considered here, but rather personal eminence: not titles but favors; what one merits, not what he inherits). This transference of a transcendental "substance" from the blood-based genealogies of feudalism (Rodríguez, *Theory*; Read, "Saving") to the individual performance of *good taste* mirrors his treatment of the Eucharist and helps pave the way for the aforementioned historical transition from an early or premodern mentality based on ritual toward a modern mentality based—ostensibly—on reason. The symbolic evacuation of the feudal social body, however, cannot do away entirely with the corpse in what ideally would be conceived as a Cartesian move toward disembodied objectivity (Damasio). Nor can Gracián's guidelines for courtly success and fame function without a series of ritual structures through which his program becomes (dis)embodied by the reader of his text. By focusing on Gracián's ritual construction of the subject of power, I will be able to look more closely at the modern, rational subject, whose ontological basis and freedom of inquiry will be shown to arise not from a substantive and self-conscious center of reflection but rather from a "demented" and "insane" lack of being. What Sánchez terms an "ontological addition" is an aesthetic effect, whose ultimate point of reference is an equally problematical, ontological *subtraction*, as at the (off-) center of Gracián's self-reflecting subject we encounter an insistent *lack* (falta).

Ritual Practice

Ritual practice, defined by Catherine Bell as an exercise of power, provides a way out of the deadlock between the two critical approaches to Gracián outlined above: the Baroque is neither *positively* resistant to modern rationalism; nor is it *negatively* "superstitious" in comparison to the Enlightenment. Rather, the Baroque is the truth of religious institutional culture insofar as the latter configures a practice of (amoral) power; and it is the truth of rationalism as a ritual, which is to say, self-legitimizing, partially blind, and embodied social practice. For Bell, the history of ritual studies is exemplary of the ritualistic nature of scientific paradigms, or ideologies, themselves. In *Ritual Perspectives and Dimensions*, she begins her survey of ritual studies by pointing out how the landmark works of James George Frazer and Edward B. Tylor reproduce one of the central historical, social, and cultural forms of modernity itself: the hierarchical and interdependent relationship between so-called primitive societies and modern civilization. Far from being an archaic residue of positivistic, "scientific" prejudices, the tendency of anthropologists, sociologists, linguists, and others to construct their own object of scientific inquiry through the activation of evolution-based hierarchies extends from Frazer and Tylor, through the debate between myth-centered and structure-centered theories such as Eliade and Levi-Strauss, and, finally, to functionalists such as Émile Durkheim and Victor Turner. In Bell's view, even the current work of Clifford Geertz privileges the "objective" stance of the anthropologist over the partially blind perspective of the ritual "practicant": for Geertz, "ritual participants act, whereas those observing them think" (*Ritual Theory* 28).

In this opposition between acting and thinking, the analytical posture of the observer disguises, or subtracts, his or her active interventions in the articulation of the object of analysis, while that which science defines as primitive is projected into the culture being studied. Looking very much like what Egginton terms the "conjuring up" of divine presence, the object of inquiry is converted into the very source of the scientific presuppositions through the self-negation of the scientist. In summary, the positive assertions of ritual researchers regarding the relationship between ritual culture and modernity are produced through a negative movement which subtracts their gaze and their bodies from the scene of their science, which in turn substantiates their scientific findings. For Slavoj Žižek, this moment of "negative self-reflection" replicates the very passage from nature to culture: "The key point is thus that the passage from 'nature' to 'culture' is not direct, that one cannot account for it within a continuous evolutionary narrative: something has to intervene between the two, a kind of 'vanishing mediator,' which is neither Nature nor Culture—this In-between is silently presupposed in all evolutionary narratives" (Žižek, *The Ticklish Subject* 36). Bell's point seems to be that in anthropology this vanishing mediator is the scientist him- or herself, whose analysis both marks off and rationalizes the qualitative difference between primitive and modern culture even as it effaces the active imposition of qualitative hierarchies.

The Baroque is much more sophisticated in its rationalism than is generally recognized. Witness Gracián's self-conscious inscription of the activity of the *ingenio* into the nature of the reality that it wittily transforms into a conceit: "Es un acto del entendimiento que exprime la correspondencia que se halla entre los objetos" (*Agudeza*, Discurso II, 33) (It is an act of understanding that expresses the correspondence that is found between objects). I say self-conscious because his treatise *Agudeza y arte de ingenio* repeatedly demonstrates how these correspondences can be made up, invented where none is readily apparent. Once the invention takes hold, however, the relation passes back into the object: "Están ya en los objetos mismos las agudezas objetivas" (*Agudezza*, Discurso LXIII, 538) (objective witticisms are already in the objects themselves). It is this strategic manipulation that ultimately leads us to the political nature of Gracián's ritual structure, which brings us back to Bell.

According to Bell, the goal of ritualization is to maintain and strengthen a sense of *redemptive hegemony*, which she defines in the following way:

> [R]itualization does not simply act, unseeingly, to bring the social body, the community, and the largest image of reality into some reassuring configuration of coherent continuity. More fundamentally, it also appropriates this coherence in terms of the interests of persons or groups. The coherence is rendered and experienced as *redemptive* for those empowered by the schemes of the ritual. (*Ritual Theory* 115; my emphasis)

This definition of ritualization resonates strongly with Spadaccini and Talens's characterization of Gracián's writings as an attempt "to develop a methodology to prepare the elites for power" ("Introduction" xxiii). Bell's emphasis on the active dimension of ritual power also enriches Maravall's observation concerning the shift from medieval to baroque-guided culture: "What we might call a simple *static guidance controlling by presence* had to give way before a *dynamic guidance controlling by activity*" (68). In Gracián, the gradual and strategic embodiment of expedient schemes and dispositions describes the entire trajectory of Andrenio in the three books of *El Criticón*, as he moves from passive spectator to active participant through the internalization of prudent schemes of knowledge formation and self-representation. This constant making and remaking of the self and the cosmos unveils the ritual nature of Gracián's extensive and difficult guide for pilgrims, a process tied to the ages of man and one which stages what Bell terms the "unrecognized primacy of the body" in ritualization (*Ritual Theory* 96-98).

As in baroque art in general, the modern obsession with the body is ritualistically concealed behind a material disgust, which is both the source and limit of aesthetic taste (Cascardi, "Gracián"): "No hagas caso, no, de essa material vida en que los brutos te exceden" (*El Criticón* III, 12; 794) (Give no heed, at all, to that material life in which the brutes [ignorant] outdo you). As such, the best way to approach Gracián's reconstitution of the social body is through the philosophy of *desengaño*. Maravall, Fernando R. de la Flor, and Juan Carlos Rodríguez all argue that, far from being a residue of medieval religious culture, *desengaño* is an early modern ideology whose primary function is to mediate between the univocal cosmological hierarchies of the Middle Ages and the political, economic, social, religious, and artistic transformations that accompany the onset of modernity. In the progressive destabilization of the medieval cosmos, which was based on the substantial *influence* of God in the world, presence gives way to an exaggerated absence, wherein the human condition is portrayed as constitutively eccentric and finite, condemned by and limited to its temporal-corporeal nothingness. The ideological thrust of this philosophy becomes clear with the realization that any attempt to overcome this state of (non-) existence is perceived as vain or blind or both (R. de la Flor). What Victor Turner terms "anti structure" thus functions as a strategic support for structure. In a sense, one redeems one's own nothingness by participating in activities, or more specifically, in *rituals*, which redeem the nothingness of the Church and the State.

Gracián treats this insuperable obstacle in a much different way, and instead of a sign of absolute interdiction, it is made to appear as positive possibility. The very validity of earthly activity—political, artistic, historical—is seen to arise from its categorically immanent and lacking condition. As Žižek argues in his explanation of the moment of absolute negativity that precedes the assemblage of the Cartesian transcendental subject, "what appears as an *epistemological limitation* of our capacity to grasp reality (the fact that we are forever perceiving reality from our finite, temporal standpoint), is the positive *ontological condition* of reality itself" ("Introduction" 5). Similarly, Gracián offers a way to redeem human knowledge (and history) and its validity through the absolute realization of the doctrine of *desengaño*, making its "condition of impossibility" the very basis for legitimate activity: "Hanse de procurar los me-dios humanos como si no huviesse divinos, y los divinos como si no huviesse humanos" (*Oráculo* 250 and 237) (Human means should be adopted as if there were no divine means, and divine as if there were no human). By taking *desengaño* to its logical conclusions, Gracián deals a definitive blow to organicist, presence-based notions of social hierarchies and their role in the legitimization of political privilege and power: "Noble hay que sacan dél hilo de estopa, y plebeyo que sacan [dél] hilo de plata y aun de oro" (*El Criticón* III, 11, 762) (There are nobles from whom one can pull a thread of course hemp, and commoners from whom one can pull a thread of silver or even of gold).

Under the backdrop of the decay of imperial might and the destabilization of its organicist discourses of natural right by political and material necessity, Gracián's modern translation of the medievalized social body results in the articulation of a new type of social body based on taste rather than on a sublimated figuration of blood.[5] The sanguine residue of feudal society, which heretofore had been distilled through genealogical rituals tied to family honor, is now combined, contaminated as it were, with "oil, ink, and labor (sudor)" (*El Criticón* I, 13, 276). The ingenious transfusion of *artificial* fluids into the feudal corpse reconstitutes the social body and the role of art, whose primary criterion for aesthetic perfection will now be the success with which the artist accumulates praise and favors by *tastefully* differentiating himself from the rest. In a sense, the subject moves from rituals that construct and guarantee presence and sameness (of blood) to ones that suggest depth (*caudal*) and difference. As David Castillo observes, however, this difference never places the new subject of power outside the social body. Note the echoes of *redemptive hegemony* in Castillo's description of Gracián's cosmos: "eminent men do not waste their lives attempting to change the world, instead they learn how to accommodate to its current circumstances" ("Gracián" 200).

The Organized Body of Taste

The Graciánesque *fábrica*, or *empresa*, of strategic, ingenious, witty, and tasteful concepts is a living, breathing, eating, and birthing corpus that penetrates and is in turn penetrated by other *bodies* on the political stage of the court. Like the physical body, the *persona* has its "sweet" and "kingly" defects, and is fecund in its conceptually procreative act; moreover, its goal is to become the object of desire of the foreign, admiring gaze, which it attracts and amazes with the impression of substantial depth. Although humanity itself is categorically rejected as a "sack of filth" (*El Criticón* I, 11, 239), the language of taste is overdetermined by corporeal metaphors and analogies which reveal that we are looking at a social or politically informed body. Pierre Bourdieu describes how the ritual creation of the *socially informed body* involves much more than the five conventional senses:

> [T]his principle is nothing other than the *socially informed body*, with its tastes and distastes, its compulsions and repulsions, with, in a word, all its *senses*, that is to say, not only the traditional five senses—which never escape the structuring action of social determinisms—but also the sense of necessity and the sense of duty, the sense of direction and the sense of reality, the sense of balance and the sense of beauty, common sense and the sense of the sacred, tactical sense and the sense of responsibility, business sense and the sense of propriety, the sense of humor and the sense of absurdity, moral sense and the sense of practicality, and so on. (124)[6]

What we see throughout Gracián's *oeuvre* is the conversion of bodily organs into a spiritual, or aesthetic, body of *tropical* machinery, one which produces and judges conceptual creations in the movement of time and space. As both Malcom Read and Juan Carlos Rodríguez have noted, this new organized body reflects the new "freedom" of labor in modernity, as the subject is freed from his material body in order to remake himself according to the demands of the marketplace: in Gracián's terms, "Concebir de sí y de sus cosas cuerdamente" (*Oráculo* 194 and 208) (To conceive of oneself and of one's things sensibly). The advantage of this new body for the decrepit political elite of the Spanish State is that it is infinitely replicable by those subjects who possess the material and intellectual requisites for redeeming the status quo, while denying them a substantive legitimacy on which to base a project of real social change (Castillo, "Gracián"; Spadaccini and Talens). The disembodiment of power means that it can be everywhere and nowhere all at once.

Gilles Deleuze adroitly observes in *The Fold* that the folding of the bodily organs into the spiritual faculties is not the end of the process; the self-conceived organs are themselves endlessly folded into one another: "ojos en los mismos ojos, para mirar cómo miran; ojos y más ojos y reojos, procurando ser el mirante en un siglo tan adelantado" (*El Criticón* II, 1, 294) (eyes inside the same eyes, in order to look at how they are looking; eyes and more eyes and glances, aspiring to be the overseer in such an advanced century). Wit is "un cuerpo entero" (a whole body), but it is also "pasto del alma" (food for the soul) and "alimento del espíritu" (sustenance for the spirit) (*Agudeza* 27). Witty conceits feed the soul and the spirit but in other places pass for life and spirit themselves: "Son los conceptos, vida del estilo, espíritu del decir y tanto tiene de perfección, cuanto de sutileza" (*Agudeza* 510) (Conceits are, the life of style, the spirit of speech and have as much perfection as they do subtlety). In the end, the coincidence between aesthetic, intellectual, and bodily organs is impossible to disentangle, as in the case of those truths that are much sweeter in the mouth than in the ear (*El Criticón* III, 3, 609).[7] For Bell, this embodiment of expedient schemes and practices is the key to understanding the workings of ritual:

> Essential to ritualization is the circular production of a ritualized body which in turn produces ritualized practices. Ritualization is embedded within the dynamics of the body defined within a symbolically structured environment. (*Ritual Theory* 93)

In *El Criticón*, each of the three books meticulously describes the remaking of the social body, i.e., *persona*, beginning with Andrenio's grotesque account of his bestial birth in nature (*madrastra del hombre* [step-mother of man]), which is opposed to Critilo's remaking of himself after he is shipwrecked: "Viéndome sin amigos vivos, apelé a los muertos, di en leer, comencé a saber y ser persona (que hasta entonces no había vivido la vida racional, sino la bestial)" (I, 4, 109) (Seeing myself with no living friends, I hailed the dead, I immersed myself in reading, I began to know how and to be a *persona* [as up until then I had not lived the rational life, but the animal life). Bodily death becomes not an end but rather the beginning of the "universal reform" of man into an intellectual being (II, 1, 287).

This process begins in earnest in the *crisi octava* of book I:

> Es el arte complemento de la naturaleza y un otro segundo ser que por estremo la hermosea y aun pretende excederla en sus obras. Préciase de haber añadido un otro mundo artificial al primero; suple de ordinario los descuidos de la naturaleza, perfeccionándola en todo: que sin este socorro del artificio, quedara inculta y grosera. (I, 8, 171)

> (Art is the complement of nature and another second being that greatly improves the latter and even aspires to exceed it in its own works. It holds itself in high regard for having added another artificial world to the first; it habitually disguises the oversights of nature, perfecting it in everything: as without this help from artifice, it (nature) would remain unrefined and course.)

This description of a nature that is lacking, as in the case of the Eucharist, might seem surprising, until we remember that Gracián is talking about human nature: "Ninguna de las cosas criadas yerra su fin, sino el hombre" (I, 9, 188) (Nothing in all of creation errs from its own purpose, except man). Consequently, the first steps toward personhood consist of a series of recognitions of the eminently "deceived" and lacking nature of man: "reconozcámonos todos y entendamos que somos unos sacos de hediondez" (I, 11, 239) (let us all recognize ourselves and understand that we are but sacks of filth). All of the senses, starting with sight, are subsequently dematerialized and interiorized, turned away from sensual delights and the physical world in order to start the transformation toward being in the political world: "haze fin del deleite y de la vida haze medio para el gusto" (I, 10, 205) (he puts an end to pleasure and makes of life a means for taste). Here pleasure and taste are actually contradictory phenomena, which shows us just how far away we are from the sensual world. The eyes must learn how to see everything in the world *al revés*, or even through "ojos ajenos" (II, 1, 293) (estranged eyes). The ear becomes an intellectual sense by playing deaf (I, 8, 195); while smell is painstakingly attuned to more spiritual emanations: "discierne el buen olor del malo y percibe que la buena fama es el aliento del ánimo" (I, 8, 197) (it discerns the good scent from the bad and it understands that a good reputation is the breath of the spirit). Following the work of Foucault, Bell has argued that this process is best understood as a ritual fabrication of dispositions: "the social body is the active sight of 'dispositions, maneuvers, tactics, techniques, functionings,' it is a 'network of relations, constantly in tension' for which the proper metaphor would be a 'perpetual battle' rather than 'the conquest of territory'" (*Ritual Theory* 203). Gracián's description of life as "una milicia a la malicia" (a studied war on malice) immediately comes to mind, bringing us right back to Turner's ritual dramatization of the struggle between structure and anti structure, although without Turner's pastoral respite of *Communitas* (*El Criticón* II, 9, 457).[8]

Unlike Bakhtin's carnivalesque, grotesque body of becoming, the *persona* in the state of political becoming must convert his sensual organs into a site of perpetual *un*becoming, whose perfection, or completion, coincides with the physical death of the subject: "Muere el hombre cuando había de començar a vivir, cuando más persona ... assí que nace bestia y muere muy persona" (III, 11, 763) (Man dies when he should have started to live, when most successful ... thus he is born a beast and dies very rational). Exemplary of this abasement of the physical, material body, Gracián's works repeatedly and meticulously—ritualistically—erase any positivistic notions concerning truth and the subjective "content" of the courtly actor in order to arrive at a completely *immaterial*, *absent*, or *different* notion of subjectivity and artistic activity, one exclusively interested in arranging and occupying courtly stages of representation. Even colors lose their substance due to their origins in the same dust out of which the nothingness of man emerges: "el verde no es verde, ni el colorado

colorado, sino que todo consiste en las diferentes disposiciones de las superficies y en la luz que las baña" (III, 6, 652) (green is not green, nor red red, rather everything consists of different dispositions of surfaces and of the light that bathes them). In effect, Gracián configures a series of machine-like, intellectualized organs of taste designed to attract, provoke, and manipulate the desire of other subjects in the public representation of the "hombre con fondos" (the profound man).

As we have seen in the case of ritual studies and its preoccupation with the movement from nature to culture, Hans-Georg Gadamer and Anthony Cascardi likewise track the "passage from sensuous to social body" in Gracián, in which procreative and degustative metaphors become the linguistic and conceptual building blocks for Enlightenment notions of artistic creation and sensibility (Cascardi, "Gracián" 257). What is less well understood are the nature and location of the subject of taste with respect to the organized social body. If on the one hand it is clear that the intellectual and sensible faculties are constantly interacting with and interpenetrating each other and the ingenious performances of other subjects, the primordial "center" out of which all this activity is directed is decidedly more obscure by comparison. Spadaccini and Talens, for example, describe Gracián's courtly subjects as "those who practice a strategy and technique of prudence, of hiding their *true selves* . . . [and] control their own destinies" ("Introduction" xi; my emphasis). This Cartesian-based concept of the *true self* is problematic in Gracián, as he reconverts the human subject into a locus for positive activity, not by rejecting the pessimistic view of human agency and the institutions that employ it for repressive (even nihilistic) ends, but by seeing the possibilities in it for the individual subject of the court to advance and triumph in the world of appearances. If it is *true* that "No son las cosas más de como se toman" (*El Criticón* III, 5, 652) (things are nothing more than what they are taken to be), or that "no hay cosa que tenga estado" (*El Criticón* III, 10, 747) (nothing remains the same), then the search for truth—and *true* subjectivity—becomes a contingent and illusory game of artistic appearances: "Una cosa es ser falso y otra no poder ser verdadero" (Checa 118) (it is one thing to be false and quite another to not be able to be true). What is on the one hand lamented as man's *difference* with respect to God's once immaculate and now fallen creation, is now celebrated as the source of a new anti-body of creation: in Žižek's words, "'subject' is nothing but the void, the gap, opened up by the failure of reflection" ("The Cartesian" 263). Gracián's movement is difficult, and devious, and belies Žižek's suggestion that this void necessarily acts as a limit for the unbridled will to power of the State. If, as I stated earlier, the State itself is seen to occupy a similar void (*La vida es sueño*), then its incompleteness mirrors that of the subject (Maravall), and any move toward plenitude—or substance—be it material or transcendental in nature, compromises the play of surfaces and light in which reality is theatrically rendered. Thus, when Gracián speaks of "penetrating" the surface, his object is not the *real thing* but rather the real void, or desire, that motivates the public representation of any subject.

In the last chapter of *Agudeza y arte de ingenio*, Gracián approaches what are most accurately described as postmodern theories of subjectivity when he looks to Seneca for an explanation of what he means by an "anomalous" subject:

> todo ingenio grande tiene un grado de demencia. Suele estar de día, y tener vez, de modo que él mismo se desconoce; altérase con las extrínsecas y aún materiales impresiones; vive a los confines del afecto, a la raya de la voluntad y es mal avecindado el de las pasiones. (537)

> (every great genius has a measure of madness. It tends to follow the day and the hour, such that it misrecognizes itself; it alters itself with extrinsic and even material impressions; it resides toward the margins of the affect, toward the radius of the will and is poorly accompanied by the passions.)

This is perhaps the most precise definition of the *ingenio* that Gracián formulates, and its thesis hinges on the *demented* nature of the greatest thinkers, which for Gracián would primarily be those listed in his genealogy of authors of *philosophical truths*, all of whose works are indirect, or allegorical, in nature.[9] Seneca returns in *El Criticón*, declaring that "no hay entendimiento grande sin vena" (II, 13, 526) (there is no understanding without inspiration). Santos Alonso clarifies Gracián's meaning by noting that "Vena de loco, se entiende" (*El Criticón* II, 13; 526n39) (A mad fancy, it is understood). In the exchange of insults between a German and a Frenchman that follows this stoic *sentencia*, a Spaniard performs a quick clarification of *locura* (madness), which is the insult that the German has hurled at the Frenchman: "la locura es falta y la embriaguez es sobra" (II, 13, 526) (madness is want and inebriety is excess). Thus, we move from madness to fancy and, finally, to lack.

The echoes of Huarte de San Juan's *ingenio caprichoso* are hard to miss, but we must emphasize once more the alterations that Gracián introduces.[10] In his reading of ingenious madness, the *ingenio* never coincides with itself; it is always other to its affect, its will, its passions . . . in the end, "it misrecognizes itself." Even its greatest powers were taken from another faculty: judgment. In an emblem by Juan de Borja, the *ingenio* is represented by a "machine" or "crane" which lifts a heavy weight. The motto of the emblem reads "Ingenium vires superat" (El ingenio vence a la fuerça [wit triumphs over force]) (I, 102–3). In the *pictura*, the *ingenio* appears only in the tools it employs and the weight it lifts; it is present only as an absent intention that drives the performance of the event. The effect—or *special* effect, if we think of the importance of similar devices in Golden Age theater—of wit's influence is moved to the material locus of the weight, while wit itself disappears. This is a very godly sort of relationship between creator and creation. We get a similar image of "art" from the second *empresa* of Diego de Saavedra Fajardo, which shows a blank canvas set up in a landscape of seemingly infinite proportions. On the left-hand side is a cloud, and from the cloud a hand emerges holding a palette and several brushes. The *inscriptio* reads, "Ad omnia" (para todo [for all things]), while the first line of the commentary says, "Con el pincel y los colores muestra en todas las cosas su poder el arte" (Saavedra Fajardo 2, 202) (with brush and colors art manifests its power in all things). When placed alongside the emblem by Borja, the structural relationship between *ingenio*, art, and power stands revealed, even as the force and ultimate truths that both produce and are produced by the mechanism of taste remain purposefully veiled.

What is striking here is not the secrecy concerning the ultimate locus of power behind its representation, but rather the foreignness of the *ingenio* with respect to the subject himself, which becomes not so much an effect as an imperative for the courtly *persona* (Forcione 40; Read, "Saving" 121). The *persona* is a permanently self-estranged subject, which results in a subject of power who shares a constitutive trait with the State, and, ultimately, with God himself (Nancy 59). Just as God fabricates a human body to negatively reflect himself (through his absence) and to be recognized in the substantial lack behind his reflection, so too does Gracián's *persona* require a socially informed body in order to exercise its obscure will (Žižek, *The Puppet*). This decentered, or redoubled, point of enunciation endows the subject with a certain independence and self-consciousness through which it may manipulate language and perception to its own advantage. This linguistic freedom, however, does not lead to substantive changes in baroque society, as Maravall points out: "Only in the latter areas ['artistic and poetic caprice'] could there be acknowledgment of that 'freedom of ingenuity' exalted by Gracián" (139). This independence also isolates the subject from all other subjects and necessitates the individual encounter with ideology and power. "Visto un león, están vistos todos, y vista una oveja, todas; pero visto un hombre, no está visto sino uno, y aun ésse no bien conocido" (*El Criticón* I, 11, 225) (If you see one lion, you've seen them all, and if you see one sheep, all the rest; but when you see a man, you've only seen one, and even that one is poorly known). More importantly, the following advice that Critilo gives to Andrenio demonstrates that baroque "freedom" is not to be understood as a positive movement into the world but rather as a cautious and closed resistance to "being in the world" (Egginton, *How the World*): "Procura de ir con cautela en el ver, en el oír y mucho más en el hablar; oye a todos y de ninguno te fíes; tendrás a todos por amigos, pero guardarte has de todos como de enemigos" (*El Criticón* I, 3, 100) (Attempt to proceed cautiously in what you see, hear, and above all in what you say; hear everyone and trust no one; all will be your friends, but guard yourself from everyone as if they were your enemies). In book II this idea is universalized by *el Valeroso*: "la mayor valentía de un hombre consiste en no empeñarse ni verse obligado a sacarla" (*El Criticón* II, 8, 445) (the greatest valor of man consists of not committing himself nor of seeing himself obligated to use it [his valor]). In both cases, freedom can only be understood as a negative resistance to complete identification; indeed, this gap is necessary to the subject's ability to consent to his utilitarian and inferior role within the hegemony of the State. Or as Maravall puts it, "Choice was the freedom to guide one's own behavior, and, as behavior assumed a mode of working in the outside world, this signified that choice was the equivalent of choosing one's own behavior or at least freely attempting to direct one's behavior physically, following the line established by one's own will" (171).

Through the ritual embodiment of schemes of social positioning, Gracián creates a practice through which individual subjects may amass personal power and prestige without directly threatening the existing sociopolitical organization, all of which achieves Bell's *redemptive hegemony* precisely by shifting the exercise of power toward the individual. As such, Bell's model of ritualization, like Maravall's notion of baroque rationalism, does not separate freedom from the workings of power; rather, the two are mutually constitutive and informative, as agency becomes the site of an embodied subject of power: "Embodiment, like consensual participation in the objectification processes of the rite, is *experienced* as a negotiated appropriation, not as a total and indiscriminate absorption or social molding" (*Ritual Theory* 208). Slowly but surely, Andrenio's voluntary, material disembodiment becomes constitutive of his reembodiment as a subject of power and fame: "Ninguno parece hasta que desaparece" (III, 12, 787) (No one appears until he disappears). Moreover, the constantly folding and unfolding hierarchy of *ingenio, entendimiento, alma, espíritu*, etc., is placed in perpetual motion so that the subject can activate a sense of universal totality: "En Dios todo es infinito, todo inmenso; assí en un Héroe todo ha de ser grande y magestuoso, de suerte que todas sus acciones, y aun razones, vayan revestidas de una trascendente grandiosa magestad" (*Oráculo*, 296 and 258) (In God everything is infinite, all is immense; thus in a Hero everything should be grand and majestic, in such a way that all his actions, and even his rationales, go about adorned by a transcendent grandiose majesty).

As we have seen in the emblems of "art" and "*ingenio*," this immanent majesty functions through self-difference, always leading the adoring or circumspect gaze to where it is not: "tan manifiesto en sus criaturas y tan escondido en sí . . . . Con todo esso, está tan oculto este gran Dios, que es conocido y no visto, escondido y manifiesto, tan lexos y tan cerca; esso es lo que me tiene fuera de mí" (*El Criticón* I, 3, 94) (so manifest in his creatures and so hidden in himself . . . . That being said, this great God is so hidden, that he is known and not seen, hidden and manifest, so far away and yet so near; that is why I am beside myself). The common ground that Gracián establishes between God and man is that of the relationship between immaterial—or absent—substance, and external attributes and creations. Critilo "finds himself" not in himself but in an absent God, just as those who surround the prudent subject are amazed (suspended) and guided by a calculating political *Hero* who gauges their "palates," "inclinations," and "wills," and in so doing convincingly performs "learned" roles with the learned and "saintly" roles with the saintly: a "discrete Proteus," who represents all things for all subjects (*Oráculo* 77, 145). In the end, the Hero is as absent as God himself: "el gran primor es no ser y parecerlo, esso sí que es saber" (*El Criticón* II, 6, 433) (the great beauty is to not be and yet to appear to be, that is indeed wisdom). The reasons for the Church's discomfort with Gracián's thought become clear here, as his radically orthodox treatment of *desengaño* underlines a heretical nihilism at its dogmatic center. In short, the politics of self-abasement and obedience at the heart of Ignatian meditative practices can also be used to destabilize all earthly edifices, including the laws of genealogical purity, or even the Church and State themselves. In such a desubstantialized world, art is not the *reflection* of the subject's positive, yet hidden truth; nor can we separate its technical aspects from the achieved effect of political success; rather, art *is* the system of politically motivated self-representation. Similarly, taste is the name given to a ritually structured *ecosystem* (Rappaport) in which individual bodies of taste—agents—sustain and are in turn sustained by a social body whose primary ontological and epistemological product is not truth or substance, but power. If we replace "Ritual" with "Art," we get the following statement from Bell: "*Art* is the thing itself. It is power; it acts and it actuates" (*Ritual Theory* 195).

Conclusion

At the end of *El Criticón*, Critilo and Andrenio, accompanied by *el Peregrino*, cross over to the Island of Immortality, where *Merit* asks the pilgrim for his *manifest* ("patente": understood here as a pass or "papers"). "Manifest" on the manifest is the entire history of their journey, which is also the journey of the reader through the three books. When the two heroes step onto the isle, however, the reader is left standing at the threshold. For those readers who want to see how the story ends in all its details, the narrator leaves the following advice: "Lo que allí vieron, lo mucho que lograron, quien quisiere saberlo y experimentarlo, tome el rumbo de la virtud insigne, del valor heróico, y llegará a parar al teatro de la fama, al trono de la estimación y al centro de la inmortalidad" (III, 12, 812)[11] (What they saw there, and all they achieved, whosoever wants to know these things and experience them, should follow the path of remarkable virtue, and he will arrive at the theater of fame, to the throne of esteem and to the center of immortality). Put another way, the only way to follow these heroes over the threshold is to actively take up, or embody, Gracián's text, which becomes a guide no less imposing and all-encompassing than St. Ignatius's own *Spiritual Exercises*. Both texts seek the active and voluntary engagement of the reader, and neither text is complete without the ritualized embodiment of the practicant, whose goal in each case is immortality.

If Gracián can be said to be "prefiguring" or "anticipating" the transcendental subject of modernity, I think it must be emphasized that this subject's secular and disinterestedly "empirical" gaze on the world is activated through a *demented* disengagement from that same world. As Žižek remarks, "the ontological necessity of 'madness' resides in the fact that it is not possible to pass directly from the purely 'animal soul,' immersed in its natural environs, to 'normal' subjectivity, dwelling in its symbolic virtual environs—the 'vanishing mediator' between the two is the 'mad' gesture of radical withdrawal from reality, which opens up a space for its symbolic (re)constitution" ("The Cartesian" 259). Whether we are referring to Descartes's momentary immersion into radical doubt, the ritual theorist's subtraction of his own gaze from the production of his evolutionary discourse, or Gracián's radicalization of baroque *desengaño*, the modern subject arises from a moment of absolute negativity and madness. Through a progressive disembodiment, Gracián's subject of power obfuscates the fabrication and application of its power, placing it in a labyrinthine movement whose infinite will and disembodied violence can never be scrutinized, since, ontologically, they cannot be said to even exist. Neither Lazarillo's penetrated and half-starved body nor Sancho Panza's anti utopian degustation and elimination, nor even Maria de Zayas's tortured and dismembered female corpses can become materially present within the confines of tasteful conversation. Truth and substance give way to issues of form and taste, and knowledge becomes a question of multiplying and manipulating disembodied perspectives. In effect, all discourses, including vivid images of corporal violence, become subject to, and the subjects of, competing and *in*substantiated points of view. If the body itself is emptied of substance and significance, any and all violence committed on it can be repeatedly and ritualistically justified in the name of a disembodied ideal. Such madness is at the heart of Gracián's rituals of modernity.

Notes

1. All translations from the Spanish in this article are my own.
2. I have borrowed William Egginton's distinction between the "full space" of Medieval dramatizations of primordial events and the "empty and homogeneous space" of Renaissance perspective and modern theatricality in order to distinguish between the "full taste" of a self-sufficient god and the "empty taste" of the imperfect, "undeceived," human subject of the Counter-Reformation. He writes, "the Middle Ages experienced space in a fundamentally different way: as full, impressionable and substantial, whose dimensions existed relative to observers and, more specifically, participants, as opposed to being empty and independent of them—an experience that, for instance, would not necessitate a notion of 'ether' in order to explain action at a distance" (*How the World* 37).
3. For a simultaneously detailed and sweeping study of the transformation from the feudal (blood-based) "matrix" of socio-economic production to the capitalist "matrix" and its subsequent production of a "free" subject, and the importance of this transition in the creation of literary culture, see Juan Carlos Rodríguez's *Theory and History of Ideological Production* and *El escritor que compró su propio libro*.
4. Maravall connects the artistic technique of incompleteness with the dramatic creation of suspense and novelty: "a procedure wherein the incomplete serves as the means for leading to a state of suspension, to the public's active intervention, and to contact with and psychological action upon this public, thus inclining it toward certain desired objectives" (218). See also Castillo, *(A)wry Views*, 10–17.
5. I have opted for the term "medievalizing" as opposed to "medieval," following José Antonio Maravall's reading of the deployment of archaic notions of organicist social organization by the "monarchical-seigniorial segments" of early modern Spain in the attempt to anchor their claims to power in universalist notions of blood purity and genealogical heredity. A similar movement can be seen in the *Comedia nueva*, where what were once "popular" theatrical practices become popularizing discourses of

power in the massively conceived and directed aesthetics of Lope de Vega and others (see Maravall; see also Molho).

6. One of the strongest indications of this ritual transformation is the movement from material to immaterial organs, exemplified most strikingly by the transformation of the mammalian breast into the reservoir of the memory: "Thus I believed that the savage who fed me at her breasts (pechos) was my mother" (*El Criticón* I, 1, 71), gives way to "[the greatest splendors are achieved] by taking things from the chest (senos) of history and passing them to the understanding" (*El Criticón* III, 6, 655).

7. For Renata Salecl, the movement from the moment of negative self-reflection, i.e., *desengaño*, to the construction of a social universe opens onto the constitutive role played by the partial drives that "symptomatically" arise when the subject is introduced into language: "The subject is determined on the one hand by these partial drives, and on the other hand by the field of the Other, the social symbolic structure" (180). Is not the ideology of taste an exemplary case of the linking of the drives of the subject to the power of the State?

8. Turner's "organic" model of structure and anti-structure goes as follows: "It is as though there are here two major 'models' for human interrelatedness, juxtaposed and alternating. The first is of society as a structured, differentiated, and often hierarchical system of politico-legal-economic positions with many types of evaluations, separating men in terms of 'more' or 'less.' The second, which emerges recognizably in the liminal period, is of society as an unstructured or rudimentarily structured and relatively undifferentiated *comitatus*, community, or even communion of equal individuals who submit together to the general authority of the ritual elders" (96). When antagonisms erupt in structure, the stricken individuals move or are moved to the borders, where they perform ritual dramas that re suture, or restructure, societal relations. As in most post-Durkheimian models, the goal is to preserve the "sanity" of social organization at the expense of antagonistic breakdowns.

9. Gracián's catalogue of "sages" of philosophical truths reveals the oblique, indirect, *allegorical* nature of truth in his oeuvre: "Homer with his *Epics*, Aesop with his *Fables*, Seneca with his *Sentences*, Ovid with his *Metamorphosis*, Juvenal with his *Satires*, Pythagoras with his *Engimas*, Lucian with his *Dialogues*, Alciato with his *Emblems*, Erasmus with his *Proverbs*, Bocalinni with his *Allegories* and the prince Don Juan Manuel with his *Stories*" (*Agudeza* 476).

10. Huarte writes, "A los ingenios inventivos llaman en lengua Toscana *caprichosos*, por semejanza que tienen con la cabra en el andar y pacer. Esta jamás huelga por lo llano; siempre es amiga de andar a sus solas por los riscos y alturas, y asomarse a grandes profundidades; por donde no sigue vereda ninguna ni quiere caminar con compañía" (344–45) (They call the inventive geniuses in the Tuscan language *capricious*, due to their likeness to a goat in walking and grazing. The latter never takes pleasure in the easy path; (s)he always prefers walking alone through the crags and heights, looming over the great depths; whereby (s)he never follows any path nor wants to travel in company). Note Huarte's use, once again, of the degustative metaphor *pacer*. Also

note the negative withdrawal of the *ingenio* as it stares from the heights of inspiration into the abyss of nonidentity represented by the *vulgo* (Read, *Visions*).

11. I owe this last observation to an e-mail "conversation" with one of the editors of this volume, David R. Castillo.

Works Cited

Ayala, Jorge M. *Reflejo y reflexión: B. Gracián. Un estilo de filosofar.* Zaragoza: Centro regional d estudios teológicos de Aragón, 1979.

Bakhtin, M. M. *Rabelais and His World.* Trans. Helene Iswolsky. Cambridge, MA: MIT Press, 1968.

Batllori, Miguel, and Ceferino Peralta. *Baltasar Gracián en su vida y en sus obras.* Zaragoza: Institución Fernando el Católico, 1969.

Bell, Catherine. *Ritual Perspectives and Dimensions.* Oxford: Oxford University Press, 1997.

———. *Ritual Theory, Ritual Practice.* Oxford: Oxford University Press, 1992.

Bernat Vistarini, Antonio, and John T. Cull. "Las edades del hombre en los libros de emblemas españoles." *Criticón* 71 (1997): 5–31.

Borja, Juan de. *Empresas morales.* Ed. Carmen Bravo-Villasante. Madrid: Fundación Universitaria Española, 1981.

Bourdieu, Pierre. *Outline of a Theory of Practice.* Cambridge: Cambridge University Press, 1977.

Calderón de la Barca, Pedro. *El gran teatro del mundo: El gran mercado del mundo.* Ed. Domingo Ynduráin. Madrid: Istmo, 1974.

Cascardi, Anthony. "Gracián and the Authority of Taste." *Rhetoric and Politics: Baltasar Gracián and The New World Order.* Ed. Nicholas Spadaccini and Jenaro Talens. Minneapolis, MN: University of Minnesota Press, 1997. 255–86.

———. *Ideologies of History in the Spanish Golden Age.* University Park, PA: Penn State University Press, 1997.

———. "The Subject of Control." *Culture and Control in Counter Reformation Spain.* Ed. Anne J. Cruz and Mary Elizabeth Perry. Hispanic Issues 7. Minneapolis, MN: University Minnesota Press, 1992. 261–30.

Castillo, David R. *(A)wry Views: Anamorphosis, Cervantes, and the Early Picaresque.* Purdue Studies in Romance Literatures 23. West Lafayette, IN: Purdue University Press, 2001.

———. "Gracián and the Art of Public Representation." *Rhetoric and Politics: Baltasar Gracián and The New World Order.* Ed. Nicholas Spadaccini and Jenaro Talens. Minneapolis, MN: University of Minnesota Press, 1997. 191–208.

———. "Horror (vacui): The Baroque Condition." *Hispanic Baroques: Reading Cultures in Context.* Ed. Nicholas Spadaccini and Luis Martín-Estudillo. Nashville, TN: Vanderbilt University Press, 2005. 87–104.

Checa, Jorge. "Alegoría, verdad y verosimilitud en *El Criticón*." *Documentos A* 5 (1993): 116–26.
Correa Calderón, E. *Baltasar Gracián: su vida y su obra*. Madrid: Gredos, 1961.
Daly, Peter M. *Literature in Light of the Emblem: Structural Parallels between the Emblem and Literature in the Sixteenth and Seventeenth Centuries*. Toronto: Toronto University Press, 1979.
Damasio, Antonio R. *Descartes' Error: Emotion, Reason, and the Human Brain*. New York: Quill, 2000.
Deleuze, Gilles. *The Fold: Leibniz and the Baroque*. Trans. Tom Conley. Minneapolis, MN: University of Minnesota Press, 1993.
Echeverría, Bolívar. *La modernidad de lo Barroco*. Mexico, D.F.: UNAM, 1998.
Egginton, William. "Gracián and the Emergence of the Modern Subject." *Rhetoric and Politics: Baltasar Gracián and The New World Order*. Ed. Nicholas Spadaccini and Jenaro Talens. Minneapolis, MN: University of Minnesota Press, 1997. 151–69.
———. *How the World Became a Stage: Presence, Theatricality, and the Question of Modernity*. Albany, NY: State University of New York Press, 2003.
Forcione, Alban. "At the Threshold of Modernity: Gracián's *El Criticón*." *Rhetoric and Politics: Baltasar Gracián and The New World Order*. Ed. Nicholas Spadaccini and Jenaro Talens. Minneapolis, MN: University of Minnesota Press, 1997. 3–70.
Gadamer, Hans-Georg. *Truth and Method*. New York: Continuum, 1975.
Gracián, Baltasar. *Agudeza y arte de ingenio*. Buenos Aires: Espasa-Calpe, 1942.
———. *Arte de ingenio, tratado de la agudeza*. Ed. Emilio Blanco. Madrid: Cátedra, 1998.
———. *El Criticón*. Ed. Santos Alonso. Madrid: Cátedra, 1993.
———. *El Héroe; El Discreto*. Madrid: Espasa-Calpe, 1980.
———. *Oráculo manual y arte de prudencia*. Ed. Emilio Blanco. Madrid: Cátedra, 1997.
Gumbrecht, Hans Ulrich. *Production of Presence: What Meaning Cannot Convey*. Stanford, CA: Stanford University Press, 2004.
Horozco y Covarrubias, Juan de. *Emblemas morales*. Çaragoça: Alonso Rodrigues y Juan de Bonilla, 1603.
Huarte de San Juan, Juan. *Examen de ingenios para las ciencias*. Ed. Guillermo Serés. Madrid: Cátedra, 1989.
Loyola, S. Ignacio de. *Ejercicios espirituales. Directorio y Documentos. Glosa y vocabulario de los ejercicios por P. José Calveras, S. I*. Barcelona: Balmes, 1944.
Maravall, José Antonio. *The Culture of the Baroque: Analysis of a Historical Structure*. Trans. Terry Cochran. Minneapolis, MN: University of Minnesota Press, 1986.
Molho, Maurice. *Cervantes: raíces folklóricas*. Madrid: Gredos, 1976.
Nancy, Jean-Luc. *Au fond des images*. Paris: Galilée, 2003.
Pelegrin, Benito. *Ethique et esthétique du Baroque: L'Espace jésuitique de Baltasar Gracián*. Arles: Actes Sud, 1985.
Rappaport, Roy A. *Ecology and Meaning, and Religion*. Richmond, CA: North Atlantic Books, 1979.

Read, Malcolm. "Saving Appearances: Language and Commodification in Baltasar Gracián." *Rhetoric and Politics: Baltasar Gracián and The New World Order.* Ed. Nicholas Spadaccini and Jenaro Talens. Minneapolis, MN: University of Minnesota Press, 1997. 91–124.

———. *Visions in Exile: The Body in Spanish Literature and Linguistics.* Amsterdam: J. Benjamins, 1990.

Rodríguez, Juan Carlos. *El escritor que compró su propio libro: para leer el* Quijote. Barcelona: Random House Mondadori, 2003.

———. *Theory and History of Ideological Production: The First Bourgeois Literaturas (the 16th Century).* Trans. Malcolm K. Read. Newark, DE: University Delaware Press, 2002.

R. de la Flor, Fernando. *Barroco: Representación e ideología en el mundo hispánico (1580–1680).* Madrid: Cátedra, 2002.

Saavedra Fajardo, Diego de. *Idea de un príncipe político cristiano representada en cien empresas.* Ed. Sagrario López. Madrid: Cátedra, 1999.

Salecl, Renata. "The Silence of the Feminine Jouissance." In *Cogito and the Unconscious.* Ed. Slavoj Žižek. Durham, NC: Duke University Press, 1998. 175–97.

Sánchez, Francisco. "Cultura y persona en Gracián." *RLit* 122 (1999): 375–88.

———. "Symbolic Wealth and Theatricality in Gracián." Spadaccini and Talens 209–29.

Spadaccini, Nicholas and Jenaro Talens. "Introduction: The Practice of Worldly Wisdom: Rereading Gracián and the New World Order." *Rhetoric and Politics: Baltasar Gracián and The New World Order.* Ed. Nicholas Spadaccini and Jenaro Talens. Minneapolis, MN: University of Minnesota Press, 1997. ix–xxxii.

———. eds. *Rhetoric and Politics: Baltasar Gracián and the New World Order.* Minneapolis, MN: University of Minnesota Press, 1997.

Turner, Victor. *The Ritual Process: Structure and Anti-Structure.* Fwd. Roger D. Abrahams. New York: Aldine de Gruyter, 1969.

Žižek, Slavoj. "The Cartesian Subject versus the Cartesian Theater." In *Cogito and the Unconscious.* Ed. Slavoj Žižek. Durham, NC: Duke University Press, 1998. 247–74.

———. ed. *Cogito and the Unconscious.* Durham, NC: Duke University Press, 1998.

———. "Introduction: Cogito as Shibboleth." In *Cogito and the Unconscious.* Ed. Slavoj Žižek. Durham, NC: Duke University Press, 1998. 1–10.

———. *The Puppet and the Dwarf: The Perverse Core of Christianity.* Cambridge, MA: MIT Press, 2003.

———. *The Ticklish Subject: The Absent Centre of Political Ontology.* London: Verso, 1999.

5

An Unreasonable Journey?
The Place of Europe and Italy
in Francesco Negri's *Viaggio settentrionale*

Nathalie Hester

When middle-aged priest Francesco Negri left his hometown of Ravenna in 1663 and undertook a three-year voyage in Scandinavia, he became the first continental European to make an extensive journey through these northern regions. A mostly self-funded and certainly self-styled scientist-investigator who dedicated most of his life to tending his parish, Negri eschewed the better-known itineraries of European and world travel for a less beaten path.[1] Not only was his choice of destination unusual, but so was too, as is evident in his *Viaggio settentrionale* (Northern Travels, 1700), his presence abroad as an independent Italian traveler. Negri faced the growing reputation of Italians as less fervent adventurers, and, for example, at the court of King Frederick III in Copenhagen before returning home, he notes the monarch's surprise at seeing an Italian in the far north:

> [The king] soggiunse che la maggior curiosità... era che un italiano, nato in un clima de' più dolci del mondo, avesse avuto tanto ardire e forza d'intraprendere e compire un viaggio de' più aspri e pericolosi che siano, e in tale stagione. (379)

> (The King added that the most curious thing was that an Italian, born in one of the mildest climates in the world, had had such desire and determination to undertake and complete a voyage of the harshest and most dangerous kind, and in such a season.)[2]

Frederick III's words, of course, offer an ideal opportunity to underscore Negri's tenacity as well as the originality of his endeavor. However, for the King, the most curious aspect—"curiosities" being a principal attraction of cross-cultural encounters of the time—is neither the difficulty of the journey nor Negri's success at extreme travel, but rather that Negri is out of *place*. The king implies that it is unexpected, even if all the more heroic, for Italians to leave their temperate zones to seek out extreme conditions. Negri has in effect been geographically unreasonable in the sense that there seems to be no *reason* for Negri to travel. Logic would dictate that climatically privileged Italians are better off at home.

Frederick III's surprise might also reflect the reality that, by the time Negri set off on his journey, Italy was in many ways the first early modern European "has been," and Italians were considered lesser players within the broadening scope of European mobility.[3] With much of Italy under Spanish domination, the Italian peninsula construed more as a host country to Grand Tourists than the departure point of explorers, and with Venetian and Genoese commercial shipping eclipsed by English, Dutch, and Spanish-Portuguese companies, Italians no longer figured as prominently as travelers in the European cultural imaginary.[4] Although they continued to go abroad, primarily as missionaries, diplomats, and merchants, they did not and indeed could not participate in the now dominant European paradigm of proto-national expansionism.[5] In fact it was when they left a culturally and politically fragmented peninsula that Italians such as Negri found the most direct indications that Italy now occupied the margins of contemporary culture.

Certainly travel literature, an inherently malleable and interdisciplinary form of writing, can function as an excellent gauge of cultural currents and shifting paradigms for making the world comprehensible. A kind of narrative in which history, geography, ethnography, astronomy, economics, literature, and natural philosophy readily intermingle and which is not traditionally bound by constraints of genre, travel writing offers an ideal space for discursive explorations. More significantly, early modern travel accounts, as they multiplied in numbers and in scope, also had a profound effect on approaches to knowledge by privileging experience—the direct observation of place—over classical authority. According to Norman Doiron, travel accounts were at the source of a "veritable epistemological revolution," moving readers and thinkers from the *autoritas* of the book and humanistic culture toward the book of the world whose complexity perhaps could still be contained. For Doiron, Descartes's *Discours de la Méthode* (1634) (*Discourse on Method*), replete with metaphors of the journey, owes much to the approaches to *scientia* in the travel narratives and guides the philosopher read and adapts the centrality of experience put forth by travelers to the domain of philosophy.[6]

Published in a time where there was no monolithic approach to ordering the explosion of data collection and dissemination, the *Viaggio settentrionale*, while heavily invested in the authority of direct experience, nevertheless represents a crossroads of sometimes competing methodologies for understanding the world. These methodologies circulated concurrently in the seventeenth century and coexisted without clear hierarchies establishing their authority and acceptability in relation to others. In the same way that certain phenomena were often explained through analogy and metaphor,[7] the multitude of approaches to knowledge and information in the *Viaggio settentrionale* seems to reflect the analogous complexity as well as the daunting breadth of natural phenomena and human diversity that had yet to be satisfactorily explained and understood. Reason—not in its Cartesian manifestation, but in the sense of justification or explication—could and indeed did include its own contradictions. In this sense, Negri's account is a sign of its times, a period in which multiple, competing ways of categorizing knowledge could coexist in a single work without compromising the validity or credibility of its representation of reality.

If a modern or postmodern reader is to find a more convincing *reason* behind the *Viaggio settentrionale*, it is in the ends, not the means. This epistolary account presents an ideal case study for considering how multiple and sometimes contradictory discourses, old and new, mingle in a single text to serve a principal purpose: to justify Italian participation in travel culture and, more broadly, to prove that Italy lies at the geographical (and therefore cultural) center of Europe and the world.[8] While seventeenth-century Italian travel writing participates in general European developments and changes, many narratives illustrate culturally specific responses to Italy's diminishing role in international mobility. These texts represent an especially rich terrain of investigation, because it is precisely when Italy moves off the map of European influence that Italian travel narrative more overtly and relevantly reflects the anxieties constitutive of the early modern and eventually the modern Italian condition: the preoccupation with the place of Italy and its relationship to Italian cultural identity.[9] The cosmopolitan, exportable, classical-humanist "deterritorialized" Italian identity and culture that had functioned successfully in the early Renaissance become especially problematic when the new, emerging models for proto-national identity base themselves on politically and geographically integrated territories and participation in worldwide economic and colonial enterprises.[10] In conveying the authoritative "Italian" point of view of an Italian traveler and travel writer of 1660s Europe, the *Viaggio settentrionale*, as much as it relies on still widely accepted classically based notions of geography, anthropology, and natural science, also reflects an impetus to create novel or to recraft preexisting discourses that can establish Italy, in relation to Scandinavia, as a geographically cardinal and spatially integrated *place*.

As I will argue, Negri's sometimes incongruous methodologies for observing and explicating foreign lands, whether based on classical history or Galileian science, may serve the reasonable or at least comprehensible purpose of attempting to retrieve or carve out a cultural niche both for Italy and Italian travel. His quest to put Italy back on the European map of influence takes him on a variety of discursive paths: first, he recuperates the explorer-ethnographer model to characterize his journey as one through remote and unknown regions populated by "primitive" peoples. Then, in discussing militarily powerful Sweden, he abruptly switches logical gears and makes the unprecedented case that Swedes and Italians share essential characteristics because of their common Gothic origin. Finally, while he acknowledges the value of experimental science and stresses the importance of up-to-date, direct investigation of natural phenomena, Negri ultimately favors modified Classical paradigms of climate theory to position Italy in a globally advantaged place.

The *Viaggio settentrionale*, a text recounting travels primarily through Sweden and Norway 1663–1666, is comprised of eight letters and begins *in medias res*, when Negri has already reached Lapland. Following a lengthy itinerary whose final destination is the North Cape, Negri first travels up the east coast of Sweden to the northern tip of the Gulf of Bothnia and investigates Lapp culture.[11] When land travel becomes too difficult in the fall of 1663, he goes back down to Stockholm, where he stays for approximately one year, and then makes his way to the North Cape by Norway, stopping in Copenhagen on his way there and back. The letters do not depict in detail Negri's movement along his chosen itinerary, but rather focus on topographical, zoological, and ethnographic elements of the areas he visits, including information on local pastimes, language, natural wonders, and hunting and fishing techniques.[12] Negri quotes extensively from numerous classical sources and more contemporary authors such as John Barclay and Olaus Magnus. He expresses admiration for the moderate behavior and social organization in some of the areas he visits. Coming from an Italy devastated by plagues, famines, and over-taxation, he often makes positive remarks concerning the lack of disease, poverty, and hunger in Scandinavia. For instance, he commends Swedes who "amministrano con maggior facilità al mantenimento della vita umana che nelle più deliziose provincie del mondo [i.e., Italy], non trovandosi qui chi mendichi, come in quelle, né chi si muoia di fame in tempo di carestia, o tremi di freddo l'inverno" (150)

(They administer the preservation of human life better than in the most pleasant provinces of the world [Italy], and one cannot find here people who beg, as in those regions, or people dying of hunger during a famine, or trembling of cold during the winter). Furthermore, Negri is eager to demonstrate his openness to the scientific trends of his time and is often critical of ancient authorities; for example, he dismisses Aristotle in his erroneous descriptions of glacial zones.[13] He also states the need for experimentation on the properties of ice and cold climates in general and emphasizes the importance of direct observation, criticizing writing by geographers who do not personally verify information because, "non volendo lasciare gli agi della patria scrivono ciò che non hanno già mai veduto nè ben inteso da altri" (346–47) (unwilling to leave the comforts of their hometown, they write of that which they have never seen nor well understood from others).

While Scandinavia might at first glance seem an unusual or unexpected destination for Negri, as it did for Frederick III, in fact the itinerary is ideally suited for his purpose of reinscribing Italy as a significant European place and as a departure point for intrepid travelers. The choice of Scandinavia allows this traveler to engage in a crucial strategy of avoidance: he can claim status as an Italian making a bold journey while at the same time downplaying any reminders of Italy's changed role on the European stage. It is an area less well known to southern Europe, and Negri's movement in effect redirects European paradigms of traveling south (to Italy) or on an East-West axis (to Asia, to the Americas). It is also a safe option in that it includes territory for the most part neither disputed by continental European powers nor threatened by Eastern civilizations. In the textual representation of Scandinavia, the area is just spatially far enough to be characterized as exotic, but culturally near enough not to incite fear or anxiety.

Negri's text does not reproduce discourses of religious conversion or economic exploitation when representing "exotic" Scandinavia, and this is not simply because he travels through an area which, even if considered remote, is nevertheless still European and therefore does not lend itself to discourses of appropriation. More significantly, his perspective reflects his unique position as an Italian traveling for personal reasons and not representing a political, economic, or religious institution. Negri is excluded from, and indeed cannot participate in, a colonial mentality or set of cultural practices. He never engages in explicit acts of possession, to refer to Stephen Greenblatt's use of the term regarding Columbus, but rather focuses on observation and explanation.

Negri's careful sidestepping of potentially controversial subjects, or subjects that might point to Italy's decline, is most obvious in his discussions of religious rituals in Sweden, whose official religion was Lutheran. Through an ethnographic lens, he describes Swedish marriages and funerals in great detail, glossing over issues of religious doctrine. He finally concedes: "Non s'è detto ancora cos'alcuna della Religione; onde brevemente dirò, che la sola Luterana qui si professa [. . .] Tra tanti popoli, che nel secolo passato si disunirono dalla nostra, anzi sua antica Religione, i meno da essa remoti sono i Luterani" (120) (I haven't yet said anything about their religion; so I'll say briefly that only Lutheranism is practiced. Of so many people who, in the last century, divorced themselves from our, or rather their, ancient Religion, the least remote from the Church are the Lutherans). In line with his tendency to characterize similarity and difference in spatial terms, Negri qualifies Lutheranism as "least remote" from Catholicism, essentially refusing to address such explosive issues as the status of the Christian religion.[14] Scandinavia, in the narrator's portrayal, must remain ideologically unproblematic, even if it involves a form of denial, so that he can more freely explore possible discursive practices to bolster Italy's status.

One principal discursive practice of Negri's in demonstrating his authority as an Italian traveler—which he borrows from accounts of travel to the other continents—is to create an image of Scandinavia as a mysterious *terra incognita*, a European "other." This allows him, especially when visiting the more isolated areas of Scandinavia, to take on the role of a courageous discoverer-chronicler of new lands. For instance, using Pliny as an authority, he declares toward the end of his narrative, "E' tanto differente dunque questo regno, o piuttosto questa Scandinavia, dall'altre parti d'Europa che pare che ad essa piuttosto sarebbe convenuto quel detto: *Divisa ab orbe Scandinavia, che Britannia*" (238) (Scandinavia is so different from other parts of Europe that Pliny should have said that Scandinavia, instead of Britannia, is separate from the world).[15] Using a lexicon stressing alterity ("so different," "separate") Negri reinforces an impression of Scandinavia as occupying another universe unto itself, allowing him to place himself within the "we" of a dominant European travel culture.

Because Negri is most concerned about place, his narrative consists of an intricate combination of spatial discourses inasmuch as the text produces a variety of spatial relationships, or explains cultural similarities and differences through spatial means.[16] In characterizing Scandinavia, Francesco Negri recasts in a multitude of ways the distance or proximity between the European continent and its northernmost zone, between Italy and Scandinavia, and between Italy and the rest of continental Europe and even the world. For instance, Negri characterizes Scandinavia as a distant site of "harmless exoticism," and, recuperating elements of early European accounts of indigenous Americans, he sometimes associates Scandinavians with the mythical Golden Age or biblical times. Scandinavians are admirable for their excellent health and extraordinary longevity, characteristics often associated with the inhabitants of the Americas: "Superano ogni altra nazione d'Europa più meridionale in lunghezza di vita.... Quasi in ogni parocchia, nelle parti norlandiche, si trova chi con prosperità passa cent'anni" (150, 151) (They surpass every other more southern European country in length of life. In almost every parish of the northern areas, one finds someone who has leisurely passed one hundred year, of age).[17]

In Lapland especially, Negri, again painting a picture of harmless and unthreatening difference, characterizes the natives as "noble savages" whose pacificity and simplicity offer an appealing alternative to the complexities of civilization.[18] These very notions of barbarism and civilization are at the heart of his representation of the Lapps. Despite his criticism of some of their pagan superstitions, Negri likens the Lapps' way of life to that of the Golden Age and waxes nostalgic for their uncomplicated existence, again referencing discourses from the Age of Exploration. In their frozen world, they are untouched by either excessive virtue or excessive vice, and embody the *aurea mediocritas* ideal:

> Non sarebbe alieno dal vero chi dicesse, che le qualità dell'animo di questi abitatori corrispondono a quelle della loro terra, che non produce né frutti, né spine. Essi non hanno né virtù né vizii. Pare in un certo modo, che goda delle qualità del secolo d'oro questa nazione, che o poca o nulla ha notizia dell'oro. (128)

> (It would not be far from the truth were someone to say that the qualities of spirit of these populations correspond to those of their land, which produces neither fruits nor thorns. These people have neither vice nor virtue. It seems that in a certain way the people of this country enjoy the qualities of the Golden Age in that they have little or no knowledge of gold.)

With a play on the word "oro," he defends the Lapps' innocence and praises their adherence to natural law and the resulting well-being and social harmony.[19] In terms of character, extreme location has produced a total—and for Negri's purposes, safe—moderation in its inhabitants. The Lapps occupy a kind of *degré zero* of potential and occupy a place outside of or removed from more mainstream paradigms of good and bad.

On the subject of physical characteristics, however, Lapps are anything but moderate. When describing their appearance, Negri does so by focusing on their radical alterity within a European framework and also likens them to populations of other continents. The Italian traveler's logic of analogies between location and ethnic or cultural characteristics allows him both to "distance" Lapps and to "center" Italy. After discussing the Lapps' hut-like living quarters, he comments on their physical size:

> I nostri Lapponi . . . sono di statura i più piccoli dell'Europa . . . e l'istesso è degli Sciti, o Tartari Asiatici . . . . Costituiscono dunque i Lapponi due estremi insieme con gli Olandesi, che sono i più grandi e grossi in Europa, e massimamente le donne. (73)

> (Our Lapps are the smallest of stature in Europe, and this also goes for the Scythians, or Asians Tartars. The Lapps and the Dutch are the two extremes of Europe in that the Dutch are the tallest and most solid Europeans, especially Dutch women, who often surpass the norm in weight and size.)

In his quirky anthropological map of the world, Negri acknowledges that Lapps are European ("the smallest of stature in Europe") and opposes them to the larger-sized Dutch on a European scale. He equates Lapp physique, however, with that of non-European populations such as Scythians and Tartars. The Lapps may be European geographically speaking, but their diminutive size categorizes them under a rubric relative to eastern peoples.

Negri, it is true, uses a possessive ("our Lapps") when characterizing Lapps and thus places them in a European perspective, i.e., one of ours. Nevertheless, when commenting on Lapp skin color, he infers that he is part of an *Italian* group that defines the norm or average for human size and coloring.

> La piccolezza però de' Lapponi non è tanta, come de' Pigmei, che stimo favolosi, o de' Nani; ma i più grandi eguaglieranno appena un mediocre de' nostri . . . essi sono i più bruni di tutti gli altri, che tramezzano tra noi e loro, perché sono intirizziti, o quasi abbruciati dal freddo della zona glaciale, siccome gli Etiopi sono i più negri di tutti gli altri, che tramezzano pure fra noi e loro, per esser adusti dal calore della zona torrida. (75)

> (The smallness of the Lapps is not as great as that of Pygmies, which I believe to be fictitious, or of dwarfs, but the largest of them would barely equal in height an average one of ours. These people have a darker complexion than the people who live between their region and ours, due to their close proximity to the polar region. They are numbed and almost burned by the bitter cold, much like the Ethiopians (the darkest of all people between their region and ours) are burned by the heat of the torrid zone.)

"I nostri" means Italians and not Europeans because Negri here excludes Lapps, whom he has just acknowledged as European, from the category of "ours." He continues to play with the notion of Scandinavia as both inside and outside of Europe. In this passage, "an average one of ours," an average Italian, is the measuring stick with which to assess the height of the Lapps. Similarly, he explains that the extreme ("the darkest") Lapp skin color results from their far northern location relative to an Italian middle ground, just as Ethiopian skin color results from an extreme southern location vis-à-vis the *we*. The degree of distance from the presumed Italian center determines the degree of darkness. Once more Lapps occupy a realm of alterity that lies outside of any concept of European-ness and that renders them closer to the inhabitants of other continents.

According to Negri's argument, Lapps and Ethiopians can be grouped together precisely because they have a similar "extreme" skin color (Lapps brownish, Ethiopians black). By the same token, the small size of Pygmies and Lapps—not opposite but identical characteristics—can *also* be explained by their inhabiting extreme, even if opposite, geographical areas. In other words, opposite climates produce similar physiques. Negri's tendency to interpret phenomena by relating seemingly contradictory components, while scientifically questionable, effectively highlight Italy's presupposed central position.[20] Because for Negri, Italy lies indisputably at a spatial nexus; in other words the conclusion is presumed to be true, then any argument leading to that conclusion can be a reasonable and valid one.

Negri appears to reject the premises of his argument when, after initially describing Scandinavia as remote, he establishes later on an unexampled cultural connection between Italians and Swedes. This temporary nearing of Italy to Sweden involves rather unreasonable historical interpretation, but it is in fact a parallel strategy or means to justify Italy's importance. One again, a dubious premise perfectly serves Negri's goal of placing Italy and Italians in a positive light by associating them with Sweden's military strength and ability to resist invasion.

Certainly Sweden held a significant position on Europe's political and cultural map, having fought successfully against the Holy Roman Emperor in Germany before the Peace of Prague in 1625.[21] Furthermore, the cultural connection of Sweden to Italy in the seventeenth century was manifest, especially in the figure of Queen Christina of Sweden. An eminent humanist who gained international fame when she abdicated the throne in 1654, converted to Catholicism, and established herself at the papal court, she held famed literary meetings with a circle that would found the Arcadia literary academy later on in 1690. Negri himself has been witness to Christina's offical entry into Rome: "Ci andai [to Rome] non per veder Roma, ma il felice e fausto ingresso di sua Maestà, allora che vi fu accolta colla magnificenza a tutto il mondo nota dal Sommo Pontefice Alessandro VII" (220) (I went not to see Rome, but for the joyful and festive entry of her Majesty, when she was welcomed with a magnificence known to all by the Great Pontiff Alexander VII).[22] Bent on conveying positive common attributes in Swedes and Italians, Negri insists on their shared Gothic pedigree. He defines Swedes as Goth-Swedes ("questo popolo Svero-Goto") (134) who owe their military might to Gothic ancestors best known for their conquests:[23] "Non fu mai soggiogato il paese [Sweden] da stranieri con aperta guerra, ma bensì i suoi popoli arrivarono già sotto il nome di Goti a dominare la dominazione del mondo, Roma" (135) (This country was never conquered by foreigners in open war, and instead her people, under the name of Goths, were even able to dominate the world's dominator, Rome).[24] Implicit in Negri's remarks are the reference to Italy's subjugation to Spain and the yearning for an Italy free of foreign domination. In his attempt to associate Italy with Sweden's defensive capabilities, Negri focuses on cultural correspondences resulting from a common history and proximity, not on differences related to climatic and geographical variations.

To make his argument "reasonable," however, Negri not only unequivocally dismisses the traditional Italian early modern nostalgia for Rome's far-reaching influence, but also overlooks the fact that the Goths were themselves invaders and contributed to the demise of the Roman Empire. In his interpretation, Goths become benevolent dictators: "se giammai godè l'Italia felice governo, ciò fu sotto il regno de' Goti" (136) (If Italy ever enjoyed a good government, it was under the reign of the Goths). In this unprecedented historical re-reading, Italy's resilience and courage stem from its northern heritage, not from a triumphant and glorious Roman past. Negri goes as far as invoking Charles V's respect for Gothic conquerors to support his claims of Italy's heroic Gothic heritage:

> Non isdegnò quel grande eroe l'imperatore Carlo V di dichiararsi di discendere dalla prosapia degli antichi Goti . . . e così possono fondatamente dire gli abitatori di Ravenna, stata regia sede de' re Goti; anzi l'Italia tutta se ne può pregiare, particolarmente in quelle parti, che conservano i costumi degli antichi Goti. (157)

> (That great hero, the Emperor Charles V, did not disdain declaring himself a descendant of the ancient Goths. And the citizens of Ravenna can say the same with good reason about the ancient seat of the Gothic Kings. All of Italy can take pride in that, especially in those areas that have kept ancient Gothic customs.)[25]

That Negri is eager to create a powerful and dignified past especially for himself becomes clear in his recalling that the Goths who settled in Italy established the center of their reign in Ravenna. However farfetched his argument, Negri's narrative does provide a completely novel cultural and spatial *rapprochement* of southern and northern Europe. For a brief moment in the text, then, the Italian peninsula has shifted northward, and Italy's newly defined Swedish heritage allows Negri to transfer to his homeland the worthy attributes of the country visited.

In a cultural climate in which natural philosophy is gaining recognition, Negri also incorporates references to "new" scientific methodologies, once again in the service of nearing Italian culture to northern Europe. A correspondent of Lorenzo Magalotti, the secretary of the Galileo-inspired scientific *Accademia del Cimento*, Negri is familiar with general concepts of the scientific culture and with the only publication of the Academy, the *Saggi di naturali esperienze* (1667) (*Examples of National Experiments*), which Magalotti spent years writing and revising for publication.[26] Negri does not mention Galileo by name, but his knowledge of the use of inductive technique and his willingness to challenge traditional scientific doctrine are Galilean in flavor.

However, to Negri, the role of "new" science seems as much of a methodological imperative and "reasonable" investigative practice as a means to bring Italian culture closer to prominent northern European scientific centers. As Marco Biagioli writes, "it is undeniable that, by 1680, the centers of European science were no longer Padua or Florence, but Paris and London."[27] The *Saggi di naturali esperienze*, which presumably would be Negri's principal source for practicing experimental science, betrays an underlying anxiety about Italian contributions to science in its regular references to its investigations as part of a pan-European project.[28] Magalotti's comments on the importance of scientific investigation is typical: "per dare il suo pieno a così nobile e giovevole intraprendimento, niun'altra cosa ci vorrebbe, che una libera comunicazione di diverse adunanze sparse, come oggi sono, per le più illustre e più cospicue regioni d'Europa" (60–61) (to give full scope to such a noble and useful enterprise we should wish for nothing else but a free communication from the various Societies, scattered as they are today through the most illustrious and notable region[s] of Europe). Or, on an experiment with quicksilver performed by an Italian scientist, he said: "E' nota oramai per ogni parte d'Europa quella famosa esperienza dell'argentovivo, che l'anno 1643 si parò davanti al grande intelletto del Torricelli" (80) (That famous experiment with the quicksilver that in 1643 presented itself before the great intellect of Torricelli is now known in every part of Europe).

This awareness of a European playing field with which to contend is evident in Negri's own explanation of his decision to travel in Scandinavia:

> [N]on può, per dire il vero, parere che strano, che noi Europei trascuriamo parti così curiose nella nostra Europa, intenti più tosto ad investigar con diligenti osservazioni i remoti paesi dell'Oriente e dell'Austro, e insin del Nuovo Mondo, al presente tanto noti e praticati; e ignoriamo poscia le stesse nostre regioni. (52)
>
> ([In truth, it can only seem strange that we Europeans ignore such intriguing parts of our own Europe, intent rather on investigating with diligent observations the remote countries of the East and the South and even the New World, all of which are by now so well-known and traveled; and we then ignore our own regions.)

Conveniently casting sea and land travel to other continents as unimaginative and repetitive—in other words the travel undertaken by the principal powers of Spain, England, France, and the Netherlands—Negri can make the case for the absolute necessity of his trip. His use of pronouns to include himself in European patterns of mobility ("we Europeans") and the repeated possessives ("our own Europe," "our own regions") serve to place himself within the dominant travel culture of continental Europe, since his statement necessarily excludes a possible Scandinavian point of view. He constructs a similar perspective when he mentions the lack of information on Scandinavia and "il non trovarsi, per quanto io sappia, alcun autore che abbia scritto della Scandinavia come testimonio oculare dopo di averla osservata tutta, e massimamente le sue parti boreali" (52) (One cannot find, as far as I know, any author who has written about Scandinavia as an eyewitness after having observed all of it, and especially in its northernmost areas). Again, Scandinavians don't appear to fit in the category of European eyewitnesses, and Negri's focus seems to rest on the authors and authorities of areas of cultural prominence in northern Europeans countries such as the ones mentioned by Biagioli.

Negri's insistence on the importance of direct, experimental inquiry becomes less reasonable when, perhaps responding to the references in many travel accounts to unusual and wondrous flora, fauna, and geological formations, he also confirms, through what he claims to be reputable sources, the existence of trolls, elves, and miraculous occurrences, such as the revival of men and animals after lengthy submersions in ice-covered waters. The pull of the marvelous, still requisite elements in tales of "exotic" travels, excludes the possibility of following any one distinct methodology. However, this turning away from a consistent scientific approach in favor of more aesthetic considerations—including the taste for the curious and the bizarre—can also be seen in Magalotti's scientific writing and in the activities of the Accademia del Cimento. When describing one of the Academy's specially ordered coil-shaped thermometers, Magalotti admits:

> [è] fatto questo strumento più tosto per una bizzarria e per curiosità di veder correre l'acqua le decine di gradi, mossa dal semplice appressamento dell'alito, che per dedurne giuste ed infallibili proporzioni del caldo e del freddo. (49)

> (This instrument is rather made for a whim, and through curiosity to see the liquid run through tens of degrees when it is simply breathed on, than for finding out with it the just and unfailing proportions of heat and cold.)[29]

For Negri, like for the members of the Accademia del Cimento, the pleasure and marvel of science are never completely removed from the practice of it.[30] In this particular manifestation of seventeenth-century natural philosophy, scientific precision does not necessarily take precedent over or interfere with amusement, pleasure, or an impulsive, fanciful, and certainly unreasonable *bizzarria*.

While "new" science lets Negri make the case for being an up-to-date traveler who participates in the latest modes of investigation, he turns to classically-derived climate theory to create his *mappamundi* and "prove" that Italy is the world's geographical point of reference. Principally, climate theory offers the perfect "scientific" method for Negri to consider Scandinavia and Italy within a *global*, and not just European discourse. Again according to Norman Doiron, climate theory is fundamental to seventeenth-century travelers' search for a totalizing discourse ("discours totalisateur") which can account for and categorize all variety and difference on earth.[31] Negri seeks to define Scandinavia and Italy as part of a totalizing discourse, in other words, in relation to the rest of the world. He uses this "global" perspective to explain the impact of the cold on humans and even animals by contrasting the Scandinavian conditions to various torrid climates such as those of India and China. His correlation of extremes reflects widespread notions of the consequences of living in cold or hot climates, according to which those living in cold areas are more vigorous and those from warmer regions weaker.[32]

When Negri focuses on the "extremes" in terms of binary oppositions of frigid-torrid, calm-fierce, and corrupt-uncorrupt, implicit in this discourse is the Aristotelian notion that a temperate climate can provide ideally balanced conditions for human beings. Despite his laudatory commentary on Scandinavian vigor and restraint, the Italian traveler argues that Italy has the ideal climate, and in doing so diverges from the climatic and geographical preferences of his classical predecessors. Although basic tenets linking climate and human behavior were common to many classical and early modern texts, the specific location of the ideal climate remained in the eye of the beholder. Aristotle, of course, favored Greece, and Ptolemy favored those regions between 28 and 34 degrees north. As can be expected, Negri declares that the areas lying at the 45th parallel—Ravenna's latitude being 44'25" north—have the most salutary climate. Such a place is most favorable for humankind's potential to flourish:

> Ritrovo che quelle nazioni, che sono egualmente distanti dalla zona torrida e dalla glaciale, cioè circa al grado quarantesimo quinto, producono, se non unitamente nell'istesso soggetto, almeno disgiuntamente in varii, le persone più belle e gli ingegni più acuti, e per conseguenza più virtuosi o più viziosi, che l'altre provincie, che s'accostano all'estremità, nella quale si verifica regolarmente il detto del Filosofo: *Homines regionum frigidarum plus habent virium, minus consilii; calidarum e contra.* (157)

> (I find that those countries equidistant from the torrid and frigid zones, that is at about forty-five degrees, produce, if not together in the same person, at least separately in various persons, the most beautiful people and the sharpest minds, and by consequence the most virtuous or the most full of vice, than the other areas close to the extremities, in which one can consistently validate the saying of the Philosopher: Men of the cold regions have spirit but lack intelligence; the opposite is true for those of the hot regions.)[33]

Just as he indicates when describing the Lapps, acute cold may prevent excess vice, but it also prevents excess virtue. Negri, in a manner reminiscent of his description of Lapps as "noble savages," uses opposing hyperbolic characteristics—that is the tendency toward extreme vice and extreme virtue—to characterize one people. Scandinavians are less subject to sin than Italians, but they are accordingly unable to achieve either the greatness or even the physical beauty of those from Negri's self-defined ideal climate.[34]

The theory of "extreme vice and virtue" also provides a built-in *reason* for Italian failures and successes, since these attributes are two sides of one latitudinal coin. Italy, because of its moderate climate, is a site for great potential, unlike areas of intense heat or intense cold. This rather ingenuous line of logic does the service both of accounting for Italy's decline in the seventeenth century *and* explaining Negri's decision to take on a treacherous journey. His trip becomes a "reasonable" one, then, whose origins lie in the Italian possibility of achieving great virtue, in this case through audacious exploration and thorough investigation of lesser-known lands.

Negri pays a more expected and traditional homage to Italy's Classical past when he praises Italy and Greece as homes to the finest minds: "L'esperienza ci dimostra, che i migliori ingegni del mondo sono provenuti dalla Grecia e dall'Italia, e dalle parti d'Europa a quelle corrispondenti ne' climi, e particolarmente in quelle, nelle quali si producono buoni vini e acque sottili" (158) (Experience shows us that the best minds in the world have come from Greece and Italy, and from those parts of Europe with a corresponding climate, and particularly those areas in which good wine and delicate waters are produced). By characterizing Italians as having the highest potential intelligence of any populations, he also implies that they have the capacity at least to match, if not to surpass, other Europeans in their travels and explorations abroad. Given the premise of Italian superiority, it logically follows that Negri himself, as an Italian living in Ravenna, is particularly well-suited to undertake and write about such a challenging but warranted journey. Having firmly placed Italians at the center of civilization, he can confidently declare: "mi parebbe di non esser italiano, se non avessi avuta questa curiosità" (238–39) (I wouldn't seem Italian, if I had not had this curiosity).[35] According to Negri's logic, then, Frederick III's surprise at seeing an Italian abroad is based on flawed assumptions about climate and character. For Negri, his travels are in fact reasonable—that is to say, within expected and comprehensible parameters of behavior—simply because he is Italian.

The *Viaggio settentrionale* is in essence an attempt to construct a "totalizing discourse," to return to Doiron's term, through the representation of travels to a single region of Europe. In this, Negri's ambitions and motives for travel are reasonable, but his methodologies for representing them and Scandinavia are ultimately unreasonable. The logical inconsistencies in the text reflect a tension between a pseudo-objective, "new" scientific and more "universal" perspective on the one hand, and, on the other, a desire to claim authority and recognition through the narrator's connection to a specifically defined area—the Italian peninsula and even Negri's hometown, or *patria*, of Ravenna. Negri may pose as a natural scientist at the forefront of developing European currents of investigation, but "new" science does not provide him the means to his end, which is to explain *cultural* phenomena in a way that highlights Italian contributions to contemporary Europe.

In the end, the distinction of the *Viaggio settentrionale* lies neither in the quantity nor in the accuracy of the factual information and argumentations, but in this Italian observer's innovative techniques of notation, categorization, and explanation of the far north. His travel account is in part the reflection of the variegated and ultimately incompatible forms—old and new—of ordering knowledge that are circulating in an increasingly international culture, and in part the product of a self-conscious traveler's reaction to Italy's progressive exclusion from a Europe growing more powerful precisely because of its international mobility. If Negri does not furnish a truly scientific or logically consistent inquiry with experimentation and calculation, he exercises his methodological freedom and surpasses empirical guidelines by letting permeate through them the real meaning of his undertaking, namely, to prove that Italy and especially Ravenna are at the true center of the world.

Notes

I thank the Oregon Humanities Center for a research fellowship which enabled me to complete this article. I am also grateful to Leah Middlebrook for her invaluable comments and suggestions.

1. Francesco Negri (1624–1698) may have been to England and Poland on diplomatic church missions, but there are few documents attesting to other travels abroad besides those to Scandinavia. See, for example, Caravita's irksomely fragmented but informative text. When Negri left for Scandinavia, the most authoritative source of information was *Historia de gentibus septentrionalibus* (1555) (*History of northern peoples*) written by Swedish scholar Olaf Manson (1490–1557). See Ricci. After Negri returned to Italy, Johannes Scheffer in 1673 published *Lapponia (Lapland)*, from which Negri quotes. Also see Chiodo.
2. Translations are mine unless otherwise indicated. A brief and rudimentary version entitled "Lapponia" appeared in the travel anthology *Il genio vagante: Biblioteca curiosa di cento e più relazioni di viaggi stranieri de' nostri tempi*, Valerio Zani, ed. (Parma: Giuseppe dall'Oglio e Giuseppe Rosati, 1690–1692). A counterfeit of the first integral edition, published posthumously, (Padua: Stamperia del Seminario, 1700) came out in 1701 (Forlì, G: Dandi). The first letter of the text was published as *La Lapponia Descritta* in 1705 (Venice: Albrizzi). The *Viaggio settentrionale* has two modern editions: Bologna: Zanichelli, 1883, and Milan: Alpes, 1929. A facsimile of the 1700 edition was published by Bergamo: Leading Edizioni, 2000.
3. As Daria Perocco writes, "ci si rende conto della diminuzione dell'importanza strategica e politica del paese d'origine, del fatto che l'essere italiano non è più sufficiente carta di presentazione e di credito" (20) (Italians become aware of the diminishing strategic and political importance of their own country and the fact that being Italian no longer suffices as a letter of presentation or credit). Giovanni Francesco Gemelli

Careri, traveling some twenty years later in Europe, characterizes Italians as "svogliati e timidi nel slontanarsi da patrii lidi" (1) (reluctant and timid about distancing themselves from home shores).

4. The Peace of Westphalia, which put an end to the Thirty Year's War in 1648, played a significant role in cutting off Italy from its increasingly powerful northern neighbors. Pope Innocent X rejected the treaty, exacerbating Italy's isolation from the rest of Europe. Furthermore, the geographical break between Atlantic and Mediterranean worlds entailed the redefinition of European centers and margins. The Italian peninsula, which had dominated Mediterranean sea travel and trade, was now on the outer edge of the new Atlantic-directed European map. See Prosperi and Viola, 94.

5. The missions of the Roman Catholic church had a large Spanish and Portuguese component, making it difficult to conceive of those projects as "proto-national" or somehow representative of an "Italian" form of travel. In terms of secular travel, Italy did not have an equivalent of (national) identity-forming paradigm of the Grand Tour favored by the English. For an overview of early modern European travel and tourism, see Maczak.

6. See Doiron, 89 and 92–93. Doiron calls travel a metaphysics in which the seventeenth-century traveler wants to encompass the whole world: "Le voyage étant une métaphysique, le voyageur veut englober (méta) dans la carte qu'il dessine, dans le récit qu'il compose, et tout le monde et tous les discours" (Travel being a metaphysics, the traveler wants to encircle [meta] all of the world and all discourse in the account that he composes and in the map that he draws). Doiron focuses more on the impulse of seventeenth-century travelers to be comprehensive and encyclopedic in their methodology rather than necessarily "rational" or "scientific." See Doiron, 90.

7. For example, the movement and speed of sound were explained through the visual image of concentric circles of water moving out from the spot where a stone has been dropped in a pond. See Lorenzo Magalotti's *Saggi di naturali esperienze* (1667) (*Examples of Natural Elements*), which will be discussed later, in which the experimenters of the *Accademia del Cimento* criticize inaccuracies in the analogy.

8. Certainly most travel narratives directly or indirectly presume the superiority of the traveler's country and culture of origin. Nevertheless, Negri's constructions of spatial and geographical relationships represent a specifically Italian phenomenon.

9. Even though in their time many seventeenth-century Italian travel narratives enjoyed wide international readership, their association with Italy's exclusion from dominant travel patterns and the decline in Italy's international status translated into less scholarly attention. Francesco Negri is mentioned diligently in literary histories and anthologies and has enjoyed somewhat of a recent revival locally in Ravenna, but most of the studies of his life and works are of a strictly historical or geographical nature.

10. See Cachey.

11. The modern designation for the inhabitants of Lapland is the Swami people, however, for the purposes of this analysis, I translate Negri's term "Lapponi" as "Lapps."

12. Negri's extant letters to Antonio Magliabechi, Grand Duke Cosimo III's librarian,

attest to the traveler's concern with factual accuracy and document his plans to have illustrations prepared for the account as well as his efforts to find a publisher. Negri mentions Valerio Zani's support for publication and that of Athanasius Kircher, the Jesuit polymath settled in Rome, who proposes to send Negri's work to a Dutch publisher. Negri also mentions geographers such as the Venetian Vincenzo Coronelli, founder of the *Accademia Cosmografia degli Argonauti*, who was to send him accounts of Scandinavia written by Venetian ambassadors. Negri's letters, held at the Biblioteca Nazionale in Florence, are edited by Wis Murena. The narrative includes several amusing anecdotes from his travels, including what is probably the earliest account of a (failed) ski lesson.

13. After explaining the Scandinavian treatment of victims of the extreme cold, Negri chides the ancients for claiming the truth of phenomena not personally witnessed: "Tutta questa lezione io l'ho imparata da questi libri dell'esperienza che ho narrato, i quali non erano noti al tempo di Aristotile e di Galeno. Che se quei grandi uomini gli avessero letti, gli avrebbero intesi meglio la natura. Se camminassero sopra al mare agghiacciato, non lascierebbero scritto che il mare non può agghiaccarsi" (284–85) (I learned this entire lesson from the book of experience that I have narrated, books which were unknown at the time of Aristotle and Galen. For if these great men had read them, they would have better understood nature. If they had walked upon the frozen seas, they would not have written that the sea cannot freeze over). The metaphor of the "book of nature," rendered famous in late Renaissance Italian culture by Tommaso Campanella (1568–1639) and Galileo, is a clear reference to "new" science.

14. Negri receives help and hospitality from members of the Catholic church in Scandinavia and, when in Stockholm, stays with the French almoner to Louis XIV.

15. The quotations do not correspond to the writings on Britain in Pliny's *Natural History*, which say simply that Britain "is situated to the north-west, and, with a large tract of intervening sea, lies opposite to Germany, Gaul, and Spain, by far the greater part of Europe" (350). Negri's view of Scandinavia as a different world may refer to Pliny's description of Scandinavia as an island: "the most famous among [the northern islands] is Scandinavia, of a magnitude not as yet ascertained: the only portion of it all known is inhabited by the nation of the Hilleviones, who dwell in 500 villages, and call it a second world" (343).

16. Negri's travel account could be read as a form of "cartographic writing," to use Tom Conley's term, which relates visually discernible spatial discourses of maps and texts to the construction of the early modern self. See Conley.

17. Hayden White observes in commentary on indigenous Americans, "The natives apparently enjoy the attributes formerly believed to have been possessed only by the Patriarchs of the Old Testament: robust health and longevity of life" (187).

18. As Joan-Pau Rubiés notes, following the discovery of the "New World," ethnographic writings attempt to categorize different peoples according to the sophistication of their culture and their perceived character and moral qualities: "Human nature and history were in fact newly defined on the basis of the description of diversity and change

in travel literature and historiography .... The comparison of different systems of behavior and beliefs ultimately led to a new hierarchical classification for peoples in terms of barbarism and civilization" (85, 90).
19. Even when Negri acknowledges that Lapps might find ridiculous certain Italian customs, he does so by using a European/non-European binary opposition. For instance, after positing that Lapps would laugh at the use of the plural pronoun "voi" to address formally one person, he writes: "Simil occasione di risa reciprocamente verte tra molte nazioni: *non minus illis Europoei, quam Europoeis illi ridiculi sunt*; così scrive il P[adre] Maffei, mentre racconta molti costumi tra di loro contrario de' Cinesi e degli Europei" (82) (A similar occasion for laughter can be seen among many nations. They are no less ridiculous to the Europeans than the Europeans are to them. So writes Father Maffei when he tells of the many customs that are opposite in the Chinese and the Europeans). Drawing a parallel between European-Chinese reciprocal laughter and Italian-Lapp reciprocal laughter, Negri implies that the cultural and geographical distance between Italy and Lapland is comparable to the distance between Europe and China. Giovanni Pietro Maffei is the author of *Historiarum indicarum libri XVI* (Florence: Giunti, 1588).
20. Prosperi and Viola, 424–25.
21. The Italian traveler also had an audience with Christina of Sweden after his journey and mentions that he spoke with her of his "patria Ravenna, residenza degli antichi re de' Goti" (200) (hometown Ravenna, residence of the ancient kings of the Goths).
22. Negri insists in the same vein: "Questa è una nazione delle più bellicose che veda il sole . . . . E realmente può dirsi che la natura abbia fatto questi popoli per conquistare, il paese per non esser conquistato, comunicando a quelli un animo dotato di straordinario coraggio e robustezza di corpo" (134) (This is one of the most bellicose nations under the sun. And one can truly say that nature has made these people for conquering, and their country for not being conquered, giving them a spirit of extraordinary courage and physical robustness).
23. Negri uses "Goth" as a generic term for invaders from the north. The Ostrogoths, who occupied much of Italy during the medieval period and made Ravenna their principal Italian stronghold in the Fifth and Sixth centuries, actually originated from regions near the Black Sea. These were a separate group from the southern Scandinavian-German Goth tribes. See the *Atlante storico Garzanti*, 114–19.
24. At at a dinner with Swedish clergymen, Negri proudly proclaims, as a native of Ravenna, his descendance from Gothic roots: "Ed essi pur godevano di interrogarmi dei nostri paesi, e mi facevano istanza particolarmente quando mi udivano dire che io sono Italo-goto, cioè la mia patria esser Ravenna, l'antica residenza già dei re Goti, le cui memorie e gli edificii de' medesimi tuttavia l'illustrano" (170) (And they enjoyed questioning me about our countries, and their interest was particularly peaked when they heard me say that I'm an Italian-Goth, that is that my hometown is Ravenna, the ancient residence of the Gothic Kings, whose memory and whose buildings still make her illustrious). Negri even submits that the Goths were fair-minded invaders and not

"barbarians" because they never purposely demolished Roman temples and buildings: "Parmi che sia che i veri guerrieri, come i Goti, cercano di batter generosamente chi li può battere, e non le statue e macchine insensate" (138–39) (It seems to me that, like true warriors, the Goths seek to beat generously those who can beat them, and not statues and constructions in a senseless manner).

25. The Academy, active from approximately 1657 to 1667, was founded by a student of Galileo's, Vincenzo Viviani, and sponsored by the Grand Duke Ferdinand II of Tuscany. While acknowledging its Galilean origins, the Academy avoided experiments in astronomy, gravity, and tidal forces that might have been risky given the Church's widespread control and censure of scientific investigations and publications. For an informative study of the Accademia del Cimento in English, see Middleton. The book includes a translation, from which I draw, of the *Saggi di naturali esperienze*.

26. Biagioli, 12.

27. It is Negri's predilection for terms such as *esperienza*, along with his eagerness to explain and not just report different phenomena, that marks the presence of scientific culture in the account. For example, after positing that reindeer are the fastest animals in Europe, he concludes: "l'esperienza però ne darebbe la total certezza" (94) (an experiment would provide complete certainty). Or, when confirming the existence of a symbiotic relationship between certain indigenous species of trees, he confesses: "non ho fatto l'esperienza, perché solamente dopo la mia partenza da Lapponia ho fatta questa riflessione" (99) (I did not do the experiment, because it was only after my departure from Lapland that the notion came to me).

28. These thermometers are viewable at the Museo della Scienza in Florence, and color photographs of them are published in Paolo Galluzzi's book.

29. Marziano Guglielminetti identifies lingering elements of baroque literary aesthetics in the *Viaggio settentrionale*, and likens some of Negri's lists of flora and fauna to Giambattista Marino's *Adone* (1623) (256).

30. Doiron's comments on French travel narratives are applicable here: "le voyageur classique dresse des catalogues de raretés, et son récit est un *recueil* contenant, en abrégé, toute l'histoire du monde. La dispersion qui suivit la chute de Babel trouve sa plus profonde expression dans la *théorie des climats* .... C'est donc la diversité des climats qui impose aux voyageurs la tâche de recueillir par leurs parcours les qualités éparses propres à chaque lieux" (98) (the traveler of the 1600s makes catalogues or rarities, and his narrative is a collection, in abbreviated form, of the entire history of the world. The dispersion that followed the fall of Babel finds its deepest expression in climate theory. It is the diversity of climates that imposes upon the traveler the task of gathering through his routes the varied qualities particular to each place). In using climate theory to argue for Italy's still-privileged position, Negri picks up on a key component of early modern anthropological thought and the "critical debate about relativity of customs and behavior" (Rubiés 95).

31. See Tooley, 73. Vigor is linked to a healthy appetite, as Negri points out: "Insomma questi climi settentrionali portano seco la disposizione ad esser più abbondante nel

mangiare e bere che in altri; e ciò lo provo in me stesso" (84–85) (In short, these northern climates bring about a disposition to eat and drink more abundantly than in others; and this I have experienced myself).
32. Negri's quotation comes from Aristotle's *Politics*, VII, ch.7 on climate and character.
33. Negri also quotes from John Barclay's *Icon animorum* (1614), a treatise on the character of people and nations, to support his argument: "Nihil autem tam arduum sedulitatis humanae, ad quot Italici acuminis praestanti a non tollatur. Ad extremum non alibi sanctiorum virtutum exempla, pejorumque facinorum, quam in italicis animis, cernas" (158) (There is no challenge to human intelligence so great that the Italians' superior acumen does not rise to the occasion. In the end, you will not find elsewhere examples of the most saintly virtues and the worst crimes, as in Italians).
34. By the sixteenth century, curiosity was considered an acceptable motive for travel, and Negri's intentions could easily be construed as "virtuous." See Stagl.

Works Cited

Aristotle. *Politics: Books VII and VIII*. Trans. R. Kraut. Oxford: Clarendon, 1997.
Biagioli, Marco. "Scientific Revolution, Social Bricolage, and Etiquette." *The Scientific Revolution in National Context*. Ed. Roy Porter and Mikulas Teich. Cambridge: Cambridge University Press, 1992. 11–54.
Cachey, Theodore, Jr. "An Italian History of Travel." *Annali d'Italianistica* 14 (1996): 55–64.
Caravita, Gregorio. *Francesco Negri: il prete ravennate che ha scoperto gli sci*. Ravenna: Tipolitografia Artestampa, 2004.
Chiodo, Carmine. "Il Viaggio settentrionale di Francesco Negri." *Campi immaginabili* 7–8 (1993): 59–103.
Conley, Tom. *The Self-Made Map: Cartographic Writing in Early Modern France*. Minneapolis, MN: University of Minnesota Press, 1996.
Doiron, Normand. "L'art de voyager: Pour une définition du récit de voyage à l'époque classique," *Poétique* 73 (1988): 83–108.
Galluzzi, Paolo, ed. *Scienziati a corte: L'arte della sperimentazione nell'Accademia Galileiana del Cimento (1657–1667)*. Florence: Sillabe, 2001.
Gemelli Careri, Giovanni Francesco. *Viaggi per l'Europa*. Naples: Raillard, 1693.
Greenblatt, Stephen. *Marvelous Possessions: The Wonder of the New World*. Chicago: University of Chicago Press, 1991.
Guglielminetti, Marziano. *Storia della civiltà letteraria italiana: Manierismo e Barocco*. Turin: UTET, 1990.
Hilgemann, Werner and Herman Kinder. *Atlante storico Garzanti*. Milan: Garzanti, 1999.
Maczak, Antoni. *Travel in Early Modern Europe*. Trans. Ursula Philipps. Cambridge: Polity, 1995.

Magalotti, Lorenzo. *Saggi di naturali esperienze (1667)*. Ed. Teresa Poggi Salvani. Milan: Longanesi, 1976.

Middleton, W. E. Knowles. *The Experimenters: A Study of the Accademia Del Cimento*. Baltimore, MN: Johns Hopkins University Press, 1971.

Negri, Francesco. *Viaggio settentrionale*. Ed. Enrico Falqui. Milan: Alpes, 1929.

Perocco, Daria. *Viaggiare e raccontare: narrazione di viaggio ed esperienze di racconto tra Cinque e Seicento*. Alessandria: Edizioni dell'Orso, 1997.

Pliny the Elder. *Natural History, Book IV.* Trans. John Bostock and H. T. Riley. New York: George Bell and Sons, 1893.

Prosperi, Adriano and Paolo Viola. *Dalla rivoluzione inglese alla rivoluzione francese: Storia italiana*. Turin: Einaudi, 1998.

Ricci, Virgilio. "Sci e alpinismo nel Seicento. Francesco Negri, l'ardito romagnolo che ubbidì al grande richiamo delle nevi scandinave." *Le Alpi* 61 (Jan.-Feb. 1924): 79–90.

Rubiés, Joan-Pau. "New Worlds and Renaissance Ethnology." *Facing Each Other: Part I*. Ed. Anthony Pagden. Burlington, VT: Ashgate, 2000. 81–121.

Stagl, Justin. *A History of Curiosity: The Theory of Travel 1550–1800*. Chur, Switzerland: Harwood Academic Publishers, 1995.

Tooley, Marian J. "Bodin and the Mediaeval Theory of Climate," *Speculum* 28 (1953): 64–93.

White, Hayden. *Tropics of Discourse*. Baltimore, MD: Johns Hopkins University Press, 1978.

Wis Murena, Cristina, ed. "Le Lettere di Francesco Negri ad Antonio Magliabechi dal Giugno 1678 al Giugno 1696." *Atti dell'Accademia Pontaniana: Nuova Serie* 34. Naples: Giannini, 1986.

◆ 6

Baroque Sapphic Poetry: A Feminist Road Not Taken

Dianne Dugaw and Amanda Powell

Women's love poetry to women in the baroque era opens a window onto a publicly vaunted feminism quite at odds with the post-Enlightenment legacy that has defined modern feminisms. The pan-European mode of sapphic poetries appearing in Italy, France, and the Netherlands as well as Britain, Spain, and New Spain represents a philogynist "road not taken" by later modernity.[1] Such "queering" poetry (in our parlance) proposes women's active cultural agency—an authority of wit and soul—as well as passionate same-sex eroticism; both are forwarded through (often satirical) manipulation of masculinist traditions. Considering here examples in Spanish and English, we hope to encourage exploration of sapphic poetry in the many language traditions of the early modern era for which it held prestige.[2] Sapphic courtings of women by women emerge from the thought of an early modern world that saw transcendent power in the Virgin Mary, worldly and secular might in abbesses, and an approach to divinity in the power and stature of earthly queens. The neo-platonic model underlying this sapphic mode is an hermaphroditic self theorized in a tradition extending back to Plato (Laqueur) that offered women possibilities (as well as limitations) markedly different from those of later feminisms. Such modes of reason became the unacceptable unreasons of a later time.

Relegated out of marketplace, guild, and ecclesiastical and court authority, later women lost even the memory of ways of thinking known to their predecessors in the medieval and early modern period as the institutions and ideologies of modernity took shape. Engendered from within these structures and modes of thought, modern feminisms work their way out from an imposed domestic space and an apparently naturalized heterosexual imperative. Thus, for example, *Vindication of the Rights of Women* (1792) by Mary Wollstonecraft, a fountainhead of modern international feminism, cannot keep from being betrayed by its assumptions as it demands women's right to move from an infantilizing identification with a "naturally" subservient "Eve" to achieve the reasoning powers of "Adam."[3] The *Vindication's* model for citizenship and subjectivity, defined *against* earlier aristocratic and religious values, is foundationally male, bourgeois, and property-owning: the quest for egalitarian terms remains haunted by Adam's householding rule of a relationally and heterosexually defined Eve.[4] Sapphic feminism inhabited an earlier world, one now all but lost to us. Moreover, its championing of women's passions and reasons together addresses issues that now confront us in post-modernity.

Early modern women poets who erotically address other women draw on a courtly world and work salient changes on the petrarchan literary imaginary. Features that distinguish what we identify as sapphic poetry include: (1) loving address by a woman to a woman, often framed as wooer-to-beloved; (2) homage to women of (or in terms of) high social status, emphasizing courtly flourish and context; (3) erotically charged, not just affectionate, language that often plays with the reader's possible discomfort at such woman-to-woman ardor; (4) stock vocabulary, imagery, and modes from the petrarchan tradition; (5) humorous and parodic turns on standard (male-authored) lyric; (6) obvious play with gender roles that mocks assumptions of male superiority and insists on female agency; and (7) dynamic interpersonal intimacy between speaker and addressee that implies or states the equality of subject and object, and contrasts to the speaking-male-to-silent-female conventions of petrarchan address. This celebration of women's affective bonds interrogates men's exclusive discursive agency and undoes women's silence or incapacity.

Baroque sapphic poetry poses an unapologetic erotic rhetoric between women that challenges the heterosexual normativeness customary to our modern era. Equally startling, the Hispanic poets tend to be nuns; the English poets tend to be royalists with Catholic leanings or allegiances. However, we should recall that Catholicism held up, in contrast to the subservient Eve of Protestant iconography, a heroic ideal for women in the Virgin Mary—"Mother of God," "Queen of Heaven"—a powerful as well as beloved intercessor. Catholic tradition also conceptualized an androgyny of the soul that imagined monastic men as well as women as "brides of Christ." As we will show, instructive feminist voicings of desire and critique emerged from the—to today's eyes—"backward" and "unreasonable" settings and ideologies of convent and court, petrarchism and neo-platonism.

Baroque sapphic poems boldly voice women's equality to men. Their authors unabashedly draw (figurative) swords and fence their way into the role of poet, courtier, and swain-at-courtship. The temerity in the poems corresponds to other expressions of ambition and self-valorization by these writers. The English dramatist Aphra Behn declares in her preface to *The Lucky Chance* (1686):

> All I ask, is the Priviledge for my Masculine Part the Poet in me, (if any such you will allow me) to tread in those successful Paths my Predecessors have so long thriv'd in, to take those Measures that both the Ancient and Modern Writers have set me, and by which they pleas'd the World so well: If I must not, because of my Sex, have this Freedom, but that you will usurp all to your selves; I lay down my Quill, and you shall hear no more of me . . . I value Fame as much as if I had been born a *Hero*; and if you rob me of that, I can retire from the ungrateful World, and scorn its fickle Favours. (Behn VII, 217)

Nothing wilts or defers as Behn claims her "Masculine Part," as if she "had been born a *Hero*" whose self-assurance contrasts Wollstonecraft's embattled recourse to the domestic sphere.

Behn's entitlement to an assertive "Masculine" self partakes of the ideal of the *femme forte*, an ambivalently gendered icon of female heroism and leadership, prominent in early modern arts, that hovers behind the courting role of the petrarchan poetry of women wooers of women.[5] An ambitious fragment by English poet and painter Anne Killigrew (1660–1685) renders this ideal in verse rich with images. Alexander and the Greeks "come up to th' *Amazonian Band*" of Thalestris and make "a Hault and a respectful Stand" (Killigrew 4). The women forcefully embody their warrior role: "Down from their shoulders hung a Panthers Hide, / A bow and Quiver ratled by their side; / Their hands a knotty well try'd Speare did bear, / Jocund they seem'd, and quite devoid of fear" (3). Eye-to-eye, the two armies "Did each on other with deep silence look" (4), until Thalestris—"Th'Heroick Queen (whose high pretence to War / Cancell'd the bashful Laws and nicer Bar / of Modesty, which did her Sex restrain)" (5)—strides "boldly" to address her counterpart, Alexander the Great. Thalestris epitomizes the *femme forte*, and the parity in this representation is striking. She enacts an hermaphroditic ideal of human heroism that expresses a "Masculine Part" fully equivalent with the Greek hero and his men.

Sor Juana Inés de la Cruz (1648?–1695), who wrote from court and then convent in New Spain (later Mexico), similarly assumes this parity. A *romance* (literary ballad) addressed to the Countess of Paredes speaks more obliquely but no less firmly:

> Ser mujer, ni estar ausente,
> no es de amarte impedimento;
> pues sabes tú, que las almas
> distancia ignoran y sexo. (Obras completas I, 54–59)

> (Your being a woman, your being gone
> cannot pose the slightest hindrance
> to my love, for you know our souls
> have no gender and know no distance.)[6]

Sor Juana engages a neo-platonic understanding of the "sexless"—we would say genderless—soul that elides masculine and feminine.

Sor Juana's *Answer* or *Respuesta a sor Filotea* (1691), a public defense of her intellectual life in the convent, presents a more careful, ironic statement than Behn's preface. Yet, invoking the centuries-long *querelle des femmes*, she summons a lineage of heroic classical, biblical, and historic women, renowned for political and military power as well as learning:

> Porque veo a una Débora dando leyes, así en lo militar como en lo político, y gobernando el pueblo donde había tantos varones doctos. Veo una sapientísima reina de Sabá, tan docta que se atreve a tentar con enigmas la sabiduría del mayor de los sabios, sin ser por ello reprendida, antes por ello será juez de los incrédulos. Veo tantas y tan insignes mujeres: una adornadas del don de profecía, como una Abigaíl; otras de persuasión, como Ester; otras, de piedad, como Rahab; otras de perseverancia, como Ana, madre de Samuel; y otras infinitas, en otras especies de prendas y virtudes. (*Answer* 76–77)

> (I see a Deborah issuing laws, military as well as political, and governing the people among whom there were so many learned men. I see the exceedingly knowledgeable Queen of Sheba, so learned she dares to test the wisdom of the wisest of all wise men with riddles, without being rebuked for it; indeed, on this very account she is to become judge of the unbelievers. I see so many and such significant women: some adorned with the gift of prophecy, like an Abigail; others, of persuasion, like Esther; others, of piety, like Rahab; others, of perseverance, like Anna [Hannah], the mother of Samuel; and others, infinitely more, with other kinds of qualities and virtues.)

As Sor Juana notes, the Judeo-Christian tradition ranks among its heroes women who exercise wit and agency, both with and over men. She implies the question always found on the philogynist side of the *querelle des femmes*: Why should this standard not be applied in her time?

Sor Juana wrote an even more assertive private defense to a confessor, Antonio Núñez de Miranda, who decried her "profane" public writings and sought to stop them. This letter disputes his entitlement to bend her will in any way:

> ¿... qúal era el dominio directo que tenía V.R. para disponer de mi persona y del alvedrío ... que Dios me dió? ... Tócale a V.R. mi correpción por alguna razón de obligación, de parentesco, crianza, prelacía o tal que cosa? ("La carta" 623–24)
>
> (... what direct authority ... did you have to dispose of my person and the free will given to me by God? ... Does Your Reverence have some rightful say in chastising me by reason of obligation, familial relationship, responsibility for my upbringing, Church authority, or any such thing?)

She acknowledges rightful obedience in formal hierarchical relations, but she denies male rights of dominance over her *as such* ("La carta" 626). It does not occur to her to identify—as it inevitably will Wollstonecraft and the moderns—or to argue against imposed domesticity or infantilism. While she came of age to limited options, they did include the convent as alternative to marriage, a community as opposed to private domesticity, and sacralized celibacy as opposed to a defining heterosexuality. She asserts a worldview by which the laws of the church govern her; the determinations of a self-constituted male supremacy do not. Such *apologiae* by Sor Juana, Behn, and others evince a "resistant" consciousness at once suggestively modern, yet oddly "other": constituted within echoing religious and biblical contexts, in confidently "unreasoning" appeals to authority, in presumption of a public arena of reference with room for them, and in "manly" boldness of address.

Early modern sapphic verse implicitly or explicitly voices a gender-consciousness consistent with the passages above, adding a playfulness that satirizes notions of female obeisance and male prerogative. The authors participate in culturally prestigious forms and forums—that is, "as if [they] had been born a *Hero*." In lyric poetry as in prologues or letters, Behn, Sor Juana, and their fellow/sister poets lay claim to powers of thought and action that in their literary-cultural world are embattled, but not secondary to those of male poets. Stepping into intellectual and aesthetic spaces that will close off after them, these women speak with an unsubmissiveness that later generations will be at pains to regain.

Seventeenth-century sapphic love poetry reworks petrarchan tradition within the conceptual frame of early modern platonism, an ontology that included an erotically coded ideal of the indivisible Beautiful and Good. This homoerotic *kalos* of Greek tradition becomes identified with and accessible to women with the Renaissance rediscovery of Plato. The baroque world, in ways almost masked to us now, offers cultural sites that include a valorized (though disputed) homoeroticism and a heroic female "Good" of learning and nobility.

Platonism was a complex inheritance.[7] Platonic and Aristotelian thought reached pre-modern Europe through the writings of Plotinus of Alexandria (284/5–270 CE) by way of mystical writings by Christian, Jewish, and Islamic authors of the Arab world—Proclus of Constantinople (410?–85), Avicenna (980–1037), Ibn Ezra (1089–1164), Ibn Tufayl (c.1116–1185), and others (Baldwin and Hutton 1–51).[8] This legacy of the eastern Roman empire and the medieval Arab world emphasized the mystical bent of both Plato and Plotinus: their intellectual formulation of the highest human aspiration as *desire* for the divine. Not until the nineteenth-century German dominance of philosophic historiography, did this ontology receive the (somewhat pejorative) designation "neo-platonism." As Aaron Hughes observes, the neo-platonic worldview is "a hybrid—part philosophy, part mysticism, part poetry, part aesthetics" (17) working as "an interface between the visible and the invisible, the particular and the universal, and the transcendent and the ephemeral" (4). Flourishing in baroque literary, visual, musical, and ritual arenas, this worldview underlay the seventeenth-century dispute regarding the "Ancients" and the "Moderns" and infused petrarchan tradition and its sapphic reworkings. In the postmodern era this dynamic, polysemous, and refractory ontology may rise more visibly on our horizon when relativity and quantum physics permeate thinking even at the popular level.

Key tenets recur in the texts of Plato, presenting ultimate human aspiration as notably engaged and embodied: *love*, rather than knowledge or thought. Moreover, the imagined union with the "Beautiful/Good" is profoundly homoerotic, premised on Socratic desire for the exquisite young man of classical Athenian culture. Christian thought reimagines this platonic "highest good" as divine. However, deeply operative remains the idea of an elevating homoerotic union of likeness with another, an ascent of the soul, within a cosmos that phenomenalizes itself in echoing patterns of resemblance—what Hughes terms the "microcosmic-macrocosmic relationship that is at the heart of Neoplatonism" (159). The similarity-premised longing for divine Beauty/Good engages an aesthetically oriented imagination that responds not only rationally, but sensually, to the incarnational presence of a beloved *kalos*.[9] The eroticism and sensuality of this theory, emphasizing mystical experience rather than reason, have continued to vex interpreters. Kenneth Dover notes in much that is written of Platonism,

> an uncritical enthusiasm for the abstract and immutable, as if such an enthusiasm always and necessarily afforded better access to the truth about man [sic], nature and divinity than is afforded by a love of the particular, material and perishable. One consequence of this is that Plato is sometimes welcomed as an ally by people who would not like what they found if they attended less selectively and more precisely to what he actually says. (viii; also 7–8)

Such discrepancy arises already in the Renaissance rediscovery of platonic thought. For enthusiastic humanists of fifteenth-century Italy—Ficino who translated the newly uncovered writings of Plato and Plotinus; his influential supporter and friend Petrarch; and their learned and literary circle—Plato proved eye-openingly exciting *and* troubling.

Discussing translations of the newly (re)discovered platonic manuscripts from Ficino through the sixteenth century, Jill Kraye describes an increasing "straightening-out" of the manifestly "queer" (in our terms) Plato and his thought—a "transformation of Platonic love from an embarrassing liability into a valuable asset" through the altering of the "homosexual and pederastic orientation" (76). Indeed, the translation-adaptation history of Plato's *Symposium* demonstrates how, in explicit ways, the beloved of platonic thought becomes a woman. By 1505, Bembo heterosexualizes the text's ideal and Christianizes this male-female love from the sexual to the spiritual plane—similar to allegorical readings of the biblical Song of Songs. With *The Courtier* (1528), Castiglione replaces the desirable young man found in Plato, Ficino, Pico, and others with "a non-sexual, safely heterosexual Platonic love," as Kraye puts it (85), which nonetheless retains elements of the tutelage in Plato's relationship—an influential rationale for courtly emphasis on women's learning.[10] Petrarchan lyric took up this program of heterosexualizing revision. Nevertheless, flashes of platonic homoeroticism light through the tradition, as in Michelangelo's ardent sonnets to Tommaso de Cavalieri or Shakespeare's to "The Young Man." Women, too, drew on this same-sex eroticism in the poetries of Italy, Spain and New Spain, France, the Netherlands, and England.

Sor Juana's epistolary poems to her viceregal patrons display the confident voice and ennobling address characteristic of the "other" feminism of sapphic discourse. In the poem to "*Divina Lysi mía*" (my divine Lysi, a pastoral name for the vicereine), Sor Juana highlights her dedicatee's aristocratic prestige, while the poem offers metalinguistic justification for her audacity in naming "my Lysi" with the possessive pronoun. The seeming appropriation of the other as "mine" is ironically reversed ("'my jail,' says the prisoner"). Dialectical play here subtly overturns a masculinist petrarchism in the mutually ennobling homoerotic paradigm:[11]

> Error es de la lengua,
> que lo que dice imperio (10)
> del dueño, en el dominio,
> parezcan posesiones en el siervo.
> Mi rey, dice el vasallo;
> mi cárcel, dice el preso;
> y el más humilde esclavo, (15)
> sin agraviarlo, llama suyo al dueño.
> Así, cuando yo mía
> te llamo, no pretendo
> que juzguen que eres mía,
> sino sólo que ser tuya quiero. (20)
> . . .
> Que mirarte tan alta, (26)
> no impide a mi denuedo;
> que no hay Deidad segura
> al altivo volar del pensamiento.
> . . .
> En fin, yo de adorarte
> el delito confieso;
> si quieres castigarme, (35)
> este mismo castigo será premio. (*OC* I 210–11)
>
> (This is an error of language
> for what it terms the dominion
> of the master, to express ownership,
> seem to be possessions of the servant.
> "My king," says the vassal;
> "my jail," says the prisoner;
> and the lowliest slave,
> giving no offense, says "my master."
> And so when I call you
> mine, I make no claim
> to have others think you mine;
> it is only that I wish to be yours.
> . . .

And seeing you so high above me
in no way hinders my daring;
for no Deity is proof
against the lofty flights of thought.
. . .
In sum, I confess my crime
to be this: that I adore you;
if you wish to punish me,
that punishment will be my reward.)

Platonically, the perfection of the love object elevates the subject. The poem vibrates with a flirtatious confidence underscored by its hyperbole. In Sor Juana's feminist voicing, both women merit a degree of honor that has no awareness of the resistance to infantilism that we see in Wollstonecraft.

"*Divina Lysi mía*" accentuates a complex dynamic of desire-within-dependence as the poet praises the noble woman in terms of address usually reserved for *her* superior, the "lord" or man above her.[12] Another poem addressed to the vicereine highlights the literary convention of positing the "lady" as "lord" (*OC* I 212). "¡Qué bien, divina Lysi, / tu sacra deidad sabe . . . !" (l. 25) (How well, divine Lysi, your sacred holiness knows) calls the vicereine "divino Dueño" and "hermoso Dueño" (l. 30) (lovely master). The convention reaches back to troubadour poets who customarily addressed the lady, a social superior, as *senhor* (in fact, María Luisa is a countess). Purity, nobility, perfection, an enrapturing distance in the beloved, all enhance the desirability of the other and ennoble both women: a cross-dressing feminism in a more "lordly" key than we recognize readily.

Love poems in English by women to women similarly voice the advocacy and agency of this feminist "road not taken" by later generations. The mirroring neoplatonic worldview pervades such poems even as they develop two themes: (1) flexibility with regard to gender and sexuality as the devotion of the poet for her beloved follows an eroticized androgynous ideal of wooing and union; and (2) the enlistment of the *femme forte* and the Amazons of classical antiquity as heroic models. Katherine Philips (1631/2–1664) lived the greater part of her short life in Wales. Talented and ambitious, the young Philips was poised to move into London literary circles at the time of her death (Thomas 17–20). She wrote many amorous addresses to and celebrations of women. "Mutual Affection between Orinda and Lucasia" is a song of the 1650s set to music by Henry Lawes, court composer for King Charles I and Queen Henrietta Maria. "Lucasia" was the pastoral name for Philips's friend and beloved, Anne Owens.

Both text and tune playfully recast verities in the metaphysical style of John Donne.[13] Philips's poem threads the courtship trope through paradoxical juxtapositions of disparate realms—religious, political, alchemical—weaving together startling figures for the power of love between two women. She declares the "subjectivity" of equal "selves" in an explicit parody of Donne. "Come, my *Lucasia*, since we see, / that miracles men's faith do move / By wonder and by Prodigy, / To the dull, angry world let's prove / There's a religion in our Love" (Philips 90, ll.1–5).

Through six stanzas, the song steps from one antithetical, Donne-like field of institutional reference to another, pervaded by the mirroring strategies of neoplatonic correspondence among these spheres. Stanza 1 calls on the theological concept of miracles as evidence; the figure equates "Religion" and woman-for-woman "Love" and invokes "wonder" and "prodigie" to constitute proof. The playfully irreverent argument conflates paradoxes conventional to theological polemic and those of petrarchan devotion through references to religious "election," alchemical transformation, "thrones," and "captivity." The fifth stanza notably reformulates masculinist and imperial "She is all States, and All Princes I" from Donne's "The Sunne Rising" (27, l. 21). A "rebound" of the women's love "shuffles titles" so as to make this devoted couple equals: "We are our selves but by rebound, / And all our titles shuffled so, / Both Princes, and both Subjects too" (ll. 23–25). Philips empowers herself and her beloved with this pointedly feminist reworking. The characterization of both women as "Princes" underscores simultaneously the courtly frame of reference and the flexibly gendered ideal; the conflation of "Princes" and "Subjects" indicates the mirroring reflexivity of platonism as well as the equalizing reformulation of Donne's image.

Philips's "Friendship in Emblem, or the Seale, to my dearest Lucasia" works as a double conceit ekphrastically describing an emblem—probably a material item—that in turn represents the friendship (106–108). The poem reverberates with the multi-sensory, microcosmic-macrocosmic correspondences of neoplatonism to visualize designs inscribed on an object that emblematizes the love. Like "Mutual Affection," "Friendship in Emblem" reworks to feminist effect a well-known image from Donne—here, the compass of "A Valediction: Forbidding Mourning" (54–55), wherein two souls "which are one" are (paradoxically) two "As stiffe twin compasses are two" (l. 26). In Philips's poem a "Seale" with flaming hearts is surrounded by "compasses that stand above" to "Express this great immortall Love" (ll. 21–22). However Philips pointedly reimagines the emblem of male domination in Donne's address to his mistress:

"Thy soule the fixt foot, makes no show / To Move, but doth, if th'other doe." Philips's image gives both parties agency: "The steddy part does regulate / And make the wanderer's motion streight" (ll. 31–32). The "friendship" also serves the *topos* of the *femme forte* as it "teach[es] the world heroique things" (l. 40) even as it steers a steadily erotic course. Just when the verse seems about to flee embodiment, it reaffirms the bodily world of sensory experience: "Their points, like bodys, separate, / But head, like soules, knows no such fate. / And as each part so well is knit, / That their embraces ever fitt" (ll. 51–54).

Sor María de Santa Isabel (mid-seventeenth century) collected her poems under the martial pseudonym "Marcia Belisarda" in a carefully prepared manuscript that shows intent to publish, although this was never realized.[14] Born in Toledo, Spain, Belisarda became a nun, began to write verse at twenty-seven years of age, and was still alive in 1646. She composed several gallant love poems to women and throughout her poetry employs the whole range of grammatical gender modes for speakers and addressees (Powell). The sonnet "Si no impide mi amor el mismo cielo" (If heaven itself does not impede my love) responds to an assigned topic for a poetry contest.[15] The theme, *no desmayarse* (not fainting away) in the face of *un desdén* (disdain) reflects a well-worn petrarchan complaint on the beloved lady's coldness. However, Belisarda deftly gives feminist dimensions to "not fainting away." Rebuff by the beloved is requisite to petrarchan tradition. On one level, this poetic speaker faces—and faces down—confrontation with the "rigores" (1.2) (cruelties) of "Jacinta" that are a masculinist legacy. Typical of petrarchism, the speaker will stay true to love, even if "en vez de amor me pagas con enojos" (l. 11) (instead of love you repay me with vexations).

Subtle indications point to another discursive level, however, that lifts the poem out of its assigned conventionality and gives a larger dimension to love. The poet confronts a literary and social culture that would cast her, *qua* female, as spoken-of, not speaking. However, Belisarda refuses to faint away. The term "disdain" derives (in English as in Spanish) from the Latin *dedignare* or "rehusar como indigno" (Corominas 207) (to reject as unworthy). The poetic speaker here rejects such denial of herself. Her initial insistence that only "el mismo cielo" (heaven itself) can "imp[edir] mi amor" (l. 1) (impede my love)—regardless of petrarchan resistance from the beloved—suggests that the writer will not be deterred from her "beloved" poetic vocation, whatever "rigores" she may encounter. As if to underscore this feminist subtext, the poem introduces the multivalent term "querellas" (l. 12) (complaint, objection), which includes dispute raised in court or self-defense. The speaker argues not only for the right to enjoy the beloved's beautiful eyes. Belisarda claims a full poetic capacity that assumes her capability and reasoning: after all, her love—poetic in many senses—is "en razón fundado" (l. 4) (founded in reason).

Sor Violante del Cielo (1601?/07?–1693) wrote in Spanish and Portuguese from a Dominican convent in Lisbon. Her extensively woman-centered poems evoke a Catholic setting and courtly connections, and display the features of sapphic verse: eroticism, playfulness, female advocacy, and petrarchan and neo-platonic lineage. The prominence of love poems to women in her *Rimas varias* (Rouen, 1646) suggests their prestige: a sonnet-sequence opens the book with dedication to female objects of love and admiration (sonnets 1–4 and 6–9).[16] Author, patron, and publisher position these examples of a prestigious mode prominently to woo and win readers.

Violante also has a title-shuffling, female-empowering approach in address to women interlocutors. Her poems to women present problematic as well as valued sides to the love and friendship—and without reference to male presence (or absence). In the *romance* "Amada prenda del alma" (Beloved treasure of my soul), an all-female love triangle implicitly calls into question the hegemony of heterosexuality and its corollary, male entitlement to possession of women. The speaker hyperbolically praises her beloved (both grammatically female) with petrarchan vocabulary and neo platonic elevation: "treasure," "zone of heaven," "lovely sun," "planet," and "prize" (ll. 1–13). The complex relationship between speaker, beloved, and a third woman named "Nise" is vital and absorbing—rife with the ironies, tensions, and satisfactions of courtship. The final stanza underscores this completeness of female-female relationship: "Todo, en fin, sois, prenda mía; / pues hallo junto en vos, / si premios para el deseo, / lazos para el corazón (ll. 61–64) (In sum, you are all things, my lovely: / for I find joined in you / not only rewards for desire, / but bonds to knit the heart). This worldview neither rejects men nor finds them necessary—a feminist position all the stronger for its understatement, especially in contrast to later generations' need for combative defensiveness to claim intellectual and creative space.

Aphra Behn (1640?–1689), a playwright, poet, novelist, and translator active in London literary and court circles, was the second-most-produced playwright of her generation. A number of addresses to women—some of them extremely erotic—are found in Behn's poetry and merit consideration in terms of the themes posed here. As in the love triangle portrayed by Sor Violante, Behn's "To My Lady Morland at Tunbri[d]ge" proposes a wry alternative to female competition. Hyperbolic praise is lavished on the addressee, who now receives the adoration of the speaker's own former suitor, "Amyntas Faithless Swain" (Behn I, 61–62). An extravagant epic simile (ll. 1–13) opens the poem, identifying the conquering Cloris with the *femme forte*. "As when a Conqu'rour does in Triumph come, / And proudly leads the vanguish'd Captives home," the poem begins, and then continues for a dozen lines of description of a triumphant "Prince" entering as "the Joyful People croud in ev'ry Street." Behn's extended figure draws on the cross-gendering and boldly stated equivalences of the *femme forte* tradition to convey the power of such "Beauty." But in the sapphic mode, these conquering "Marvels" and "Beauty" sweep the speaker too into adoration as the elaborate simile resolves in an enrapturing sapphic moment: "So when the Marvels by Report I knew, / Of how much Beauty, *Cloris*, dwelt in you; / . . . I wish'd to see, and much a Lover grew" (ll. 13–17). Such love surmounts rivalry: "I came and saw, and blest my Destiny; / I found it Just you should out-Rival me" (ll. 19–20). However, typical of such poems, the conventions sprout with a baroque excess that ripples with humor and parody. Nonetheless, "To My Lady Morland" at its center advocates, like Sor Violante's *romance*, a wry female agency and alliance.

Even more explicitly neo platonic and playful—in a mode reminiscent of Sor Juana—is Behn's "To the fair Clarinda, who made Love to me, imagin'd more than Woman" (Behn I 288).[17] Though the poem is frequently anthologized and commented upon, its parodic character—especially vis-à-vis the petrarchan framework—and its relationship to neoplatonism and pan-European sapphic poetry need to be recognized. Behn's erotic title recasts the conventional apostrophe to the alluring but aloof petrarchan mistress to characterize the dual, or ambiguous, gender of the beloved "Clarinda" (whether a physical or figurative hermaphroditism or androgyny remains unclear). Bi-gendered epithets frame the courtly address to this ambiguously gendered "mistress": "Fair lovely Maid" . . . "Lovely Charming Youth." Behn plays on the conventional seduction of the literary pastoral with the ambisexuality of "Clarinda": "While the bright Nymph betrays us to the Swain." The poem then works out feminist implications of this "betrayal."

At midpoint Behn advocates the advantage of love with such a "mistress": "That we might Love, and yet be Innocent." A startling serpentine image then interjects phallic resonance—especially in our post-Freudian context—and the iconography of the Edenic Fall: "For who, that gathers fairest Flowers believes / A Snake lies hid beneath the Fragrant Leaves." The satanic "Snake" and Edenic "Leaves" invoke the religious shaping of sexual mores that for Behn's generation certainly carried overtones of the biblically inspired "reforms" of Puritan policy and, of course, the anti-feminist Eden of Milton's *Paradise Lost*.

A more liberatory feminist resolution to Behn's poem opens up a neoplatonic space for a "third sex" and a freer love as the text releases its pastoral and biblical tensions into a flight of classical allusion (l. 18). "Thou beauteous Wonder of a different kind," the speaker exclaims, lifting us to an admiring neo-platonic awe. Leaving behind anxieties about "hidden Snakes," the final sestet shifts from the abstract pronominative *thou* and *thee* to a double-naming of the paradoxical "Clarinda" as "Soft *Cloris* with dear *Alexis* join'd." Both names carry transgressive and homoerotic implications from antiquity: "Chloris" signifies a prostitute as well as the goddess of flowers, and "Alexis" is the youth beloved by the shepherd of Virgil's unabashedly homoerotic second eclogue (Lempriere 162 and 39). "We" are called at the poem's end to "extend" our "noblest Passions" in a final chiasmic allusion to the ancient classical world: "The Love to *Hermes, Aphrodite* the Friend." In the passionate clasp of "Love" and "Friendship" stands the hermaphroditic Clarinda, resonant evocation of the beloved *kalos* of platonic tradition. Clarinda rises before us, "this beauteous Wonder"—homosexual, intimate, paradoxical, ennobling.

Like other sapphist poets, Behn steers directly, if parodically, into traditions that she inherits: the culturally privileged petrarchan paradigm of address to the mistress, the related pastoral *topoi*, the realm of biblical allusion, and the final neo platonic move to the homoerotically inclined realm of classical mythology (Hammond 46–61). At the same time, a feminist Behn voices the poet as a woman, a NOT silent mistress, stepping out of the conventional female silence and lack of agency pervading these traditions. Indeed, we cannot assign solely feminine or masculine gender even to the speaker, who after all shares with the richly ambiguous addressee, membership in "our sex"—which now has to include the "third."

We propose a coherent, alternate feminism voiced in this corpus of love poems by women to women in the lyric discourse of early modern Europe.[18] Particular well-wrought poems—for example Behn's "Fair Clarinda" or Sor Juana's *romance* 19—have become known and intensively studied, with fascination for the same-sex passion they evoke. But critical consideration has treated them as idiosyncratic phenomena. We suggest that these poems belong in a tradition that presents a conscious, shared reworking of the petrarchan literary imaginary that early modern women employed, but which modernity has not sufficiently recognized. The majority of such poems—for example, those by Belisarda—remain in obscurity, unpublished, and critically unexplored. Further, as a tradition, these sapphic poems work cumulatively to convey a feminist message that carries strengths unfamiliar to us, based as they are upon a different set of premises for thinking about gender and women's advancement. These cheeky, bold, ironic, and passionate voicings of women's love offer elements that the post-Enlightenment valorization of incorporeal "reason" and modern feminism's identification with bourgeois (heterosexual) citizenry have shied away from: confident assumptions of equivalence with men; strong agency; passionate eroticism; ennobling oneself in surrender to love for a reflectingly noble other.

The cross-dressing eroticism of this courting poetry steers directly into that "sexual character" that has been used to denigrate women and that has haunted and intimidated the feminism of Wollstonecraft's era and since. The flirtatiousness and buoyant humor exercised by Sor Juana and Aphra Behn construct—as they both note—a kind of parity. Proceeding from a neoplatonic worldview that has remained all but impossible for moderns to comprehend, baroque sapphic poetry evokes a more inter-resonant, more polysemous, and more dynamic universe whose ennobling of women strides free of the anxiously relational apologetic of Wollstonecraft's time and later. With the eye-to-eye forcefulness of Killigrew's Thalestris, the accomplished yet mysteriously obscure Belisarda declares in her manuscript prologue, "que quien dio alma a la mujer la dio al hombre, y que no es de otra calidad que ésta aquélla, y que a muchas concedió lo que negó a muchos" (Olivares and Boyce, *En desagravio*) (that the One who gave a soul to woman gave the same to man, and that the former soul is of no different quality than the latter; indeed, that One granted to many women what was denied to many men). Far from abject, these women-authored voices that desire and celebrate women display a confident sense of divine and noble right. They command our attention.

Notes

We wish to thank the University of Oregon Center for the Study of Women in Society and the Oregon Humanities Center for their generous support of this project.

1. Writers of such poems include, in Italian, Isabella di Morra (1515/20–1548?), Laura Terracina (1519–1577?), Isotta Brembate (1530?–1586), and Tarquinia Molza (1542–1617); see Jaffe, 144, 163ff., 280ff., and 320ff. In French, they are Anne de Rohan (1584), Mme. de C*** (n.d.), and Pauline de Simiane (1676–1737); see Stanton, 71 and 96–99. In Flemish and Dutch, they are Katharina Questiers (1631–1669), Cornelia Van Der Veer (1639–1702?), Katharina Lescailje (1649–1711), and Titia Brongersma (late seventeenth century); see Meijer, 59–61, and van Gemert, whose study reveals features suggesting that this mode is pan-European.
2. The term "sapphic" usefully conveys the presence of a classical past associated with a valorized homoeroticism. Sapphic poems constituted a fashion in several senses

of that word: as a "prevailing style or custom, as in dress or behavior," something in "the current mode," or the "style characteristic of the social elite" (*American Heritage Dictionary*, 4th ed., 2000).
3. Writing from an Anglo-Protestant background, Wollstonecraft critiques the idea of woman's "natural" inferiority in John Milton's *Paradise Lost* (1667) wherein Eve addresses Adam: "God is *thy law, thou mine*: to know no more / Is woman's *happiest* knowledge and her *praise*." Wollstonecraft objects: "These are exactly the arguments that I have used to children" (101). Wollstonecraft's text is foundational to European feminisms.
4. An increasingly capitalist, Protestant-influenced Europe founded individuals' "rights" in terms of a relational, heterosexual pairing (Milton's Eve and Adam) that relegated women to the domestic sphere. According to Wiesner-Hanks, "'Domestic' or 'relational' feminists [in the post-Enlightenment era] . . . thus acknowledged [we would say 'conceded'] the private nature of the household" as women's subordinate sphere; she continues, "One wonders if in the long run a continued assertion of the public nature of women's domestic responsibilities might have proved a more secure base for the expansion of women's political rights" ("Women's Authority" 35–36). She further observes that Protestantism "set up a uniform ideal of sexual life, with marriage and parenthood as essential for both sexes, while Catholicism and Orthodoxy endorsed a range of options" (*Christianity* 265).
5. See Barash, *English Women's Poetry,* 32ff. and Dixon, 158ff. On gender ambiguity and the *femme forte*, see Baumgärtel, 97–117. On the waning of the warrior heroine, see Dugaw, *Warrior Women*, 65–90.
6. *Obras completas* is henceforth *OC*. Translations are by the authors unless otherwise noted.
7. For a survey, see Wiener, 371–78 and 495–515.
8. An influence on St. Augustine of Hippo, Plotinus's reworkings of Plato (426?–347 B.C.E.) and Aristotle (384–22 B.C.E.) shaped medieval philosophy. Until the modern era, works by Plotinus were thought to be by Plato and Aristotle; see Hughes, 51 and 154. The legacy of Arabic thought was reworked by the Dominican Thomas Aquinas (1225–1274) who turned Christian philosophy in an Aristotelian direction. The nearly contemporary Franciscan theologian John Duns Scotus (c.1266–1308) maintained a more "Plato/Plotinus-friendly" Christianizing of the ancient systems of thinking. Hebreo and Arabic traditions of platonism in Spain may have influenced the mystical spirituality of Teresa of Avila, John of the Cross, and Ignatius Loyola.
9. See also Roe, Medcalf, Robb, and Orgel and Strong (19ff. and 47ff.). Ignatius of Loyola designed his *Spiritual Exercises* to lead the practitioner to such a neoplatonic "ascent" as we outline here. Significantly, he used the verb "*sentir*' for a neoplatonically *felt* knowing of the divine.
10. The Renaissance negotiation of the "queerness" of Plato becomes apparent when the prevalent *trattori de amore* form is taken up by a woman. Tullia d'Aragona's dialogue

is cast between herself and the cleric, Benedetto Varchi, who defends the homoerotic ideal even as she attacks such "lascivious love for youths" (95). Heterosexualizing the platonic same-sex union so that woman becomes the beloved counterpart, Tullia asks: "I should still like to know why a woman cannot be loved with this same type of love?" (97). Varchi was reprimanded by ecclesiastical authorities for his relations with university students. He repeatedly defended their spiritual character. Tullia's remarks strike a tone that we today would find "homophobic" (95ff.).

11. On this petrarchan parody in Sor Juana, see Bergmann and Middlebrook, 153–56; in baroque sapphic poetry in general, see Dugaw and Powell.
12. Reiger states, "Although the troubadour's predominantly 'normal' address for his lady is *(ma) domna* or *bona/bella domna*, it is often replaced by the masculine form *mi dons*"; she concludes that the medieval Bieris could not have been a lesbian (74). For a refutation, see Sautman and Sheingorn, 30–31. Some of Sor Juana's poems taken to be addressed to men should be considered indeterminate; they may have been addressed to women.
13. On parody in the musical setting, see Dugaw and Powell.
14. Manuscript 7469, Biblioteca Nacional, Madrid. For a selection, see Olivares and Boyce, *Tras el espejo*.
15. Manuscript 7469:18r: "A consonantes forzosos sobre que habían escrito sonetos con asuntos diferentes diferentes personas, diéronme por asunto no desmayar a vista de un desdén" (To obligatory rhymes, with which various people had written sonnets with different themes, they gave me the topic of not fainting away at being treated with disdain).
16. For a modern edition, see Mendes; selections are in Olivares and Boyce, *Tras el espejo*.
17. Many readings of Behn and Philips discuss homosexuality. See Andreadis; Barash, *English Women's Poetry* and "Political Possibilities"; and Wahl, 130–70.
18. Sor Juana's literary models were almost entirely European (classical Roman and Spanish); her sociohistorical identity as a *criolla* ("pure" Spanish descent in the "New" world) in relation to her intellectual self-positioning is examined by Martínez-San Miguel.

Works Cited

American Heritage Dictionary, 4th ed. (Boston: Houghton Mifflin, 2000).
Andreadis, Harriette. *Sappho in Early Modern England*. Chicago: University of Chicago Press, 2001.
Baldwin, Anna, and Sarah Hutton, eds. *Platonism and the English Imagination*. Cambridge: Cambridge University Press, 1994.
Barash, Carol. *English Women's Poetry, 1649–1714*. Oxford: Clarendon Press, 1996.

———. "The Political Possibilities of Desire: Teaching the Erotic Poems of Behn." in Fox, Christopher, ed., *Teaching Eighteenth-Century Poetry*. New York: AMS Press, 1990. 159–76.

Baumgärtel, Bettina. "Is the King Genderless? The Staging of the Female Regent as Minerva Pacifica." in Dixon, Annettee, ed. *Women Who Ruled: Queens, Goddesses, Amazons in Renaissance and Baroque Art*. Ann Arbor, MI: University of Michigan Museum of Art, 2002. 97–117.

Behn, Aphra. *Works*. Ed. Janet Todd. Columbus: Ohio State University Press, 1992–96.

Bergmann, Emilie, and Leah Middlebrook. "La mujer petrarquista: 'Hollines y peces.' Poética renacentista de la óptica de sor Juana," Ed. Iris M. Zavala. *Breve historia feminista de la literature española (en lengua castellana)*. Vol. II, *La mujer en la literatura española: Modos de representación desde la Edad Media hasta el siglo XVII*. Barcelona: Anthropos, 1995. 145–58.

Corominas, Joan. *Breve diccionario etimológico de la lengua español*. Madrid: Gredos, 1980.

Dixon, Annette, ed. *Women Who Ruled: Queens, Goddesses, Amazons in Renaissance and Baroque Art*. Ann Arbor, MI: University of Michigan Museum of Art, 2002.

Donne, John. *John Donne: A Selection of His Poetry*. Ed. John Hayward. New York: Penguin, 1985.

Dover, Kenneth, ed. *Plato: Symposium*. Cambridge: Cambridge University Press, 1980.

Dugaw, Dianne. *Warrior Women and Popular Balladry, 1650–1850*. Chicago: University of Chicago Press, 1996. First published 1989 by Cambridge University Press.

Dugaw, Dianne and Amanda Powell. "Sapphic Self-Fashioning in the Baroque Era: Women's Petrarchan Parody in English and Spanish." *Studies in Eighteenth-Century Culture* 35 (2006): 129–162.

Fox, Christopher, ed. *Teaching Eighteenth-Century Poetry*. New York: AMS Press, 1990.

Hammond, Paul. *Figuring Sex between Men from Shakespeare to Rochester*. Oxford: Clarendon Press, 2002.

Hughes, Aaron. *The Texture of the Divine: Imagination in Medieval Islamic and Jewish Thought*. Bloomington, IN: Indiana University Press, 2004.

Jaffe, Irma, with Gernando Colombardo. *Shining Eyes, Cruel Fortune: The Lives and Loves of Italian Renaissance Women Poets*. New York: Fordham University Press, 2002.

Juana Inés de la Cruz. *The Answer / La Respuesta*. Ed. and trans. Arenal, Electa, and Amanda Powell. New York: Feminist Press, 1994.

———. "La *carta* de sor Juana al padre Núñez (1682)." Ed. Antonio Alatorre. *Nueva revista de Filología Hispánica* 35 (1987): 591–673.

———. *Obras completas*. Ed. Alfonso Méndez Plancarte. 4 vols. México City: Fondo de Cultura económica, 1994.

Killigrew, Anne. *Poems*. London: Samuel Lowndes, 1686.

Kraye, Jill. "The Transformation of Platonic Love in the Italian Renaissance." in Baldwin, Anna and Sarah Hutton eds. *Platonism and the English Imagination*. Cambridge: Cambridge University Press, 1994. 76–85.

Laqueur, Thomas. *Making Sex: Body and Gender from the Greeks to Freud.* Cambridge, MA: Harvard University Press, 1990.
Lempriere, John. *Lempriere's Classical Dictionary.* London: Bracken, 1984.
María de Santa Isabel ("Marcia Belisarda"). Manuscript 7469. Biblioteca Nacional, Madrid.
Martínez-San Miguel, Yolanda. *Saberes americanos: subalternidad y epistemología en los escritos de Sor Juana.* Pittsburgh, PA: Instituto Internacional de Literatura Iberoamericana, University of Pittsburgh Press, 1999.
Medcalf, Stephen. "Shakespeare on Beauty, Truth, and Transcendence." in Baldwin and Hutton: 117–25.
Meijer, Maaike, ed. *The Defiant Muse: Dutch and Flemish Feminist Poems from the Middle Ages to the Present.* New York: Feminist Press, 1998.
Olivares, Julián. *En desagravio de las damas: Studies on Women's Poetry of the Golden Age.* Ashville, NC: Pegasus Press, forthcoming 2006.
———. *Tras el espejo la musa escribe: Lírica femenina de las Siglos de Oro.* Madrid: Siglo Veintiuno, 1993.
Orgel, Stephen, and Roy Strong. *Inigo Jones: The Theatre of the Stuart Court.* 2 vols. Berkeley: University of California Press, 1973.
Paden, William D. *The Voice of the Trobairitz.* Philadelphia: University of Pennsylvania Press, 1989.
Philips, Katherine. *The Collected Works of Katherine Philips.* Vol.1, *Poems.* Ed. Patrick Thomas. Stump Cross, UK: Stump Cross, 1990.
Powell, Amanda. "'*O qué diversas estamos, / dulce prenda, vos y yo!*' Multiple Voicings in Love Poems to Women by Marcia Berlisarda, Catalina Clara Ramírez de Guzmán, and Sor Violante del Cielo." in Olivares, Julián. *En desagravio de las damas: Studies on Women's Poetry of the Golden Age.* Ashville, N.C.: Pegasus Press, forthcoming 2006.
Reiger, Angelica. "Was Bieris de Romans a Lesbian?" in Paden, William D. *The Voice of the Trobairitz.* Philadelphia: University of Pennsylvania Press, 1989. 73–94.
Robb, Nesca. *Neoplatonism of the Italian Renaissance.* London: George Allen and Unwin, 1935.
Roe, John. "Italian NeoPlatonism in the Poetry of Sidney, Shakespeare, Chapman, and Donne." in Baldwin, Anna and Sarah Hutton, eds. *Platonism and the English Imagination.* Cambridge: Cambridge University Press, 1994. 100–16.
Sautman, Francesca Canadé, and Pamela Sheingorn. *Same Sex Love and Desire among Women in the Middle Ages.* New York: Palgrave, 2001.
Stanton, Domna, ed. *The Defiant Muse: French Feminist Poems from the Middle Ages to the Present.* New York: Feminist Press, 1986.
Thomas, Patrick. "Introduction: Biographical Note." in Philips, Katherine. *The Collected Works of Katherine Philips.* Vol. 1, Poems. Ed. Patrick Thomas. Stump Cross, UK: Stump Cross, 1990. 1–39.

Tullia d'Aragona. *Dialogue on the Infinity of Love.* Ed. and trans. Rinaldina Russell and Bruce Merry. Chicago: University of Chicago Press, 1997.

van Gemert, Lia. "Hiding Behind Words? Lesbianism in Seventeenth-Century Dutch Poetry." *Thamyris* 2 (1995): 11–44.

Violante del Cielo/do Ceu. *Rimas varias.* Rouen [Ruán], France: Maurry, 1646.

———. *Rimas várias.* Ed. Margarida Vieira Mendes. Lisbon: Presença, 1993.

Wahl, Elizabeth. *Invisible Relations: Representations of Female Intimacy in the Age of Enlightenment.* Stanford, CA: Stanford University Press, 1999.

Wiener, Philip, ed. *Dictionary of the History of Ideas.* 5 vols. New York: Charles Scribner's Sons, 1973.

Wiesner-Hanks, Merry. *Christianity and Sexuality in the Early Modern World: Regulating Desire, Reforming Practice.* London: Routledge, 2000.

———. "Women's Authority in the State and Household in Early Modern Europe." in Dixon, Annette, ed. *Women Who Ruled: Queens, Goddesses, Amazons in Renaissance and Baroque Art.* Ann Arbor, MI: University of Michigan Museum of Art, 2002. 27–39.

Wollstonecraft, Mary. *A Vindication of the Rights of Woman.* Ed. Miriam Brody Kramnick. New York: Penguin, 1975.

Part II
Of Houses and Cities: Early Modern Spaces and the Aporias of Baroque Reason

♦ 7

The Foreigner and the Citizen:
A Dialogue on Good Government in Spanish Naples

John A. Marino

> I return therefore to say that the city of Naples, by
> not having taken care to have written its own
> history, is subject to the lies of foreigners; those
> foreign, badly informed writers with little love for
> Naples have spoken of her without conforming to
> the truth, but according to their various passions.
> —Tommaso Costo, *Apologia Istorica del Regno di Nagoli*[1]

To whom does history belong, and for whom will the story of the past become a part of their present? History does not belong to the actors who make it, but rather to those who write it. In the Renaissance commonplace, fame yields to time; and thus, Achilles gives way to Homer, who memorializes the warrior's deeds. But when foreigners write the history of a place or a people not their own, whose truth do they tell? Are they subject to distortions and lies, ruled by their passions rather than reason? On the other hand, what authorizes the native, rather than the other, to tell the truth?

In full baroque fashion, Giulio Cesare Capaccio (1552–1634) uses the conceit between a foreigner/stranger newly arrived by ship in Naples and a Neapolitan citizen/guide to write a 1,024-page dialogue, *Il Forastiero*. Capaccio considers that the dialogue form, with its introductory frame of praise for the contemporary city and its many luminaries, the disputations, and numerous digressions of a Neapolitan insider and foreign outsider, is better than narrative history, because traditional history does not provide a sufficient style to explain his ideas. The dialogue alone allows him to offer such a great vastness of new thoughts and so many things that a curious man would judge worthy of taking account. The form of conversational exchange allows Capaccio to relate the marvels of Naples in their universal variety of descriptions, reports, unexpected royal events, governments, wars, memories of ancient things, the succession of states, encomia of families and persons worthy of honor, and a thousand similar things which entertain a beautiful creativity to draw lessons, and which are useful for a variety of ways of knowing.[2] His dialogue, then, can transcend history to become, in the best tradition of Renaissance humanism, philosophical disputation and moral instruction for the ruling class.

The authority of Capaccio's dialogical scene depends on his long lists and seemingly interminable details in a standard Counter-Reformation rhetorical theory that derives from Giambattista Manso (ca. 1560-1645), the leader of the Neapolitan Accademia degli Oziosi, to which Capaccio is a founding member. Manso's *Del dialogo: Trattato del Marchese della Villa* (1628) pays lip-service to their common mentor Tasso and Tasso's *Discourse on the Art of the Dialogue* (1585).[3] Like Manso, Capaccio downplays the delight and pleasure in the re-created conversation of dialogue in order to emphasize the overriding purpose of a dialogue as effective, persuasive didacticism for a beneficial moral lesson. Capaccio's dialogue hides no heterodox opinions and harbors no comic irony, but instead relies on esoteric analysis through long discourses by the *Cittadino*. The *forastiero*, a word that literally means someone from the wilds of the woods rather than the civilization of the city, is hardly a rustic interlocutor, but such an erudite literatus that he presents himself as traveling around the world for curiosity to learn many things that not everyone has a taste for, such as the origin and beauties of cities, the customs of peoples, the way of life of men, the movements of war, the varieties of dominions, the intrigues of governments, the provisions of laws, the practices of knights, the goings-on of citizens, buildings, paintings, statues, the policing of inhabitants, and every other similar thing that occurs in a noble city, and particularly in the famous city of Naples, which is envied by all the other most famous (cities) of Europe. Yet, the foreigner is merely a stage prop who asks leading questions and responds in knowing approval to the Citizen-Capaccio, who is *un virtuoso di tutte le discipline*.[4] In *Il Forastiero*, Capaccio bows in imitation of Tasso's own voice as a Forestiero Napolitano in many of his dialogues; for example, in *Il Malpiglio overo de la corte* (1585) (The Malpiglio, or the Court), Tasso employs a Forastiero Napolitano as the chief interlocutor on court life by explaining how to win grace from princes and avoid the envy and ill will of courtiers to Vincenzo and Giovanlorenzo Malpiglio, father and son in the court of Ferrara.[5] Back in Capaccio's scene in Naples, the tables are turned as a visiting Forastiero meets the Cittadino Napolitano, but the knowledgeable and polished Neapolitan courtier is still the center of attention as he explains things to his dialogic partner.

Late sixteenth-century local Neapolitan antiquarian studies and historical writings established a necessary context for Capaccio's foreigner-citizen dialogue. What makes this half-forgotten dialogic history important, however, is not only its creation of a national history for the city and Kingdom of Naples, but also its attempt to resolve the Renaissance debate on the problem of good government.[6] The political and philosophical debate on the nature of the state finds the Counter-Reformation Neapolitan historians in the Catholic anti-Machiavelli camp, both in their rethinking of the origins of ancient Italy and their use of examples for contemporary Naples circa 1600. Prioritizing Naples raises it above Rome, which in turn changes the relationship between its papal prince and the Spanish monarch, who at one and the same time as king of Naples was required to present the annual tribute of a white horse, the *chinea*, to his papal lord.

Pandolfo Collenuccio's 1498 *Compendio de le istorie del Regno di Napoli* (Summary of the Histories of the Neapolitan Kingdom), which saw fifteen partial or complete Italian editions between 1539 and 1613—four of them commented upon, corrected, and continued by Tommaso Costo (1545?–1612) in his *Giunta*—is the starting point for sixteenth-century Neapolitan historiography.[7] The crisis of the French invasions of 1494 and the loss of the Kingdom's independent monarchy lay behind Collenuccio's original inquiry back to ancient and medieval times from the ancient Greek origins of Naples to 1459. His experience as an ambassador from his native Pesaro to Rome and Venice, from the Este court in Ferrara to Rome and the Empire, and as *podestà* of Florence and Bologna led Collenuccio to regard Florence and Ferrara as model states; whereas Naples had succumbed to internal chaos and foreign conquest, above all, because of the papacy's meddling in the political affairs of its southern neighbor. That Collenuccio, a foreigner who had never even visited Naples, holds pride of place in this historiographical tradition explains much about Costo's castigation of lying foreigners and Capaccio's later didactic instruction of the curious, pliant *forastiero*. The brief against Rome, nevertheless, became the centerpiece of Neapolitan historiography—as the anonymous 1607–08 descriptive history of Naples makes clear in its terse opening phrase: Naples existed about two hundred years before the building of Rome.[8]

After the political realities of the Aragonese fall from power had displaced the fifteenth-century humanist historians patronized by Alfonso the Magnanimous (1442–1458) and his son Ferrante (1458–1494), not even the great Giovanni Pontano could find much of an audience in the century after his death. Only one work of Pontano, his lone history, the 1499 *De bello napolitano* chronicling the baronial revolt against Ferrante's succession (1458–1464), was reissued and published in vernacular translation in 1590.[9] Why was Pontano translated in 1590 and for whom? In the introduction by the translator, Giacomo Mauro, *uno erudito giovenetto*, it is clear that his patron, Don Luigi Carafa, Prince of Stigliano, had commissioned the work to commemorate the fact that he now occupied the same estate in Terra di Lavoro as Pontano and that the usefulness and pleasure of history as moral philosophy and consolation against mortality were eternal truths. No correspondence to the present political exigencies of contemporary Naples is invoked. In fact, Pontano's panegyric on the city of Naples in the concluding Book 6 makes the memorial character of this translation all the more clear. Naples stands out for its man-made monuments (castles, palaces, and beautiful churches) and its natural environment (mild climate, incomparable site, and abundant fertility). While Pontano's generalizations about the dark side of human nature and Ferrante's unexpected success in establishing peace after war and outrageous fortune might conjure up the complexity of human affairs, in no way did they address the problem of Naples.

That problem—the perceived political instability of Naples—could only be found in Collenuccio's return to the long-term history of the Kingdom and its recurrent structural defects—the character of its inhabitants, its weak or ineffectual monarchs, the legacy of Byzantine lordship, the Angevin-inspired wars of succession, and the interference of the papacy and high clergy. This stereotypical litany excludes the feudal nobility, who find themselves praised as defenders of local privileges instead of blamed for their wanton self-interest. Quite rightly, Neapolitan humanism has been called feudal humanism since its patrons and their praise lie at the heart of a rhetorical program that favored rule by the optimates, the humanisticly educated and piously faithful nobility.[10]

Little wonder, given Tommaso Costo's feudal allegiances and courtier orientation, that he took Collenuccio's compendium history, albeit correcting its errors, as the starting point for his own narrative which began in 1563 after Collenuccio's previous continuation by Mambrino Roseo from 1459–1557 and Colantonio Pacca from 1557–1562. The events chronicled by Costo's *Giunta* first edition of 1588 continued from 1563 until 1582; the second edition of 1593 extended the history through 1586, and eventually through 1610 in subsequent editions that included such local Neapolitan events as the 1585 *popolo* riot and murder of their city council representative, Giovan Vincenzo Starace.[11] This quarter century of Philip II's rule in Costo's first edition proved to be critical in the cultural development of Naples because it marked the first appearance and eventual elaboration of the ideas of the city's three most influential late sixteenth-century intellectuals, Giambattista della Porta, Bernardino Telesio, and Torquato Tasso (its adopted son born in exile across the bay in Sorrento).[12]

Soon after the second Neapolitan edition of the *Giunta*, Costo published a short seventy-one-page *Memoriale delle cose più notabili* in 1592.[13] In brief chronicle form he summarized the history of Naples from 412 in four parts to 1302 in ten pages, from 1302 to 1408 in eight pages, from 1408 to 1500 in thirteen pages, and from 1500 to 1588 in thirty-seven pages. Immediately thereafter, in 1593 with a second edition in 1595, Costo prepared a structural overview of the Kingdom in schematic form. Included were lists of the Kingdom's towns and castles by province, lists of the Kingdom's bishops and archbishops, a short review of the kings by dynasty, a summary of governors and viceroys from the time of the Byzantine occupation in 545, a list of the seven major offices, princes, dukes, marchesi, counts, and extinct members of the noble neighborhood districts; all chronicle the glory past and present of Naples. All this antiquarian lore of civic pride in a noble frame was collected not to make the lessons more forceful nor to instruct newly arrived Spanish viceroys on their short, three-year term, but for the ideal nobleman's education.[14]

Costo's nemesis and rival in this genre of local history, Scipione Mazzella, had been publishing on the history of Naples from 1586. Mazzella's *Descrittione del Regno di Napoli* (Description of the Kingdom of Naples), grew in size from its first edition in 1586 to a big book of 711 pages by its second edition in 1597, as it established itself as the most popular history of Naples. The first edition was devoid of any analysis of historical events, as it provided a descriptive historical-geographical compendium of lists and details on people (monarchs and nobility), places (towns and castles), and things (offices and administration) in the Kingdom. Mazzella's initial success spawned an expanded narrative history of the lives of the Neapolitan kings, which was published independently in 1594 and later incorporated in the second and subsequent editions of the *Descrittione*.[15] While preparing *Le vite dei re* (The Lives of the Kings), Mazzella published a 147-page text in 1591 on ancient Pozzuoli and the Campi Flegrei to the west of Naples, where the first settlement and origins of the capital are traced to ancient Cuma.[16]

All this antiquarian collecting found vituperative criticism from Costo in his *Ragionamenti* (Thoughts) of 1595.[17] Costo derided Mazzella for being derivative, for copying from other writers, and for perpetrating frauds and lies. He engaged in a long discussion on rhetoric, both writing in general and history in particular, only to find himself hauled by Mazzella before both a civil and ecclesiastical court, one of which condemned him to a short prison term.

The first edition of a turn-of-the-century Counter-Reformation history of the three principle cities in the world—Jerusalem, Rome, and Naples, published in Naples in 1598 by Michele Zappullo—brings together Naples's classical inheritance (founded 408 years before Romulus's Rome) and its Christian faith (established three centuries before Rome's) in the common view of successive epochs.[18] Zappullo recounts world history as a progression of ages in the fulfillment of God's plan for mankind. According to Zappullo, whereas the Jews of Jerusalem remained God's chosen people until their rejection of Christ and the destruction of the temple by Titus, Rome was the seat of a Gentile empire whose cults of false gods and idols ruled there until Constantine accepted Christianity publicly in 325. Naples, on the other hand, proved to be the first city of Europe converted to Christianity, the refuge of Christianity during the persecution of the primitive church, and since then has remained steadfast in her ancient faith with more holy places than any other city in the world in order that the intercession of the just and their good works might placate the wrath of God. Naples was the New Jerusalem, a religious center with priority and fidelity in the West before Rome.

Such local historiographical investigations culminated in 1601–1602 in Giovan Antonio Summonte's definitive 1,143-page first two volumes of the *Dell'Historia della Città e Regno di Napoli*.[19] Summonte narrated the city's foundation up to the mid-fifteenth-century Aragonese conquest. He was an admirer of Mazzella, a most diligent observer of (Neapolitan) antiquity and a lover of virtue, who had given Summonte an ancient incription gratefully acknowledged in volume one.[20] The last two volumes of Summonte, another 1,037 pages which continues his history from the Aragonese conquest of the Kingdom in 1443 through Philip II's reign to 1590, only appeared in 1640 and 1643.[21]

In 1596 Costo published *Il Fuggilozio* (Leisure Flight), a literary text which marked the high point of this exemplary moral literature produced for court society.[22] Costo's Leisure Flight is a collection of 522 short anecdotes, examples, or attributed sayings each ending in a proverb, which are organized in a Boccaccesque frame of eight days, told by a company of ten (eight men and two women) with a moral message worthy to be read by every gentleman. Costo himself resided and participated in the fullness of court culture. He served as secretary for a number of prominent Neapolitan noble families and would write a treatise on the secretary in 1602, as had Capaccio before him.[23] Costo's early literary studies included a 1582 Neapolitan edition of Tasso's *Gerusalemme liberata*, whose appendix included a Capaccio letter. Costo's and Capaccio's contemporary careers are not just parallel, but deeply intertwined and nowhere more so than in their aristocratic sympathies, political opinions, and historical studies.

In 1602, the fifty-year-old Capaccio received recognition for his already distinguished career in literary studies and local historical-archeological erudition with the appointment as secretary of the city of Naples.[24] In the tradition of city chancellors and secretaries drawn from provincial roots such as the Florentine chancellor Leonardo Bruni Aretino who became passionate propagandists for their adopted capital city,[25] Capaccio was born in Campagna d'Eboli in the modern province of Salerno (the place where, according to Carlo Levi, Christ stopped). Capaccio produced an authoritative two-volume Latin history of his adoptive city in 1607, as well as the much-more accessible, vernacular, dialogue version with the posthumous publication many years later in 1634 of *Il Forastiero*.

Capaccio's description of the wonders of the marvelous city recounts persons, places, and actions in the dominant baroque aesthetic of awe and admiration associated with the literary style of the great Neapolitan poet of international reputation, Giambattista Marino (1569–1625). The word *maraviglia* (wonder) or its derivatives *maravigliosa* and *maravigliosissima* appears seven times in Capaccio's opening four-page dedication to his patron, the Neapolitan viceroy (1631–1637), Don Emmanuel de Zuñiga, Count of Monterey and double brother-in-law of the Conde Duke Olivares. Capaccio, in fact, makes explicit the symmetry between the city's gifts of nature (its serene air, tranquil sea, and sublime site) and its gifts of fortune (its foreign commerce, large population, and the splendor of its ancient and powerful nobility) with the intellectual gifts of its viceroy, by nature (his sublime intelligence, divine judgment, and lively memory) and by fortune (his network of correspondents, universal praise and celebrity, and glorious family).[26] Although published a third of a century after he became city secretary, *Il Forastiero* reflects the conservative political-religious program put in play in Naples in the 1590s that sees the viceroy's virtues as the mirror-image of the city's glories, and can only be understood as the fruition of that formative moment in the establishment of a Counter-Reformation paideia for the Neapolitan nobility and the culmination of Capaccio's lifetime of service to the Spanish government of Naples.

After studies in law and theology, travels and friendships throughout Italy, writings as a professor of sacred theology on preaching and as a literary critic on Tasso and poetry, Capaccio scored two literary successes: *Il Secretario* (1589) on the art of the secretary, and the form and content of letter-writing; and *Delle Imprese* (1592), a book in three parts: on the practices of printing, on the neoplatonic tradition of interpreting hieroglyphics as symbolic representations, and on emblems.[27] He then returned to Naples in 1593 as the newly appointed *provveditoria dei grani e degli ogli* (superintendent of wheat and oil), one of the city's sources of indirect revenue, which placed him in charge of two public works projects—construction of the grain depository and a new large olive oil cistern. Two literary works produced during that period immediately before becoming city secretary are extremely important in understanding Capaccio's participation in the rich public culture of 1590s Naples.

In imitation of Sannazzaro's *Arcadia*, Capaccio published *Mergellina*, a collection of piscatorial elegies in Venice in 1598. Besides alternating prose and poetry in a pastoral mode that elevates fishermen rather than shepherds, Capaccio's poetry shows influences from Tasso and marks him as part of the end-of-the-century anti-Petrarchan movement. The emergent new baroque aesthetic that was to develop from such influences and experiments emphasized sharp and sudden insight, overwhelming stupor created by the sublime and all-powerful, and in short, the faith and commitment to God and king that reflected and reinforced the program of post-Tridentine political-religious reform. These emotive and expressive literary exaggerations and elaborations found enthusiastic proponents such as Capaccio in Naples who infused the new style with the color of local religiosity and the content of Counter-Reformation spirituality.

Capaccio's 1602 *Gli Apologi*, an emblem book, demonstrates that marriage in ornate style and moral message *par excellence*. Capaccio claims to be writing as a *vero Filosofo, e non Apologista*, and later editions in 1607 and 1619 add a sub-title that clarifies the issue: The *Apologues*, moral sayings with almost true-life details in the Courtier mode.[28] Its ninety-four moral lessons are titled in emblematic, folkloric form; for example, The Clock and the Sundial; Marble and Stone; The Monkey and the Fox. For each entry, a small woodcut is then followed by an italicized poem and a one-line proverb, before a long prose section explicates the moral; for example, The Clock and the Sundial teaches us that not all virtues are given to one person alone; Marble and Stone teaches us that to become a man, one has to suffer many difficulties; The Monkey and the Fox teaches us that many, by trying to imitate others, live lies.[29] The proverbial wisdom of such emblems had its roots in manuals of court manners, where the pithy phrase and elaboration of etiquette prevailed. The importance of aristocratic society and noble decorum cannot be overemphasized as the dominant influence on Neapolitan learning and literature in both Latin and vernacular printed books of the late sixteenth and early seventeenth century.

The Neapolitan historiographical tradition from Collenuccio to Costo, the Costo Mazzella/Summonte controversy, and Capaccio's own antiquarian studies shaped his whole argument in the ten-day visit in the ten books of *Il Forastiero*. Days 1 and 2 developed an interpretation of the origins and foundation of Naples and of its ancient religion and wars that established noble pretensions to their freedom and their service to the state and to the Church. The myth of the foundation of the city—an old story claiming independent foundation before

Rome by Greek settlers from Pozzuoli—became part of an elaborate Counter-Reformation revival of the city nobility's prerogatives. In ancient Greek times when superstition ruled and the Sirens dominated the region, all the gods worshipped there as a holy place.[30] The emblem of the ancient Greek republic was the owl (*la civetta* or *la nottola*) because, even though it is mute, the most eloquent man in the world is the one who knows how to observe silence when necessary.[31] But that ancient Greek liberty was lost in Naples in 1130 with the crowning of the Norman King Roger II and his monarchical claims over a unified kingdom joining the mainland and the island of Sicily—in Capaccio's words, a thing to marvel at since the city of Naples after the time of the Roman Empire could never be conquered by arms, was finally subjugated with only one word.[32]

Capaccio returns to his story to describe Partenope, the founding goddess of the city of Naples, as a half-female, half-bird-legged creature, who accompanied the Sirens' song on her lyre. These two attributes point to the good government of Naples under Spanish rule and the Catholic faith. Partenope's lyre was a clear symbol of the consonance of all the things that could be imagined in this city, such as the government that had acquired its perfection with so much order over various dominions and which is recovered in these times under the most perfect harmony of the Kingdom of Spain. As vassals, the Neapolitans have united in concord to serve their lord; and the different states of plebs, *popolo*, and nobility—just as the different strings of the lyre—have come together from their diversity to make a most perfect union of faith. Partenope's nature as a bird, for its part, signified nothing other than the felicity of their king, most eager to attain greatness and to fly with the contemplation of heaven, where the new Christian religion was founded, to make [the Neapolitans] superior to any other nation.[33] Themes in later books always returned to these claims of Neapolitan priority and superiority in political organization and religious faith through Spanish good government and Neapolitan fidelity.

Capaccio follows the ancient foundations of Naples with a review of its political history and government by dynasties, from the Norman, Hohenstaufen, and Angevin kings (Day 3), the Aragonese kings (Day 4), and the Habsburgs kings (Day 5). Day 6 surveys the Neapolitan viceroys, and Day 7 surveys the governmental system of justice and administration by tribunals and councils. Day 8 describes the city's inhabitants—natives (the nobility in their residential wards or *seggi*, the nobility outside the *seggi*, the *popolo*, the plebs) and foreign residents. Day 9 describes the the city's body, that is, the corporate society of the Old Regime, its buildings, and monuments by *arte*; while Day 10 concludes with a return to the city's site, its attributes, and beauties by nature. An eighty-six-page addendum dialogue between the Foreigner and the Citizen expounds upon the *Incendio di Vesuvio* (The Fire of Vesuvius) as a metaphor for the history and tradition of Naples and the Campania. A discussion of the causes and consequences of the violent fires from mythology, geology, and history begins with the stupefying power [of Vesuvius] upon the most courageous men of the world, such that it reduces [the Foreigner] to believe that its volcanic eruption will mark the end of the world. And the dialogue ends with the Citizen's affirmation that Vesuvius, which provides perpetual illumination for the greatness of the Church, the majesty of the Spanish Habsburgs, the Holy Roman Empire, and the most faithful city of Naples, always erupts in flames of charity, love, and devotion, which are the true revolution of the planets.[34]

Violence and instability (for in the seventeenth century, "revolution" means "rotation," and not yet "revolt") are the key to understanding Capaccio's hardline descriptions of Neapolitan society and his reactionary ire against the plebs. In Day 6, Rome likewise provides the basis for comparison to understand the question of the divisions in society between nobles (who demonstrate their worth through virtuous actions), *popolo* (who distinguish themselves as landlords, civil magistrates, and merchants), and plebs (a marginalized underclass of vile, seditious rabble).[35] Disorder and disparity in the times mark the difference between past and present when it comes to the *popolo*. Placing *Il Forastiero* in the wider context of late sixteenth-century historiography shaped by the riot of May 9, 1585 around the murder and dragging through the streets of the *popolo eletto* (chosen people) Starace helps to explain Capaccio's vituperative condemnation of the growing divisions in Neapolitan society between nobles and commoners.[36] For Capaccio, the plebs were like "rabid dogs and wild beasts who sprinkled the blood of the dead Starace throughout the whole city as they dragged his corpse and reduced the cadaver to such an end that one could not find either flesh, skin, or bone, nor could one bury it, for we could say that it was buried through the whole city of Naples." With such fear and tumult, the crowd's cries in front of the viceroy's palace of *Viva il Re, e mora il mal governo* (Hurray for the King, and death to bad government) rang hollow as they then marched to sack the dead *eletto*'s house. The Citizen's narrative of events concludes by describing the public monument with niches displaying the heads and hands of the executed and by quoting the Latin epitaph on a marble stone erected on the site of the razed house and land now sown with salt of the complicit *popolo* leader, Giovan Leonardo Pisano, by order of the good government of the viceroy duke of Osuna. In response, the Foreigner quakes in expressing

Capaccio's rage and judgment: "I tremble to hear these words of just vendetta, both so appropriate and significant."[37] Later in Day 8, the Citizen will lament the changes in the relationship between the nobility and the *popolo* to the great damage of the city and the perpetuation of disorder and disparity. In their affairs, the *popolo* makes as if it is equal, and the consequent civil discord is like the dissonance in the Siren's lyre when high and low strings absorb humidity and no longer sound in tune.[38]

Day 9's discussion of the city's body, which begins with a description of Rome and a comparison with Constantinople to highlight the place that Naples holds with respect to the other great cities of the world, is exemplary of Capaccio's overall thesis.[39] Naples has changed dramatically from what it was, and just as Constantinople replaced Rome in antiquity, so too now Naples has replaced Rome in modern times. Naples surpasses Rome in both antiquity and sanctity; it deserves priority above Rome in both secular government and religious authority. Capaccio obviously did not write his book for us curious moderns, but for a contemporary Neapolitan audience which would appreciate and approve that the city's innumerable, great wonders formed one body, a veritable world of its own: one body of wall, gates, neighborhoods, castles, arsenal, particular buildings, houses, churches, banks, hospitals, schools, university, and every other thing which can form a city and make it worthy of admiration by those who contemplate and wonder at it.[40] What has come down to modern readers of Capaccio's guide to those places in the city to be most regarded is a mine of information exploited by art historians, social historians, and literary critics in their reconstruction of the culture of the early modern Neapolitan capital, but that is not why we should read or remember *Il Forastiero*.

Above all, *Il Forastiero* concerns the establishment and practice of good government, and Day 7, *Del Governo di Tribunali Regii, e Publico* (On the Government of Royal Tribunals and Public Government), begins with a long digression on *Ragion di Stato* (Reason of State).[41] For Capaccio, Reason of State was synonymous with good laws and the laws of the Church, not the impure and false teachings perpetrated by the sophistic rationalizations of Machiavelli and his Statist followers. The Citizen-Capaccio argues that there are five examples of the incorrect intentions of the Statists' theory of Reason of State: 1) it is an art of governing not by ordinary people, but known only by elite guardians with great intellect, prudence, and experience; 2) they do not follow moral or civil laws, and do not believe that governors who abide by the law follow Reason of State; 3) the prince applies the law arbitrarily and deviates from it; 4) it applies to the grave, important affairs of the prince and not to little questions; and 5) in order to conserve the prince and his state, they govern by extraordinary means, do whatever is necessary, and are not obliged to observe divine or human laws. Their rationalities were chimeras full of caprice, while the only true Reason of State, like that of the Spanish Habsburg rule of Naples, came from the humble, prudent, and just administration of the laws of God, Church, and Empire, that is, with the justice of the laws and the shame to speak of it otherwise.

For Capaccio there are two true modes of government that establish the king's greatness and his vassals' needs: imperial law adjudicated by royal tribunals, and statutes and laws administered by public courts. Heresy and ignorance are the two dangers to Christian politics from the bad intent and malpractice of Reason of State, and why the Church can be the only guide to a true Reason of State.[42] Capaccio recalls with affection his time at the court of the duke of Urbino, Federico II di Montefeltro della Rovere, and references two emblems of Alciato. Although he inverts Alciato's order, Capaccio succinctly captures the essence of good government as first, a nest of a seabird on a rock in the sea, and second, a helmet in which bees make honey, both signifying the model of a true prince who knows how to maintain the state with true reason of state.[43] Capaccio's book of emblems, *Il Principe*, dedicated to his patron, the duke of Urbino, without engraved emblems, follows Alciato's order with the latter bees' honeycombed helmet first, *Dalla Guerra la pace* (From War comes peace), and the former seabird's rocky nest second, *Dalla pace l'abondanza* (From peace comes abundance).[44] The honeycombed helmet of peace replaces the bloodstains of war, since peace should always be desired and sought. In the example of the seabird feathering his nest to bring plenty from peace, the provisioning of food establishes peace among the people; and thus, the prince is no different than a good father. But in closing his explication of the emblem, Capaccio reminds the reader with a cautionary tale attributed to the first-century A.D. Greek rhetorician and philosopher, Dion Chrysostom, that despite the good government of the prince and his provisioning against every future evil with constant labors, while the people of the republic live carefree, one day the plebs, for want of food, will knock the head off his statue!

In the city and the Kingdom, then, the Neapolitan nobility were born to rule—from antiquity, from past service in battle, from religious fidelity, and from moral rectitude. Near the end of Day 7's review of the workings of Neapolitan government in the parallel offices and administration of Kingdom and city, Capaccio's citizen identifies the Neapolitan parliament as the lone deputation combining men from both the city and the baronage.[45] In reality, a vestigial institution meeting biennially without any real power, the Neapolitan parliament's main charge was to vote monetary aids (*donativi*) in exchange for listing grievances or petitions for redress (*grazie*).⁴⁶ The viceroy inaugurated parliament with a letter written by the city secretary (another opportunity for Capaccio to show off) and concluded it with receipt of the *donativi*.

Parliament met in the former refectory of the convent adjacent to San Lorenzo Maggiore in the center of the old city. Its vault decorated under Philip III in 1600 joined together the ideas of good government on heaven and earth, a program of virtues that restated visually the humanist education program that the Neapolitan historians advocated for its best citizens, both the urban and feudal nobility. Seven virtues, which were flanked by four attendant, subsidiary virtues, presided over the twelve provinces of the Kingdom. These seven virtues provided the noble parliamentarians models of behavior to reflect upon during their debates and deliberations:

1. Gravitas attended by Constancy, Maturity, Firmness, and Perseverance;
2. Affability attended by Benignity, Grace, Courtesy, and Gratitude;
3. Clemency attended by Charity, Mercy, Peace, and Meekness;
4. Magnificence attended by Felicity, Glory, and Honor (with the fourth virtue now lost);
5. Magnanimity attended by Victory and Nobility (with two virtues no longer visible);
6. Providence attended by Hope, Vigilance, Counsel, and Fortune; and
7. Royal Authority attended by the four moral virtues Justice, Temperance, Fortitude, and Prudence.

The moral life defined the public life for the ideal noble in Counter-Reformation Naples, as an old nobility of blood was to be a nobility of virtue.

A large group of Neapolitan imprints on local history and geography linked Counter-Reformation spirituality with the ancient history of the city in order to emphasize the distinctiveness of its noble citizens' contributions and continuing commitment to the Church and the state. Capaccio's *cicerone* for the Foreigner, thus, was really a humanist primer for the Citizen. Excluded from such a noble citizen's consciousness were both *popolo* and plebs, who would soon rise up against their lords, both monarch and nobles, in the 1647 revolt, only to find themselves all the more repressed by the moral imperatives of that same virtuous nobility. The other in Spanish Naples was not so much the lying foreign historian or the curious foreign visitor out to see the world, but rather the resident commoners—the *popolo* and plebs—whose unfaithfulness and unreason challenged noble governance and authority.

Notes

1. Tommaso Costo, *La Apologia Istorica del Regno di Napoli contra la falsa opinione di coloro che biasimarono i Regnicoli di inconstanza e d'infedeltà* (Naples: Gio. Domenico Roncagliolo, 1613), 4: "Torno dunque a dire che la città di Napoli, per non essersi curata di havere scritta proprio delle sue cose, è in corsa nella calumnie de gli stranieri, i qualie male informati, e poco amorevoli di lei ne hanno parlato non conforme al vero, ma secondo le loro varie passioni."
2. Giulio Cesare Capaccio, *Il Forastiero* (Naples: Gio. Domenico Roncagliolo, 1634), vii: "mi si offerì una sì gran vastità di novi pensieri, e furono tante le cose che giudicai degne di tenersene conto da gli omini curiosi in questa occasione, che mi ritrovai immerso dentro il pelago d'una Enciclopedia che nell'universal varietà di descrittioni, relationi, accidenti Regali, governi, guerre, memorie di cose antiche, successi di Stato, encomij di famiglie, e di persone degne di onore, e mille altre cose simili che trattengono nella lettione i belli ingegni, e che sono utili alla varietà del sapere, mi ferono dubitare se dovessi formarne istoria, o pure con altro genere di dire spiegare i concetti miei." (In that occasion I was given such a great vastness of new thoughts, and I observed so many things deserving to be considered, that I found myself immersed in the sea of an Encyclopedia. The universal variety of descriptions, reports, regal accidents, government, wars, memories of ancient things, successes of state, praises of families, and of individual deserving honor, and a thousand of other similar things, made me doubtful about the opportunity of recounting their story, or explaining my ideas in another mode of discourse). For an explication of this passage as a reflection of the concept patria, see Pasquale Novellino, "Le filigrane culturali della 'fedeltà' nella storiografia napoletana tra fine Cinquecento ed inizio Seicento" (paper, École française de Rome-Casa de Velázquez Seminar, Histoire sociale des institutions), Fidelitas I, (21 May 2004): 5–6.
3. Jon R. Snyder, *Writing the Scene of Speaking: Theories of Dialogue in the Late Italian Renaissance* (Stanford, CA: Stanford University Press, 1989), 185–97. Manso's treatise on dialogue appears as an appendix in *Erocallia, ovvero dell'amore e della bellezza* (Venice, 1628), 1033–64. For Tasso on dialogue, see Snyder, 146–80; for the Italian text of Tasso's *Discorso dell'arte del dialogo* with facing English translation, see Torquato Tasso, *Tasso's Dialogues: A Selection, with the Discourse on the Art of the Dialogue*, trans Carnes Lord and Dain A. Trafton (Berkeley and Los Angeles: University of California Press, 1982), 15–41. For Manso in *Il Forastiero*, see 8–9 and 750–51; for Tasso, see 3–4, where he is equated with Homer, Virgil, and Ariosto.
4. Capaccio, 1–2: "di andar atorno per il mondo per curiosità di saper molte cose di che non tutti han gusto, come sono origine, e belezze di città, costumi di popoli, usanze di genti, movimenti di guerra, varietà di dominij, maneggi di governi, provedimenti di leggi, esercitij di Cavalieri, andamenti di cittadini, fabriche, pitture, statue, politia di habitanti, & ogni altra simil cosa che ad inclita città convenga, e particolarmente à Napoli città famosa che fa invidia à tutte l'altre famosissime di Europa." (To go around

in the world for curiosity of knowing many things not interesting for everybody, such as origin, beauties of cities, morals of peoples, customs, movements of war, variety of dominions, intrigues of governments, provisions of laws, armies of Knights, trends of citizen, buildings, paintings, statues, politeness of inhabitants, and every other similar thing that pertains to a noble city, particularly to the famous city of Naples which all other most celebrated European cities envy).

5. Tasso, *Tasso's Dialogues*, 151–91 provides the Italian text and facing English translation.
6. Raffaele Colapietra, "La storiografia napoletana del secondo '500," pts. I and 2 *Belfagor* XV (1960): 415–36; XVI (1961): 416–31; and Eric Cochrane, *Historians and Historiography in the Italian Renaissance* (Chicago: University of Chicago Press, 1981), 155–59, 270–75.
7. Pandolfo Collenuccio, *Compendio de le istorie del Regno di Napoli*, ed. Alfredo Saviotti (Bari: Laterza, 1929). See also the study of Giorgio Masi, *Dal Collenuccio a Tommaso Costo: vicende della storiografia napoletana fra Cinque e Seicento* (Naples: Editoriale Scientifica, 1999).
8. "Napoli descritta ne'principii del secolo XVII," *Archivo Storico per le province napoletane* 7 (1882): 73: "Fu Napoli a ducento anni prima dell'edificio di Roma."
9. Giovanni Gioviano Pontano, *Historia della guerra di Napoli* (Naples: Giuseppe Cacchi, 1590).
10. Jerry H. Bentley, *Politics and Culture in Renaissance Naples* (Princeton, NJ: Princeton University Press, 1987) limits his discussion of Neapolitan humanism to Latin-based authors, whereas I have extended it to include vernacular authors with the same classical reference base and value structure.
11. Tommaso Costo, *Addizioni e note al Compendio dell'istoria del Regno di Napoli*, P. Collenuccio, M. Roseo e C. Pacca (Naples, 1583; Naples, 1588; Venice, 1613); see Masi, Appendix I.
12. Della Porta (1535–1615) first published *Magia naturalis (Natural Magic)* in four books in 1558, and in a revised, second Neapolitan edition in twenty books in 1589. Telesio (1508–1588) had published the first two books of his *De natura juxta propria principia (On The Nature Of Things According To Their Own Principles)* in 1565, with the complete edition of the *Rerum natura* in 1586.
13. Tommaso Costo, *Memoriale delle cose più notabili accadute nel Regno di Napoli dell'incarnazione di Cristo per tutto l'anno MDLXXVI* (Naples: Salviani, 1594).
14. Cochrane, 275, summarizes the general thrust of publications in both content and format. Henrico Bacco, *Effigie di tutti i Re, che han dominato il Reame di Napoli da Ruggiero I Normano in sino ad oggi* (Naples: Carlino, 1602) and the numerous editions of his later popular guide books are a good example. Cochrane is mistaken, however, about the purpose of these late sixteenth-century books, since newly appointed Spanish viceroys prepared themselves with Spanish language *avvertimenti*. See Manuel Rivero Rodríguez with examples of the genre transcribed in Giuseppe Congilio, *Declino del viceregno di Napoli (1599–1689)* (Naples: Giannini, 1990); Istruzioni di Filippo III al

vicerè conte di Lemos, (20 April 1599), 71–143; and Istruzioni di Filippo III al vicerè di Napoli conte di Benavente, (17 September 1602), 174–241.

15. Scipione Mazzella, *Descrittione del Regno di Napoli*, 1st ed., 2nd ed., and 3rd ed. (Naples, 1586; 1597; 1601) and *Le vite dei re di Napoli con le loro effigie naturale* (Naples: Giuseppe Bonfadino, 1594).

16. Scipione Mazzella, *Sito et antichità della città di Pozzuolo e del suo amenissimo distretto*, 1st ed. (Naples: Salviani, 1591); 2nd ed. (Naples: Stigliola à Porta Regale, 1595).

17. Tommaso Costo, *Ragionamenti intorna alla descrizzione del Regno di Napoli et all'antichità di Pozzuolo di Scipione Mazzella* (Naples: Stigliola à Porta Regale, 1595).

18. Michele Zappullo, *Sommario Istorico ... di tre gran Città, cioè Gerusalem, di Roma, e di Napoli* (Naples: Carlino and Pace, 1598). In the second and subsequent edtions (Naples, 1602; Vicenza: Giorgio Greco, 1603; Naples: Carlino and Vitale, 1609), Zappullo adds Venice because of its long history of liberty not subject to its enemies and the Indies as the hope and fulfillment of the spread of God's word to all mankind. I have used the third edition (Naples, 1609), ix–x and 253–330.

19. Gio. Antonio Summonte, *Dell'Historia della Città e Regno di Napoli*, 2 vols. (Naples: Carlino, 1601–02).

20. Ibid., 1:27: "un'altro marmo con l'iscrittione che nel suo luogo si ponerà, à noi dato dal Signor Scipion Mazzella diligentissimo perscrutatore dell'antichità di questa Città: & amator di virtù."

21. Ibid., vol. 3 (Naples: Francesco Savio, 1640) and vol. 4 (Naples: Giacomo Gaffaro, 1643).

22. Tommaso Costo, *Il Fuggilozio* (Naples: Carlino and Pace, 1596; mod. ed., ed. Corrado Calenda, Rome: Salerno editrice, 1989). For biographical details, see Calenda, xxxvi–xlv and S. Lettere, "Costo, Tommaso," in *Dizionario Biografico degli Italiani* 30 (1984): 411–15.

23. Tommaso Costo and Michele Benvenga, *Il Segretario di lettere*, ed. Salvatore S. Nigro (Palermo: Sellerio editore, 1991), orig. in Costo's *Lettere* (Venice, 1602; Naples, 1604). See also Salvatore Nigro, "The Secretary."

24. See S. Nigro, "Capaccio, Giulio Cesare," *Dizionario Biografico degli Italiani* 18: 374–80; Amedeo Quondam, "Dal manierismo al barocco," *Storia di Napoli* 5: 368–72 and 503–33 (Naples, 1972); and Quondam, *La parola nel labirinto: Società e scrittura del Manierismo a Napoli* (Rome and Bari: Laterza, 1975), 187–225.

25. Donald J. Wilcox, *The Development of Florentine Humanist Historiography in the Fifteenth Century* (Cambridge, MA: Harvard University Press, 1969).

26. Ibid., iii–iv. See also *Novellino*, 7–10

27. Giulio Cesare Capaccio, *Il Secretario* (Rome, 1589; Venice, 1591, 1594, 1597, and 1607) and *Delle Imprese* (Naples: Salviani, 1592).

28. Giulio Cesare Capaccio, *Gli Apologi*, 1st ed. (Naples: Carlino, 1602); 2nd ed. (Venice: Barezzo Barezzi, 1619). The later editions add the subtitle: *con le dicerie morali ove quasi con viri colori al modo Cortegiano*.

29. Ibid., 1 and 99: "Horologio da ruote, e da Sole, moral Non tutte le virtù sono date

ad un solo"; 2 and 100: "Marmo, e Pietre, moral Per divenir huomo, si han da soffrir molti disaggi"; 3 and 102: "Simia, e Volpe, moral Molti per farsi imitatori altrui, s'ingannano."
30. Capaccio, *Il Forastiero*, 64. On the cult of the ancient god Hebone, associated with the sun, see Pasquale Novellino, "*Il culto di Hebone: 'enciclopedia' classica e visibilità contemporanea ne Il Forastiero di Giulio Cesare Capaccio*," Res publica litterarum 24 (2001): 106–36.
31. Capaccio, *Il Forastiero*, 14.
32. Ibid., 56–58: "per cosa di maraviglia che Napoli città qual dopo il Romano Imperio mai non potè esser vinta col ferro, fusse finalmente soggiogata con una sola parola."
33. Ibid., 64–65: "La Lira fù chiaro simbolo della consonanza di tutte le cose che si fussero potuto imaginar in questa Città così del governo che dovea con tanto ordine di varij dominij, acquistar la sua perfettione, in che si ritrova in questi tempi, sotto la perfettissima armonia del Regno di Spagna.... L'esser partecipe poi della natura di uccello, altro no significò che la felicità de i loro Re, velocissimi all'acquisto di tutte le grandezze; & al volare con la contemplatione al cielo, ov'era per fonder la nova Religione Cristiana per farsene superiori a qualsivoglia natione."
34. Capaccio, *Il Forastiero*, immediately following 1024, *Incendi di Vesuvio*, 1: "ch'in vero novità cosi maravigliosa haveria stordite le menti de i più coraggiosi homini del mondo, mi ridussero à credere che all'hora fusse venuto il fine di quello"; and 85–86: "Et in tanto arda Vesuvio, per far perpetua luminaria alla grandezza della Chiesa . . . ; alla Maestà di casa d'Austria . . . ; alla Maestà dell'Imperio . . . ; & alla fidelissima Città di Napoli, la qual sempre erutta fiãme di carità, di amore, e di divotione, e queste sono la vera rivolutione di pianeti."
35. Capaccio, *Il Forastiero*, 770–87, esp. 742 and 783–84.
36. Ibid., 484–89. See Corona, "" in BNN, MS. XV.F.47, 100–115 and transcribed in *Archivio storico per le province napoletane* 1 (1876): 131–38. Two detailed descriptions of the incident drawn from wider sources are available in English: Eric Cochrane, ed., *The Late Italian Renaissance, 1525–1630* (New York: Harper & Row, 1970); 305–30; Rosario Villari, *The Revolt of Naples*, trans. James Newell (Cambridge: Polity Press, 1992), 19–29.
37. Capaccio, *Il Forastiero*, 487: "All'hora come cani arrabbiati, e come fiere indomite . . . e ridussero il cadavero a tal termine, che non trovandosi, nè carne, nè pelle, nè ossa, nè se gli potè dar sepoltura, se non vogliamo dire che gli fù sepolcro tutta la città di Napoli"; and 488: "Tremo in sentir queste parole piene di giusta vendetta, e così proprie, e significanti."
38. Ibid., 780–81.
39. Ibid., 799–802.
40. Ibid., 802.
41. Ibid., 561–73. See Maurizio Viroli, *From Politics to Reason of State* (Cambridge: Cambridge University Press, 1992).
42. Capaccio, *Il Forastiero*, 561–63, 561: "E per questo dal ragionar che faremo ho' gi sco-

priremo i due veri modi di governo che stabiliscono la grandezza del Re, & il bisogno di vassalli." (And through this discussion that we will have today, we will discover the two true forms of government that establish the power of the king and the need of vassals.)

43. Ibid., 568–69: "l'una fù, un nido dell'Alcione sopra uno scoglio in mare, l'altro un Cimiero dentro il quale faceano il mele l'Api, ambedue significatrici del modello di un vero Principe, che sappia con vera ragion di stato, mantener lo stato." For Andrea Alciato, *Emblematum liber* (1621), see *www.mun.ca/alciato/index.html*, Emblem, 178 and 179.

44. Giulio Cesare Capaccio, *Il Principe . . . tratto da gli emblemi dell'Alciato, con ducento, e più avvertimenti politici e morali utilissimi à qualunque Signore per l'ottima eruditione di Costumi, Economia, e Governo di Stati* (Venice: Barezzo Barezzi, 1620), 370–75, Avvertimenti CLXIX and CLXX: "Pace sempre deve esser desiderata, e procurata" and "Il vero stabilimento di pace co i popoli è la provisione dell'annona, che ad ogni modo stà a carico del Principe . . . . che niente differisce il buon Principe dal buon padre."

45. Capaccio, *Il Forastiero*, 660–62.

46. Guido d'Agostino, *Parlamento e società nel regno di Napoli. Secoli XV–XVII* (Naples: Guida editori, 1979).

Works Cited

Alciato, Andrea. *Emblematum liber* (1621). The Memorial Web Edition in Latin and English. *www.mun.ca/alciato/index.html*.

Bacco, Henrico *Effigie di tutti i Re, che han dominato il Reame di Napoli da Ruggiero il Normano in sino ad oggi*. Naples: Carlino, 1602.

Bentley, Jerry H. *Politics and Culture in Renaissance Naples*. Princeton, NJ: Princeton University Press, 1987.

Capaccio, Giulio Cesare. *Delle Imprese*. Naples: Salviani, 1592.

_____. *Il Forastiero*. Naples: Gio. Domenico Roncagliolo, 1634.

_____. *Gli Apologi*. (1st ed. Naples: Carlino, 1602; 2nd ed. Venice: Barezzo Barezzi, 1619.

_____. *Il Principe . . . tratto da gli emblemi dell'Alciato, con ducento, e più avvertimenti politici e morali utilissimi à qualunque Signore per l'ottima eruditione di Costumi, Economia, e Governo di Stati*. Venice: Barezzo Barezzi, 1620.

_____. *Il Secretario*. Rome, 1589; Venice, 1591, 1594, 1597, and 1607.

Cochrane, Eric. *Historians and Historiography in the Italian Renaissance*. Chicago: University of Chicago Press, 1981.

_____. *The Late Italian Renaissance (1525–1620)*. New York: Harper Brow, 1970.

Colapietra, Raffaele. "La storiografia napoletana del secondo '500." Pts. 1 and 2. *Belfagor* XV (1960): 415–36; XVI (1961): 416–31.

Collenuccio, Pandolfo. *Compendio de le istorie del Regno di Napoli*. Ed. Alfredo Saviotti. Bari: Laterza, 1929.

Congilio, Giuseppe. *Declino del viceregno di Napoli (1599–1689)*. Naples: Giannini, 1990.
Costo, Tommaso. *Addizioni e note al Compendio dell'istoria del Regno di Napoli.* scritto da P. Collenuccio, M. Roseo e C. Pacca. 1st ed. Naples, 1583; 2nd ed. Naples, 1588; 3rd ed. Venice, 1613.
_____. *La Apologia Istorica del Regno di Napoli contra la falsa opinione di coloro che biasimarono i Regnicoli di inconstanza e d'infedeltà*. Naples: Gio. Domenico Roncagliolo, 1613.
_____. *Il Fuggilozio*. Naples: Carlino and Pace, 1596. Modern edition, ed. Corrado Calenda, Rome: Salerno editrice, 1989.
_____. *Memoriale delle cose più notabili accadute nel Regno di Napoli dell'incarnazione di Cristo per tutto l'anno MDLXXVI*. Naples: Salviani, 1594.
_____. *Ragionamenti intorna alla descrizzione del Regno di Napoli et all'antichità di Pozzuolo di Scipione Mazzella*. Naples: Stigliola à Porta Regale, 1595.
Costo, Tommaso, and Michele Benvenga. *Il Segretario di lettere*. Ed. Salvatore S. Nigro. Palermo: Sellerio editore, 1991.
D'Agostino, Guido. *Parlamento e società nel regno di Napoli: Secoli XV–XVII*. Naples: Guida editori, 1979.
Lettere, S. "Costo, Tommaso." *Dizionario Biografico degli Italiani* 30 (1984): 411–15.
Manso, Giovanni Battista. *Erocallia ouero Dell'amore e della bellezza dialoghi 12. Di Gio. Battista Manso marchese della Villa. Con gli argomenti a ciascun dialogo del caualier Marino*. In Venice: Deuchino, Evangelista, 1628.
Masi, Giorgio. *Dal Collenuccio a Tommaso Costo: vicende della storiografia napoletana fra Cinque e Seicento*. Naples: Editoriale Scientifica, 1999.
Mazzella, Scipione. *Descrittione del Regno di Napoli*. 1st ed., 2nd ed., and 3rd ed. Naples, 1586; 1597; 1601.
_____. *Sito et antichità della città di Pozzuolo e del suo amenissimo distretto*. 1st ed. Naples: Salviani, 1591; 2nd ed. Naples: Stigliola à Porta Regale, 1595.
_____. *Le vite dei re di Napoli con le loro effigie naturale*. Naples: Giuseppe Bonfadino, 1594.
Nigro, Salvatore. "Capaccio, Giulio Cesare." *Dizionario Biografico degli Italiani* 18 (1976): 374–80.
_____. "The Secretary." *Baroque Personae*. Trans. Rosario Villari and Lydia Cochrane. Chicago: University of Chicago Press, 1994. 82–99.
Novellino, Pasquale. "Le filigrane culturali della 'fedeltà' nella storiografia napoletana tra fine Cinquecento ed inizio Seicento." (Paper, École française de Rome-Casa de Velázquez Seminar, Histoire sociale des institutions) *Fidelitas* I (21 May 2004).
_____. "Il culto di Hebone: 'enciclopedia' classica e visibilità contemporanea ne *Il Forastiero* di Giulio Cesare Capaccio." *Res publica litterarum* 24 (2001): 106–36.
Pontano, Giovanni Gioviano. *Historia della guerra di Napoli*. Naples: Giuseppe Cacchi, 1590.
Quondam, Amedeo. "Dal Manierismo al Barocco." (From Mannerism to Baroque) *Storia di Napoli* 5 368–72 and 503–33. Naples: Soc. Ed. Storia de Napoli, 1975.

———. *La parola nel labirinto: Società e scrittura del Manierismo a Napoli.* Rome and Bari: Laterza, 1975.

Rivero Rodríguez, Manuel. "Doctrina y práctica política en la monarquía hispana; Las instrucciones dadas a los virreyes y gobernadores de Italia en los siglos XVI y XII." *Investigaciones Históricas* 9 (1989): 197–213.

Snyder, Jon R. *Writing the Scene of Speaking: Theories of Dialogue in the Late Italian Renaissance.* Stanford, CA: Stanford University Press, 1989.

Summonte, Gio. Antonio. *Dell'Historia della Città e Regno di Napoli.* 4 vols. Naples: Carlino, 1601–02; Francesco Savio, 1640; Giacomo Gaffaro, 1643.

Tasso, Torquato. *Tasso's Dialogues: A Selection, with the Discourse on the Art of the Dialogue.* Trans. Carnes Lord and Dain A. Trafton. Berkeley and Los Angeles: University of California Press, 1982.

Villari, Rosario. *The Revolt of Naples.* Trans. James Newell. Cambridge: Polity Press, 1992. First published in Italian in 1967.

Viroli, Maurizio. *From Politics to Reason of State.* Cambridge: Cambridge University Press, 1992.

Wilcox, Donald J. *The Development of Florentine Humanist Historiography in the Fifteenth Century.* Cambridge, MA: Harvard University Press, 1969.

Zappullo, Michele. *Sommario Istorico . . . di tre gran Città, cioè Gerusalem, di Roma, e di Napoli.* Naples: Carlino and Pace, 1609.

◆ 8

The Baroque Public Sphere

William Childers

Introduction: Habermas and the Baroque

The regulation of public life by rational dialogue has often been seen as a hallmark of modernity. Currently, the most influential statement of this view, which privileges the Enlightenment as the moment when the modern world came decisively into being, is Jürgen Habermas's notion of the bourgeois public sphere, first presented in *The Structural Transformation of the Public Sphere*. This essay uses discursive practices in Hapsburg Spain to exemplify an alternative model of the public sphere, focusing in particular on two fundamental aspects: the epistemology of rumor and the performance of religious identity. Ultimately, the Baroque emerges here as a distinctive modernity, challenging the equation of the modern with post-Enlightenment reason.

The point of departure for theoretical models of the public sphere remains Habermas' claim that the spread of such practices as coffeehouse discussion and newspapers and periodical literature was a condition of possibility for the emergence of modern representative democracy. In his account, an expansion of historical agency to ever-larger segments of the population was made possible by free access to debate conducted in accordance with principles inherent in human communication. In "Further Reflections on the Public Sphere,"

Habermas clarified that his theory "intends to bring into the open the rational potential intrinsic in everyday communicative practices" (447). Responding to the events of September 11, 2001, Habermas once more reiterated his view that everyday interaction "rests on a solid base of common background convictions, self-evident cultural truths and reciprocal expectations," while "insincerity and deception," constitute second-order distortions that can lead to misunderstandings, erupting in violence ("Fundamental Terror" 35).

In this idealized view of bourgeois culture, discussion among reasonable people mediates between private feelings and policy decisions. Habermas contrasts this state of affairs both with "feudal" public life prior to the eighteenth century, and with the mass society forged by the culture industries of the twentieth century. Pre- and postmodern public spheres seem to him equally to deny agency to all but a small elite by casting the majority of the population in the role of passive spectators. He casts high bourgeois culture as a golden age in which the public sphere served to facilitate a high level of participation by individual citizens in the political process. The only form of public sphere that he recognizes prior to the eighteenth century is the "representative publicness" of ostentatious displays of power by feudal lords or, later, absolute monarchs ("Structural Transformation of the Public Sphere" 5–14). In this context he dismisses "Baroque festivity" as a concentration of "publicity of representation" at court, aiming only at endowing authority with an "aura" ("Structural Transformation of the Public Sphere" 9). Ritualized performance of status confirms the already existing order, and the public's role is confined to that of passive spectators. This is not a true public sphere, since it is "completely unlike a sphere of political communication" ("Structural Transformation of the Public Sphere" 8).

The following account of the public sphere of baroque Spain contrasts at nearly every point with the bourgeois public sphere theorized by Habermas. In the Baroque a full-fledged public sphere takes shape, in which individuals and groups attain political agency without the transparency of rational debate or any pretense of equal participation. Its prominent features include asymmetrical access, distortion of public discourses due to their hidden or partially hidden relations to power, and internal divisions between "modern" and "archaic" practices. Rather than an idealized, timeless abstraction, the public sphere of the Baroque is a hybrid, compromise formation, made up of a blending of earlier and later practices, technologies, and social structures.

As we will see, the baroque public sphere is indeed characterized by spectacle, but the audience's role is far from passive. Through performance, power is negotiated and status redefined in a complex play of display and concealment. Rumor plays a fundamental role in setting the stage for this performative dimension. Whereas the bourgeois public sphere is grounded in a distinction between public and private, in the Baroque, the opposite of "public" is "secret." The separation between that part of the self that is in the public domain and that which is not is simply that the latter is hidden, at least for the moment, and at least as far as the person in question is aware. Anything is fair game for the public realm, then, once it becomes openly known; and everything secret functions as a kind of submerged dimension of the public sphere, for obviously *someone* knows it and may make use of that knowledge, for instance by passing it along as a rumor. Despite its opacity and apparent disorder, however, this public sphere allows the individual actor to behave rationally within it, though according to a logic quite distinct from the one prevailing in the social world of high modernity.

A Roadmap of the Baroque Public Sphere

The Baroque is a period of transition, in which earlier elements persist, even as emergent technologies and the nascent modern state incorporate them into a new order that transforms their meaning. Imperial expansion and the slow consolidation of the absolutist state bring together sectors of society and geographical areas that were formerly isolated. They are incorporated into the framework of a public sphere that, though externally joined in a loose network, remains fragmented and internally divided along multiple lines: ethno-religious, class, regional, urban vs. rural, etc.

Particularly characteristic of the Baroque is the coexistence of practices which, from a high modern perspective, would seem to belong to different epochs. The printing press, for example, does not simply displace the manuscript; rather, as Fernando Bouza's research has shown, it produces a shift in its functions. Manuscripts could still be preferred as a way to get around censorship or to avoid legal responsibility, for example in the case of libelous texts. At times the same book might circulate in two different versions, with certain chapters being altered or excised in the printed edition (Bouza 27–83). The side-by-side juxtaposition of manuscript and printed book contributes to the duplicitous structure of the baroque public sphere. Within the state-sanctioned institution of book publishing, texts circulated freely in a transparent space; yet they were "shadowed" by manuscripts whose circulation was clandestine. This duplicity, a consequence of the transition to modernity, is typical of the baroque public sphere in general.

Another example of this overlapping of premodern and modern practices can be found in the impact of the rapidly expanded judiciary on town life. Despite increased access to the king's justice, local power relations based on intimidation, strategically employed violence and insults, and the code of honor persisted. Reconstructions by José Manuel de Bernardo Ares and other historians of the *régimen local* reveal the extent to which the absolutist monarchy was always a negotiated settlement. State power extended itself by incorporating local oligarchies into a judicial structure that at the same time gave legitimacy to the political aspirations of their opponents, both *hidalgos* and *pecheros*. The expansion of litigation in Spain studied by Richard Kagan resulted from the strategic convergence between myriad local rivalries and the crown's interest in consolidating its own power. One powerful clan could obligate another to initiate a costly *pleito de hidalguía* in the Chancery at Granada or Valladolid simply by starting a rumor concerning their purity of blood. In this way the higher judicial bodies of the monarchy came to function as arbiters in struggles for legitimacy within the *régimen local*. Yet the use of symbolic street violence to damage rivals' reputations through acts of public humiliation continued unabated, with the same families turning at one time to the "archaic" approach of public insult and at another employing the "modern" one of taking their opponents to court. Indeed, the practice of violent intimidation through publicly staged scenes of dishonor parallels judicial recourse in exactly the same way as the circulation of manuscripts parallels that of printed books.

Thus a basic structuring element of the baroque public sphere is the epistemological instability resulting from the lack of transparency in such fundamental modern institutions as printed books and legal proceedings. Since what is "public" is only the tip of the iceberg, and there is no way any one individual can know how much more is "secret," the game of public interaction in the Baroque is always played under the sign of an uncertainty arising from not knowing how much the other person might be hiding, or how much of what one knows it would be prudent to reveal. In the bourgeois public sphere, for something to be public knowledge means everyone has access to the information and accepts its accuracy. In early modern Spain, to say that something is public knowledge—*público y notorio*, as the documents often express it—means that there is a rumor going around to that effect. The epistemology of rumor dominates public discourse in our period.

A feature shared by all the emerging practices in the preceding review is the active role of state power. In this sense, at least, the Spanish Baroque indeed corresponds to the *cultura dirigida* (guided culture) described by José Antonio Maravall. But this role of the state is mitigated by the persistence of residual practices, all of which to a certain degree exceed such control. Frequently, the same individuals engage in both, calculating which better serves their needs in a given situation. As a result, the distinctions between localized vs. state power, secrecy vs. transparency, and exclusivity vs. accessibility, rather than being the stable basis on which to construct a public sphere, serve as variables within it. Participants in the state-sponsored practices (e.g., book printing, litigation) must be in a position to at least make a show of loyalty to the crown, religious orthodoxy, and honor (grounded in *limpieza de sangre*). These categories do not regulate the other practices in the same manner, so the residual elements become an ambiguous zone of dialogue and confrontation between official and alternative positions. The status of any display of officially sanctioned qualities is radically undermined by awareness that the same person who makes it may elsewhere be engaging in a partially hidden, but still public, practice, with quite a different meaning. Terms such as duplicity, hypocrisy, and dissembling imply a moral judgment that impedes our full understanding. The most useful term for understanding the nature of participation in the baroque public sphere is *performance*. Certainly, this performative dimension is inseparable from the enormous popularity of the theater at this time. But it is also in this context, as I will argue below, that we must learn to see the negotiation of religious identities and the partially submerged practices nowadays referred to as crypto-Judaism and crypto-Islam.

The theorist *par excellence* of the baroque public sphere is Gracián, whose *Oráculo manual* brilliantly describes the functioning of self-interested reason in the context of theatricalized competition for status. In this respect, his position is analogous to that later occupied by Kant, who theorized the role of disinterested reason in the bourgeois public sphere. It is suggestive in this context that for William Egginton the recognition of self-interest in Gracián's morality was precisely what had to be repressed for the Enlightenment ethics of Kantian disinterestedness to come to the fore, making Gracián a crucial figure in the emergence of the modern subject, but one whose role had to be eclipsed (165–67). Gracián effectively analyzes the behavioral modalities of this play of hiding and revealing, of donning one or another mask according to context, and of speaking or remaining silent depending on access to this or that discursive practice. In the *Oráculo manual*, the courtier's goal is to regulate the judgment others make of him by seeing himself as they see him. We are instructed to cultivate a degree of interiority, not for its own sake, but in order to control more effectively the image we project. Interiority is an element in the social game of appearances, since without some depth it is impossible to hide anything (Egginton 154). The counterpart of dissembling one's own secondary and tertiary intentions is inferring those of the interlocutor, leading to a spiraling complexity of feints and counterfeints, similar to a game of chess. There simply is no private self from which the gaze of the other is excluded. Aphorism 297, "Obrar siempre como a vista," ([the prudent courtier] acts as if he were always in full view of everyone) states a basic principle underlying the entire *Oráculo*, to do everything as if you were being watched, because sooner or later, you will be. The prudent courtier "even when alone, acts as if he were in full view of everyone, for he knows that all will be known, and he thinks of those who will later hear the rumor (*noticia*) as if they were direct witnesses now" (259). As we have seen, the opposite of public is not private, but secret, at least for now. The difference between performer and spectator is here a matter of chance: at any given moment the performing subject becomes the judging interlocutor and vice versa. Only the constant back-and-forth movement remains. Such is the performativity of the Baroque.

Habermas's description of the public sphere emphasizes the positive values associated with the bourgeois model: individual autonomy, transparency, equality, universality, and rationality. By contrast, the agency of the person who performs in the baroque public sphere is necessarily fragmented and situational. It is the agency, not of an autonomous, private citizen, but of a member of a specific status group. The social space in which this agent operates is not a unified, transparent arena of rational debate, but a maze of distinct possibilities. While a rational actor can be postulated, à la Bourdieu, developing strategies to maximize available options, one cannot even begin to describe this actor's behavior without specifying socioeconomic class, ethnic group, gender, and other aspects of codified social identities. The bourgeois ideal of an open forum for representing mutually transparent positions simply does not exist. The baroque public sphere does not "add up" to such a forum, but instead remains internally fragmented in separate spaces, overlapping and interpenetrating, yet often mutually opaque to one another, through which subjects move, sometimes visible, sometimes hidden or half-hidden. Nonetheless it is my contention that these fragments do in fact constitute a single public sphere by virtue of the interlocking continuum into which they are articulated. This is especially true because of their shared connection to the growing state power. In this above all consists the modernity of the baroque public sphere.

The Inquisition and the Harnessing of Rumor

In the Baroque, fact and hearsay, which high modernity devotes so much effort to keeping apart, are exasperatingly intertwined. In print media, one finds, among the tremendously popular forerunners of modern journalism known as *relaciones de sucesos*, a hopeless mix of factual and fanciful accounts, propaganda, prophecy, and speculation.[1] A whole series of epistemologically ambiguous discourses flourish, among them interpretations of portentous events (monstrous births were especially popular); unabashedly propagandistic accounts of Spanish victories (without reports being published of the defeats); and elaborate hoaxes such as the *libros plúmbeos* of Sacromonte. These apocryphal texts, written in Arabic on circular lead plates and hidden in Sacromonte in 1595, purported to be the lost writings of a group of Arab martyrs who supposedly preached Christianity in Spain long before the Islamic invasion of 711. The aim of the hoax was clearly to incorporate the Moriscos into a myth of national origin as a way of counteracting their exclusion from the emerging definition of Spanish identity. The *libros plúmbeos* are thus a fascinating attempt to harness the power of rumor. Hiding them and arranging for them to be "found," the counterfeiters provided them with the anonymity of an accidental "discovery," and let rumor do the rest.[2]

Rumor, the dominant social discourse of the Baroque, is the antithesis of the rational debate that characterizes the bourgeois public sphere. Habermas's idealized notion of human communication assumes the reciprocal good faith of participants, an implicit mutual agreement to frankly state what both sides sincerely believe to be true, and perhaps most importantly, a willingness to take responsibility for what is said. Rumor's social efficacy depends precisely on the opposite: ambiguity, uncertainty, and above all, anonymity, for a rumor never expresses the speaker's own claims or views, but only what an unnamed, collective "they" are saying. As Hans-Joachim Neubauer puts it in *The Rumour: A Cultural History*:

> [W]hat everyone says is not necessarily a rumour. Rather a rumour is that about which it is said that everyone is saying it. Rumours are quotations with a loophole. It can never be determined who is being quoted; and nobody knows who it was who originally set it in motion. (3)

The epistemology of rumor corresponds precisely to the flexible, evasive play of hiding and revealing that typifies communication in the baroque public sphere. We must not be too quick to dismiss it as a crude form of news, as if rumor flourished only because modern journalistic accountability and critical evaluation of sources have not yet been achieved. As Guha has shown with respect to rumors of rebellion in colonial India, "rumour belongs to a class apart from news" (260). Its anonymity not only allows one to repeat it without fear of reprisal; it also means everyone who repeats it can alter its meaning:

> [R]umor functions as a free form liable to a considerable degree of improvisation as it leaps from tongue to tongue. The aperture which it has built into it by virtue of anonymity permits its message to be contaminated by the subjectivity of each of its speakers and modified as often as any of them would want to embellish or amend it in the course of transmission. (Guha 261)

Constantly changing, not subject to any authority, rumor spreads like wildfire, generating as it goes a sense of solidarity among those who help to transmit it (Guha 257). Its ability to evade control makes it an especially important communicative mode wherever increasing centralization of power is taking place. As Neubauer points out, early modern images of rumor often depicted it as a many-tongued monster, or, as in Thomas Campion's 1615 masque, wearing a traveling cloak covered with tongues (72–80). Its constitutive ambiguity made it a powerful tool for sedition, and public authorities feared its influence; but by the same token, it was tempting to think the state might be able to make use of it. In his unfinished essay "Of Fame," Francis Bacon, having warned against the dangers and unreliability of rumor, adds a crucial comment: "But now if a man can tame this monster, and bring her to feed at the hand, and govern her, and with her fly other ravening fowl and kill them, it is somewhat worth" (quoted in Neubauer 78).

The most successful early modern experiment at taming rumor was undertaken by the Spanish Inquisition. In addition to maintaining a vast network of informers, inquisitors carried out regular visits to the towns of their jurisdiction, during which an *edicto de la fe* would be read inviting residents to come forward and declare anything they had seen *or heard* against the faith.[3] The visit was, in large part, an operation of recording as much rumor and hearsay as possible in *libros de testificaciones*, to be digested in the comfort of the tribunal's headquarters, eventually putting on trial only the most promising cases. Only a few *libros de testificaciones* from Cuenca and Toledo have survived. What they reveal about the discursive practice of informing on one's neighbors to the Inquisition provides significant insight into the functioning of the baroque public sphere among the peasant population.[4]

Obviously, gossip existed and exists today in rural Spain, as it always has in agrarian communities the world over. Gossiping about one's neighbors can be understood as a local form of social control, existing alongside a series of practices in which "normal" civility is flouted, such as public insults, shaming, and blasphemy. The *libros de testificaciones* amply demonstrate that such practices, including blasphemy, continue unabated despite fear of the Inquisition. Nonetheless, the inquisitor's presence transforms the local institution of gossip into a denunciation to the king's representative. Most of the conversations reported have taken place within a period of five years preceding the visit, but cases in which witnesses claim to give verbatim what people said over twenty years before are not uncommon. Multiple layers of discussion accumulate over time. For example, a witness reports what someone else overheard, adding the comments made by those who shared in the gossip, giving their names so the inquisitor can call them in or perhaps claiming not to remember who was present. Always, the final layer is the present act of denunciation before the inquisitor. Frequently, in fact, the reading of the *edicto de la fe* provokes the penultimate of these layers, as a witness declares he or she has come forward because after mass some parishioners were discussing the list of offenses in the edict, and someone remembered what so-and-so had said a year or two before. To a certain extent, then, it is the inquisitor's arrival that adds the social tension needed to turn ordinary gossip into fast-moving, protean rumor.[5]

Not surprisingly, the rumors that begin to fly when the inquisitor comes to town often concern Conversos or Moriscos. Because spreading rumors generates a feeling of solidarity, encouraging a secret practice of denouncing the heresies of religious minorities was a way of getting people to identify their own status as *cristianos viejos* with the active rejection of these groups. One gets the impression, reading their testimony and considering the time frames involved, that townspeople developed mental collections of accusations, filing them away until the inquisitor came to visit their town or even some nearby town to which they could easily travel and return home the same day. Over decades, this develops into a habit of vigilant spying.

In Quintanar de la Orden, a town that had about 2,500 inhabitants in 1575, a group of Converso families were subject to their neighbors' scrutiny for a period of roughly one hundred years, from the late fifteenth century until the 1590s, when a series of trials for crypto-Judaism did away with the Converso community there.[6] In every generation members of the Mora and Villanueva families were tried by the Inquisition based mainly on hearsay. Their neighbors developed strategies for testing them to see if they ate pork, and for entering their homes on Saturdays to catch them resting and on Sundays to catch them working. All the information they collected was duly reported to the inquisitors and eventually shows up in their trials, no matter how trivial. Alongside reports of their cleaning the house and lighting candles on Fridays and wearing new clothes on Saturdays, one also finds improbable, made-up rumors. In a particularly puerile example, witnesses recalled that someone had once overheard Alonso de Mora and his wife Mari Juárez talking inside their walled garden, plotting to rub an apple on her vagina and then place it where an unsuspecting passerby would find and eat it. Such absurd projections onto Conversos of pure malice toward Christians smack of medieval popular anti-Semitism, but the rumor was duly recorded and preserved (Archivo Deocesano de Cuenca leg 781, exp 2313).

The arrival of the Morisco refugees from the War of the Alpujarras provided both potential allies against the Conversos and another target for Old Christian xenophobia.

In 1585 several *quintanareños* traveled six miles to "unburden their consciences" to the inquisitor who was visiting Villanueva de Alcardete. Juan de Hiniesta, a *regidor* from Quintanar, heard that Angelina, a *morisca* who sometimes helps out in the Mora home, says they often do housework on Sundays (ADC *Libro* 325, fols. 127r–128r). A few days later, Catalina Patuda, seventeen years old, comes forward to tell the story of how Brianda, a *morisca* who runs errands for Conversos, supposedly went to Francisco de Mora's yard to buy a basket of grapes and came upon him whipping a crucifix (ADC *Libro* 325, fol. 131). Since this is a serious offence, the inquisitor calls in Brianda to question her. Her testimony is revealing:

> Asked if she knows or presumes the cause of her being called before this Holy Office, she said she presumes she has been called because they say in Quintanar that she says she saw a certain Francisco de Mora, resident in Quintanar, whipping a crucifix, and that *she has seen no such thing*. (ADC *Libro* 325, fols. 139r–140r; emphasis added)

Under pressure, she sticks to her version and explains that she tried herself to find out the origin of the rumor five years earlier when it began to circulate, confronting those who she had heard were going around saying she had seen Francisco de Mora whipping a crucifix. Nobody admitted even having passed the rumor on, and she never cleared up how it got started. That Brianda knew perfectly well why she had been called in shows how current the rumor was. Despite her consistent refusal to confirm it, the story was included as part of the evidence against Francisco de Mora, who was executed for Judaizing in 1592. Rumor has a life of its own, independent of the truth or falsity of the affirmation it conveys. Unfounded hearsay alone was not enough for the Inquisition to convict suspected heretics, but it could be the basis for arresting and torturing them until they confessed. Thus the Inquisition successfully integrated preexisting local discursive practices into its thoroughly centralized, rationalized judicial procedures, transforming rumor into an instrument of royal power.

But even as the Inquisition harnessed rumor, the documentation shows that it also created new opportunities for resistance. This is especially the case as more attention was focused on policing the speech and conduct of the *cristianos viejos* themselves. After the Council of Trent, widely held folk beliefs that clashed with Catholic doctrine were reclassified as *delitos contra la fe* (crimes against the faith). Two in particular account for a consistently high percentage of the accusations made during visits: the view that extramarital intercourse was not a sin, provided the woman received payment (referred to as *simple fornicación*) and the explicit claim that marriage was as pleasing to God as membership in a religious order which required celibacy (*estados* or *error sobre estados*). The declarations found in the *libros de testificaciones* display a regularly repeated pattern: a group of people is gathered, at someone's home or in the fields, and the conversation turns to a topic that holds out the opportunity to publicly display a transgressive attitude. Where *simple fornicación* is involved, one person usually asks someone directly whether they consider intercourse a sin if the woman gets paid, whereupon the second person says no, and someone else who is present responds, how dare you say such a thing? At this point the one who had said simple fornication was not a sin remains utterly silent. Often, a qualifier, such as "for me, it's not a sin" or "I do not hold it to be a sin" accompanies the negative response. In the case of *estados*, a married person usually says in the presence of a *beata*, who has taken a public vow of chastity but lives at home rather than in a convent, that the state of matrimony is no less pleasing to God than her chastity. She insists that this is not the view of the Church, whereupon, again, the one who pronounced the heretical proposition keeps silent.

These conversations reveal a practice of using heretical statements whose repression had recently come under inquisitorial control as a way of marking a distinction between pious and irreverent factions in the community. These statements appear to serve to "test the waters" to see how those present would respond to a little irreverence. The specific issue marking the boundary between folk beliefs and official doctrines is raised in a very deliberate way. The silence of those whose error is pointed out is also interesting. Though there are instances in which they retract what they said, and others in which they strenuously insist upon it, silence is the most frequent response and seems to reflect both a stubborn refusal to accept the orthodox view and a prudent decision not to continue voicing the heretical opinion.[7] Here a dividing line is being drawn between two groups who challenge one another's claims to authority. On one side, there are those who align themselves with the external monarchical and ecclesiastical powers of the nascent modern state, represented in the town directly by the inquisitor. On the other, there are those who continue to defend the local autonomy of a community accustomed to the de facto religious freedom resulting from centuries of benign neglect. Gradations of piety and irreverence had existed in rural Castile long before the Council of Trent.[8] But it is the Inquisition's intervention in town life, the institutionalization of rumor, that incorporates such otherwise banal disagreements into the baroque public sphere, magnifying their meaning by attaching greater consequences to such "errors of faith" than they had previously had.

Occasionally, one finds more extreme examples of individuals who cultivate an aggressive irreverence, openly rejecting fundamental tenets of Christian doctrine and espousing a consistently skeptical attitude. Mari Díaz was quoted in one declaration as saying, around 1575, that Hell was only invented to frighten us ("dijo que no había infierno, que por meternos miedo lo decían") (ADC *Libro* 325, fol. 130r). In 1590, she was denounced for denying the virgin birth. After a sermon concerning Joseph's doubts when Mary told him she was pregnant, she asked her friends, "But didn't they sleep together?" ("¿Pues no se acostaban juntos?") (ADC *Libro* 326, fol. 169v). In both cases, the inquisitor called in an additional witness to confirm the accusation, but there is no record of Mari Díaz of Quintanar ever having been tried by the Inquisition. In an age of increasing control over religious practice and belief, when her Converso and Morisco neighbors were subject to close scrutiny, she apparently went around for over fifteen years occasionally making such scandalous statements, presumably as a provocation to sincere believers. Though an Old Christian by birth, she carved out a public role for herself as a religious skeptic. And the Inquisition did not judge her performance of that role worthy of a major intervention, though they kept a record of the denunciations against her. Such cases, though relatively rare, require us to consider religious identity in early modern Spain in the light of baroque performativity.

Performing Religious Identities in the Baroque Public Sphere

Let us imagine for a moment that we have been transported back in time to around 1600, and that we are attending mass in a Spanish town—let us say for example, Quintanar de la Orden. Looking around at those present, we can readily divide them into certain groups: *beatas* at the front, along with members of leading families like the Ludeñas or Villaseñores, whose ancestors are buried in luxurious chapels they endowed at great expense; then folk of more modest means, some of them at least overtly pious, such as the members of local *cofradías*. But over here is a man known for getting drunk and pronouncing scandalous blasphemies; and there is Mari Díaz, the *picarona* who sometimes makes sly skeptical comments with a wink and a laugh (many in the town think she's mad). A number of Converso families, most notably the Moras and Villanuevas, attend mass in a church where the *sambenitos* of their grandparents and great-grandparents are displayed. The perennial rumor about them is that they are really practicing Jews. And in back are the Moriscos, brought here forcibly thirty years ago from Granada and an object of suspicion ever since, though among them there are those whose commitment to Christianity is such that ten years from now they will avoid expulsion by offering themselves as "slaves" to the Virgin in perpetuity.[9]

Are all of these people engaging in the "same" practice? Conceptually, how can we clarify what is going on here? There is a set of obligatory institutionalized behaviors (attending mass, reciting prayers, annual confession) around which are grouped many aspects of social life: genealogy, family tradition, deeply held beliefs about ultimate reality, social status, etc. At the height of the Counter-Reformation, certainly, nothing one does or says in relation to this field will be seen as neutral. But as the above discussion shows, there are subtle ways of communicating alternative positions—and some not-so-subtle ways. An ongoing war of position exists between religious authorities and their official or unofficial "agents," on the one hand, and the various groups or individuals who try, in their own small way, to resist the pressure to adhere to an ever-narrower orthodoxy are on the other. More than a single set of beliefs or practices, religion in Counter-Reformation Spain has become a complex field of interacting positions, through which individuals and groups perform identities on which to a large extent their status depends. In the following examples, I have chosen to focus on performative aspects of the religious identity of the Morisco minority, though a similar analysis might be made for any social group.

In the *libros de testificaciones* as well as in full-scale trials before the Inquisition, the statements Moriscos that are accused of making are often calculated to be reversible and ambiguous. One such type is the attempt to claim a minimum of status by distinguishing oneself from Jews and thereby implicitly from known or reputed Conversos. Luis de Murcia, a Morisco from Granada and resident of Corral de Almaguer, was reported to have said that Islam (*la ley de los moros*) was superior to Judaism (*la ley de los judíos*) because, although the Muslims did not recognize the virgin birth, they did believe in God. Above all, he argues to the inquisitors, Jews, not Muslims, crucified Christ. Clearly his intention was to compare his own ethno-religious minority with the Conversos, and witnesses quoted him as saying, "We [the Moriscos] do not believe in the virgin birth." But even under torture he insisted that he used the third person, not the first person plural, that he never meant to identify with the Islamic beliefs he was describing, and that he never approved of Islamic teachings (*la ley de los moros*). Though they got no more out of him, the tribunal considered his having said Islam was superior to Judaism somewhat heretical (*malsonante*) and required him to abjure his statement in a public *auto de fe* (ADC Inq leg 305 num 4410).

That the Moriscos's cultural and religious identity tended to conform more closely to Christian orthodoxy in public, with any vestiges of Muslim customs and practices being confined mainly to the private sphere, is obvious. But if we pay close attention to specific cases, a more complex picture emerges. In 1588, Christian friends of Angela Hernández, a *morisca* resident of Priego (Cuenca), presented themselves before the inquisitor on his visit to complain that her husband was trying to force her to follow Muslim dietary laws (ADC *Libro* 326, fols. 1–3). In other cases, a young woman's stepmother or her mother-in-law might take on the responsibility of imposing Islamic practice. Isabel de Gálvez, twenty years old, a sincere Christian and evidently a troubled young person, tired of pretending to be a Muslim at home, finally denounced her own father, her stepmother, and a number of family friends, leading to fourteen trials for crypto-Islam in Campo de Criptana, beginning in 1589 (ADC Inq leg 317 exp 4581). With no separate public sphere of their own, the Morisco community had to try to define itself under Christians' watchful eyes. Confusion and uncertainty surrounded their ethnic identity and the attempts at least some of them made to preserve it. In a case from Socuéllamos a young Morisco, Luis López, becomes furious with his new bride when he discovers, after the marriage, that she does not speak Arabic. If he had known, he tells her, he never would have married her (ADC, Inq. leg 283, num 3945).

The necessity of maintaining a public façade of Christian practice made it impossible even for the Moriscos themselves to know what members of their community were doing secretly. Generalizations about how widespread crypto-Islam might have been, whether made by a sixteenth-century prelate or a twentieth-century historian, amount to spreading rumors. An honest look at the documentation suggests a situational adjustment, directed toward one or another public or private audience. Thus we have only multiple levels of performance, including the performance that a Morisco accused of being Muslim might put on in the torture chamber of the Inquisition. Certainly, there was considerable solidarity among the Moriscos as a group—hardly surprising given their shared marginal status—and this could sometimes manifest itself as hostility toward Christians and, by extension, Christianity. A typical example of this was the fact that Moriscos often celebrated the news of Turkish or Algerian victories over Christian forces, thus antagonizing their neighbors (García Arenal 87–88). Another is the trial of Lorencio Hernández, who publicly said, "My law is better than yours" (apparently referring to Islam) to a Christian. The circumstances under which he said it were that he had come to the defense of a *morisca* who was being taunted and intimidated by a group of Christians when she went to buy fruit from a wagon in town, and one of the men had called Hernández *perro*, provoking his angry response. The extent to which he was really publicly revealing a previously hidden Muslim identity can perhaps be measured by his chief defense: drunkenness. As corroborated by witnesses, he had been drinking wine at a makeshift bar where many Moriscos of Corral de Almaguer spent their idle hours (ADC, Inq., legajo 252 expediente 3404).

In no other document are the malleability and reversibility of Morisco identity more powerfully demonstrated than in a curious report on events that took place in Manzanares, another town of la Mancha, in August of 1600. Like other towns and cities throughout New Castile, Manzanares had received a sizeable contingent of Moriscos from Granada. The local church being in need of funds to gild the *retablo* (altarpiece), someone suggested they raise money by staging a festival of *moros y cristianos*, and that the Moriscos could play the part of the Moors, their ancestors. The idea won the approval of local authorities, who gave their permission and enthusiastically supported the project from the outset. Though normally it was strictly forbidden for the Moriscos to carry arms, the forty-three who participated in this festival were outfitted with swords, daggers, halberds, and five arquebuses. They paraded every Sunday for about six weeks, waving a flag adorned with five crescent moons, brandishing their swords, firing the guns, and calling the Moorish war cry of "li, li." When the big day arrived, they held the most of the principal citizens of the town "captive" in a makeshift "castle" erected for that purpose on the town square. After sharing a banquet with their captives, they released them upon payment of a "ransom," which went toward gilding the *retablo*. They raised more than 800 *reales*. People came from miles around to enjoy the spectacle, which the organizers and the Moriscos alike deemed a success.

Having the Moriscos impersonate the exotic indomitable Moors of literary fame was a bold step. Some might even say an imprudent one, given the fact that many viewed them as intransigents who could never be integrated into Spanish society. It was believed that at least some of the Granada Moriscos who participated in the rebellion of the Alpujarras had blended in with the deported refugees, and rumors abounded of secret alliances between the Moriscos and the Ottoman Empire. There is certainly a delightful paradox in asking them to pretend to be Muslims for the purpose of enhancing the decoration of the local Christian shrine. Arguably, the event even points to a possible integration of the Moriscos, not through a gradual forgetting of their past, but in full recognition of their cultural otherness. Apparently, a few residents of Manzanares found this simulacrum of war too close to the real thing for comfort. We know what we do about the festival, in fact, because an alarmist faction within Manzanares, seeing no local authority opposed to it, sent word to the Consejo de Órdenes, which initiated proceedings against the local officials of the town. The official sent to investigate, Juan Gutierre de Villegas, prepared a report of some 68 folios (AHN, OO MM, AHT 36.658) in which he includes interviews with a number of townspeople, all of whom agree there was no scandal provoked by the event. People enjoyed watching the Moriscos dress up as Moors, and they knew it was for a good cause. Gutierre de Villegas recommended some penalty for the two *alcaldes* that authorized the mock battle, perhaps a fine and a period of banishment, but the documentation makes no mention of any such action being taken. The festival held in Manzanares was probably not unique, though it may be uniquely well documented.[10] It reveals that, although constrained both by royal power and local opposition, it was still possible as late as 1600 for the proud display by a group of Moriscos of their Muslim heritage to be incorporated as a central element in a Christian celebration. It does not reveal anything at all, however, about the Moriscos's own religious beliefs or what elements of Muslim practice, if any, they secretly maintained.

Religious identity in the Baroque—like other forms of identity—is partly predetermined by birth and partly negotiated in the public sphere. In this process of negotiation, as we have seen, individuals and groups can achieve a modicum of self-determination through performance. The constant presence of rumor, however, conditions the reception and interpretation of the identities to which they thereby lay claim. Thus the interplay of rumor and performance constitutes a crucial dynamic of baroque publicity. The modern ideology of secularization has tried (and it seems, ultimately, failed) to make religion a matter of personal belief, marginal to the public sphere. Yet if we are to understand the role of religious controversies in early modern Spain—and Europe generally—we must abandon attempts to ground our understanding in terms of the beliefs held intimately by individuals or even groups, examined in isolation from the larger social context. Such issues as the Morisco question or the cultural role of Conversos cannot be understood purely on their own terms, but rather must be looked at within the baroque public sphere as a whole.

Conclusion: Then and Now

Before the institution of the bourgeois public sphere, the role of the populace in public life was much more active than Habermas has argued. Far from restricting agency in social and political matters to a tiny elite, the Baroque multiplied opportunities for all social groups to articulate a relation to state power. As Michel Foucault taught us to understand in *Discipline and Punish*, however, such articulation, even when it takes apparently benign forms, is always double-edged. Actively seeking their own benefit, individual subjects do not necessarily perceive the degree to which they are extending the reach of the institutions of power, integrating previously independent spheres of social life into an ever more comprehensive system.

Where the baroque public sphere differs most sharply from its post-Enlightenment equivalent is not, then, in the degree of agency, but in the forms that agency takes and the means used to represent it. The baroque public sphere was in many ways the opposite of the order ushered in by the Enlightenment. In the Baroque, the *self* was rendered transparent by the other's unrelenting gaze, but *knowledge* was opaque, endlessly fragmented, and deferred by rumor. Those mirror fragments in turn reflected back upon the transparency of the self, shattering it into shards of personality from which a temporary, makeshift whole could only be forged in dramatic confrontation with the other. The subjectivity underlying archival documents and cultural artifacts left behind by the Baroque thus differs from that of autonomous bourgeois individuals, divided into public and private selves.

Before mass communications, as Nancy Fraser has argued, access to the public sphere was in practice restricted almost entirely to propertied white men. The deterioration of bourgeois society over the course of the twentieth century has done away with the illusion of social harmony made possible by such exclusions, and few today mourn the loss. We nonetheless retain normative expectations of open debate and rational discourse, even as baroque performance and the ubiquity of rumor have resurfaced. Our public sphere is a hybrid combining baroque and bourgeois elements.

In our current predicament, it is helpful to remind ourselves that the Baroque was also a kind of modernity—a modernity, moreover, that was always in some respects present beneath the surface of bourgeois culture. Modern bourgeois culture's pretense of disinterested, rational debate was itself a performance, despite which rumors reached the metropolis that what was happening in the colonies was not altogether pretty. Unfortunately, that pretense is still with us, though the cynicism of the performance shows through more plainly than it used to. And unfortunately, we still rely on rumors to know what is really being done in the name of Progress, but at least now those rumors circulate faster than ever.[11]

Notes

1. In *Literaturas marginadas* María Cruz García de Enterría laid the theoretical groundwork for the recent explosion of studies of *relaciones de sucesos*. Ettinghausen's articles, along with his anthology, focused on tales of the monstrous and fantastic, and have also helped to open this new direction for Golden Age studies. Augustín Redondo's use of *relaciones* as background for the study of *Don Quijote* shows how much can be done with the rich store of information they contain.
2. In addition to Hagarty's edition, the most comprehensive studies of the *libros plúmbeos* are Godoy Alcántara's still useful *Historia crítica de los falsos cronicones* (1868), Darío Cabanelas's sympathetic portrait of Alonso del Castillo, one of the most likely participants, and Carlos Alonso's *Los apócrifos del Sacromonte*, a detailed narrative of the controversy running from their discovery in 1595 to definitive Papal judgment of their inauthenticity, signed by Pope Innocent XI on January 28, 1682.
3. Jiménez Montserrín has transcribed and annotated instructions for carrying out visits and *edictos de la fe* (291–94, 499–539).
4. Dedieu briefly discusses the *legajos* containing such *testificaciones* from the Inquisition of Toledo in *L'administration de la foi* (183–90). My remarks here are based on *Libros* 325, 326, and 327 of the Archivo Diocesano de Cuenca (ADC).
5. Beginning with Jaime Contreras's 1992 *Sotos contra Riquelmes*, Inquisition studies have increasingly turned toward the examination of how inquisitorial activity dovetailed with pre-existing social tensions. An immediate precedent for the position I take here is Gretchen D. Starr-LeBeau's view that inquisitorial intervention in late fifteenth-century Guadalupe imposed rigid distinctions among religious identities where fluid positionings had prevailed.
6. Charles Amiel has reconstructed what he considers a homegrown Manchegan variety of *marranismo* based on the trial records of the *conversos* from Quintanar. The population statistic quoted here comes from his study as well (213).
7. Peter Burke discusses the importance of "prudent silence" and dissimulation among

elites in early modern Spain and Italy, emphasizing the "rise of silence in the political domain" as a consequence of the "increasing number of spies in government service" (123–41). Essentially, the inquisitors, with their network of *familiares* and *comisarios*, were among these spies and contributed to the politicization of ordinary conversation in even the most out-of-the way towns and villages.

8. Employing a *libro de testificaciones* from the late fifteenth century, John Edwards has shown such gradations were present from the earliest introduction of the Inquisition in Soria.
9. Félix San José Palau gives a description of the chapels of the parish church of Quintanar with the dates of their foundation and the surnames of some of those buried in them (91–95). Juan Martín de Nicolás includes a transcription of the document by which Isabel Hernández, widow of Ginés Pérez, and her children were made slaves of the Virgen de la Piedad, patroness of Quintanar, in 1610 (36–39).
10. In the final letter accompanying his report, Gutierre de Villegas excuses the Moriscos in part by commenting that "such festivals in which these same [Moriscos] from that kingdom [of Granada] are extremely common in this province, in almost every town in [Campo de] Calatrava and in the county seat which is Almagro, for many years now" (ANH OO MM AHT36.658).
11. The archival research on which this essay is based was carried out under a grant from the Whiting Foundation.

Works Cited

Archivo Diocesano de Cuenca Inquisición.
Archivo Histórico Nacional, Sección de Ordenes Militares, Archivo Histórico de Toledo.
Alonso, Carlos. *Los apócrifos del Sacromonte: Estudio histórico*. Valladolid: Esudio Agustianiano, 1979.
Amiel, Charles. "Les cent voix de Quintanar: Le modèle castillan du marranisme." *Revue de l'histoire des religions* 218 (2001): 195–280, 487–577.
Bernardo Ares, José Manuel de. "El régimen municipal en la corona de Castilla." *Studia historica: Historia moderna* 15 (1996): 23–61.
Bouza, Fernando. *Corre manuscrito: Una historia cultural del Siglo de Oro*. Madrid: Marcial Pons, 2001.
Burke, Peter. *The Art of Conversation*. Cambridge: Polity Press, 1993.
Cabanelas, Darío. *El morisco granadino Alonso del Castillo*. Granada: Universidad de Granada, 1965.
Contreras, Jaime. *Sotos contra Riquelmes: Regidores, inquisidores y criptojudios*. Madrid: Anaya and M. Muchnik, 1992.
Dedieu, Jean-Pierre. *L'administration de la foi: L'Inquisition de Tolède, XVIe–XVIIIe siècle*. Madrid: Casa de Velazquez, 1989.

Edwards, John. "Religious Faith and Doubt in Late Medieval Spain: Soria circa 1450–1500." *Past and Present* 120 (August 1988): 3–25.

Egginton, William. "Gracián and the Emergence of the Modern Subject." *Rhetoric and Politics: Baltasar Gracián and the New World Order.* Ed. Nicholas Spadaccini and Jenaro Talens. Minneapolis, MN: Minnesota of University Press, 1997. 151–69.

Epalza, Mikel de. *Los moriscos frente a la Inquisición. En su visión islámica del Cristianismo.* Madrid: Pliegos de Encuentro Islamo-Cristiano, 2001. Re-impression from Vol. III of the *Historia de la Inquisicion en España y América* published by the Biblioteca de Autores Cristianos in 2000.

Ettinghausen, Henry. "The News in Spain: *Relaciones de sucesos* in the Reigns of Philip III and IV." *European History Quarterly* 14 (1984): 1–20.

———, ed. *Noticias del siglo XVII: Relaciones españolas de sucesos naturales y sobrenaturales.* Barcelona : Libros Puvill, 1995.

———. "Sexo y violencia: noticias sensacionistas en la prensa española del siglo XVII." *Edad de Oro* 12 (1993): 95–107.

Foucault, Michel. *Discipline and Punish: The Birth of the Prison.* Trans. Alan Sheridan. New York: Vintage, 1977.

Fraser, Nancy. "Rethinking the Public Sphere," *Habermas and the Public Sphere.* Ed. Craig Calhoun. Cambridge, MA and London: MIT Press, 1992. 109–42.

García Arenal, Mercedes. *Inquisición y moriscos. Los procesos del Tribunal de Cuenca.* Madrid: Siglo XXI, 1978.

García de Enterría, María Cruz. *Literaturas marginadas.* Madrid: Playor, 1983.

Godoy Alcántara, José. *Historia crítica de los falsos cronicones.* Madrid: Real Academia de la Historia, 1868. Facsimile edition. Madrid: Alatar, 1981.

Gracián, Baltasar. *El oráculo manual y arte de prudencia.* Ed. Emilio Blanco. Madrid: Cátedra, 1997.

Guha, Ranajit. *Elementary Aspects of Peasant Insurgency in Colonial India.* Durham, NC and London: Duke University Press, 1999.

Habermas, Jürgen. "Fundamentalism and Terror." Interview with Giovanna Borradori. Giovanna Borradori. *Philosophy in a Time of Terror: Dialogues with Jürgen Habermas and Jacques Derrida.* Chicago: University Chicago Press, 2003.

———. "Further Reflections on the Public Sphere," *Habermas and the Public Sphere.* Ed. Craig Calhoun. Cambridge, MA and London: MIT Press, 1992. 421–61.

———. *The Structural Transformation of the Public Sphere.* Cambridge, MA: MIT Press, 1989. First published as *Strukturwandel der Öffentlichkeit.* (Neuwied and Berlin: Luchterhand, 1962.)

Hagarty, Miguel José, ed. *Los libros plúmbeos de Sacromonte.* Granada: Comares, 1998.

Jiménez Montserrín, Miguel. *Introducción a la inquisición española.* Madrid: Editora Nacional, 1980.

Kagan, Richard L. *Lawsuits and Litigants in Castile, 1500–1700.* Chapel Hill, NC: University North Carolina Press, 1981.

Maravall, José Antonio. *La cultura del Barroco*. Barcelona: Ariel, 1975.
Martín de Nicolás, Juan. *La Piedad: Historia y devoción de Quintanar de la Orden*. Quintanar de la Orden: Mayordomía de Nuestra Señora de la Piedad, 1996.
Neubauer, Hans-Joachim. *The Rumour: A Cultural History*. Trans. Christian Braun. London and New York: Free Association, 1999.
Redondo, Augustín. *Otra manera de leer el* Quijote. Madrid: Castalia, 1998.
San José Palau, Félix. *Miscelánea quintanareña*. Quintanar de la Orden: Asociación Cultural Moros y Cristianos San Juan, 1997.
Starr-LeBeau, Gretchen D. *In the Shadow of the Virgin: Inquisitors, Friars, and Conversos in Guadalupe, Spain*. Princeton, NJ: Princeton University Press, 2003.

9

Reason's Baroque House
(Cervantes, Master Architect)

William Egginton

If it ain't *Baroque*, we might say, don't fix it; yet, if it is Baroque, it can't be fixed, because the desire to fix is part of what's Baroque. In this admittedly silly (and hackneyed) play on words we find the traces of a paradox central to early modern reason. The Baroque is the cultural expression of a deep and abiding anxiety regarding the nature and extent of human reason. In its philosophical expression, this anxiety takes the form of a paradox that hinges on the problem of truth as a function of appearances. Does the veil of appearances that besieges the senses represent in some altered form a truth, a reality that in itself persists in an unaltered, and hence different, form? If so, does piercing the veil of illusion give one access to this unadulterated truth? Or does the very access to the truth pervert it yet again, in that, in appearing to us, it is reduced to appearance and hence to the very thing that hides from us its essence? Modernity has hung haplessly on the horns of this baroque dilemma since the perfection of its cultural expression in the seventeenth century, and perhaps every age or movement since can be read as an attempt—more or less successful in propagating itself as the final answer—to transcend or at least circumvent its grasp.

Conceiving of baroque cultural artifacts as in some profound way responding to the original provocation of this dilemma suggests several strategies for the construction of those artifacts. On the one hand, such artifacts can be seen as affirming the promise of appearances, that they are indeed the way to the uncorrupted truth, and that perseverance along this path will lead to glory. At the apex of this tendency lies a neoplatonic religious discourse, embraced by Reformation and Counter-Reformation representatives alike, that equated terrestrial life with appearance and hence with deception and degeneracy and proposed that the truth lay in another dimension altogether. The tempting mistake to make here has been to associate the baroque style exclusively with the Counter-Reformation. The fact is that the radical negation of the ephemeral espoused by the reformist churches is not opposed to the superficial opulence of Counter-Reformation ritual; the two stylistic tendencies are responding to precisely the same urge. Both Reformation and Counter-Reformation ideology confront the conflation of life itself with the suspect world of appearances that is at the heart of the Baroque, but while the one responds by negating the lived world, the other responds by emphasizing its theatricality, and hence ultimate emptiness, in relation to a determining but previously unknown ground.

The other strategy is less common, the necessary but often unnoticed inverse to this major strategy of modern reason. It is what we could call a minor strategy, borrowing the term from Deleuze and Guattari's theorization of a minor literature. Minor literature is writing that deterritorizalizes the ordinary use of language, leaving behind the normal structures of sense by following the lines of flight or escape that such language inevitably carries with it (*Kafka* 21). Unlike the Baroque's major strategy, which affirms the promise of appearances whether by negating the world or ostentatiously theatricalizing it, the minor strategy suggests that the promise of purity behind the veil of appearances is itself already corrupted by the very distinction that gave birth to it, and hence that reason's house is built on shifty ground, in some sense always already baroque(n). The shearing away of appearances is, from this perspective, an infinite process, once one buys the initial premise that appearances are deceptive and hide from us a purer, uncorrupted truth. The insight of the minor strategy would thus seem to correspond to the central insight of deconstruction, which the late Derrida posed in the apparently paradoxical formulation "essential corruptibility."[1] Corruption is not a secondary, belated process that attaches onto a pristine subject; rather, essence is at heart already corrupted by time, change, decay. In a similar way, according to the minor strategy, the truth hidden by the veil of appearance is already corrupted by the appearances, and is itself nothing but appearance, but without the ultimate support of an ever-receding ground of unmitigated self-identity.

I want to emphasize, however, that the identification of such a strategy at the heart of the Baroque should not be discarded as the merely ahistorical imposition of a late twentieth-century fad on seventeenth-century cultural artifacts. One should not, properly speaking, ever "apply" deconstruction to anything; rather, deconstruction can be shown to be already at work in texts. But one of the reasons it can and is so often shown to be working in the texts of modernity is that modernity is organized philosophically around the baroque dilemma, whose minor strategy is a relentless deconstruction of its major strategy's pretensions.

Just as "every text of metaphysics carries within itself, for example, *both* the so-called 'vulgar' concept of time *and* the resources that will be borrowed from the system of metaphysics in order to criticize that concept" (Derrida, "Ousia" 61), in the same way every baroque text carries within itself both the major strategy and the resources that will be borrowed from the baroque system in order to criticize that strategy. This is not to say, however, that the texts are therefore subject to the sort of leveling reading that would make them all minor in the same way and to the same extent. Nor are we led to claim the opposite, that a cultural product somehow depends for its strategic position vis à vis major baroque culture on the explicit intention of its author. Here lies, as Julio Baena has already indicated, the one weakness in the important discussion between himself and David Castillo on the subject of the aesthetic value of Cervantes' *Los trabajos de Persiles y Sigismunda*. The *Persiles*, Baena had argued in his *El círculo y la flecha*, "fails as a novel where it intends [*pretende*] to triumph as a utopia."[2] In his review of Baena's book, Castillo countered this claim at the level of its content with an equally agile reversal, arguing rather that it "triumphs as a novel where it intends [*pretende*] to fail as a utopia" (quoted in Baena, *Discordancias* x, my translation). It does not, in other words, claim or intend to be a utopia, but is rather a full-blown critique of utopia,[3] and therein lies its literary value. Literary value, therefore, is associated with irony, self-awareness, and distance from the model it imitates, in this case the Byzantine novel. The difference between Baena's and Castillo's positions comes down to whether that distance is there or not, the presence or absence of which they both implicitly equate with whether Cervantes intends (*pretende*) it to be there: Castillo says he does, Baena says he does not.[4] In what concerns an evaluation of the *Persiles*, I ultimately come down agreeing with Castillo. Whereas Baena says of the *Persiles* that it is a novel he likes "less each time he has to read it" (*Discordancias* xii, my translation), I think the *Persiles* is a marvelous novel, and my reason for thinking so is based on the same reasons Castillo argues for: namely, it subverts the genres it appears to be imitating rather than merely imitating them. Nevertheless, in my view this subversion has absolutely nothing to do with what Cervantes *intends*. If *Persiles* is a great novel, it is because it *really*, *objectively* subverts the genres it imitates; but unlike the new critical, objectivist notion of irony I am recalling here, the objective subversion of Cervantes' text relies entirely on its immersion in historical context. Here I may quote again either Baena's or Castillo's typically cogent formulations: *Persiles* exhibits "la obligada excentricidad de lo pretendidamente centrado," or, "an anamorphic mirror that inverts or ... distorts the symbols of Counter-Reformation culture." In my view, the *pretensión* implicit in Baena's formulation is not Cervantes' but that of the major strategy, with which Cervantes' texts are in a relation of *structural excentricity*. Cervantes' texts, in other words, are subversive in that they consistently deploy the minor strategy in a structural relation to the Baroque's major strategy. I could demonstrate what I mean using the *Persiles*, but I think both Castillo, in *(A)wry Views*, and Baena in his books have done that in a decisive way,[5] regardless of their surface disagreement. Instead, I will look at several of the *Novelas ejemplares* in which Cervantes, master architect of the Baroque, shows us what is involved in making, and unmaking, the baroque house of reason.

The House and Its Walls

A baroque house, Deleuze writes in his analysis of Leibniz, has neither windows nor doors (*Fold* 3–13). This is because the Leibnizian house, the monad that is the soul, inflects the entire world in the folds of its walls. Its walls are expressive of the world; no change goes unregistered in the universe that laps up against its walls. But this house, we should recall, is multi-layered. It has an upstairs that corresponds to the monad proper; but it also has a foyer downstairs that would correspond to the monad's form of communicability with the world. It is a paradoxical communicability, at once blind and omniscient, hermetically sealed and vibrantly exposed to the world.

A baroque house, Cervantes explains in his novella *El celoso extremeño* (The Jealous Extremaduran), has more than one set of walls:[6]

> compró una [casa] en doce mil ducados, en un barrio principal de la cuidad, que tenía agua de pie y jardín con muchos naranjos; cerró todas las ventanas que miraban a la calle y dióles vista al cielo, y lo mismo hizo de todas las otras de la casa. En el portal de la calle, que en Sevilla llaman casapuerta, hizo una caballeriza para una mula, y encima della un pajar y apartamiento donde estuviese el que había de curar della, que fue un negro viejo y eunuco; levantó las paredes de las azuteas de tal manera que el que entraba en la casa había de mirar al cielo por línea recta, sin que pudiesen ver otra cosa; hizo torno que de la casapuerta respondía al patio. (103–4)

(he bought [a house] for twelve thousands ducats, in a good part of the city, which had running water and a garden with many orange trees; he closed all the windows that looked out on the street and gave them a view up to the sky, and he did the same with all the other windows in the house. In the entryway to the house, which in Seville they call the *casapuerta*, he made a stall for a mule, and above it a straw loft and apartment where the one who would care for it could stay, who was an old, black eunuch; he raised the level of the terraced roofs such that one who entered into the house would have to look directly at the sky without being able to see anything else; he made a gate going into the patio to correspond with the *casapuerta*.)

The idea of this plan recalls to some degree Deleuze's reconstruction, in that the doubled structure of the walls and the space separating them guarantee simultaneous communicability and insulation. That the inhabitant of the intermediate space be black and castrated guarantees in Carrizales's mind that the very means of necessary communication—namely the entryway for provisions—be facilitated by one whose being and status hinder or make impossible communication. As a black man Luis represents the most culturally alien being for Extremadura's provincial society; as a eunuch Luis represents the deadening of that most dangerous of forces, sexual desire.

The doubling of Carrizales's walls resonates throughout the text in the word that more than any other characterizes his condition as *celoso* (jealous): *recato*. A word popular both to Cervantes and the writing public of his time as a mode of description for the *care* one should take for all things regarding one's honor, *recato* takes on a doubly important role for Carrizales. *Recato* (first recorded usage of *recatado* 1605), defined as *honestidad* or *modestía*, results itself from the doubling of *cato*, of what one does when one sees, is aware, pays attention. The redoubling of this awareness is at the same time a reflexive, self-constituting act, as self-consciousness is to consciousness, or the ego to the libidinal investment that first cathects objects, in Freud's telling. *Recato* also connotes something like the *recinto*, the second wall formed by surrounding something, wrapping or taping it.

According to the dynamics of a baroque house, however, all these efforts at reinforcement are to naught. The physics of baroque architecture would seem to work contrary to those laws we are comfortable with, and with which the jealous worries of a man like Carrizales consoles himself. For these laws suggest that what one wants to protect one should hide from the outside world with the redoubled protection of *re-cato*, an awareness turned back onto itself; but the physics of baroque architecture decree that the very walls that one doubles up, in the interest of protecting an interior purity, have the intensely disturbing effect of rendering that interior space impure, and of doing so, apparently, to an extent exactly proportionate to the intensity of the protection.

Carrizales's plan would seem to be perfect: build a house with two walls; let the interior space be inhabited only by virgin women;[7] let no man ever pass beyond the interior wall; and let communication between the walls be mediated by a man with no contagions, either cultural or sexual. As Cervantes writes regarding the extent of Carrizales's banishment of masculinity from the inner recesses of his house:

> aun no consintió que dentro de su casa hubiese algún animal que fuese varón. A los ratones della jamás los persiguió gato, ni en ella se oyó ladrido de perro; todos eran del género femenino. De día pensaba, de noche no dormía; él era la ronda y centinela de su casa y el Argos de lo que bien quería. Jamás entró hombre de la puerta adentro del patio. Con sus amigos negociaba en la calle. Las figuras de los paños que sus salas y cuadras adornaban, todas eran hembras, flores y boscajes. Toda su casa olía a honestidad, recogimiento y recato. (106)

> (he did not even consent that animals enter in his house if they were male. No cat ever chased the rats of the house, nor was the barking of a dog ever heard in it; all were of the feminine gender. By day he pondered, by night he did not sleep; he was the watch and sentinel of his house and the Argos of what he loved. No man ever entered the door to the patio. With his friends he did business in the street. The figures on the clothes that adorned the rooms and stalls were all females, flowers, and woods. All his house smelled of honesty, seclusion, and *recato*.)

And yet despite—or better, precisely because of—Carrizales's supreme *recato*, his greatest fear is realized, and his prize possession, the virgin child he calls his wife, is spoiled. (Albeit not technically, as Leonora's honesty ultimately exhausts even her young, energetic suitor; but it is enough that he be found in the inner sanctum, if not *in flagrante delicto*.)[8]

The difference between "despite" and "because of," however, is a great one, and it thus makes sense to pin this point down. When we first meet the undoer of Felipo's honor, Cervantes gives us a clue as to his motivation: "Uno destos galanes, pues, que entre ellos es llamado *virote*, mozo soltero, que a los recién casados llaman *mantones*, asestó a mirar la casa del recatado Carrizales, y viéndola siempre cerrada, le tomó gana de saber quién vivía dentro; y con tanto ahínco y curiosidad hizo la diligencia que de todo vino a saber lo que deseaba" (107) (One of those young men who among themselves is called *virote*, bachelor [the word emphasizes his *virility*], who calls the recently married *mantones* [shawls], began to watch the house of the *recatado* Carrizales, and seeing it always locked, got the urge to know who lived inside; and he did his work with such enthusiasm and curiosity that he came to know everything he desired). The tension between two explanations is clear: either the threat is entirely external—the *virote* who ridicules the institution of marriage; or it is due to the very fact of Carrizales's *recato*, which gives birth to the curiosity and desire to enter a house defined by its state of permanent closure. While the major strategy of baroque mores demands the former (and thus Don Juan's shadow haunts a society built on women's *honestidad*), Cervantes' minor proclivity keeps upsetting the show. His way finally cleared through his picaresque seduction of *el negro* Luis's social and musical desires, *el virote* Loaysa sings in his first performance to the gathered virginity of the inner sanctum the following verse:

> Madre, la mi madre,
> guardas me ponéis,
> *que si yo no me guardo,*
> *no me guardaréis.*
> Dicen que está escrito,
> y con gran razón,
> ser la privación
> causa del apetito;
> crece en infinito
> encerrado amor;
> por eso es mejor
> que no me encerréis;
> *que si yo* etc. (125)

> (Mother, my mother,
> you put guards on me,
> *but if I don't guard myself,*
> *you won't guard me.*
> They say it is written,
> and it is certainly true,
> that privation
> is the cause of appetite;
> it grows to be infinite,
> enclosed love;
> that's why it's better
> not to close me in;
> *since if I don't etc.*)

Although these lines could be simply read as the persuasive rhetoric of our energetic *virote*, we should not fail to note that the choice of songs is not his own but is rather that of the *dueña*—ultimately responsible for safeguarding Leonora's honor, whose own desire for Loaysa will eventually be the key to delivering her ward to his clutches—and is enthusiastically seconded by the audience of damsels.

The damsels, in other words, are perfectly aware of what Freud would theorize somewhat later as an inherent transgressivity to desire, when he remarked, for example, in his *Three Essays on the Theory of Sexuality* that the "sexual instinct in its strength enjoys overriding" (18) such social and somatic barriers as disgust or, in the case at hand, the honesty of virgins. But as Freud also argued in his later treatise on prohibition and its discontents, Totem and Tabu (*Totem and Taboo*), the desire to transgress taboo (of which the honor code is a clear example), is fundamentally an ambivalent one: "Diese [the *Tabuvölkern*, the people of the taboo] haben also zu ihren Tabuverboten eine *ambivalente Einstellung*; sie möchten im Unbewußten nichts lieber als sie übertreten, aber sie fürchten sich auch davor; sie fürchten sich gerade darum, weil sie es möchten, und die Furcht is stärker als die Lust" (323) (the people of the taboo thus have an ambivalent attitude toward their taboo; they would like nothing more than to transgress it, but they are also afraid of it; they fear precisely because they would like to, and the fear is stronger than the desire). Now it is clear in what sense the honor code in literature does not function like a taboo in Freud's sense: in literature the fear of breaking a taboo is *always* overridden by the pleasure thereby produced. Nevertheless, Freud's emphasis on the ambivalence of effect produced by the taboo resonates suggestively with Cervantes' architectural imagination. According to the major strategy, virginal purity must be guarded, and doubly so, against its corruption through external forces. But Cervantes' minor strategy reveals a desire in relation to prohibition as always ambivalent: purity at once fears intrusion *and* desires it. But if such desire coexists with its enclosure, purity can hardly be called pure.

The minor strategy often emerges to greatest effect in Cervantes in the narrative voice, which by and large confines itself *at the level of its utterance* to aping the conventional dictates of the genre or social mores in which the narrative finds its context. But what is offered in the utterance, in classic Cervantine irony, is immediately undermined in the enunciation, as in this case in which the narrator discusses Carrizales's hypothetical discovery of his honor's destruction:[9]

Bueno fuera en esta sazón preguntar a Carrizales, a no saber que dormía, que adónde estaban sus advertidos recatos, sus recelos, sus advertimientos, sus persuasiones, los altos muros de su casa, el no haber entrado en ella, ni aun en sombra, alguien que tuviese nombre de varón.... Pero ya queda dicho que no había para qué preguntárselo, porque dormía más de aquello que fuera menester; y si él lo oyera, y acaso respondiera, no podía dar mejor respuesta que encoger los hombros y enarcar las cejas y decir: "¡Todo aqueso derribó por los fundamentos la astucia, a lo que yo creo, de un mozo holgazán y vicioso, y la malicia de una falsa dueña, con la inadvertencia de una muchacha rogada y persuadida! . . ." Libre Dios a cada uno de tales enemigos, contra los cuales no hay escudo de prudencia que defienda ni espada de recato que corte. (129)

(It would be good at this moment to ask Carrizales, if we didn't know he was sleeping, where were now his well warned *recatos*, his suspicions, his warnings, his persuasions, the high walls of his house, the not having let in even the shadow of one who would have the name of male.... But we've already said that there was no reason to ask him, because he was sleeping more than necessary; and if he heard it, and perhaps responded, he couldn't give a better answer than shrug his shoulders and arch his eyebrows and say: "All this was brought down to its foundations by the cleverness, I believe, of a pleasure-seeking and vicious youth and the malice of a false governess, along with the carelessness of an importuned and persuaded girl! . . ." God free us from each of these enemies, against whom there is neither shield of prudence that defends nor sword of *recato* that cuts.)

The paragraph is a masterful example of the master architect's style, its tropological dynamics reinforcing his architectonics at every turn. The entire paragraph is hypothetical, because, as he reiterates, Carrizales was sleeping and hence completely out of the loop. And yet we are treated to both what we might ask him, and what he might respond, were it the case that he were not so soundly asleep. This next level, then, contains both the tut-tut of the conventional narrator's admonitions and the accusations toward the usual suspects in cases of honor's deceit. This litany, however, is not only undermined by the narrator's own repeated observation that the question and answer are irrelevant, insofar as Carrizales is sleeping, but also by the apparent affirmation his last words lend to the charges against these "enemies, against whom there is neither shield of prudence that defends nor sword of *recato* that cuts." That there can be no defense against these enemies is perhaps, then, the entire point, because the sword of *recato* is one that cuts both ways, its reflexive return inscribing in the purity of its defendant the ambivalence so fundamental to all objects of taboo.

Carrizales, at least when awake, does not, it turns out, answer in the same way the narrator of convention would have him answer. Although foolish in life, his fatal sorrow has learned more wisdom than that. Instead of the bloody revenge for which the honor code provides as the appropriate response to its violation, Carrizales blames only himself, as having "yo mismo . . . sido el fabricador del veneno que me va quitando la vida . . ." and having, like "el gusano de seda, [fabricado] la casa donde muriese" (133) (myself been the maker of the poison that is now taking my life; like the silkworm, made the house in which I will die). And is this not the answer that the narrator in some sense seeks when, appearing for the first time in first person in the last paragraph of the story, he declares himself stumped by Leonora's silence as to her ultimate innocence? For her innocence was, in fact, never the point. Carrizales built himself a baroque house, and now he must die in it.

The Force of Baroque Blood

It may strike us as readers of Cervantes' fiction that his work—and his *Exemplary Novels* are exemplary of just this—shuttles back and forth between the conventional (or even down right conservative) and the subversive. We modern literary critics naturally appreciate the latter and feel somewhat embarrassed by the former. Hence the debates over the value of the *Persiles* I cited above, and the tradition of apologies for Cervantes' first foray into fiction, the pastoral *Galatea*. Even within the frame of the novellas this distinction appears to be at work, with more or less openly critical works like *El celoso extremeño* (The Jealous Estremaduran) and *El Licenciado vidriera* (The Glass Graduate) facing off against more modest and seemingly traditional fare like *La fuerza de la sangre* (The Force of Blood).[10] It would seem counterintuitive to call subversive a story that seems to extol the force of blood in a society obsessed with the discriminating potential—in terms of class, religion, and overall privilege—of that force. But if what I have claimed about Cervantes as being the producer of a work that is structurally minor in relation to a major cultural context has validity, then evidence of the minor strategy's preeminence must be apparent to a greater or lesser degree in all his work, especially that work dating from the same period.

La fuerza de la sangre is the tale of a young woman of good but poor stock who is raped by a young nobleman and gives birth to his son, unbeknownst to either the nobleman or his parents. At the age of seven, the boy, having already shown signs of his noble heritage, is hit by a horse in the street and suffers a serious head wound, from which his noble blood flows. The boy and his blood are seen by none other than the boy's paternal biological grandfather, who is moved by his semblance to his own son, who has been living in Italy for these last seven years. The denouement is obvious for any reader of Golden-Age literature: the boy's mother is reunited with his biological father, and her honor thereby repaired. In this way, it seems, the distinction of blood is reaffirmed, and the crime of rape overlooked, if not justified.

And perhaps this reading would suffice, were it not for Cervantes' architectonics, which are at work laying out blueprints even in a story that is not explicitly about building houses. Judging from the frequency of expressions relating to it, if there is a central concept or theme to this story, it is *secrecy*. On more than twenty occasions Cervantes uses the word *secreto* or some variant suggesting the hidden, the feigned, the dissimulated. The motive of the secret is the safeguarding of honor, and it is the role of the force of blood to pierce the secret by restoring honor to its rightful place. Blood's force, then, is equated to honor; it restores what has been dishonored, and what for that very reason has required secrecy. But the minor structure of Cervantes' story never ceases to upset and question this dichotomy, and to interrogate that very honor that would seem to be the source of blood's force. In this way it is not too far off to draw again a parallel with Derrida's thought, and suggest that the title *The Force of Blood* be read in much the same vein as Derrida's *Force of Law*, namely, as a demonstration that the force underlying the rule of any set of conventions is never pure, self-identical, but rather itself always already an effect of the conventions it apparently founds.[11] And just as the force of law, justice, is a force that must disrupt with its precipitating violence the symmetry of the legality it (in an essential ambivalence) sustains, the force of blood that is honor turns out—in the hands of Cervantes' minor strategy—to be the disruptive force of that very legality it sustains. And the minor strategy reveals this precisely by way of honor's own essential ambivalence.

Although it would appear that everything in this story is a secret—beginning with the name of the perpetrator, "que por ahora, por buenos respectos, encubriendo su nombre, le llamaremos con el de Rodolfo" (77) (whom we will for the time being, for reasons of respect, covering his name, call with that of Rodolfo)—the secret at the heart of all the others is that of the dishonor that serves as the story's source and motive. Already on the second page, Leocadia's parents (as that is the name we are told to call her) hide the fact of her abduction from the forces of justice, "temerosos no fuesen ellos el principal instrumento de publicar su deshonra" (78) (fearful that they would be the principal instruments in publicizing their dishonor). The theme of the publicity of dishonor is a common one in Golden-Age literature, with variants gracing the titles of several theatrical standards of the age. With Cervantes' minor strategy, however, the theme is treated to its full paradoxical extent. In the darkness of the room into which she has been secreted, Leocadia wishes the darkness to become her eternal resting place, "pues es mejor la deshonra que se ignora que la honra que está puesta en opinion de las gentes" (79) (since dishonor that goes unknown is better than honor exposed to the opinion of people). The same theme is developed in slightly different language later in the story, when her father counsels her to keep the story of her violation a secret:

> Y advierte, hija, que más lastima una onza de deshonra pública que una arroba de infamia secreta. Y pues puedes vivir honrada con Dios en público, ne te penes de estar deshonrada contigo en secreto: la verdadera deshonra está en el pecado y la verdadera honra con la virtud. (84)

> (And beware, daughter, that more damage is done by an ounce of public dishonor than by a sackful of secret infamies. And since you can live in public in an honored way with God, don't worry about being dishonored with yourself in secret: true dishonor is in sin and true honor is in virtue.)

The paradoxical nature of the honor code achieves its full expression in these two sentences and is displayed in even greater detail when they are mapped against the preceding formulation. The final sentence of the above quotation corresponds to the major strategy of what we could call, borrowing a term from Barbara Fuchs, baroque transparency.[12] According to this strategy, the world of appearances is denigrated with respect to the true world of sin and virtue, damnation and salvation. Honor is translated out of its worldly context and into its otherworldly context, and thus made dependent on these truths known to God and to our souls. The sentence immediately preceding it, of course, expresses exactly the opposite sentiment; an ounce of public dishonor is worse than a sackful of secret dishonor. The second, in this light, becomes merely the overt justification for the first. In other words, precisely because public dishonor is such a bad thing, let us use the language of virtue and vice to justify keeping your dishonor secret.

Here we witness one possible trope of the minor strategy: simply taking the major strategy at its word and letting it work against itself. While both the sentences are examples of common pieties of the major strategy, in laying them out side by side Cervantes allows them to draw a "line of flight" leading to their mutual dissolution. In a similar way, aligning the two sentences dealing with the relative damage of public and private dishonor precipitates a line of flight toward the very disintegration of any coherent notion of honor:

a) Dishonor that goes unknown is better than honor exposed to the opinion of people.
b) More damage is done by an ounce of public dishonor than by a sackful of secret infamies.

As the argument is somewhat complex, I will present it in schematic form, as follows:

a) [-H] > H or, hidden dishonor is better than exposed honor (honor exposed to the danger of its own loss)
b) -H < [-H] or, exposed dishonor is worse than hidden dishonor

What we see from this schematic treatment is that, while the value of hidden dishonor remains the same in both equations (namely, as "better than" or at least "not so bad"), the side of the equation carrying the negative value reverses its charge without thereby changing its value relative to the other side. What this means is Cervantes has established a relative equality between honor and dishonor *insofar as what is assumed is its exposure*. There is, in other words, no such thing as honor, only the fear of exposure, a fear, obviously enough, coterminous with enclosure and secrecy.

As in the case with Carrizales's baroque house, the house Cervantes has built for honor has a distinctly minor feel. Its walls are made of secrecy and dissimulation, as if to hide, to protect an honor whose redemption through the force of blood will render those walls obsolete. Inside the walls are innocence, virtue, and nobility. But the minor strategy undoes all that. Within its walls we are treated not to innocence and purity; instead, piercing those walls reveals to us the theater of how the promise of purity was dependent all along on its very enclosure, just as its corruption was a function of our desire to protect it from corruption. For this reason it cannot be a mere coincidence that the scene of Leocadia's dishonor is referred to in theatrical terms. Upon returning to her parents, "[d]íjoles lo que había visto en el teatro donde se representó la tragedia de su desventura" (83) (she told them what she had seen in the theater where was represented the tragedy of her misfortune). But more than that, her very tragedy was a masterpiece of acting. As she tells Rodolfo as he prepares to rape her for a second time, "[d]esmayada me pisaste y aniquilaste; mas ahora que tengo bríos, antes podrás matarme que vencerme: que si ahora, despierta, sin resistencia concediese con tan abominable gusto, podrás imaginar que mi desmayo fue fingido cuando te atreviste a destruirme" (81) (when I was in a faint you stepped on me and destroyed me; but now that I have my wits about me, you'll have to kill me before conquering me: because if now, awake, I were to concede to your so abominable desire without resistance, you might imagine that my faint was put on when you dared to destroy me). In other words, in the very moment of resisting a second violation, what Leocadia fears is not the violation itself, but the impression her failure to resist might give her attacker about the nature of their first encounter: that her faint was, well, a feint.

Like deconstruction, the minor strategy works from the inside of a textual and social tradition, undermining the established models of truth that support its idea of reason. If honor as the force of blood constituted a powerful ideologeme of the day, a tool in the box of a powerful propagandistic effort to promote the interests of an entrenched elite (Maravall), the major strategy was one that sustained and supported that effort, and it did so primarily through a kind of myth of eventual transparency (Fuchs). This is the strategy of sustaining the promise of essence against the ephemera of appearances. In this view, the force of blood is driven by a truth not subject to the whimsy of appearance, the necessary secrets, and dissimulations of social life. In this view, innocence is guarded against corruption, which approaches from outside the walls of a baroque house. But the minor strategy churns away at the heart of this pretension. This strategy feeds on these illusions, not in order to carve them away and reveal, at last, that long-sought truth; rather, the minor strategy reveals only a minor truth, a truth with a small *t*. That truth is the other side of baroque reason, the shifty ground on which the modern house is built.

Notes

1. See Hägglund's discussion in "The Necessity of Discrimination."
2. Cervantes, Baena writes, "aferrándose a la ciencia de entonces, quiere que su libro sea el mejor jamás escrito, de la misma manera que todo dictador quiere crear la sociedad perfecta: controlando sus menores ángulos. Que lo consiga o no es otra cosa: es precisamente *la otra cosa*, la obligada excentricidad de lo pretendidamente centrado, lo que marca al *Persiles* como un enorme *fracaso*, en lo que estribaría su grandeza, como la del *Quijote* estribaba en haber fracasado rotundamente en sus pretensiones." (30) (fastening onto the science of the age, wants his book to be the best ever written, in the same way that any dictator wants to create the perfect society: by controlling its smallest angles. Whether he achieves it or not is another thing: it is precisely *the other thing*, the necessary excentricity of the desired centrality, which marks the *Persiles* as an enormous *failure*, in precisely that which should have been the seat of its greatness, just as the greatness of the *Quijote* lies in having roundly failed in its desires).

3. As Castillo puts it in his own reading, *(A)wry Views,* the *"Persiles* is a counter-utopian narrative . . . an anamorphic mirror that inverts or . . . distorts the symbols of counter-Reformation culture" (94–95).
4. Baena notes in his response in *Discordancias* that "[lo] débil de lo que ambos decimos está en ese verbo *pretender*" (xi) (the weakness in what we each say is in that verb *pretender*), and, indeed, begins his whole discussion in *El círculo* with Cervantes' own send-up of the intentional fallacy in the *Quijote* (25). Thus, if I disagree with Baena's aesthetic judgment concerning the novel, it is in no way via a disagreement with his theoretical articulation of the stakes, which are impeccable. Similarly, in *(A)wry Views,* Castillo's reading is anything if not anti-intentionalist, focusing on what he specifies as the "effect—if not necessarily the intention—of much of Cervantes' writing" (106). Indeed, in his extremely positive review of the book, it is precisely Castillo's distinction between intention and effect that Clamurro identifies as a possible source of controversy for some critics (187).
5. As have such critics as Ruth El Saffar, Diana de Armas Wilson, and Amy Williamsen, each in their own way.
6. All translations of the *Novelas* are mine. The house has been at the center of much of the criticism on *El celoso extremeño,* the eminent Casalduero going so far as to call the house the story's protagonist (171). Molho discusses the three different versions of the tale in Cervantes' oeuvre and analyzes the house in terms of its sexual dimensions: "nos hallamos, pues, ante un edificio de doble dimensión: horizontal y vertical. La penetración ha de realizarse horizontalmente, pero la plena posesión requiere que se penetren las profundidades de la casa, adueñándose de las verticalidades" (755) (we find ourselves, then, before a building of double dimensions: horizontal and vertical. Penetration must take place horizontally, but full possession requires that one penetrate the depths of the house, taking ownership of its verticalities). Later he refers to "esa especie de esclusa vaginal que es la *casapuerta,* o *cazzo-puerta*" (that species of vaginal passage that is the *casapuerta,* or *cazzo-puerta*); the latter etymology—suggesting a door for the penis (*cazzo*)—is creative, if not entirely confirmable. Forcione focuses on the aspect of "confinement" in the house (35–36). See as well Áviles's review of the criticism that focuses on the house (71–72). His own argument is that the space of the house "nos obliga a pensar el comportamiento del lenguaje desde la perspectiva de la alegoría" (72) (obliges us to think the behavior of language from the perspective of allegory). Percas de Ponseti also reads the novella as an allegory, namely, for "el abismo que existe entre la verdad absoluta y la verdad individual" (137–38) (the abyss that exists between absolute truth and individual truth).
7. Or at least hermaphroditic. See Molho's reading of Marialonso's name (743).
8. This represents a change between the Porras de la Cámara manuscript and the 1613 edition, which gave Américo Castro reason to berate Cervantes' conformism. See Castro, 244, quoted and discussed in Williamson, 793.
9. Here I agree with Castillo's emphasis in seeking the anti-ideological (what he calls "anamorphic") potential of Cervantes' narrative style in the relation between enuncia-

tion and utterance. As he puts it in his reading an apparent "*anti-morisco* diatribe" in *Persiles*, "[t]he choice of subject of enunciation—which is but the victim himself—forces us to reassess the meaning of the racist statement from an oblique viewpoint" ((A)wry Views 112). Percas de Ponseti makes a similar claim about the novella's ending.

10. Forcione sums up at least part of the criticism in referring to the novella as "an example of bad taste and unintelligibility" (328). Slaniceanu mentions its "reputation as a repository of idealistic statements concerning virtue, honor, and marriage" (101), but sees in it herself "strong overtones of social criticism" (102), and finally interprets it as "undermining the authority of those figures normally associated with [marriage's] formalities" (109). For Welles, critics have admired its form while deploring "its lack of psychological verisimilitude" (240). She herself privileges the "literal level" of the rape itself, and argues that Cervantes has subverted the "typical rape narrative" (241). El Saffar privileges instead the allegorical level and speaks of the novella as presenting an "abstract combination of forces" (128). Howe reads it as a contribution into the debate around *honor y honra* (64–65), a debate which, as I argue below, I see Cervantes rather as deconstructing in its entirety. Friedman argues that it is the "countergeneric recourses" common in Cervantes that drive the novella, namely "deviation from the norm and from readerly expectations" (147–48), and De Rentiis reads the structure of the novella as ultimately vindicating freedom of perspective (170). Baena focuses his "discordant" reading on the "error" found in the novella's last lines, in which the couple are said to spend the rest of their days enjoying themselves [*gozaron de sí*] as opposed to each other; an error that, if taken as "intended," does much to undo the conventional construction of marriage and the honorable ending (181–82).

11. In one section Derrida describes the problem in the terms of speech act theory, saying, "[i]t is true that any current performative supposes, in order to be effective, an anterior convention. A constative can be *juste*, in the sense of *justesse*, never in the sense of justice. But as a performative cannot be just, in the sense of justice, except by grounding itself on conventions and so on other performatives, buried or not, it always maintains itself with some irruptive violence. It no longer responds to the demands of a theoretical rationality. And it never did, it was never able to; of this one has an a priori and structural certainty. Since every constative utterance itself relies, at least implicitly, on a performative structure . . . the dimension of *justesse* or truth of theoretico-constitutive utterances (in all domains, particularly in the domain of the theory of law) always thus presupposes the dimension of justice of the performative utterances, that is to say their essential precipitation, which never proceeds without a certain dissymmetry and some quality of violence" (256). The mere question of the rightness or wrongness (*justesse*) of a constative utterance, Derrida argues, must implicitly invoke the dimension of "justice," which he situates in this essay beyond the stability, the theoretical rationality, of calculable questions of legality. The parallel is also present with Deleuze and Guattari's notion of minor literature: "Finally, it is not the law that is stated because of the demands of a hidden transcendence; it is almost

the exact opposite: it is the statement, the enunciation, that constructs the law in the name of an immanent power of the one who enounces it—the law is confused with that which the guardian utters, and the writings precede the law, rather than being the necessary and derived expression of it" (*Kafka* 45).

12. See Fuchs's reading of what she calls Cervantes' critique of transparency, 87–110.

Works Cited

Avilés, Luis F. "Fortaleza tan guardada: casa, alegoría, y melancolía en *El celoso extremeño*." *Cervantes: Bulletin of the Cervantes Society of America* 18.1 (1998): 2–95.

Baena, Julio. *Discordancias cervantinas*. Newark, DE: Juan de la Cuesta, 2003.

_____. *El círculo y la flecha: principio y fin, triunfo y fracaso del Persiles*. Chapel Hill, NC: University of North Carolina Press, 1996.

Casalduero, Joaquín. *Sentido y forma de las Novelas ejemplares*. Madrid: Editorial Gredos, 1969.

Castillo, David R. *(A)wry Views: Anamorphosis, Cervantes, and the Early Picaresque*. West Lafayette, IN: Purdue University Press, 2001.

_____. Review of *El círculo y la flecha: principio y fin, triunfo y fracaso del Persiles*, by Julio Baena. *Cervantes: Bulletin of the Cervantes Society of America* 17 (1997): 145–48.

Castro, Américo. *El pensamiento de Cervantes*. Madrid: Imprenta de la librería y casa editorial Hernando, 1925

Cervantes, Miguel de. *Novelas ejemplares*. Vol. 2. Madrid: Cátedra, 1985.

Clamurro, William H. Review of *(A)wry Views: Anamorphosis, Cervantes, and the Early Picaresque*, by David Castillo. *Cervantes: Bulletin of the Cervantes Society of America*. 22.1 (2002): 184–87.

Deleuze, Gilles. *The Fold: Leibniz and the Baroque*. Trans. Tom Conley. Minneapolis, MN: University of Minnesota Press, 1993.

Deleuze, Gilles, and Félix Guattari. *Kafka: Toward a Minor Literature*. Trans. Dana Polan. Minneapolis, MN: University of Minnesota Press, 1986.

De Rentiis, Dina. "Cervantes's *La fuerza de la sangre* and the Force of Negation." *Cervantes's "Exemplary Novels" and the Adventure of Writing*. Hispanic Issues 6. Ed. Michael Nerlich and Nicholas Spadaccini. Minneapolis, MN The Prisma Institute, 1989. 157–74.

Derrida, Jacques. "Force of Law: The 'Mystical Foundation of Authority.'" *Acts of Religion*. Trans. Mary Quaintance. Ed. Gil Anidjar. New York and London: Routledge, 2002. 228–98.

_____. "Ousia and Grammé: Note on a Note from *Being and Time*." *Margins of Philosophy*. Trans. Alan Bass. Chicago: University of Chicago Press, 1982.

El Saffar, Ruth. *Novel to Romance: A Study of Cervantes's* Novelas ejemplares. Baltimore, MD: Johns Hopkins University Press, 1974.

Forcione, Alban. *Cervantes and the Humanist Vision: A Study of Four Exemplary Novels*. Princeton, NJ: Princeton University Press, 1982.
Freud, Sigmund. *Three Essays on the Theory of Sexuality*. Trans. James Strachey. New York: Basic Books, 1962.
———. *Totem und Tabu*. Studienausgabe. Band IX. Frankfurt: Fischer Verlag, 1994. 287–444.
Friedman, Edward H. "Cervantes's *La fuerza de la sangre* and the Rhetoric of Power." *Cervantes's "Exemplary Novels" and the Adventure of Writing*. Hispanic Issues 6. Ed. Michael Nerlich and Nicholas Spadaccini. Minneapolis, MN The Prisma Institute, 1989. 125–56.
Fuchs, Barbara. *Passing for Spain: Cervantes and the Fictions of Identity*. Urbana and Chicago: University of Illinois Press, 2003.
Hägglund, Martin. "The Necessity of Discrimination: Disjoining Derrida and Levinas." *Diacritics* (Forthcoming).
Howe, Elizabeth Teresa. "The Power of Blood in Cervantes' *La fuerza de la sangre*." *Forum for Modern Language Studies* 30.1 (1994): 64–76.
Maravall, José-Antonio. *Poder, honor y élites en el siglo XVII*. Madrid: Siglo Veintiuno de España, 1979.
Molho, Maurice. "Aproximación al *Celoso extremeño*." *Nueva Revista de Filología Hispánica* 38.2 (1990): 743–92.
Percas de Ponseti, Helena. "El 'misterio escondido' en *El celoso extremeño*." *Cervantes: Bulletin of the Cervantes Society of America* 14.2 (1994): 137–53.
Slaniceanu, Adriana. "The Calculating Woman in Cervantes' *La fuerza de la sangre*." *Bulletin of Hispanic Studies* 64.2 (1987): 101–10.
Welles, Marcia L. "Violence Disguised: Representation of Rape in Cervantes' 'La fuerza de la sangre.'" *Journal of Hispanic Philology* 13.3 (1989): 240–52.
Williamson, Edwin. "El 'misterio escondido' en *El celoso extremeño*: una aproximación al arte de Cervantes." *Nueva Revista de Filología Hispánica* 38.2 (1990): 793–815.

10

Spanish Mannerist Detours in the Mapping of Reason: Around Cervantes' *Novelas Ejemplares*

Julio Baena

In his prologue, the author of the *Novelas ejemplares* invites the reader to consume his novellas together, as a totality or textual whole, or to read each individual piece in isolation ("así de todas juntas como de cada una de ellas de por sí"). It may be said that the *Novelas* acquire full meaning (or a surplus of meaning) only when we read them together, as moving parts of a meaning-producing machine; but this is also how they become a problem, a monstrous octopus. They begin with a lack—the lack of that hand with which the prologuist threatens to chop off his other hand—and end with a lack, namely, the void of the second part of the *Coloquio*. In their middle, we find lack after lack or, from another angle, discarded bit after discarded bit, just like the cut-out corners of the playing cards of *Rinconete y Cortadillo* (Rinconete and Cortadillo).

In this essay I reflect on this "marginal self-positing" of the *Novelas* in the context of a reexamination of mannerist aesthetics. I propose to look at the textual world of the *Novelas* and other Cervantine "places of unreason" in light of Adorno and Horkheimer's investigation into the structure of Reason (its dialectical ties with totalitarianism), and especially Deleuze and Guattari's explorations of the fetish of subjectivity. In reading the *Novelas ejemplares* as an image of *(re)territorialization* (Deleuze and Guattari "Anti-Oedipus"), I will be opposing reason to Reason, following the dialectics of pre- and post-philosophy

(Heraclitus) and the work of Spanish theoreticians García Calvo and Sánchez Ferlosio.

Predating by a few decades Foucault's date of the Great Confinement, as established in the first chapters of his *Madness and Civilization*, we can see by 1615 an intriguing Spanish distribution of Cervantine lunatics, both internal and external. Besides Don Quixote himself, two madmen have their stories told in the Prologue to *Don Quixote II*. We find another madman whose story is told by the priest in Chapter 1. The *Novelas'* Vidriera is yet another famous madman. And, finally, there is Avellaneda's Don Quixote. In all these cases, it is apparent that the internal/external paradigm is at this time already inextricably linked to reason/unreason. Unless their story is told by a priest (or Avellaneda), the madmen roam the streets free. For Avellaneda and the priest, then, the outside is the place of Reason; the inside is that of unreason. For the other Cervantine narrators, however, the distribution is reversed. Moreover, madmen are confined when their story is told *inside* a text, but they roam free when the stories are told *outside* the text—in a prologue, or in *a book with no walls*: a book like the *Novelas ejemplares*.

We find the main madman, Cervantes' Don Quixote, at the juncture at which confinement becomes a possibility: he is overcome by desire to *break out* and, unlike the priest-dependent Neptune paranoiac—or Avellaneda's own Don Quixote—he will break out. Pending our reading of the end of *Don Quixote* as either the ultimate re-territorialization, or the ultimate escape, out goes the hidalgo into the world of dogs and madmen—into the Greek agora where the madman met the dog, and melted with it into the cynic philosopher—the *kynikos*. The dogs, of course, accompany the non-confined madmen in the prologue stories, or in the *Novelas*, if we read them as wall-less spaces.

Before Foucault, Heraclitus had already placed reason in the context of a dialectics of fence-erection. In fragments of his book, he sees the Law as applying to those inside the city walls, and therefore those walls cut out reason from every outside (39–40; 269–70). The common, thus subdivided, is Logos, but submits to the rule of fencing: it becomes *Idée Phronesis*. Reason defies reason by acquiring a subject, by tracing a territory. The foundational Murder in Roman mythology occurs when Remus jumps over the walls—just *traced* by Romulus. Tracing (writing) ensures, but it also brings Death, as Derrida often said.

Quevedo, the self-proclaimed Christian Heraclitus, has no better image of the decline of the self—with his phallic *báculo* or his defeated sword—than that of the crumbling walls of the Polis: "Miré los muros de la patria mía / si un tiempo fuertes ya desmoronados" (31) (I looked at the walls of the Fatherland, strong long ago, now crumbling). The enclosure has been breached. To the baroque defender of reason—and attacker of mannerist Gongorian indefinition—this was the ultimate defeat.

Don Quixote crosses the *limits* of reason by traversing a wall: when he actually gets *out* of his corral, it is through the *puerta falsa* (false door). His are not "Part One" or "Part Two," but First, Second, or Third *Salida* (outing). The Housekeeper—she is, after all, in charge of the integrity of the inner space—says it precisely to Sansón Carrasco, the Licentiate, the keeper of sanity: "que mi amo se sale; ¡sálese sin duda!" (*Quijote* II, 7: 623) (My master is getting out; without a doubt he is getting out). In Spanish, *salirse* can also be interpreted as "to leak," hence the Licentiate's answer, which, like Foucault, or Heraclitus, constitutes a precise connection between reason as a matter of enclosure, and reason as a matter of subjectivity. Turning the walls of the hidalgo's house into the walls of reason itself, Carrasco answers to the good Ama: "Y ¿por dónde se sale, señora? [. . .] ¿Hásele roto alguna parte de su cuerpo?" (Where does he leak from? Is any part of his body broken?).

Reason and unreason are thus complexly related to containment and leaking. Foucault's Ship of Fools (3–37) is an ironic dry island navigating a liquid world. It is also ironic that Don Quixote's brains leak, for they were dry to the bone: "His brains dried up" is the diagnosis of the narrator *(Quijote* I, 1; 34), following Huarte de San Juan (77, 94–96, 109, 113, and 130). Throughout her autobiography, Teresa de Jesús expresses often her chronic "dryness" and her search for "water" in association with her living outside herself: "Vivo sin vivir en mí." Quevedo goes "outside" to find the water he knows not to be there anyway: "Salíme al campo. Vi que el sol bebía / los arroyos del yelo desatados" (31) (I went out to the country, and I saw how the sun drank up the streams released from the ice). San Juan de la Cruz exits, just like Don Quixote, through the back door, slipping out—"Salí sin ser notada" (424) (I slipped out without being noticed)—into a journey at the end of which s/he will drink from the loved one's cellar. For the mystics, though, as for Don Quixote, this crossing of the walls is not the Quevedan disaster; rather, it is a desired *wound* that reunites the inside and the outside.

We cannot over emphasize the similarity between the mystics desire-producing mechanisms and those of Don Quixote. The hidalgo's dried-out brains, which the Housekeeper fears will leak, *do* leak, in fact, in the episode of the cottage cheese (*Quijote* II, 17: 297–8), right before the knight tempts God in the ultra-mad Adventure of the Lions (701). While a bone protrudes from Loyola's leg (which he will chop off, just as the Prologuist of the *Novelas ejemplares* threatens to do with his hand [Rivadeneira 13ff.]), Teresa suffers from vomits—ironically, like her always-pregnant mother—all her life. The bodies of the mystics and the madman seem to want to push out of themselves.

Those defiant of reason, then, are *out of their minds*; that is, they are out of their containment spaces, as drawn by the map that precedes any territory and marks it as conquered space—because all maps are, essentially, military maps: apprehension machines. The art-historical name given to the historical period in question, Mannerism, points to the perception of the issue as a manner, almost a mania and certainly a nervous tic: the *symptom*—rather than the name—of something that remains unexpressed. And it is intimately related to defiance of the map. The *maniera* hides all *matter* as well as all *form*. Mannerists insist on expressing each thing with its contrary at the same time, not knowing which comes first. In this, language, or the picture canvas, failed them: the former because it is linear; the latter, because in its frame the canvas reproduces the Heraclitean Law of the City (everything inside the walls must be subject to the same Logos), and therefore it favors *haploschematism* over *palinschematism* (Sánchez Ferlosio, *Las semanas* I 52–68), straight perspective over anamorphosis (Castillo), and cleanliness over "stain" (Huergo).

A painter's problem in saying two things at the same time is that every outside is going to be re-territorialized by a *frame* (Derrida 71ff.). Because of the inescapable enclosure, the weak spot in *The Burial of the Count of Orgaz* is going to be that *border* between heaven and earth; its center, that "soul" of the Count, is barely a smudge, a stain. How to conceive the inconceivable? How *not to draw* a border between the visible and the invisible, the paintable and the non-paintable? How to distinguish, in a framed canvas, allegory from representation, metaphor from metonymy?[1]

Classical painting, before and after Mannerism, rarely allows for double spaces. Only one here-and-now is allowed; we are either on earth or in heaven. Mannerist art, on the other hand, constitutes an (ultimately failed) effort to de-territorialize the last border of the gods.[2] In Mannerism, it is the juncture that becomes apparent, against the wishes of reason.[3] The discovery of heterotopies that cannot be overcome by a juncture that resists invisibility is what fascinates mannerist authors, who resort to double-imaging, as in El Greco, or anamorphosis, as in the artists studied by Castillo.[4] Music's problem in saying two things at the same time has a name: polyphony. Those who develop it are great mannerists such as Palestrina or Victoria. And more often than not, their work also ends in disjunction, as in Victoria's beautiful *Ave Maria a 4 voce*, which has to combine heaven with a *chaconne*.

To be able to say two things at a time, poets such as Góngora use a double tongue (Huergo 848), or refer to "the road" as nonsense ("un desatino") (Gerli

10; Hauser 17) or, as in the *Soledades*, "errant steps." The mystics dwell in "the place to get lost" (Certeau Ch. 1) and complain of messengers who are not knowledgeable enough to tell them what they want, "que no saben decirme lo que quiero" (60) (for they know not how to tell me what I want). The map—a machine for not getting lost—is for them both useless and undesirable. At this time of consolidation of the modern nation, before the Baroque deifies the State, Mannerism cries for internationalism (Hauser 19). Musicians give new meanings to Heraclitean metaphors (bow and lyre) such as to explore *discord* as a form of harmony; painters paint both heaven and earth in the same space; and Cervantes—as I have written in *Discordancias cervantinas*—says and un-says, making Heraclitean reason speak through the holes and the scars, as much as from the thread of his textile.

But it is perhaps the *Novelas ejemplares*—with their shattered frame in need of repair—that are the symbol, even more than the *Quixote*, of the discomfort of reason's best-fitting coat.[5] Without a margin, they are marginal; without a surrounding membrane, they are not a body. If they are a body, it is one "sin pies ni cabeza, ni entrañas" (51) (without feet, or head, or guts), which means also "nonsensical." At times there will be no body between a head and two feet, but rather only head and feet—or hands—which is to say, as both the Prologuist and Cipión fear, a cephalopod, an octopus (53 and 319). By being all head and "feet"—or "hands" or "tails": the dogs are not too sure—it makes no sense: *no tiene pies ni cabeza*. It lacks the human(ist) body between the head(er) and the foot(er); it is not built in the image of Man. These *inhuman Novelas*, therefore, embody the very mannerist culture that stumbled upon humanism as crisis for the first time (see Nerlich; Forcione 337).

The mannerist feels the pressure of the territory, or the map, while the Baroque spends lavishly in re-territorializing.[6] The baroque "guided culture" tends toward the simulacrum—in the sense that Baudrillard has given the concept—for modern cultural artifacts. Mannerism adopts, rather, a "negative falsehood," what Hauser called "a lack of naiveté" (14). In the Baroque, the map precedes the road, and the monster is pre-fabricated according to precise specifications. Following the Jesuit trend vis-à-vis the Bible, for example, the audience—more and more a mass audience—will be given not the original, but the copy. And just like Hollywood did with Mary Shelley's Frankenstein, the mass-audience universe substitutes its version for the original.

Trying to give both copy and original, Mannerism fights the map. The mannerist poets are no different in this from the painters or the musicians. Villamediana amplifies his *Phaeton* precisely at the point at which the Sun penetrates Hades (593–97). Only then does Zeus intervene. Before that ultimate invasion, when it was only the fruits of human labor that had been scorched by the out-of-control chariot, the gods simply looked on, amused and even delighted. But when it is the *limes* of the gods themselves that are in danger, when it is the Fatherland—"los muros de la patria mía" (the walls of my city) —that is permeable, we have a *casus belli*, and the arrogant semi-god must be destroyed. Paul Julian Smith, in his seminal "Barthes, Góngora, and Nonsense," shows how the "Gongorian text" is the scandalous mark of the disappearance of the deepest boundaries. Poetry, more than any other form of writing, and like Cervantes' prose, is *re-writing*: it reads *as* it writes; it writes as an act of reading. In doing that, it shows itself in *deliberate disjunction*, or deviation (Gerli 4–6; Dudley, Introduction). This reading-as-writing-as reading activity situates the end product *within* epistemology, and therefore outside of the grasp of truth with its totalitarian underpinnings.

One crucial point of connection, then, between Cervantes' texts and the works of Victoria or El Greco, or with the poets, is that of the *failed juncture*. Just as in Victoria's music, in Villamediana's failed enlightment of Hell, or in El Greco's painting, the *line* that separates the parts is visible. In Cervantes there is an ongoing *scar* in the form of *error* or disjunction that posits always an alternate text to the one the reader is supposedly reading. By remaining in the realm of *error*, the Cervantine text escapes re-territorialization. Cervantine *errors* and disjunction constitute the textual equivalent of anamorphic perspective, in the sense in which David Castillo uses the term and applies it to mannerist writing. Cervantine error is an *errancy* that belies both the tyranny and the uselessness of the map.

But the *Novelas ejemplares*, perhaps more than the *Quixote*, take the (suicidal) obsession with the outside to its limit. The *Quixote*, after all, begins and ends; its many interpolated stories are framed by a main narrative. In the *Novelas,* in contrast, there is no fixed road from beginning to end. As I wrote in "Los naipes" Rinconete's deck of cards is the picture of an unbound book: *Rayuela avant-la lettre.* The *Novelas ejemplares* allow themselves to be reshuffled time and again, allowing for chance and chaos to infiltrate the strict rules of the game. There is neither beginning nor end in a deck of cards, and yet the cards themselves are a rigidly ordered system: nothing but number and value, accompanied by gender and value. Nevertheless, less is more (when *one* is also *Ace*), and the binary opposition King/Queen is complicated by the *Sota*—Jack. Finally, the protagonist's names are *what is discarded* progressively from the oval cards. They are not the *ergon*, but the *parergon*.

The *Novelas,* according to the Prologuist, are to be read as one book, or as separate pieces of fiction. This in itself is an invitation to enclose or leave out, as the whims of the reader tell her. If the *Quixote I* was, in many ways, a loose collection of stories put together in connection to the magic place of Palomeque's inn—just as in Montemayor's *Diana*—merely framed by the "main" story of the mad hidalgo, the *Novelas* simply dispense with the tenuous frame. As María Rey López eloquently put it, "they shatter the box." The *Novelas* "se salen" (they get out of; they leak from their container) like don Quixote did, to the terror of his housekeeper; at the same time, they will become nothing more than container themselves: *parergon*, margin, "una mesa de trucos." In them an inside is negated by stepping out—into nowhere. They are about—and follow the rules of composition of—marginal society, absolute others (the gypsies of *La gitanilla*, witches, dogs, syphilitics, thieves, renegades, cleaning maids, English Spaniards, madmen). Moreover, in the *Novelas* the outside is permeated and deformed by an inside, at least as much as the other way around.[7]

The jealous Extremadurian actually puts Leonora on tempting display through the very excess of the enclosure he builds around her. Normal society's will to destroy all desire, to rid of it, as with the gypsies in *La gitanilla*, intensifies the desire to escape. Normal society will *surround* Monipodio's courtyard to the point of having the thieves keep score of the deeds commissioned by "decent people." In *El amante liberal* (The Liberal Lover) we find Christians turned Muslim turned who-knows-what, the *renegado* being the central figure. In *La española inglesa* (*The Spanish-English Lady*) we find from the title the erasure of national—and religious—boundaries. Cleaning maids do not clean, nor are rogues rogues in *La ilustre fregona* (The Illustrious Scullery Maid), where we find that donkeys have *five* quarters. The moral of the story of *Las dos doncellas* (*The Two Ladies*) is so clear that it has to be restated at the end, just as the excursion to the outside made by the young Basques in *La señora Cornelia* is a trip to nowhere and a re-affirmation of endogamy. *El licenciado Vidriera* (The Glass Graduate) represents the risks of confusing container with contained, among many other dangers of reason, while *La fuerza de la sangre* (*The Force of Blood*) discovers the ultimate infamy in the law, by making Leocadia marry *and be happy with* her rapist. Such is the fate of marriages, seen as the knot that ties the individual to the social, and hence reason to Reason, by involving *both* exchange mechanisms: that of desire, and that of money.

Money abounds in the *Novelas ejemplares*, tying them all up, threading them with the sign of signs. If there is a path that can be followed from *La gitanilla* to *El coloquio*, it is the path of money. And *all* money is counterfeit, as Campuzano knows from *El casamiento engañoso* (The Deceitful Marriage). Hence it is time to shed all pretensions, to sweat them out in a ward of the Hospital de la Resurrección, leaving them to the ultimate takers of leftovers: the dogs of *El coloquio de los perros* (The Colloquy of the Dogs).

The *Coloquio de los perros*, ironically, functions as the *coda* to the *Novelas*. Berganza is the link among them, because he has been there, he has seen the gypsies, the thieves, the coming and going of the itinerant characters of the collection. Yet, he has not seen them all—how can he travel to Ferrara or to London?—and, therefore, cannot serve as frame but only as a fragment of a frame. By following Berganza's itinerary, you will only get halfway to your destination. Berganza is useless as a guide or as a map. All maps are military, and who knows that better than Campuzano, the soldier and composer of the *Coloquio* in the depths of delirium, fever, insanity, sin, now *straight out of Resurrection*: "*Salía del Hospital de la Resurrección, que está . . . fuera de la Puerta del Campo*" (281) (He was coming out of the Resurrection Hospital, which is . . . outside of the Country Gate).

If the *Coloquio* was the model-octopus, the *Novelas* are both illuminated and resemanticized by it. Appendices protrude from all corners of the *Novelas ejemplares*. The endings don't quite fit, or are written as an afterthought ("Olvidábaseme de decir" (134) [I forgot to say]), or in the form of a pleonasm ("gozando de sí mismos"(95) [each of them] enjoying him/herself] instead of "uno de otro" [each other]). Stories do not end or do not even "begin"; the semi-framing novella itself (*El coloquio de los perros*) is not exterior, but interior to *El casamiento engañoso*.

The Prologuist compares the *Novelas* to "una mesa de trucos" (table of tricks) as well as to "pepitoria" (stew). He uses considerable space to refer to writing as a process: something to be done with hands, pen, and table. The table, then, appears as a triple *parergon* of the *Novelas ejemplares*; a parergon of eating, writing, and playing. But there is another use for tables in the conflict of reason that we call Mannerism. The moment the *Novelas ejemplares* posit the problem of *exemplarity*—in the extremely contradictory form in which they do—we enter into the relation of that tricky table with *education*.

Maravall traces the figure of the teacher as an important landmark in the series of reconfigurations undertaken by the broken Christian corpus of the Reformation/Counter-Reformation, a time when the schoolteacher starts to compete with the priest (156ff. *La cultura*). In a Foucaultian way, colloquial English, with the beautiful expression "school's out," manages to portray education as one more in/out dialectical process. And we can see that, at the time of emergence of one of the great institutions of confinement, there is no schoolteacher in Don Quixote's town. We have a priest, a barber, a shopkeeper

(Ricote), and even a college graduate (Carrasco), but no teacher. In the *Novelas,* for Vidriera, what we see is an obsession with knowledge, an excess of teachers who will drive him not to knowledge but to insanity.

The teacher is absent from the mannerist text because, if anything, teaching is going to acquire its full significance when directed to the Baroque's "artificial men"—men already molded from teaching (Maravall 142 *La cultura*). The baroque idea of education, however, presupposes a child as *tabula rasa* (Maravall 155 *La cultura*). By studying what a table is, the entire educational construct of the Baroque can be revealed in its base. A table, being the *parergon* of both writing and eating, is essential to the creation and consumption of the world. If we add to this the ludic component in its magic limits as *world* (in/out of bounds), the Cervantine table, complementing the *tabula rasa*, will challenge the in/out paradigm of school. *A-topia* will counteract exemplarity.

Lévi-Strauss knew that the table is the battlefield of reason and unreason. The last chapter of his *Origin des maniéres de table* is entitled as "*Les régles de savoir-vivre.*" This almost-Graciánesque title points to the dialectics of eating as a dialectics of danger to/from the other. Reason, by abstracting the table and everything on it, forgets the body, specifically the *dangerous* body that menstruates—i.e., the *periodic* body, and therefore the very essence of the *now* (421). Table manners regulate the danger of the body in a double relationship. You put a clean plate between your food and the world to protect yourself from that world ("L'enfer c'est les autres") but you use a fork, and not your hands, to protect the world—including you—from yourself ("L'enfer c'est nous-mêmes") (422). The table connects you to the world, and thus its reason is common reason, related in its complexity, savageness, and horror to that body at times bleeding, at times not. Tables have manners attached to them from the beginning. Tables remain *mannerist* as long as they lead to the road that goes from Baroque to Puritanism—this road ends in the perfectly nourishing pill—and at the same time to the other road—the one that leads to "eating with your mouth open," as Lévi-Strauss puts it (413), that is, to squandering with puritanical economy, as Hauser noted. This is the noise of eating, with the open body (Sancho Panza). Recall Don Quixote's advice not to eat garlic or onions, or Dr. Pedro Recio's even more radically puritan diet. The open body, the body of the erroneous burp, that essential *falta de educación* (that is the Spanish term for both "bad education" and "bad manners") are the body of both the *Quixote* and the *Novelas ejemplares* with its scores of errors, equivocations, bad sutures, and contradictions, as I have tried to show elsewhere.

Education begins its controlling task on the figure of a table that resists the idea of being *rasa*—that is, of not existing at all. The body of the text—be it a

Kristevan body of Mother or not—resists being *rasa*. Rather than ending up as the empty space of production, Cervantes' table of tricks will be both a product and a producer. As Adorno and Horkheimer said before, the *territories* of Reason-as-Enlightenment are no different from those of the old shaman (25ff.). Vidriera cannot escape the petrifying experience of his passivity as *tabula rasa* by making himself into a "more delicate substance." In so trying, he bottles himself up. He becomes the purveyor of *idée*, not of common *logos*. In his isolation, he is the ultimate *idiotes* (García Calvo 38). In playing the (card)game of the entire collection of novellas, Vidriera assumes the specifically human form of the law of contradiction (García Calvo 70), and Cervantes, with this very portrait of insecurity, rests comfortably, unafraid of contradiction itself. Logos reshuffled becomes what was before division of labor—maybe even before the primordial division from mother through labor.

Reason is the same as unreason, and its contrary (García Calvo 116). Mannerist painters, poets, and storytellers knew this well. The disappointed or disenchanted Baroque (*desengañado*) trusts reason no more, so it encloses it, like it encloses the madman. Mannerists, on the contrary, let it speak with its own voice: as in a billiards table, with its holes (*mesa de trucos*) transcending the frame. Their works allow for reason's cryptic and dubious face to appear to the reader, provided that the reader lets go of all mistrust of its basic law (of contradiction) (118). "Person" is a thing that will be formed in the Baroque—together with its necessary corollary, mass. In order to be formed, to *be*, to have "a place in the world"—to be counted in mapping—reality must ignore contradiction. Tables should be flat and finite. *Mesas de trucos* deconstruct what *tabula rasa* so painfully tried to build.

Heraclitean reason, as logos, as language, is outside of everything, and therefore is "no thing" (García Calvo 123). But the mannerist artifact is first and foremost about the apparatus itself, about what remains outside of the finished work (Hauser 17). What El Greco wants to paint is unpaintable, just like the mystic's lover's name is unsayable, and the *Quixote*'s theme, like that of the *Novelas ejemplares*, is only bordered by negation. The *Novelas ejemplares* are the apparatus to play the game, not the game itself. Their title is a reflection on an old separation: that between the enjoyment of art and the toil of manual labor (Adorno and Horkheimer 34). Novels are on the one hand; exemplary, on the other: but those hands vow to chop each other off, impossibly, since one cannot chop itself off— thereby doubling as the hand of the artist and the hand of the moralist. Moreover, the one hand that could chop off the other has been described by the prologuist as lame: as worn off by war—that labor of labors. "Under certain conditions"—Adorno and Horkheimer remind us—"exemption from work also means disablement." The self-proclaimed disabled, then, boasts of his *productivity* (*prodesse*) as dominant over his enjoyment (*delectare*: the scandal of the song of the Sirens).[8]

But the *Novelas* deal first and foremost with money. *Preciosa*, or "pricey," opens the door for those gypsy thieves; money will go on to end the first novella falsely (it is the promise of payment that "pays" for a murder), and it continues on from there to the last one, in which syphilis will be exchanged for money, which becomes, in its turn, the delirium of "sweating it off" that finally produces the *Colloquy of the Dogs*. Money and madmen: "money and mind, the exponents of circulation, form the impossible ideal of those who have been *maimed* by domination, an image used by domination to perpetuate itself" (Adorno and Horkheimer 172). Domination as "maiming" is vengeance against that "pure circulation" that only exists in "the banker and the intellectual" (ibid.), without the *parergon* of manual work. The maimed workman wants revenge from the writer, in both Adorno's and Cervantes texts.

Superseding the enlightened—or Marxist—idea of *circulation vs. production*, Cervantes knows, like Derrida, Deleuze, or Bourdieu, that there is no original "thing" to circulate outside or before circulation. Cervantes knows that symbolic—or sexual or libidinal—capital plays the same game that money plays. *All* circulation is production (theory of surplus value), and all production is circulation (theory of language). As with the "fifth quarter" of the Asturian's donkey (*La ilustre fregona*), the end result of any human transaction is always going to be "+1," the "tail" of the donkey,[9] the excess that overflows the containment mechanisms. If the *Diana* is so close to Vives's *De anima* or Leone Ebreo's *Dialoghi d'amore* that it can be termed a *psychoanalysis*, the *Novelas ejemplares* are closer to a *schizoanalysis*.[10]

Cervantes knows that Reality, as constructed by Reason, becomes Death; their distribution circuits are identical.[11] Reason splits from the sensual in order to dominate it, in the deepest form of division of labor, which takes place within the newly formed self. Thus are Vidriera's senses crushed after eating the Toledan quince offered by the temptress. Thus Preciosa will be subjugated by her re-insertion into progressive society. Thus is the debate suppressed, in the name of Reason, concerning how dogs can speak, even if only by divine intervention. The exemplary *message* of the *Novelas ejemplares* is clear: Dogs do not speak, period. Gypsies are thieves, period. If you lose your virginity, you must marry; English cannot be Spanish; Basques marry Basques; donkeys have four quarters. Were it not for the tears in the text, as well as for the Prologue and the very disposition of the novellas, the reader would have no choice but to follow the old conclusion that they are truly exemplary, even reactionary, as Américo

Castro or Cascardi refuse to believe. In this reading, Reason has been restricted to organization and administration.[12] But that message is not what they say—or, better still, what they *do*. The *Novelas ejemplares* as "mesa de trucos" are exemplary of the one thing that unifies mannerist artifacts: the detour from the paths of mapped Reason. Their characters—like Don Quixote, like the mystics, like Victoria's beyond-human music, like Count Orgaz's soul—try to escape, with various degrees of success. Preciosa, Rinconete, Vidriera, Avendaño . . . they are all would-be escapees.

If there is a successful escape, though, it will be that of Campuzano, in that it is not believable. Peralta's strong territorialization of reason prevents reason from capturing Campuzano's deranged discourse. By reducing it to "art"— as art has become for modern man alien from the rest of the world, nice and aseptic—Peralta lets it go free. As long as Campuzano does not insist on his *tema* (theme), he may actually be reinvited to lunch, declared cured, as the poor Neptune lunatic almost managed to do.

Calderón's *El gran teatro del mundo* (The Grand Theater of the World), with God's command that everyone be the best king-or-pauper he can be, might very well be the allegorical apotheosis of the division of labor ("that great chasm upon us"—following an old Marxist idea) (Adorno and Horkheimer 29–30). For Calderón, as we all know, dreams are dreams. For Campuzano they are interchangeable with food, company, fever, dogs, or witches—they are, in other words, deterritorialized dreams.[13] The Baroque will map the world, in order to set its limits—interior or exterior. "World" or limiting Cosmos is reproduced, of course, in the family (*my* dreams, *my* fantasies) that takes the place of the dreams and fantasies that used to be there (Deleuze and Guattari, *Anti-Oedipus* 304). Utopia becomes *my* utopia.[14]

Against that divine order, Don Quixote proclaims not only a god-like "yo sé quién soy" (I know who I am), but the explanation that he can be any and all of the peers of France. Thus, Don Quixote reverses the process of the division of labor. No wonder everyone keeps telling him that he could be anything he wants, or that his real vocation is that of preacher, or that maybe he should follow a pastoral life, instead of a knightly one. When Huarte de San Juan was starting to stipulate that one and only one science fits in one type of mind,[15] Don Quixote brings out of an old closet the nostalgia for something that even modern English designates with the expression "Renaissance man." The difference, of course, is that everybody else thinks of Don Quixote as being one thing *or* another, while he insists on being all of them—a healer like Fierabrás or a poet to Dulcinea—in a utopian degree zero of the division of labor.

Far from prefiguring the models of territorialization that flourished in the

Enlightenment (à la Adorno and Horkheimer), as presented by Foucault, the key texts of Spanish Mannerism introduce an un-reason that is productive of use-value to the extent that it is *counterproductive* of exchange-value, and which complements reason in a Heraclitean manner. Far from *representing* anything, the un-reason (*sinrazón*) of these texts escapes the imposed territorializations, starting with the fundamental lines of demarcation: the inside/outside, or the one/other distinction (Deleuze and Guattari, *Anti-Oedipus* 296). Their deterritorialization begins with defamiliarization. St. Theresa, Preciosa, Don Quixote, or Lázaro de Tormes go from territory to territory after family members manage to bring them back. Theresa goes from her father's home to the Convent of St. Joseph (of all saints, she chooses the "father"). Preciosa goes from her nice family back to her nice family. Don Quixote "recovers" sanity among his family and friends.

Nevertheless, behind the failed excursion to the outside, there is a remnant *underneath* that prevents the account from *squaring off*. Preciosa's happy ending does not fit; Don Quixote's return to sanity is his greatest fantasy; Theresa cannot rest after founding the first convent (after killing the Beast—the *Endriago*—the knight does not stop).[16] Lázaro's final/resting point "at the top of [his] good fortune" is negated by his being forced to tell about it—i.e., by the very existence of *La vida de Lazarillo de Tormes*. Nobody was supposed to "hear about the case"; that was the basis of the precarious "peace in [his] house" (*La vida de Lazarillo de Tormes* 135).

When Campuzano insists that the dogs actually speak, Peralta, who up to that moment was at his same table (*comensal*), gets up and almost ends the conversation/meal (*convivium*). Campuzano has shattered all boundaries of reason, all compartments of safety. He has liberated thought from its specialization in "the professional equipment for certain branches of divided labor" (Adorno and Horkheimer 202). Because this liberated thought is "treated suspiciously as an antiquated luxury—'armchair thinking'" (ibid.), it is no wonder that Peralta leaves the chair.[17] But everything in Cervantes defies this *upstanding* mentality. Humor, for instance, refuses to be assigned its allotted place. Sánchez Ferlosio writes in *Vendrán más años,* "When humor becomes a genre it is because it has decided respectfully to part ways with serious things, so that they can engage without embarrassment their petulant tyranny" (37). When everything is becoming a *field*, a *discipline* of study, Cervantes exalts dilettantism. Monipodio, as Adorno and Horkheimer say of Sade's Julliette, "preaches on the self discipline of the criminal" (95). The atmosphere of Monipodio's realm is as stuffy and unbreathable as that of the closed logos created by the *logotetes* of the hermetic places (Barthes 7–10). Rincón and Cortado, Cervantes' picaros, leave this realm, but don't trade it for another; they simply go nowhere. One of them plans to travel to the Indies, and the other one simply disappears from the text. But even the "survivor" goes nowhere. The text ends. No more space, no more chronotope. If anything, their novella is found in the lining of the same suitcase that contained *El curioso impertinente* (The Curious Impertinent), in *Quixote I* (47:512–13). It will occupy the space of contraband, of stop-less circulation. Rincón and Cortado, as what they are (the cut-out edges of playing cards), have *no-place* (*u-topos*) to go.[18]

Notes

1. Americo Castro saw in the painting this problem as "solved" (*Cervantes y los casticismos* 107). Michael Gerli uses the image to figure a Cervantes story (*The Captive's Tale*) as capable of "blurring boundaries" in an unheard-of manner (41). I agree with both ... provided that a space in the theory is left for the obvious *scar* in the tissue, for the death-less mark of the erasure.
2. Maravall is also aware of this fight against the limits (92 *La cultura*). "Toparse con el cuadro" is his expression.
3. "Inconspicuous adjustment better than conspicuous" (quoted in García Calvo 112–13).
4. From Heraclitus: "Reality likes to hide." Stoics like Seneca elaborate: "Many things are dark, or perhaps—which is more fascinating—fill our eyes and mock them at the same time" (quoted in García Calvo 109–10). On El Greco, see Hauser's work.
5. How the *Novelas* follow an entropic road from the utopia of a protective Boccaccian frame is studied best in María Rey's still-unpublished doctoral dissertation.
6. Mannerism "squanders" space at the same time that it "economizes it" (Hauser 17).
7. Maravall notes how the Baroque sees the development of the citadel, so different from the old castle: made to defend not from the alien enemies, but from the mob (112 *La cultura*).
8. The image of Odysseus, the Sirens, and the crew is for Adorno and Horkheimer a good figure of alienation, with its roots in the division of labor.
9. See my *El círculo y la flecha*, esp. Chapter 3. See also how this "N+1" structure is one of the basic structures of capitalist productivity (Deleuze and Guattari, *A Thousand Plateaus* 17 and 21).
10. See, for example, Adorno and Horkheimer, 27, and elsewhere in their first chapter.
11. Agustín García Calvo often writes of this "distribution of death." Also see Adorno and Hokheimer, 29.
12. See Adorno and Horkheimer, 36. Profoundly enough, all Reason is *Razón de Estado*.
13. See dreams and Mannerism—and surrealism—in Hauser, 17.
14. See Maravall, *Utopía*. Let us remember that in the old utopia—the Age of Gold— "there was no such thing as 'yours' or 'mine'" (*Quixote I*, 11: 113). This "Arms and

Letters" discourse by Don Quixote occurs just before Marcela re-territorializes desire with her problematic—and modern—"I am free." Cervantes manages to make desire a contagious, rhizomatic business. This little "familiar theater"—Cervantes' text insists on the oedipal nature of Marcela—is also evident in *El retablo de las maravillas*. "[In psychoanalysis] dream and fantasy are to myth and tragedy as private property is to public property. . . . the unconscious as a stage. A whole theater put in the place of production" (Deleuze and Guattari, *Anti-Oedipus* 304–5).

15. "De muchas diferencias de ingenio que hay en la especie humana, sola una te puede caber; . . . a cada diferencia de ingenio le responde . . . sola una ciencia y no más." (Quijote 50).
16. "It is of the essence of representation to be a familial representation. But production is not thereby suppressed; it continues to rumble" . . . (Deleuze and Guattari, *Anti-Oedipus* 296).
17. See the first chapter of my *Discordancias* on the opposition between "dinner" and History-as-Domination.
18. This essay would not exist without David Castillo and Bill Egginton.

Works Cited

Adorno, Theodor, and Max Horkheimer. *Dialectic of Enlightenment.* Trans. John Cumming. New York: Seabury Press, 1972.

Avellaneda, Alonso F. de. *Segundo tomo del ingenioso hidalgo don Quijote de la Mancha.* Madrid: Aguilar, 1944.

Baena, Julio. *El círculo y la flecha: principio y fin, triunfo y fracaso del* Persiles. Chapel Hill, NC: University of North Carolina Press, 1996.

———. *Discordancias cervantinas*. Newark, DE: Juan de la Cuesta, 2003.

———. "Los naipes de Rincone(te)s Cortad(ill)os: hacia una lectura marginal de las *Novelas ejemplares*." *REH* 30 (1996): 67–80.

Barthes, Roland. *Sade, Loyola, Fourier.* Trans. Néstor Leal. Caracas: Monte Ávila, 1977.

Baudrillard, Jean. *Simulacra and Simulation.* Trans. Sheila Faria Glaser. Ann Arbor, MI: University of Michigan Press, 1994.

Cascardi, Anthony. "Cervantes's Exemplary Subjects." *Cervantes's Exemplary Novels and the Adventure of Writing.* Ed. Michael Nerlich and Nicholas Spadaccini. Minneapolis, MN: The Prisma Institute, 1989. 49–71.

Castillo, David R. *(A)wry Views: Anamorphosis, Cervantes, and the Early Picaresque.* West Lafayette, IN: Purdue University Press, 2001.

Castro, Américo. *Cervantes y los casticismos españoles.* Madrid: Alfaguara, 1966.

———. "La ejemplaridad de las novelas cervantinas." *Hacia Cervantes.* Madrid: Taurus 1957. 329–50.

Certeau, Michel de. *La fable mystique, 1*. Paris: Gallimard, 1982.

Cervantes, Miguel de. *El ingenioso hidalgo don Quijote de la Mancha.* Ed. Martín de Riquer. Barcelona: Planeta, 1980.
———. *Novelas ejemplares.* Ed. Harry Sieber. 2 vols. Madrid: Cátedra, 1981.
Cortázar, Julio. *Rayuela.* Buenos Aires: Ed. Sudamericana, 1963.
Cruz, San Juan de la. *Obra completa.* Ed. Luce López-Baralt and Eulogio Palacio. Madrid: Alianza, 1991.
Deleuze, Gilles, and Félix Guattari. *Anti-Oedipus: Capitalism and Schizophrenia.* Trans. Robert Hurley, Mark Seem, and Helen R. Lane. Minneapolis, MN: University of Minnesota Press, 1983.
———. *A Thousand Plateaus: Capitalism and Schizophrenia.* Trans. Brian Massumi. Minneapolis, MN: University of Minnesota Press, 1987.
Derrida, Jacques. *La vérité en peinture.* Paris: Flammarion, 1978.
Dudley, Edward. "The Wild Man Goes Baroque." *The Wild Man Within.* Ed. Edward Dudley and Maximilian Novak. Pittsburgh, PA: University of Pittsburgh Press, 1972.
Forcione, Alban K. "Exemplarity, Modernity, and the Discriminating Games of Reading." *Cervantes's Exemplary Novels and the Adventure of Writing.* Ed. Michael Nerlich and Nicholas Spadaccini. Minneapolis, MN: The Prisma Institute, 1989. 331–52.
Foucault, Michel. *Madness and Civilization: A History of Insanity in the Age of Reason.* Trans. Richard Howard. New York: Random House: 1988.
García Calvo, Agustín. *Razón común: edición crítica, ordenación, traducción y comentario de los restos del libro de Heráclito.* 2nd ed. Zamora: Lucina, 1999.
Gerli, E. Michael. *Refiguring Authority: Reading, Writing, and Rewriting in Cervantes.* Lexington, KY: University Press of Kentucky, 1995.
Hauser, Arnold. "El manierismo." *Historia social de la literatura y el arte,* Vol. II. Trans. A. Tovar and F.P. Varas-Reyes. Madrid: Guadarrama, 1969. 11–94.
Heraclitus. (see García Calvo, Agustín).
Huarte de San Juan. *Examen de ingenios para las ciencias.* Ed. Guillermo Seres. Madrid: Cátedra, 1989.
Huergo, Humberto. "Las dos lenguas de Góngora." *Morada de la palabra.* Ed. William Mejías López. Vol I. San Juan: Editorial de la Universidad de Puerto Rico, 2002. 842–50.
Kristeva, Julia. *The Revolution of Poetic Language.* Trans. Margaret Waller. New York: Columbia University Press, 1984.
Lazarillo de Tormes. Ed. Francisco Rico. Madrid: Cátedra, 1992.
Lévi-Strauss, Claude. *L'origine des manières de table.* Paris: Plon, 1968.
Maravall, José Antonio. *La cultura del Barroco: análisis de una estructura histórica.* Barcelona: Ariel, 1975.
———. *Utopía y contrautopía en el* Quijote. Santiago de Compostela: Pico Sacro, 1976.
Nerlich, Michael. "On the Philosophical Dimension of *El casamiento engañoso* and *El coloquio de los perros.*" *Cervantes's Exemplary Novels and the Adventure of Writing.* Ed. Michael Nerlich and Nicholas Spadaccini. Minneapolis, MN: The Prisma Institute, 1989. 247–329.

Quevedo, Francisco de. *Poesía original completa*. Ed. José Manuel Blecua. Barcelona: Planeta, 1981.

Rey López, María. *The Shattered Frame in the Boccaccian Tradition of Short Fiction*. PhD diss., University of Colorado, 1997. DAI (1997).

Rivadeneira, Pedro de. *Vida de Ignacio de Loyola.*. *B.A.E.* 60. Ed. Vicente de la Fuente. Madrid: Rivadeneira impresor, 1868.

Sánchez Ferlosio, Rafael. *Las semanas del jardín*. 2 vols. Madrid: Nostromo 1974 and 1975.

———. *Vendrán más años malos y nos harán más ciegos*. Barcelona: Destino, 1993.

Smith, Paul Julian. "Barthes, Góngora, and Nonsense." *PMLA* 101 (1986): 82–94.

Teresa de Jesús. *Las moradas* and *Libro de su vida*. México: Porrúa, 1987.

Villamediana, Juan de Tassis, Conde de. *Poesía impresa completa*. Ed. José Francisco Ruiz Casanova. Madrid: Cátedra, 1990.

Vives, Juan Luis. *Obras completas*. Trans. Lorenzo Riber. Madrid: Aguilar, 1968.

♦ 11

The Genealogy of the Sublime
in the Aesthetics of the Spanish Baroque

Anthony J. Cascardi

It has long been conceived that the category of the "sublime" is, for modernity at least, an invention of aesthetic theorists of the eighteenth century. Especially in England and in Germany, though also in France, the category of the "sublime" began to attract renewed attention just as aesthetic theory came into its own as an independent discourse, i.e., as an attempt to provide rational reflection on matters of judgment and taste, both in relation to nature and in relation to art. As aesthetic theory developed, it took as one of its central topics the representation of experiences that were somehow deemed to be "too great" for reason to grasp. Edmund Burke, for example, described sublime objects as "vast in their dimensions," and Kant characterized the sublime as the presentation of that which is "absolutely great."[1] For aesthetic theory, the category of the sublime was at once a means of putting pressure on discourse to accommodate judgments about experiences that seemed to lie beyond the bounds of reason *and* a means of legitimizing the powerful but "irrational" feelings that such experiences brought on. Sublimity became a category in which the passionate responses to overwhelming experiences sought reconciliation with the rational faculties. Indeed, the discourse of the sublime was developed, in part at least, as a way of enlarging the scope of what could be embraced within the compass of the human faculties. The ability to grapple successfully with representations that seemed to be too great for reason to grasp *cognitively* could be offered as proof of the power of reason in some higher sense, i.e., as encompassing judgments based on an affective encounter with some quasi-transcendent domain of experience. Thus, the "invention" of the sublime in the eighteenth century (better said, its reinvention) can be viewed as part of an attempt to enlarge the bounds of reason.[2]

It was not, of course, just any form of experience that presented itself in the form of the sublime as a challenge to reason but certain *kinds* of experience—many of them associated with feelings of terror, some of them akin to the *phobos* incited by ancient tragedy, and most of them associated with magnitudes that bordered on what Kant called the "absolutely great." (Like tragedy, the sublime posed the question of how something that was the source of distress for the rational faculties and even a perceived threat to bodily integrity could be judged and valued as a source of aesthetic pleasure.) But the instances of this "greatness" are surprisingly local. There has seemed to be something characteristically northern European, and modern, about the discourse of the sublime. Supercharged images of angry, storm-tossed seas, of towering cliffs and waterfalls, or of giants devouring the earth, all fall within its preferred ambit; indeed, critics have often remarked that the most typically "sublime" landscape of all is the Alps. Addison, for example, reported a particular delight related to the sublime when viewing the mountains outside Lake Geneva; it seems that in Addison's case, at least, these pleasures carried over to his experience of the Apennines.[3] Whether there is a corresponding "southern European" or "Mediterranean sublime" remains to be seen; Cervantes, for one, thought to begin his ambitious romance, the *Persiles*, in a northern climate. And while the geography of the *Persiles* is an imaginary one, I would point out that art historians have long given credence to the idea that there is a difference between the "northern" (i.e., Northern European) aesthetic sensibility and its southern counterpart. Nonetheless, that there might be a "southern" sublime, or even a Spanish sublime, is not out of the question. If there is, however, it is likely to be thoroughly entwined with the aesthetics of the Baroque.[4] My own view is that the Spanish Baroque can indeed be regarded as a form of the "southern European" sublime, or as its very close antecedent. And while historians like Maravall have argued that there was something essentially conservative about the Spanish Baroque, one of the fundamental problems it presents was how to achieve sufficient "elevation" given the cultural distance from its "archaic" roots.[5]

I will have more to say about the aesthetic configuration of sublime experience and its representation in light of its customarily *dis*avowed antecedents in southern Europe (especially Spain) in the seventeenth century, but first I want to recall that the category of the sublime has important predecessors in classical antiquity, most notably among them the treatise attributed to Longinus entitled "Peri Hypsous," often translated as "On the Sublime" but more literally rendered as "On Great Writing." One of the customary ways of figuring the difference between the sublime as Longinus treats it and the "modern" sublime can be summed up as follows: whereas early modern writers came to regard the sublime as a category of experience, with direct implications for consciousness and with relatively little concern for history, Longinus takes the sublime as a matter of rhetoric. Indeed, "Peri Hypsous" was as much a source of instruction for orators and poets about how to create great (sublime) effects in language as it was an analysis of the effects of sublime greatness (transport) in and of themselves. For Longinus, whatever is "sublime" begins as a feature of discourse; to produce a rhetoric of exalted discourse requires finding (in rhetorical terms, inventing), but also then reading and interpreting, the tropes of greatness. But whether these matters can be contained to language is far from clear. "Peri Hypsous" is itself already something more than a rhetorical treatise, and the Longinian sublime overflows the bounds of regulated discourse notwithstanding Longinus's attempt to treat "greatness" in writing as if it were a pedagogical matter. As Richard Macksey rightly pointed out, "Peri Hypsous" is not simply a discussion of " 'the high style' in the tradition common to many ancient critics of a rhetoric of stylistic gradation (e.g., High, Middle, and Low)."[6] Longinus is likewise concerned with "distinctions of conception and expression, with the sources and effects achieving a state of elevation that he calls 'transport' (*ekstasis*, in the quite literal sense of being 'carried outside' oneself)." Thus—and here may lie the crucial point—sublimity is a quality that is not at all easily stabilized. Longinus locates sublimity sometimes in the inspired author, sometimes in the "excited" discourse itself, and sometimes in its impact on the consciousness of the audience. What is clear throughout the work is that the consequences of *hypsous* are infectious and lend themselves to a rhetoric of "astonishment (*ekplexis*) and domination" (Macksey, "Longinus").

Astonishment is of course one of the very qualities that can serve to link the category of the sublime in its northern, eighteenth century versions to the aesthetics of the Spanish Baroque. ("Domination" is considerably more problematic; the question what makes certain forms of domination desirable and even pleasurable has remained open long after the initial development of theories of the sublime.) But early thoughts about a Spanish connection to the sublime were bound up with a kind of national stereotyping that sought an essentialist rather than a contextualist or philosophical understanding of the relationship between style and the formation of a collective identity. Witness Kant's assessment, in his early *Observations*, of "the Spaniard" as prone to "*exceptional and odd* actions, which *deviate from the natural*" (Kant, *Observations* 100; my emphasis). As Kant goes on to remark, "one cannot say that the Spaniard is haughtier or more amorous than anyone of another people; but he is both *in an adventurous way*, which is *odd and exceptional*. Letting the plow stand and walking with long sword and mantle up and down the tilled fields until the traveling stranger has passed; or in a bullfight, where for once the beautiful of the land are seen unveiled, to proclaim his ladylove by a special salute and then to risk his life in her honor—these are exceptional and odd actions, which deviate from the natural" (Kant *Observations* 100; my emphasis).

And yet many early modern century theorists of aesthetics, including Kant himself in his later *Critique of Judgment* (1790), sought to establish the sublime as a category of mind and of experience, *rather than* as a category of discourse and as independent of national character. This effort was consistent with the gradual disparagement of rhetoric in the aftermath of the Baroque and with the corresponding increase in the perceived importance of "poetry" as a means to tap the greatness of the human psyche. The sublime in art came to be regarded as that which could make the mind "suddenly and simultaneously aware of its miserable limitations and its infinite abilities" (Reiss 302). Indeed, one of the distinctive features of aesthetic theory in the early modern age was that it deemed the suppression of rhetoric as necessary in order to concentrate on questions of experience and truth of the largest possible magnitudes. In the course of the *Critique of Judgment*, for instance, Kant disparages rhetoric as "the art of transacting a serious business of the understanding as if it were a free play of the imagination"; poetry is by contrast the art of "conducting a free play of the imagination as if it were a serious business of the understanding" (Kant, *Critique of Judgment* 184). As he goes on to suggest, what may appear in oratory as irrational is duplicitous or dishonest: "the *orator* announces a serious business, and for the purpose of entertaining his audience conducts it as if it were a mere *play* with ideas . . . The orator, therefore, gives something he does not promise, viz., an entertaining play of the imagination. On the other hand, there is something in which he fails to come up to his promise, and a thing, too, which is his avowed business, namely, the engagement of the understanding to some end" (*Critique of Judgment* 184). Poetry is virtuous insofar as it is modest and honest: "the poet's promise, on the contrary, is a modest one, and a mere play with ideas is all he holds out to us, but he accomplishes something worthy of being made a serious business, namely, the giving of life to its concepts by means of the imagination. Hence the orator in reality performs less than he promises, the poet more" (*Critique of Judgment* 185).

And yet, as I hope to suggest below, the displacement of rhetoric in the form exemplified here could not plausibly have happened without the concomitant sense that it had reached a point of excess, that it was prone to an extremism that could have potentially dangerous consequences for matters of the psyche, for ethics, and for belief. Witness Tirso de Molina's dramatization of the figure of Don Juan. *El Burlador de Sevilla* suggests that grand baroque rhetoric could hardly be limited to matters of eloquence and diction. Discourse, and especially discourse of a heightened and enraptured kind, has the threatening ability to cloud beliefs about the truth, to dominate personal identity, and to create passionate attachments to realities that might not in fact exist. Don Juan is a powerful and threatening figure in part because he exemplifies the ability of magnified language to generate belief in what may not be "real." Just as the Longinian, rhetorical sublime could not so easily be cordoned off from the region of experience, so too the rhetoric of "enraptured" states had the ability to call into being the modes of consciousness best suited to accept them. The fear associated with Tirso's trickster is not simply that of serial seduction; it is a fear of falling rapturously into a state of false belief to which there might be no "outside."

To say that later theorists of the sublime concentrate explicitly on matters of experience and consciousness is not to say that questions of rhetoric fall outside the ambit of their concerns. Still less is it to suggest that there was an immunity to the rapturous effects of rhetoric as the theory of sublimity became more explicit. On the contrary, Kant himself was prone to a certain absorptive "quixotism" in his theorization of the sublime; in his own language he seems to have become seduced by his description of the sublime in nature. Indeed, there is a self-seductiveness in Kant's text that places it within the ambit of Don Quijote and Don Juan, even if unconsciously so. ("Bold, overhanging, and, as it were, threatening rocks, thunderclouds piled up the vault of heaven, borne along with flashes and peals, volcanoes in all their violence of destruction, hurricanes leaving desolation in their track, the boundless ocean rising with rebellious force, the high waterfall of some mighty river, and the like, make our power of resistance of trifling moment in comparison with their might," [*Critique of Judgment* 110].) Still, whatever is specifically "discursive" about the eighteenth century understanding of the sublime has mostly to be reconstructed; it must be gleaned from forms of writing that address matters of rhetoric as ancillary to problems of experience and as subordinate to problems of representation and judgment.

As is often remarked, the "rhetorical" version of the sublime—the sublime understood as a function of discourse and its tropes, rather than of consciousness or experience—was disseminated throughout early modern Europe largely as a result of the seventeenth century translation of Longinus' "Peri Hypsous" by Boileau (1647). While Boileau's was in fact the first translation of Longinus into a modern European language, and while Boileau has rightly received much of the credit for the transmission of Longinus's ideas and for the rhetorical interest in the sublime, Boileau was hardly the sole link to ancient theories of the sublime. Longinus's treatise had been rendered into Latin by Gabriel de Petra in 1612, and its *editio princeps* had been published by Robortello in Basel in 1554. Moreover, early psychologists like Huarte de San Juan had already taken up the problem of *ingenio* which, in some of its more extraordinary forms, seemed to indicate powers that were consistent with, and were even required for, the kinds of greatness that Longinus believed could be produced by rhetoric. The *Examen de ingenios* has long been recognized as relevant to Cervantes' characterization of Don Quijote in the opening chapters of *Don Quijote*, Part I (1605); in it, Huarte takes up the connection between the "extraordinary" *ingenio* and various forms of poetic "transport" which may themselves provide a possible route to truth. Huarte finds his points of support in both Plato and Aristotle, and in Plato especially in his description of the *ingenium excellens cum mania* (Huarte 202). Like the "genius," this particular form of *ingenio* is natural and cannot be learned. (The very same idea, that genius cannot be taught, appears explicitly in chapter 2 of "Peri Hypsous," even while Longinus remains committed to finding a place for instruction in the achievement of greatness in discourse.) It offers access to truths and subtleties of insight that are unavailable to the faculties of reason. Huarte believes that the extraordinary *ingenio* manifests itself best in poetry, not rhetoric: "dicen los que la alcanzan (sin arte ni estudio) cosas tan delicadas, tan verdaderas y prodigiosas, que jamás se vieron, ni oyeron, ni escribieron, ni para siempre vinieron en consideración de los hombres. Llámala Platón *ingenium excellens cum mania*. Con ésta hablan los poetas dichos y sentencias tan levantados [elevados], que, si no es por divina revelación (dice Platón), no es posible alcanzarse" (Huarte 202–3) (those who reach this level speak, without art or study, such delicate, true, and wondrous things, such as have never been seen or heard or written, nor ever entered into the minds of men. Plato calls it *ingenium excellens cum mania*. With this poets say such elevated [lofty] phrases and sayings that, Plato says, could not possibly be reached without divine revelation). Aristotle is marshaled for support when Huarte turns to address the fact that prophets and oracles may offer extraordinary insights even though they seem to speak "irrationally." Granted, Aristotle is of special interest because he understands the enraptured state of the prophets as a function of some "natural" disorder, but even so Huarte recognizes that the sublime-like "transport" of which truly great *ingenios* are capable is the source of otherwise inaccessible truths ("mejor lo hizo Aristóteles; pues, buscando la razón y causa de hablar las Sibilas de su tiempo cosas tan espantables, dijo: 'esto sucede por natural destemplanza, no por enfermedad, ni por inspiración divina'")[7] (Aristotle got this better, for while seeking the cause and reason why the Sybils of his time could speak of such frightening things he said: "this happens because of a natural distemper, and not because of illness, or because of divine inspiration").

These are among some of the most important antecedents of the discourse of the sublime, and they are especially revealing of its connection with an understanding of truth that lies outside the bounds of reason more narrowly construed. But there are other forerunners of the sublime that stand equally connected with its connection to expanded forms of rationality, and equally concerned with the dangers of its links to those non-rational states. The genealogy of the sublime runs not just through the rediscovery of Longinus, but through aesthetic forms that themselves manifest feelings and experiences that surpass what reason can grasp. The distinction between a sublime of rhetoric and a sublime of experience patently breaks down in the Baroque in the face of an aesthetics that concentrated on the rhetorical presentation of experiences that made their principal appeal to the effects and that came to mimic these as part of a discursive strategy. Moreover, insofar as the aesthetic practices of the Baroque were aligned with a rhetoric of exaggeration, of accumulation, of distortion, of excess, and of awe—all of which had implications for consciousness and belief—the distinction between the Longinian, "rhetorical" sublime and the sublime of "experience" was a manifestly unstable construct. It was at best a convenience designed with the hope of providing a layer of insulation between the discourse through which that experience was represented and its consequences for consciousness.

The fact that there was no consolidated "theory" of the sublime associated with the aesthetics of the Baroque in seventeenth-century Spain may of course raise valid questions about its affiliation with what seem to be its close cognates, ranging from tropes of hyperbole to instances of extraordinary *ingenio* to the aesthetics of *bizarría*.[8] If the matrix of eighteenth-century thought allowed for the relocation of transcendent experience in relation to a rational conception of the human faculties, then the aesthetics of the Baroque demonstrated some of the pre-secularized sources of what would become accepted as "proof" of the greatness of the human psyche. Indeed, the aesthetics of the Baroque can be deemed to constitute a version of the sublime in a pre-secular context or, better still, a version of the sublime awaiting the conceptual framework that would help establish its relationship to the secular psyche. If the Baroque concentrates on wonder and awe (*admiratio*), one of the virtues of the sublime, for a thinker like Kant, lies in the fact that it teaches "respect."

At the same time, the theory of the sublime that situates concerns about transcendence within "nature" and "experience" needs to be revised in light of the fact that the aesthetics of the Baroque was rooted in a series of increasing doubts about the orderliness and familiarity of nature. The aesthetics of the Spanish Baroque points powerfully to the theocentric controls operating in the Counter-Reformation world from which it sprang. The extremism of the Baroque reflects an increasing awareness of the need for the rhetorical reinforcement of belief in a world where the idea of a "natural order" of things seemed to be increasingly precarious. Baroque nature is not just violent and extreme but contradictory and disordered in part because the theocentric framework for understanding it seemed no longer to hold uncontested sway. Samuel Monk's claim, in his venerable 1935 study, that the mission of the sublime was to establish "a conception of nature that included the very irregularity and vastness from which the orthodox speculation of the Enlightenment instinctively shrank" (67) was equally applicable to the aesthetics of the Spanish Baroque. Robert Harbison in fact described the seventeenth century Baroque as demonstrating "a frank exhibition of energy and escape from classical restraint" (1). What needs to be recognized is that this desire for escape is also the signature of distress: the disorder of nature in the aesthetics of the Baroque bears witness to a divine plan under siege, though how and why remains to be seen. It marks anxiety over the fact that the order of nature might not provide a reliable structure for human affairs.[9] Consider Rosaura's opening monologue in Act I of Calderón's *La vida es sueño*, where the violence of nature and the extremism of her language have origins that can be traced to actions within the human sphere:

> Hipogrifo violento
> que corriste parejas con el viento,
> ¿dónde, rayo sin llama.
> Pájaro sin matiz, pez sin escama,
> y bruto sin instinto
> natural, al confuso laberinto
> destas desnudas peñas
> te desbocas, arrastras y despeñas? (I, 1–8)

(Monstrous hippogriff, peer of the wind, you're as ill conceived as a bolt of lightning without flame, a bird without color, a fish without scales, or a beast without instinct! Where do you speed off to bucking, lurching, and bolting before the obscure labyrinth of those barren crags?)

It has long been recognized that the violence described in this opening scene is a mirror of Rosaura's all-too *human* condition (her dishonor) and not simply a reflection of a natural order that has been disturbed by some hidden cause. Likewise, it seems clear that Segismundo's status as an *hombre-fiera* stems from a lack of prudence in his father's decisions. The Prince's condition is described in terms that are not simply oxymoronic, but paradoxical to such a degree that his speech itself causes Rosaura to feel the tragic-like emotions of pity and awe: "Temor y piedad en mí / sus razones ha causado" (v. 173–74) (His words have filled me with fear and pity). Ever since Aristotle it was recognized that tragedy depends upon a mixture of pleasure and pain. Hobbes observed that men take pleasure in beholding from the shore the danger of those who find themselves at sea in a storm, or in watching from a safe castle two armies charge each other in the field; he concludes that there must be more joy than grief in so doing, or men would never flock to such spectacles.[10] But whereas one of the aesthetic dilemmas of the Renaissance lay in finding ways to legitimize the astonishing and the marvelous, the problem for baroque aesthetics was to find a justification for difficult and contradictory pleasures, some rooted in astonishment and awe and some so extreme that they seemed to border on pain.

The aesthetics of what came to seem "sublime" emerges alongside a shift from the exaggerated and emphatic perspectives associated with Mannerism to the view of infinite expanses that could seem threatening in their vastness rather than reassuring in the transcendental certainties they offered. There is a tragic moment in *La vida es sueño* that has to do partly with Rosaura's dishonor (her "trágicas fortunas" or tragic fortunes, v. 2731), and partly with the opacity of nature, its illegibility; overcoming this tragedy means finding a way to act in a world that has no *inherent* points of orientation. But likewise there is a "truth" to be gleaned from the disorder of nature, and also an access to truth that is to be gained by the *aesthetic* apprehension of whatever may be "extraordinary" about it. Indeed, the Baroque stands as kin to the sublime precisely because of its insistence on the aesthetic apprehension of the truth. Rosaura's summary of her "appearances" to Segismundo, including her appearance as a "monstrous," transgendered being, are a case in point:

> Tres veces son las que ya
> me admiras, tres las que ignoras
> quien soy...
> La tercera es hoy, que siendo
> monstruo de una especie y otra,
> entre galas de mujer
> armas de varón me adornan. (v. 2712–2714, 2724–2727)

(Three times now you have beheld me, three times without knowing who I am... The third time is today, where, like a monstrous hybrid, I mix the fine clothes of a woman with the weapons of a man.)

Similarly, when Don Quijote and Sancho take flight on Clavileño, and Sancho sees the earth the size of a mustard seed (and, preposterously, the human beings on it as the size of acorns), there is a perspectival disorientation that seems troubling because it is decoupled from any a priori rules for gauging human affairs. The perspective afforded by Clavileño is of course a fiction, but this is in turn embedded in other fictions, and so on ad infinitum. This infinite regress cannot be grounded transcendentally but only arrested and transformed aesthetically. Thus it is hardly a surprise to find that the baroque aesthetics of distortion, hyperbolic accumulation, and exaggeration can lead to the grotesque as much as toward the sublime. Indeed, the "Polifemo" is a case in point. The cyclops of Góngora's poem is plainly deformed and especially deformed as regards the question of ocular perspective. And Góngora's "Polifemo" interests in part because it is itself a distortion of pastoral opened up by the fact that the natural landscape has been placed under the perspective of a single eye that seems to distort monocular human vision. Indeed, if there is a truth about human nature that is available from the aesthetics of the Baroque, it may well lie in a recognition of the necessity—or at any rate the unavoidability—of distortion in human vision: the truth is that what is "natural" about human nature lies in the fact that there something inherently "unnatural" about it. That consciousness of deformation is in turn enveloped in the literary perspective that Góngora offers on the figure whom he "borrowed" from Virgil's *Eclogues*.[11]

What is thus remarkable about the aesthetics of the Baroque is that it came increasingly to draw on the sources of "unnatural" human nature as an aesthetic means to sway belief toward invariable, transcendental truths. This was especially so in the case of orthodox responses to the challenges presented by the Protestant Reformation. Ever since the work of Werner Weisbach it has been thought that the aesthetics of the Baroque, especially in Spain, had some intimate connection with the Counter-Reformation. It is likewise known that the Jesuits played a principal role in this effort, not only in Spain but globally, in the propagation of belief by rhetorical means. But just how forceful and "ideological" these efforts were and how they stood in relation to human "nature" have sometimes been underestimated. Moreover, it is often overlooked that the most extreme forms of sacred rhetoric were susceptible to the unintended effects of their own powers. Having better control over the means of persuasion than over its ends, sacred orators could bring about unwanted effects upon themselves and their audiences. Whereas the writings of Santa Teresa and the *illuminati* were plainly recognized as dangerous—dangerous to the point that Santa Teresa was drawn to develop intimate, idiolectal ways of speaking in order to avoid political censure—the sacred oratory of the Jesuits seemed on the surface to be relatively disciplined. Jesuit practice was designed to control consciousness and culture. It played a major role in the process of subject formation. And yet even the *Ejercicios espirituales* call upon the practitioner to become absorbed in "imaginary" scenes of meditation. Robert Harbison described their effect as "hypnotic" in spite of their regularity (8). The practitioner of the *Ejercicios* was expected not just to concentrate consciously but to become lost in—to participate in—the fictional "scene" of contemplation. This is the role of the much-discussed "composition of place" (*composición de lugar*) which had a profound effect on the poetry of meditation throughout Europe. In practicing the Jesuit exercises, the "exercitant" was to make himself (for it is invariably a male subject) susceptible to a kind of "transport" that was linked to some other-than-rational state.

As is evident from Ribadeneyra's 1572 biography, Ignacio de Loyola was an enthusiast of the romances of chivalry (23). The absorptive transport that shows up in the Loyolan *Exercises* is in turn recirculated in Cervantes' parody of the transports of love built around the excesses of courtly love and the extreme sacrifices of chivalric combat. Indeed, Ribadeneyra's account of Loyola's injury and his subsequent surgery in chapter 1 of his hero's biography is a prime example of the kind of limit-case that is associated with the sublime insofar as Loyola demonstrates a strength of spirit that is portrayed as greater than the greatest imaginable physical pain. In Cervantes, all extreme experiences of pain and love are mediated by the self-consciously serio-comic effects of his ironic prose. Indeed, Cervantes commences his ironic references to the extravagant language of the books of chivalry at the very beginning of Part I. Thinking of the exaggerations endemic to the genre, the Cervantean narrator speaks tongue-in-cheek about the "clarity" of the prose writings of Feliciano da Silva: "la claridad de su prosa y aquellas entricadas razones suyas le parecían [a Don Quijote] de perlas, y más cuando llegaba a leer aquellos requiebros y cartas de desafíos, donde en muchas partes hallaba escrito: 'La razón de la sinrazón que a mi razón se hace, de tal manera mi razón enflaquece, que con razón me quejo de la vuestra fermosura.' Y también cuando leía '. . . los altos cielos que de vuestra divinidad divinamente con las estrellas os fortifican, y os hacen merecedora del merecimiento que merece la vuestra grandeza'" (Cervantes 1) (The clarity of his prose and complexity of his language seemed to him more valuable than pearls, in particular when he read the declarations and missives of love, where he would often find written: "The reason for the unreason to which my reason turns so weakens my reason that with reason I complain of thy beauty. And also when he read: . . . the heavens on high divinely heighten thy divinity with the stars and make thee deserving of the deserts thy greatness deserves.") Da Silva was known both as the author of several sequels to the *Amadís* and as the author of a *Segunda Celestina* (1534), to which the phrase "la razón de la sinrazón" (the reason for the unreason) may also refer.

That there was an "aesthetic ideology" associated with the Baroque that goes beyond the parody of "unreason" and the "unnatural" seems clear enough. That it played a significant role in the formation of subjects seems likewise clear and hardly surprising. Critics in the line of Terry Eagleton would argue that there is no aesthetic, nor any aesthetic theory, that is not embedded within some ideological framework, and indeed that the very category of the "aesthetic" was itself an ideological formation. Eagleton's thesis is potentially disarming in the case of an aesthetics with allegiances to the principle that the experience of art, and the pleasures associated with it, ought to suppress all "interest": if aesthetic pleasure purports to be of a disinterested sort, then there may indeed be some critical value in claiming that it rests on some concealed set of interests.[12] And yet the aesthetics of the Baroque can make Eagleton's claim seem odd precisely because it drew so consciously upon rhetorical resources and because its most significant effects could not easily be separated from the conscious means of "persuasion" by which they were intended to be produced. The ideological intent of baroque rhetoric was patent. What was surprising is the way in which these ideological efforts proved unable to guarantee their effects or to insulate themselves fully from their own persuasive means. The point holds equally true for rhetoric in the strictly "discursive" sense and for its extension to the visual arts and architecture. For instance, Bernini's three-dimensional representation of Santa Teresa's "ecstasy" suggests an unbounded state of transport. It is certainly one that exceeds the bounds of reason. But the sheer theatricality of the image in the Cornaro chapel serves to transform her state of transport into a spectacle and, thereby, to create a sense of privilege among the members of its intended audience (the individuals of the Cornaro family), who may not be fully aware of their complicity in the theatrical scene of her ecstasy in spite of the pleasure and power they derive from its sculptural representation.

The exaggerated language of gesture and the intensification of the expression of emotion in baroque art are closely bound up with the increasingly rhetorical orientation of the figurative arts. It was expected, by humanists and traditionalists alike, that rhetoric was the underlayment for a range of experiences and states that only later became understood as functions of distinct "faculties" of the mind. The post-Tridentine context was especially relevant in this regard. As Evonnne Levy has recently pointed out in a study of the Jesuits, the decrees on art issues at the Council of Trent emphasized the traditional, instructional use of images. These principles were elaborated in, among other places, the *Discorso intorno alle immagini sacre e profane* (Discourse Concerning Sacred and Profane Images) authored by the reform Bishop Giulio Paleotti (1582). What Paleotti hoped to offer in this long but unfinished work was "a Catholic alternative to the increasingly secularized discourse and use of the arts." But implicit in his work was the recognition that a breach in the Church's traditional justification of the arts as the "Bible of the illiterate" had been opened up by the humanistic revival of ancient rhetoric. As Levy suggests, "the history of the figurative arts in Catholic lands can be written as a consequence of Paleotti's fundamental reorientation" (50). Moreover, the heightened interest in communicating distinct emotional states, and their alignment with the powers of discourse, is emphatic in the period. "Expression" needed to be made legible if it was to play a role in persuasion. The drawings that Charles Le Brun used to illustrate his famous lecture on expression in 1668 attempted to designate the definitive physiognomic characterizations associated with specific emotional states, in part so that these could then be used in the service of rhetorical persuasion (see Levy 50). Already in Gracián the link between language and gestural expression is explicit. At the very beginning of *El Criticón* Andrenio acquires the fundamental discursive abilities: "ya comenzaba a pronunciar, ya preguntaba, ya respondía, probábale a razonar, ayudándose de palabras, y de acciones, y tal vez, lo que comenzaba la lengua, lo acababa de exprimir el gesto" (Gracián 15) (he was then beginning to speak, to ask questions, then answering, then reasoning, availing himself of words and of actions, so that and what the tongue may have begun to express was completed by gesture).

And yet here, as elsewhere, it proved difficult for discourse to insulate itself from the very effects it hoped to demonstrate. The Horatian dictum about suffering in art as stated in the Epistle to the Pisos or "Ars Poetica"—"Si vis me flere, dolendum est primum ipsi tibi" (if you would have me weep you must first feel grief yourself)—directly informed debates over the aesthetics of drama, and especially of tragedy, but had a broader set of implications than might have been expected. Rhetorical experience showed that an actor could do no better than to copy the movements of men. Juan de Guzmán addresses action and the movement of the effects as an integral part of discourse in his *Rhetórica* of 1589 (see especially the "Combite octavo").[13] According to López Pinciano this was the most secure route to truth in art: "[que] el actor esté desvelado en mirar los movimientos que con las partes del cuerpo hacen los hombres en sus conversaciones, dares y tomares y pasiones del alma; así seguirá a la naturaleza, a la cual sigue toda arte, y ésta, más que ninguna, digo la poética, de la cual los actores son los ejecutores" (289) (the actor should take care to observe the movements that people make with the various parts of their bodies during conversation, to the give and take and the passions of the soul; in this way he will follow nature, which every art must follow, and this one above all, I mean poetry, of which actors are the executives). The result was not an aesthetic of disinterest but rather one of participation, i.e., one in which the actor became absorbed in the very states that he was striving to exemplify. This practice was linked directly to ancient rhetoric; rhetorically inspired gestures were to make the "concepts" of poetry visible in a corporeally expressive way. As López Pinciano further says:

> razón es que hagan [los actores] sus acciones con muchas veras; los cuales solían hacer de tal manera los actores griegos y latinos, que los oradores antiguos aprendían de ellos, para, en el tiempo de sus oraciones publicas, mover los afectos y ademanes con el movimiento del cuerpo, piernas, brazos, ojos, boca y cabeza, porque, según el afecto que se pretende, es diferente el movimiento que enseña la misma naturaleza y costumbre; y, en suma, así como el poeta con su concepto declara la cosa, y con la palabra, el concepto, el actor, con el movimiento de su persona, debe declarar y manifestar y dar fuerza a la palabra del poeta. (284–85)

> (It is right for actors to perform with as much veracity as possible; and in fact Greek and Latin actors used to do this to such a degree that ancient orators used to learn from them about the movement of the body, so that, at the time of their public speeches, they might move affects and attitudes with the movements of their bodies, legs, arms, eyes, mouth, and head; because as befits the intended effect nature and custom teach different movements depending on the affect one wishes to assume; in sum, just as the poet declaims something with his concept, the actor, with words and ideas, must declare and show and give force to the poet's word with the movement of his person.)

To be sure, there were instances in which appeal was made to the power of the "critical" faculties in order to reduce the "extravagance" of such effects. The efforts of the Cura and the Barbero in *Don Quijote*, Part I, can be looked upon as a series of just such attempts. But it was Gracián rather than any of Cervantes' characters whose efforts were most notable in this regard, both in Gracián's attempt to classify and order the different forms of wit in the *Agudeza y arte de ingenio* and for his exploration of the tensions between wonder and critical judgment in *El Criticón*. In *El Criticón* Andrenio serves as one mouthpiece for Gracián in expressing astonishment at the marvels of the universe. Since Andrenio has been reared in a cave and only now permitted to see the world, everything appears to him as new and surprising. Critilio (critical reason) envies him for partaking of a pleasure which only the very first man must have known. Such pleasure is not simply great but incomparable to any other. And yet for this same reason there is, ironically, nothing surprising in it. Critilio strives to grasp it as the product of a divine creative power: "'¿Qué mucho (dijo Critilo) pues si aunque todos los entendimientos de los hombres, que ha habido, ni habrá, se juntaran antes a trazar esta gran máquina del mundo, y se les consultara como había de ser, jamás pudieran acertar a disponerlas, ... La más mínima flor, un mosquito, no supieran formarla. Sola la infinita Sabiduría de aquel supremo Hacedor pudo hallar el modo, el orden, el concierto de tan hermosa y perenne variedad" (17–18) (What does it matter [said Critilio] if even though all the understandings of men that have been or will be, were to be conjoined before this great world machine had been put together, and if they were consulted about how it should be they could never manage to make use of them? ... They would not know how to shape the smallest flower or a mosquito. Only the infinite Wisdom of that supreme Maker could find the way, the order, the concert of such a handsome and everlasting variety).

Gracián stands prominently among those who appreciate the powers of wonder, who acknowledge a force that stands beyond the capacity of human reason, and who consequently strive to limit the effects of unbridled wonder on human consciousness. In Gracián's case, recourse to the idea of a divine "creator" places the original moment of wonder within the context of a non-secular aesthetic. For a rationalist like Descartes, wonder that runs off the rails leads to an unwelcome form of astonishment; more specifically, Descartes defines astonishment as

> an excess of wonder, and it can never be other than bad.... We wonder too much rather than too little.... This may entirely prevent or pervert the use of reason. Therefore, although it is good to be born with some inclination to wonder, since

it makes us disposed to acquire scientific knowledge, yet after acquiring such knowledge we must attempt to free ourselves from this inclination as much as possible.... There is no remedy for excessive wonder except to acquire the knowledge of many things and to practice examining all those which may seem most unusual and strange. (354–55)

While Gracián was best known for the introduction of a discourse about taste in the *Oráculo manual*, Cervantes was no less important for the later history of that debate. Hume is well known to have been a reader of Cervantes, and in his essay on "The Standard of Taste" he drew explicitly on the case of *Don Quijote* in order to try to fathom the extent to which aesthetic judgments—judgments of taste—conform to reason or not. But if Hume's essay on taste drew him to what the *Quijote* has to say about matters of perception and judgment, his own early inclination was to regard Cervantes as posing questions relevant to the discourse of the sublime. Specifically, Hume was concerned with topics that are relevant to what might most accurately be called the "modern sublime," i.e., the sublime in a post-heroic age. His youthful enthusiasm for chivalry and knight-errantry bears sure traces of his reading of Cervantes, and his response to the question about the fate of honor in the "modern" world is suffused with an enthusiasm that seems to be both quixotic and melancholic:

> So that a Mistress is as necessary to a Cavalier or Knight-Errant as a God or Saint to a Devotee. Nor would he stop here, or be contented with a submiss Reverence & Adoration to one of the Sex, but wou'd extend in some degree the same Civility to the whole, & by a curious Reversement of the Order of Nature, make them the superior. This is no more than what is suitable to that infinite Generosity of which he makes Profession. Every thing below him he treats with Submission, & every thing above him, with Contumacy. Thus he carries these double symptoms of Generosity which Virgil makes mention of into Extravagance:
>
> *Parcere subjectis & dellebare superbos*[14]
>
> Hence arises the Knight-Errants strong & irreconcilable Aversion to all Giants with his most humble & respectful Submission to all Damsels. These two Affections of his, he unites in all Adventures, which are alwise design'd to rescue distrest Damsels from the Captivity & Violence of Giants. (Hume 60a)

Although Hume makes no explicit mention of the category of the sublime in this early essay, the magnitude of the endeavors he describes, backed by the Virgilian citation, point clearly enough in that direction. Moreover, that Hume is contemplating the fate of chivalric "greatness" in the modern world places his essay clearly enough within the ambit of *Don Quijote*. That the sublime is tied to the fate of heroism in the modern world suggests a genealogy that further links this category to the aesthetics of the Spanish Baroque. It was here that Cervantes so aptly captured both the enthusiasm that reading could bring *and* the difficulty of imagining a form of "greatness" to match what was imagined to have existed in the past. Indeed, Cervantes signals something more "modern" than many later theorists of the sublime were able to recognize. Hume comes close to this insight in his early description of the fate of epic heroism, but Cervantes seems to have known far more about the sublime than the young Hume was able to see. Perhaps better than any of its theoretical successors, *Don Quijote* epitomizes the fraught nature of the "modern" sublime and is a key link to its genealogy in the Spanish Baroque.

Notes

1. Burke, 113 and Kant, *Critique of Judgment*, 94. In this they contrast with beautiful objects which are "comparatively small." But the real difference between them, Burke goes on to say, lies in the fact that beautiful objects are a source of pleasure whereas sublime objects are the source of pain. The *Enquiry* thus turns to an old conundrum, frequently associated with the aesthetics of tragedy, viz., how something that produces pain can be a source of aesthetic enjoyment.
2. See Ashfield and de Bolla for a selection of relevant texts.
3. Addison, *Remarks on Italy*, as cited in Thorpe, 1127.
4. Indeed, Eugenio d'Ors went so far as to describe the romanticism of Goya's paintings as an example of the Baroque in art.
5. Quevedo's *España defendida* warrants special mention for the sheer exorbitance of its denial of this premise.
6. Macksey,
7. Huarte, 204–5. The reference is to the *Problemata* (XXX, 1o), attributed to Aristotle.
8. In Góngora one finds the adjective "bizarro." "En su origen 'iracundo,' 'fogoso' (Corominas) es una cualidad moral que el español convierte en cualidad descriptiva de rasgos pintorescos. Implica siempre alguna belleza o elegancia llamativa, que busca la atención del lector o del espectador: no se limita al estilo o al temperamento de tal o cual individuo, sino que se extiende al vestido y al ademán, sobre todo en la comedia" (Collard 5).
9. Hamlet's intuition, that the time is "out of joint," points to the terrible and potentially tragic consequences of this disordering.
10. Hobbes, *Elements of Law*, as cited by Thorpe.

11. To be sure, the aesthetics of ungroundable distortion stands in analogous relationship to aesthetic categories that are far less taxing. The categories of the "picturesque" and the "beautiful," along with the aesthetics of good taste, have their antecedents in the relatively placid pastoral landscapes of shepherds, in the lyrical and sometimes mournful expressions of love won and lost, and in the idyllic landscapes of Arcadian settings in which the most marvelous encounters can seem naturally magical rather than outside the bounds of reason.
12. In the case of the sublime, for instance, there is a critical value to be gained in advancing the claim that the same experiences which can prove the breadth of the human psyche are somehow motivated by ideological interests. Indeed, it would be difficult to resist the notion that there is a displaced transcendentalism operative in the aesthetics of the sublime, directly traceable to the Baroque, that underpins this new secular ideology.
13. Guzmán, 227–43.
14. "To spare the humbled and to tame the proud" (*Aeneid* VI, 853).

Works Cited

Ashfield, Andrew, and Peter de Bolla, eds. *The Sublime: A Reader in Eighteenth-Century Aesthetics*. Cambridge: Cambridge University Press, 1996.

Burke, Edmund. *A Philosophical Inquiry into the Origin of Our Ideas of the Sublime and Beautiful*. Ed. Adam Phillips. Oxford: Oxford University Press, 1990.

Calderón de la Barca, Pedro. *La vida es sueño*. Ed. José M. Ruano de la Haza. Madrid: Castalia, 1994.

———. *Life's a Dream*. Trans. Michael Kidd. Boulder, CO: University of Colorado Press, 2004.

Cervantes Saavedra, Miguel de. *Don Quijote de la Mancha*. Ed. Luis Murillo. Madrid: Castalia, 1978.

———. *Don Quixote*. Trans. Edith Grossman. New York: Harper Collins, 2003.

Collard, Andrée. *Nueva poesía: conceptismo, culteranismo en la crítica española*. Waltham and Madrid: Brandeis University and Editorial Castalia, 1967.

Descartes, René. *The Passions of the Soul*. Vol. 1, *The Philosophical Writings of Descartes*. Trans. John Cottingham, Robert Stoothoff, and Dugald Murdoch. Cambridge: Cambridge University Press, 1985.

D'Ors, Eugenio. "El arte de Goya." *Goya*. Madrid: Libertarias/Prodhufi, 1996.

Gracián, Baltasar. *El Criticón*. Ed. P. Ismael Quiles, S.I. Madrid: Espasa-Calpe, 1957.

Guzmán, Juan de. *Primera parte de la Rhetórica* (Alcalá, 1589). Ed. Blanca Periñán. Pisa: Giardini Estampi, 1993. First published 1589 in Alcalá.

Harbison, Robert. *Reflections on Baroque*. Chicago: University of Chicago Press, 2000.

Huarte de San Juan, Juan. *Examen de ingenios*. Ed. Guillermo Serés. Madrid: Cátedra, 1989.

Hume, David. "An Historical Essay on Chivalry and Modern Honours." Ed. Ernest Campbell Mossner. *Modern Philology*, 45 (1947): 54–60.
Kant, Immanuel. *Critique of Judgment*. Trans. James Creed Meredith. Oxford: Clarendon Press, 1952.
———. *Observations, Observations on the Feeling of the Beautiful and Sublime*. Trans. John T. Goldthwait. Berkeley: University of California Press, 1960.
Levy, Evonne. *Propaganda and the Jesuit Baroque*. Berkeley: University of California Press, 2004.
Longinus, "On the Sublime." *Classical Literary Criticism*. Trans. T. S. Dorsch. Baltimore, MD: Penguin Books, 1965. 99–158.
López Pinciano, Alonzo. *Philosophía Antigua Poética*. Ed. Alfredo Carballo Picazo. Madrid: Marsiega, 1973.
Macksey, Richard. "Longinus." *The Johns Hopkins Guide to Literary Theory and Criticism*. Baltimore, MD: Johns Hopkins University Press, 1994.
Monk, Samuel. *The Sublime in 18th Century England*. New York: Modern Language Association, 1935.
Paleotti, Gabriele. *Discorso intorno alle imagini sacre et profane*. Ristampata con premessa di Paolo Prodi. Bologna: Arnaldo Forni, 1990. First published 1582 in Bologna.
Reiss, Timothy. *The Meaning of Literature*. Ithaca, NY: Cornell University Press, 1992.
Ribadeneyra, Pedro de. *Vida de Ignacio de Loyola*. 3rd ed. Madrid: Espasa-Calpe, 1967.
Thorpe, Clarence DeWitt. "Addison and Some of His Predecessors on 'Novelty.'" *PMLA* 52 (1937): 1114–129.
Virgil. *Aeneid*. Trans. H. R. Fairclough. Cambridge, MA: Harvard University Press Loeb Classical Library, 1974.
Weisbach, Werner. *Der Barock als Kunst der Gegenreformation*. Berlin: P. Cassirer, 1921.

Part III
The West Wing:
America and the Frontiers of Reason

◆ 12

Sacrificial Politics in the Spanish Colonies

Fernando R. de la Flor

(Translated by Rose Seifert)

> Tal vez importa olvidar lo que es cada uno.
> —L. Ramirez de Prado, *Consejo y Consejero del Principe*
>
> (Perhaps it is convenient to forget what everyone is.)

Concealment and Deceit in the Colony

There is an object that often draws attention, shining enigmatically above any other in the cornucopia of the Baroque: it is the embalmed heart, showcased and venerated in the form of a relic behind a crystal pane; a heart that is ultimately transparent to the world, like Saint Teresa's in its shrine in the convent of Alba Torres. In contrast to this expectation of final visibility entrusted to the transparency of an urn or colored glass window (which only saints can obtain), in the Hispanic imperial empire of the Modern Age, whole nations are in fact held captive by the heavy and opaque orbit of that grave sin of concealing one's heart, a practice that even the most sophisticated forms of inquisitorial vigilance and Catholic confession are unable to uproot. Ethnic minorities and groups of dissidents who live within the layers of an empire that is only superficially unified in its ideology employ deliberate concealment as a weapon against imperial hegemony, creating a blind spot that obscures the strategies of infiltration and acculturation implemented by the imperial other.[1] In this way, these groups resist the discourses of domination privately and secretively.

In sixteenth and seventeenth century Spain, the situation of the *moriscos* necessitates the use of *taqiyya* (precaution and dissimulation) as a means of self-defense that conceals their observance of the Koran. This situation will be taken as evidence of the duplicity of an entire people whose conversion to Christianity was merely superficial, and it would become the basis for an agonizing struggle that would unfold into a drama of its own (see Bartra and Cardillac). The collapse of the cultural coexistence of the Iberian peninsula would result in the "tragic decision" of the expulsion of the *moriscos* in 1609. A print illustrating a published report that was widely distributed in the Peninsula explicitly associates the *moriscos* with the fearsome figure of the hydra, a symbol of the insurgencies and maneuverings of treacherous sedition in the political and religious spheres. What is more, the hydra is only scarcely identifiable and speaks with thousands of diverse and obscure tongues through its multiple heads. Yet, the superior eagle, the double-headed eagle of Austria, stands victoriously over the monstrous deceitfulness of the enemies of the Monarchy, as in the famous engravings of Jean de Courbes and other contemporary court artists.

Similarly, the strategies of dissimulation employed by the Jewish minority contribute to the *converso* problem. The widespread suspicion concerning the new Christians result in institutional practices aimed toward elucidating everyone's statute of blood purity (*estatuto de limpieza de sangre*). Organic intellectuals such as Bartolomé Ximénez Patón in his *Discurso a favor del Santo Loable Estatuto de Limpieza* (Speech in favor of the holy and laudable statute of purity), as well as those authors responsible for some of the great symbolic and emblematic constructs of the time such as Garau (*La fé triunfante* [The Triumphant Faith]) or Villava (*Empresas espirituales y morales* [Spiritual and Moral enterprises]), would devote much time and effort to expose and denounce the "occult" illuminati and *converso* problem.[2] The deeper these cultural minorities plunge into their world of secrecy and dissimulation the more hostility and wrath they generate among conservative ideologues and theorists of the monarchical-confessional monocracy who denounce the "double moral" (*doble moral*) of the "other": "Aunque en lo corporal y exterior nos aparezcan unánimes, estando en el espíritu diversos, fingiendo ser en lo aparente cristianos, y en lo interior observando los ritos y ceremonias del judaísmo . . . como lo hazen los infectos descendientes dellas" (Ximénez Patón 27) (Although their bodies and appearances seem common to us, their spirit is unlike ours, feigning to be Christians on the surface while secretly observing the rites and ceremonies of Judaism . . . as do their infected descendants).

In the colonial realm, the first Franciscan conceptions of the native as an essentially innocent being with the spiritual constitution of a child (*indio-párvulo*) and a natural receptivity to the Christian doctrine would change significantly as a result of the observations made by trained baroque anthropologists. They rediscover the Indian other as a greatly deceptive being, endowed with deceitful and treacherous inclinations. This change in perception precipitates, in modern terms, the "fall of the natural or primitive man"[3] caused by a loss of confidence in its inherent ingenuity. In a more profound sense, this significant change marks the collapse of the rhetoric of fraternal equality, which among the humanist principles is the one that most notoriously fails in the colonial context.

The universal nature of social behavior generates the "hidden man" (established moreover on the superior paradigm of a God that is also "hidden"), whose discovery turns out to be so explosive that it annuls the Christian foundations on which the colonial narrative would have liked to ground itself. Implicit here is the ratification of the inevitability of hate and difference, which was reproduced continually by the new Baroque anthropology despite attempts to control and censure. People become unreadable to each other because, in actuality, they have never been able to sustain a system of reciprocity founded in egalitarianism. The mission of Christianity loses here its most important battle concerning the ideal of a humanity that is truly "one."[4] This situation prefigures the condemnation and silencing that would be imposed during the Seventeenth and Eighteenth centuries on the work of the main theoretician of egalitarian and reconciliatory humanism, Fray Bartolomé de las Casas.

This radical shift of the various discourses within the anthropology of domination (from the discourse of Indian innocence during the first phase of the territorial conquest to the new discursive image of a fundamentally deceitful and treacherous primitive) takes place around some critical dates toward the end of the sixteenth century coinciding with the first collapse of the Spanish Empire. As a consequence of this conceptual change, the native is divested, deprived of his fraternal aura; we could even say metaphorically that he loses his identity of the "sheep" only to be converted into a "hyena," the wild animal that—as Gracián writes in his *Criticón*—inhabits the stables and dunghills of the world.

The discourse of Christian dogma makes visible the scandal that ensues as the original assumption of egalitarian humanity is negated, underscoring in this way the irreparable fracture between worlds that cannot possibly be reduced to the utopian unity of a "catholic planet," as Campuzano y Sotomayor and others had preached: "Y ha llegado a tanto esta disimulación o atrevimiento de los Indios que a acontecido en la fiesta del Corpus, poner una Dacha [ídolo] pequeña en las mismas andas al pie de la custodia del Santísimo Sacramento" (Arriaga 65) (And this deception or insolence of the Indians has gone so far as to place on the occasion of the feast of Corpus Christi a small *Dacha* [idol] on the very same stretcher at the bottom of the monstrance of the Holy Sacrament).

An obstinate preservation of their secret identity combined with a merely superficial adherence to imperial authority is the twofold strategy of concealment with which the natives respond to the invasion of their world. One can find evidence of this strategy in the instructions given by those who emerge as the first theoreticians of the new situation. Thus writes the Inga Don Diego de Castro Titu Cussi Yupangi in 1570: "Lo que podéis hazer será de dar muestras par de fuera de que consentís a lo que os mandan . . . si por fuerxa o por engaño os an de hazer adorar lo que ellos adoran, quando mas no pudieredes, hazeldo delante dellos y por otra parte no olvidéis nuestras xerimonias" (quoted in Mújica Pinilla *Angeles apócrifos en la América Virreinal* 87) (What you can do is pretend as though you consent to what they mandate . . . if by force or deception they have you worship that which they worship, when you reach your limit, do it before them and otherwise do not forget our ceremonies). With this the prophetic vision of Isaiah collapses resoundingly, his words thoroughly twisted, and the utopia of a *pietas concordiae*, which early Humanists had projected onto the American continent as the only possible true home for all men, is now completely destroyed: "Serán vecinos el lobo y el cordero, y el leopardo se echará con el cabrito, el novillo y el cachorro pacerán juntos, y un niño pequeño los conducirá. La vaca y la osa serán compañeras, juntas acostarán sus crías, el león, como los bueyes, comerán paja" (Isa. 11: 6–7) (And the wolf and the lamb shall be neighbors, and the leopard shall lie with the kid; the calf and the young cub and the fatling shall feed together; and a small child shall lead them. The cow and the bear shall be companions putting their young down to sleep; and the lion shall eat straw like the ox).

The paranoid Hispanic paradigm reacts to what is perceived as the double-play characteristic of the world of the other. Thus, it yields once again to the dogmatic pressure that traditionally singles out and persecutes the figures of convert culture (*marranismo*), Crypto-Judaism, fiercely combating the impermeability of the *moriscos* and *ladinos* to the Christian word, rigorously operating everywhere against the practices of *Nicodemism*,[5] and, with its own indoctrinated agents and devices, sharing in the obsession against the followers of Erasmus. Eventually, this mentality is implanted in the heart of the colonial city, projected over it through a vigilant and distrustful model of censure, which is dominated by a caste of intellectuals who abominate everything autochthonous (see Rama). The material culture of the natives will become the preferred object of this form of invasive observation once the Indian has been transformed into an essentially deceitful being (the most odious and incomprehensible of all); a figure to be added to the ones already inventoried in the metropolis, one that represents the colony as a true cesspool of humanity (see R. de la Flor, "Retórica").

Widespread suspicion plagues the colonial city, which is seen as emblematic of the insecurity and duplicity associated with the imperial periphery where the symbolic order is in danger of dissolving. This kingdom of lies and perverse deception is said to contaminate everything, making it impossible to experience our social environment as "natural." In such a place, repression and punishment may also take on convoluted and circuitous forms; they may be delayed in strict observance of the rules of occasion and timeliness, as they said at the time, for even the powerful lose their sense of security and control and openly embrace tempered and seemingly permissive policies when faced with the inevitability of a reality that is impossible to repress. Political scientists gather examples of patience and accommodation, such as Ramírez de Prado's *Consejo y Consejero* (Advice and Adviser): "Es la disimulación permitida justa, usada de los consejeros de príncipes, y no pequeña prudencia acomodarse con destreza y decoro a la representación que pasa por nosotros" (65) (Dissimulation within the permissible is justified, as employed by princely advisers, and neither is it imprudent to accommodate oneself with skill and decorum to the image that applies to us).

The Jesuits supply the court, as well as the military and administrative establishment of the colonies, with the necessary justification for the "politics of dissimulation"[6] embraced by the discourse of power, while encouraging a careful and deceiving permissibility wrapped up in evangelical rhetoric. They will soon earn the reprobation of Pascal in his *Provinciales* (Provincial Letters), a true monument of unveiled hypocrisies. In fact, Ribadeneira had anticipated many of these recipes for colonial politics: "[En los reinos de herejes] la prudencia cristiana enseña a disimular por no hacer más daño que provecho, según la doctrina de San Augustín: que no se han de desamparar los buenos por los malos, sino por los buenos tolerarse los malos" (112) ([In the kingdoms of heretics] Christian prudence teaches to dissimulate so as to not cause more harm than good, following the doctrine of Saint Augustine: good men must not be abandoned on account of the evil ones, but rather, the evil ones must be tolerated on account of the good).

Dissimulation of the "other" and of otherness is employed to prevent alterity from destabilizing the symbolic order of the aggressor.[7] But ultimately this dissimulation penetrates the body of Hispanic society contaminating its military, administrative, and religious institutions, which are forced to adopt strategic duplicity in the context of a mercantile and imperial state. Hence, the ancient military virtue of the Romans is now dismissed, along with the "classical" Justinian tactics employed to rule and to exercise violence over the "other."[8]

In 1614 Geronimo Conestaggio published in Venice a book on the Flanders wars, which would feed the black legend associated with the colonial history of Spain. Spanish violence is here described, in the words of Pedro de Valencia's censure, as mere "astucia i artificio enderezado a avaricia i ambición, sin llaneza ni verdad" (7) (astuteness and cunning directed toward avarice and ambition, without sincerity or truth). While this characterization may in fact apply to the military apparatus of the metropolis, military treason would become consubstantial with the Spanish "war machine" in the colonial realm. Beyond the issue of institutional violence, which by this time works without a precise moral code, the colonial environment itself contributes to produce an atmosphere of deceit and concealment[9] finally driving the acculturated natives to take up the same weapon employed by their colonizers: distrust. The theme resonates in the *crónicas* for a long time as it soon configures the central moral feature of the natives, who are reluctant to join the forcefully imposed civil order. Even those natives who may be regarded as fully acculturated maintain a certain attitude of mourning and nostalgia for their displaced identities. This is notoriously the case with Pomá de Ayala[10] as well as *El Inca* Garcilaso de la Vega, to provide just two examples of "melancholic" Indian mentalities.[11]

Subaltern strategies are evident in the natives' use of discretion and secrecy which are aimed to denounce and possibly to subvert the languages of domination. Natives and *criollos* will mount a true assault on these languages and their codes with the intent of turning the arguments of domination against those who display them. Baroque allegory is thus converted into a veiled vehicle for the rethinking of the principles that aided in the legitimization of the conquest and the campaigns of annexation and assimilation, a "secret" code that allows for the expression of censored ideas.[12] Thus, mutual distrust and veiled appropriation short-circuit the universe of social exchange, which is necessary for the material sustenance of the colony. The natives' withdrawal into attitudes of dignified silence becomes a serious obstacle for the colonizers. This kind of impenetrable hermetism, which is skillfully practiced by all dispossessed nations,[13] manifests itself in a certain deafness of the natives and a fear of the hegemonic language (a language that displays seemingly infinite and increasingly subtle means of persuasion).

From now on, the Indian will not open his heart to be inspected and processed by the symbolic order that has penetrated into his world. On the contrary, and in addition to this technique of dissimulation and concealment, the acculturated native of the Baroque refuses to listen to the discourse of the "other," now reduced to its plainly predatory and fatal terms, as expressed in the *Títulos* (Titles) of San Bartolomé de Capulhuac: "No consintáis que vuestros hijos se dejen aconsejar de los españoles porque por engaño les pretenderán quitar sus tierras, que los irán obligando con cariño y les darán lo que comieren; y entendiendo los naturales que es agasajo, cuando recuerden, ya les habrán ido asentando los españoles todo lo que les dieren de comer y el dinero que les dieron y, desta manera, les coxerán sus papeles y cuando vuelvan en sí, se habrán quedado sin las tierras" (quoted in Gruzinski 109) (Do not consent to letting your children be advised by the Spaniards because they will try to take away their land with trickery, obliging them with shows of affection and feeding them what they eat. The Spaniards will keep track of everything they fed them and the money they gave them, and by the time they realize what's happening, the Spaniards will have taken away their papers, and they will be left without their lands).

A print from Bonet's book *Reduction de las letras y Arte para enseñar a ablar a los mudos* (Reduction of the Alphabet and the Art of Teaching the Mute to Speak) shows a kind of padlock in the mouth of a man. *Ars* is the key that will open the fountain of his eloquence. In a cruel paradox, the civilization that "unties" the tongue of the primitive, opening the flow of speech, will ultimately dry it up and shut it off, leaving the colonial subject in an entirely implosive discursive situation (see Subirats). Some will remain silent while the words of others lose their meaning, deprived of authority by the empty space in which they fall. What follows is the ruin of the utopia of communication at the center of a Castilian language that has been hegemonically imposed. Meanwhile, it could be said that the curse of Babel reappears in these conditions driving present contingents into complete isolation and the infinite perpetuation of their differences. Only the most basic and purely denotative functions of language may be said to survive while the realm of the metaphor, i.e., the allegorical discourse of the colonizer, is faced with factual evidence that routinely undermines it or even annuls it: "Y ciertamente digo, y es assí, que con harta vergüenza se les predica a éstos [los indígenas] el Evangelio de Cristo, porque si osasen de hablar, muy justamente nos podrían decir a los españoles lo que dice el italiano: *fate, fate, non parlate*" (Mendieta 102) (And certainly I say, and it is so, that full of shame we preach the Gospel of Christ to them [the indigenous] for if they dared to speak, with good reason they might say to us Spaniards what the Italian says: act, act, do not speak).

A very particular and dense silence extends over the colonial world. And we should not forget that this "political" silence emerges as an intellectual response to censorship, the proscription of the word, which makes it impossible to display true opinions. It is, therefore, an eloquent silence, which is in itself covert, secretive, and deceptive.

American Desert

Some treatises on "American matters" are devoted to a complex task of self-legitimizing. They open up new perspectives in an attempt to escape from the moral dilemma that hovers over a Hispanic thought that is forced to process the implosive reality of an evangelizing conquest. These perspectives are expressed in the schizophrenic desire to run away from the imperial military machine, an idea impossible to rationalize from the standpoint of the most rigorous ethics, and also in the reemergence of the ideal of the desert, which begins to be seen as an alternative space to that of the colonial Babel. This eremitic ideal, which is traditionally associated with the Christian imagery of extreme austerity and penance, produces attitudes of profound antisocial behavior. While Matías de Escobar expresses this ideal in his *Americana Thebaida*, Gregorio de Matos was considered the "first American eremite," in the words of his hagiographers. He exemplifies this impulse to flee from the degraded material conditions of the contaminated colonial city. Saintly behavior is here associated with anomie and deserted spaces. Hence, the desert becomes a privileged place for the cultivation of the only Christian ideal that remains possible: a Christian exemplarity founded on suffering, penitence, and isolation. The neo-eremite no longer has feelings of attachment or participation in the material conditions of the colony (and, much less, responsibility). This is made very clear in the biography *La vida que hizo el siervo de Dios . . . en algunos lugares de esta Nueva España* (The Life Lived by the Servant of God . . . in Some Places in New Spain),[14] which calls for solipsistic and autarkic attitudes during this critical phase of the colonial enterprise.

Once the possibility of "historical intervention" has failed, revealing the demoniacal face of colonization (its irredeemable *facies hippocratica*) in the form of insurmountable contradictions, the American missionary body must now search for a solitary dialogue with the Creator. From this perspective the colonial city appears as the place that God cannot *de facto* inhabit in any way. Indeed, these visionary eremites maintain that sacred and religious circles must be constituted outside of and away from the monstrous political body created by the imperial power. Thus, the severely dislocated space of the colony begins to be visualized—dreadfully so—as a land "uninhabited by God." This is of course a radical inversion of the original missionary utopia. To be sure, allegorical discourse escapes from the prison of colonial reality thanks to rhetorical strategies that dissolve the terrible peculiarities of the local-real. The empirical reality of the failed colonial *civitas christiana* is thus sublimated into mythopoetic structures. The idea then is to elevate the moral stature of the uninhabited space, the wasteland (*el yermo*), which is sanctified in works such as Francisco de Florencia's *Descripción histórica y moral del yermo de San Miguel de las Cuevas* (Historical and moral description of the waste land of San Miguel de las Cuevas).

For the colonial operators of the symbolic, it is necessary to raise, as Calderón teaches, "de las sombras de la Historia / la luz de la alegoría" (from the shadows of History / the light of allegory). This ideology projects a serene paradigm in a place that has been materially dislocated and destroyed. The supra world thereby evoked shares in the construction of an ultra-mundane ideal, a cosmological paradigm that obscures the true social reality of the colony while raising human aspirations away from earthly matters. And yet, even as the light of allegory lifts the cosmological paradigm from the political and economic conditions of the colony, thoughts of this heavenly realm are seemingly governed in this "baroque" phase, which is far removed from the first evangelizing optimism, by the "black sun" (*el sol negro*) of melancholy, as in *Primero sueño* (First dream), Sor Juana's great poem of dreams and smoke. In effect, the *Dream* of the "tenth Muse" is first and foremost the expression of a profound paradox: namely, that the project of construction of a mechanism of such complex dramaturgy (baroque allegory) represents the reality of a struggling subject involved in a desperate fight to stabilize a crumbling symbolic order that can no longer offer knowledge of the world, only dreams.

In *Primero sueño* (First dream), as in other allegorical texts of the time, the historical violence produced by the destructive practices of colonial aggression is sublimated or redirected toward the realm of the intimate and the sublime. Yet, the anguish and personal failure that are revealed in such fictive constructs as the allegory of the pilgrim who roams a ruined land that offers no solace (a land covered in shadows from which the "soul" strives to escape) are in fact the ultimate testimony of the historical disaster of colonization.

From now on the colony will be represented in scenarios crossed by subjective positions of maximum tension. Under these conditions, the bridge of representation can only be reconstructed through the sublimation of *alegoresis*. We could say with Edmundo O'Gorman that colonial meta-stories transform human life into an allegorical spectacle: "Todo esto explica por qué [en el mundo colonial] el doblar de las campanas que marca el pausado ritmo de una vida interior avocada hacia la febril actividad de tejer un glorioso sueño, haya apagado el estruendo de las gestas y de los quehaceres pragmáticos" (quoted in Ruibal García 9) (All this explains why [in the colonial world] the tolling of the bells, which marks the slow rhythm of an inner life inclined toward the feverish activity of spinning a glorious dream, has silenced the clamoring of heroic deeds and pragmatic labor).

The failure of egalitarian evangelical reason, which is the basis of the Christian *ethos*, results from the instrumental paroxysm with which power relations are carried out in the colony. The last resort of colonial slavery is the ultimate scandal and final proof of the ethical bankruptcy of the Spanish Empire and the negative nature of its power.[15] This is sublimated, in missionary discourse, in a type of sinister allegorical story about a "fallen" world devoid of the possibility of redemption in which a humanity deprived of utopias and ideals of self-fulfillment simply awaits the end of all suffering. Such is the collapse of the Christian mission clogged up in the expansionistic logic of evangelical reason, not only in America but in the Orient as well. Thus, Japan, for example, will be similarly closed to the penetration of the Christian faith by 1639 when the *shoguns* expelled the *Compañía de Jesus* effectively ending all relations with Spain and Portugal. Statements such as the following are now possible: "Lo que haremos [los clérigos] de nuestra parte será llorar en nuestros rincones los males que sentimos, poniéndolos en las manos de nuestro Señor" (quoted in García Icazbalceta I, 33) (What we [the clerics] will do for our part is to bemoan in our corners the hardships that we suffer, offering them to our Lord). This intimate persuasion that the fulfillment of the utopia inherent in the evangelical mission is ultimately impossible results in the appearance of melancholic strategies, expressions of dereliction, tearful abandonment, despondency, and contrition. Juan Espinosa Medrano describes the situation in these terms: "Quantas veces bolvía los ojos azia las montañas de los Indios bárbaros, se atormentava, gemía, llorava amarguísimamente de ver quantas almas infieles se escapavan de los caçadores evangélicos" (Espinosa Medrano 268) (Whenever he turned his eyes to the mountains of the barbarian Indians, he tormented himself, moaned, and cried bitterly realizing how many infidel souls escaped the evangelical fishermen).

Meanwhile, the worst fantasies appear before the illuminated eyes of those who, like Jerónimo Mendieta, seek to trace an organic representation of what the chronicler calls "Indian ecclesiastical history." The year 1600 constitutes a point of inflexion in this history since, precisely at this moment, the American colonial space "lleva camino de despoblarse en breves días y de perderse en mucho más breve tiempo la cristianidad desta tierra (quoted in García Icazbalceta I, 42) (The Christianity of this land will depopulate itself in a few days and will be lost in a much shorter time). The impossibility of reconciling the interpretive structure of allegory in a general synthesis with the material entity of the actual drama that occurred *in situ* (which exceeds the possibilities of the narrative not only due to censorship but also to the very disproportions and indescribability of what happened) drives the missionary body into reclusive silence. This increasingly oppressive silence is apparent in written sources and testimonies, as well as in such ridiculous escapisms as a treatise devoted to the question of American chocolate and its relationship to ecclesiastical fasting.[16] Thus, it becomes patently obvious that, in the face of the enormity of the American question, the neo-ecclesiastics have nothing better to occupy themselves than trifles and irrelevant nimieties, implicitly creating the conditions for a rebellion against the hierarchies that maintain an abstract and idealizing theological apparatus in a virtually implosive social situation.

The discursive legitimization of the colonial enterprise that had been so effective in the early phase of the Conquest at the beginning of the sixteenth century, now arrives at a point (an essentially "baroque" juncture) at which it is no longer possible to conceal the obscene material process of colonization and the more-than-obvious reality of the "disintegration of colonial Christianity" (Dussel). Doubt corrodes the very structure that had accommodated the unfolding of the martyr mentality, which is the ultimate defense mechanism produced by the dominant discourse. Casuistry and scruple, in their neurotic forms, even manage to attach a question mark to the paradoxical offering of the missionary body, a sacrificial tribute of a somewhat paradox nature. Thus, theologians soon establish bail for the flood of potential saints and beatified martyrs by way of severe protocols that leave many of these deaths in a realm of doubt and uncertainty. The image of the colony no longer resembles the fountain of saintliness sanctioned in official rhetoric.[17]

To be sure, the deep anguish produced by the irreconcilable contradictions of a missionary conscience caught between the theological principles of egalitarian evangelical reason and the praxis of colonization give way to escapist and self-sacrificial attitudes of worldly abandonment, eremitism, anomy, silence, and martyrdom. The missions are thus transformed into emblematic figures of libidinal disintegration overtaken by the pathetic "longing" for an end without finality. In this cultural environment, words become fluid signs whose semantic elasticity stretches to the limits as the original vocabulary of victory is recycled to express feelings of extreme loss and suffering. The frequent use of the word "triumph" (*triunfo*) in the language of martyrdom makes it clear that the missionary vocabulary is now used to connote the event of a *heroic* defeat, openly evoking the world of death and the tribute of blood paid for the sake of spreading the word of Christ. A good example is Andrés Pérez de Ribas's *Historia de los triumphos de nuestra Santa Fé* (History of the triumphs of our holy faith)

(1645), which is nothing more than a meticulous account of the martyrs of the Order who died on a mission in Mexico during the turbulent years of the first half of the seventeenth century.

The sacrificial character of suffering becomes the fundamental theme underlying any representation of colonial reality from the perspective of transcendence feeding the self-victimizing discourse of all the institutions of *propaganda fide* dispersed throughout the wide land of the colony. What must then be established is the idea of a personal Pyrrhic victory resulting from the circumstances of an indisputable universal defeat. By the end of the seventeenth century the failure of the evangelical mission and its underlying rationale is evident everywhere. Missionary suffering is thus offered as compensation sublimated into the construct of a "tribute of Atonement." In the case of Japan, to speak of the other grand missionary scenario, the torture and martyrdom of the missionaries of the Order of Saint Augustine are painstakingly annotated by fray José Sicardo in *Cristianidad en el Japón y dilatada persecución* (Christianity in Japan and the extensive persecution).

In the variability of the discursive strategies employed to give account of the Christian sacrifice (all of which silence the tribute that evangelization forced unto the body of the colonized), we can in fact see the sign of a personal victory emerging that does not take into account the circumstances of the outside world. Significantly, this victory remains inscribed in the vast space of a defeat, both institutional and *historical*. The supreme pain that surfaces in the conscience and the soul of the individual cannot miraculously make up for the immense proportions of this—yes, global—failure of the sociopolitical body, whereas it presents itself to the eyes, *ad oculos*, so to speak, in the form of a spectacle. Ultimately, this pain is represented in the ancient terms of expiation and personal tribute understood as compensatory sacrifices (impossible as this notion might in fact be):

> Mas como yo, habiendo gozado (por la gracia divina) de buena parte de aquellos principios, haya visto los adversos fines en que todo esto ha venido a parar, no solo no puedo ofrecerle cántico de alabanza por fin de historia, mas antes (si para componer endechas tuviera gracia) me venía muy a pelo asentarme con Jeremías sobre nuestra indiana Iglesia, y con lágrimas, suspiros y voces que llegarán al Cielo (como el hacía con la destruida ciudad de Jerusalem) lamentarla y plañirla, recontando su miserable caída y gran desventura. (Mendieta II, 121)

> (And yet since I, having enjoyed (thanks to divine grace) a good portion of these prosperous beginnings, have seen the adverse ending everything has come to, not

only can I not offer a song of praise at the end of my story but would much rather (had I the grace to compose a lament) sit down with Jeremiah over our Indian church, mourning with tears, sighs and loud voices so as to reach the Heavens (as he did over the destroyed city of Jerusalem), recounting its miserable fall and great misfortune.)

Notes

1. In the Iberian Peninsula, the *Morisco* and Crypto-Jewish populations are compelled to adopt this kind of dissimulation to safeguard their identity. See Zorattini.
2. The connection between this and the apparatus of the Inquisition, as well as the general credibility of these sources, has been discussed by R. García Cárcel.
3. "The fall of the primitive" has been explored in these terms by A. Pagden, *La caída del hombre natural*.
4. Regarding this concept of "one humanity," see the classic study by L. Hanke.
5. Regarding this concept relating to the concealment of religious practice, see the book by C. Ginzburg.
6. This is to cite the expression used by R. Villari in his book that is mostly devoted to describing the effects of the rebellion of Naples in 1648.
7. This "colonial affect" can be found partially developed in J. T. de Silva.
8. A text which, among others, expresses the nostalgia of the Roman military order is that of V. Mut. Regarding the process of the sublimation of military and warlike violence, see R. de la Flor, "Mística."
9. This additionally helps to increase the voices calling for the truth so far negated or concealed, as in the manuscript by P. de Quiroga.
10. Beatriz Pastor identifies the author and his vindictive text with the figure of a pilgrim disillusioned with the world.
11. Máximo Hernández has studied the melancholy for the lost world portrayed by *El Inca* Garcilaso.
12. This complex issue can now be approached from the perspective advanced by Mújica Pinilla in "Identidades alegóricas."
13. Concerning the colonial "silence," see the detailed bibliography by Isabel Moraña.
14. Regarding this idea of founding an American Jerusalem far off the colonial habitats, see Milhou. For the eremite aspirations of the only American female saint Rosa de Lima, see Mújica Pinilla, *Rosa limensis*.
15. Regarding slavery and the ethical disintegration that its existence signals for the colonial city, see López García and Valtierra.
16. Regarding this issue, see the treatise by León Pinelo.
17. See the text by Torquemada quoted by Ruibal García (157).

Works Cited

Arriaga, Pablo Joseph de. *Extirpación de la idolatría del Pirú*. Lima: Jerónimo de Contreras, 1621.
Bartra, Roger. *El siglo de oro de la melancolía: Textos españoles y novohispanos sobre las enfermedades del alma*. Mexico City: Universidad Iberoamericana, 1998.
Biblia. Madrid: Biblioteca de autores cristianos, 1964.
Bonet, Juan Pablo. *Reduction de las letras y Arte para enseñar abler a los mudos*. Barcelona: Francisco Abarca de Angulo, 1620.
Campuzano y Sotomayor, Baltasar. *Planeta católico sobre el psalmo 18 a la Majestad de Filipe IIII*. Madrid: Diego Díez de la Carrera, 1646.
Cardillac, Louis. *Moriscos y cristianos: Un enfrentamiento polémico (1542–1640)*. Mexico City: F.C.E., 1979.
Castro, Diego de. *Inga Don Diego de Castro Titu Cussi Yupanqui para el Muy Ilustre Señor . . . Tocante a los Negocios que con su Majestad, en su Nombre, por su Poder de Tratar; la Qual es Esta que Sigue*. Ed. L. Millones. Lima: Ediciones de Virrey, 1985.
Díaz Esteban, Francisco. "La expulsion y la justificación de la conversion similada." *Sefarad*, 56/2 (1996): 251–63.
Dussel, Enrique. *Desintegración de la cristianidad colonial y liberación: perspectiva latinoamericana*. Salamanca: Ediciones Sígueme, 1978.
Escobar, Matías de. *Americana Thebaida: Vitas Patrum de los religiosos eremitaños de Nuestro Padre San Augustín de la Provincia de San Nicolás de Tolentino de Michoacán*. Morelia: Balsal Editores, 1970.
Espinosa Medrano, Juan. *La novena maravilla*. Valladolid: Joseph de Rueda, 1695.
Florencia, Francisco de. *Descripción histórica y moral del yermo de San Miguel de las Cuevas*. Cádiz: Imprenta de Jesús, 1684.
Garau, Francisco. *La Fé triunfante: Quatro autos celebrados en Mallorca por el Santo Oficio de la Inquisición*. Mallorca: Vda. De Gasp, 1691.
García Cárcel, Ricardo. "¿Son creibles las fuentes inquisitoriales?" *Grafías del imaginario: Representaciones culturales en España y América (siglos XVI–XVIII)*. Ed. C.A. Gonzales and Vila Vilar, Enriqueta. Mexico City: F.C.E., 2003. 96–110.
García Icazbalceta, Joaquín, ed. *Códice mendieta: Documentos franciscanos, siglos XVI y XVII*. Guadalajara: Edmundo Aviña, 1971.
Ginzburg, Carlo. *Il nicodemismo: Simulazione e dissimulazione religiosa nell'Europa del '500*. Torino: Giulio Einaudi, 1970.
Gitlitz, D.M. *Secreto engaño. La religion de los criptojudios*. Valladolid: Junta de Castilla y León, 2003.
Gruzinski, Sergei. *La colonización del imaginario*. Barcelona: F.C.E., 1995.
Hanke, Louis. *La humanidad es una*. Mexico City: F.C.E., 1974.
Hernández, Máximo. *Memoria del bien perdido: Identidad y nostalgia en el Inca Garcilaso de la Vega*. Lima: Instituto de Estudios Peruanos, 1991.

Ioly Zorratini, P. C. *L'identidá dissimulata: Giudaizzanti Iberici nell'Europa cristiana dell'etá moderna*. Florence: Universitá, 2000.

León Pinelo, Antonio de. *Questión moral: Si el chocolate quebranta el ayuno eclesiástico*. Madrid: Viuda de San Gonzáles, 1636.

López, Gregorio. *La vida que hizo el siervo de Dios . . . en algunos lugares de esta Nueva España*. Mexico City: Juan Ruiz, 1613.

López García, J.T. *Dos defensores de los esclavos negros en el siglo XVII: Francisco José de Jaca y Epifanio de Moirans*. Caracas: Universidad Católica Andrés Bello, 1982.

Mendieta, Jerónimo de. *Historia eclesiástica indiana*. Ed. F. de Solano and Pérez-Lila Madrid: Atlas, 1973.

Milhou, Alain. "Gregorio López, el iluminismo y la nueva Jerusalem Americana." *Actas del IX Congreso Internacional de Historia Americana. III*. Seville: CSIC, 1992. 55–83.

Moraña, Isabel. *Viaje al silencio: Exploraciones del discurso barroco*. Mexico City: UNAM, 1998.

Mújica Pinilla, Ramón. *Ángeles apógrifos en la América Virreinal*. México, F.C.E., 1996.

———. "Identidades alegóricas: lecturas iconográficas del barroco al neoclásico." *El barroco peruano*. Ed. R. Mújica. Lima: Banco de Crédito, 2004. 251–335.

———. *Rosa limensis: Mística. Política e iconografía en torno a la patrona de América*. México: F.C.E., 2001.

Mut, Vicente. *El príncipe en la guerra y en la paz*. Madrid: Juan Sánchez, 1648.

Pagden, Anthony. *La caida del hombre natural: El indio americano y los origenes de la etnología comparativa*. Madrid: Alianza, 1988.

Pastor, Beatriz. *El jardín y el peregrino: El pensamiento utópico en América Latina (1492–1695)*. Mexico City: UNAM, 1999, 505–27.

Quiroga, Pedro de. *Libro intitulado Coloquios de la verdad: Trata de las causas e inconvenientes que impiden la doctrina e conversión de los indios en los reinos del Pirú y de los males y agravios que padecen*. Seville: Tip. Zarzuela, 1922.

Rama, Ángel. *La ciudad letrada*. Hannover: Ediciones del Norte, 1984.

Ramírez de Prado, Lorenzo. *Consejo y consejero del príncipe*. Madrid: Luis Sánchez, 1617.

Ribadeneira, Pedro de. *Tratado de la Religión y Virtudes que deve tener el Príncipe Christiano*. Madrid: Pedro Madrigal, 1595. Reprinted, Atlas, 1952.

R. de la Flor, Fernando. "Mística de las Armas de España: El simbolismo de la violencia militar barroca." *Utopía: Espacios imposibles*. Ed. R. García, R. Navarro, and E. Núñez. Frankfurt: Peter Lang, 2003. 295–309.

———. "Retórica y conquista: La nueva lógica de la dominación humanista." *Barroco: Representación e ideología en el mundo hispánico*. Madrid: Cátedra, 2002. 301–33.

Ruibal García, A. *La santidad controvertida*. Mexico City: F.C.E., 1999.

Sicardo, José. *Cristiandad en el Japón y dilatada persecución que padeció*. Madrid: Francisco Sanz, 1698.

Silva, J. T. de. "América barroca: disimulación y contraste." *Cuadernos Hispanoamericanos* (1990): 29–37.

Subirats, Eduardo. *Memoria y exilio: Revisiones de las culturas hispánicas*. Madrid: Losada, 2003.

Valencia, Pedro de. "Censura al libro de Jerónimo Conestaggio." *Historia de la unión del reyno de Portugal a la Corona de Castilla*. Barcelona: Sebastián de Cormellas, 1610.

Valtierra, A. *Pedro Claver: El santo redentor de los negros*. Bogotá: Banco de la República, 1980.

Villari, Rosario. *Elogio della dissimulazione política: La lotta política nel Seicento*. Rome: Laterza, 1993.

Villava, Francisco. *Empresas morales*. Ed. M. Pérez. Córdoba: Universidad de Córdoba, 1998.

Ximénez Patón, Bartolomé. *Discurso a favor del Santo Loable estatuto de limpieza*. Granada: Andrés de Santiago, 1638.

◆ 13

Bartolomé de las Casas on Imperial Ethics and the Use of Force

George Mariscal

The relationship between the use of military force and the elaboration of ideological projects in foreign territories ("nation-building," in contemporary usage) has received renewed attention since the U.S. invasion of Iraq in 2003 and the subsequent occupation. To what extent can political, economic, or religious enterprises be successful when initiated by acts of overwhelming violence? On one side of the debate there are those who believe that the objective of "winning hearts and minds" is compromised by the application of military power. On the other side, force is presented as the necessary prerequisite with which to prepare the ideological terrain for the successful realization of long-term cultural, political, and economic objectives.

Almost five hundred years ago, these issues emerged in the earliest stages of Spanish colonialism. A mere two generations after Columbus's landfall in the Americas, the most dramatic manifestation of a controversy that would last several decades took shape during the debate between Juan Ginés de Sepúlveda and Bartolomé de las Casas. In their heated debate in Valladolid, both men were in fundamental agreement about the legitimacy of the Church's right to convert the indigenous people in the colonies to Catholicism. But they disagreed precisely on the issue of when and how military force ought to be applied.

In this essay I will revisit some of the main ideological currents that led up to and produced the direct exchanges between Las Casas and Sepúlveda in 1550 and 1551. By mapping the discursive fault lines that separated the strategies of the two camps within the general framework of what both sides considered to be the legitimate enterprise of mass conversion, we will begin to see the outline of an ethics of empire that continues to mark the parameters of contemporary debates about the legality of attempts by powerful nations to impose on other nations cultural and political forms thought to be superior.[1] I will draw textual examples primarily from the arguments presented over a five-day period by Las Casas at the junta in Valladolid—the *Apología*—in which the issues of sovereignty, military power, and Catholic values were articulated in an especially cogent and militant fashion.

One of the characteristics that marked the ethical core of Las Casas's entire career was the militancy with which he confronted his adversaries. Composed in a different register than the moralizing arguments of his contemporaries, Las Casas's ethical statements, while no less rooted in Catholic traditions, were noticeably sharper in their critique of the imperial project, and commentators have identified the prophetic and sometimes exaggerated quality of his interventions. I would argue that perhaps more than the actual content of his works, what makes Las Casas "modern" is precisely the way in which his experiences in America alchemized his intellectual formation to produce an uncompromising fidelity to a truth having less to do with institutionalized doctrine than with a radical idea of justice. This ethics born of the objective conditions of Spanish colonialism would drive Las Casas to challenge imperial policies at a time when most agreed that Europe itself was under attack.

On the Islamic Threat and the Christian Peace Movement

> Pues si no se le detiene a tiempo, grave es el riesgo y peligro
> que amenaza a nuestro bienestar y a nuestra libertad.
> —Juan Ginés de Sepúlveda
> (*Exhortación al Emperador Carlos V*)
>
> (For if he is not stopped in time, the risk and danger
> that threatens our security and our freedom will be grave.)

During the final years of the decade of the 1520s, Christian Europe found itself confronted by an external menace from the east. The Ottoman Turks under the leadership of Sultan Suleiman I had routed the Hungarian army in 1526 and now prepared to lay siege to Vienna. By the summer of 1529, the Turks had deployed a force of about 100,000 troops outside the Austrian capital.[2] Writing from Rome, Ginés de Sepúlveda urged Carlos V to come to the aid of the city:

"Siendo esto así y amenazándonos una guerra atroz—¿cómo amenazándonos? echándosenos ya encima—movida por el muy soberbio enemigo . . . todos los católicos cuya salvación y libertad, a ti principalmente y a tu fe confiadas, se encuentran en grave peligro y riesgo") (quoted in Losada 9) (The situation being thus and with a terrible war instigated by our arrogant enemy threatening us—what do I mean threatening us? It is already upon us—. . . all Catholics, whose salvation and freedom are mainly in your hands, will be at risk and in great danger). The general fear of an Islamic invasion was especially intense along Spain's Mediterranean coast where the Turks had made inroads in North Africa, and the Islamic city-states carried out attacks against major cities with impunity.[3] Within Spain, the perception that collaborationist cells might be embedded in *morisco* communities had forced Carlos V in 1526 to decree a ban on Islamic practices and the use of Arabic. In political and religious circles there was a shared consensus that a gathering danger was about to engulf Europe.

From Sepúlveda's perspective, however, there was a second challenge to the security of the Christian nations. Circulating throughout the student community in Italy, especially at the prestigious college known as San Clemente de Los Españoles in Bologna, was an antiwar discourse that questioned the compatibility of Catholic and military values. The students were reacting at least in part to the controversy initiated by Luther who in 1518 had stated that the Turkish menace was a divine punishment for Christendom's vices and therefore should not be resisted.[4] By the time Erasmus entered the debate with a written statement, more rational arguments had emerged, but the public discussion was already awash in distortions and innuendo. In his "On the War against the Turks" (1530), the Dutch thinker rejected as "slander" the charge that he believed that "the right to make war is totally denied to Christians" (318). Taking a position that would later resonate in the writings of Las Casas and other Spanish *erasmistas*, he argued:

> My message is that war must never be undertaken unless, as a last resort, it cannot be avoided; war is by its nature such a plague to man that even if it is undertaken by a just prince in a totally just cause, the wickedness of captains and soldiers results in almost more evil than good. St. Bernard goes further, in calling "malicious" the "militia" of this world; he designates it "of this world" because so often the call to arms is provoked by ambition, anger or the hope of plunder; the man who falls in wars of this kind, he says, is dead for all eternity, while he who kills and conquers lives on—as a murderer. (318)[5]

Many in the highest ranks of ecclesiastical and military circles, however, found Erasmus' clarification to be unconvincing and they continued [willfully?] to misread Erasmus as a strict pacifist who opposed the use of force under any circumstances. From the point of view of the traditional elites, the student movement was moving dangerously close to a pacifist position and held the potential to create a generation of "conscientious objectors" precisely at the moment in which Christian Europe found itself locked in mortal combat with a potent Muslim army to the east and Muslim naval forces to the south.

In his text addressed to Carlos V, Sepúlveda had reacted to the student protest movement with a noticeably impatient and mocking tone. Responding to concerns about the lack of precedent in the New Testament for military action, he wrote: "Pues si porque ni Cristo ni los Apóstoles hicieron la guerra no debiéramos nosotros hacerla por ningún motivo, ya que su vida y acciones deben ser nuestra doctrina, ¿acaso porque Cristo no condenó como reo a la adúltera hemos de pensar, por lo mismo, que están permitidos a los cristianos los adulterios?" (quoted in Losada 11) (For my response to the claim that just because Christ and the Apostles never waged war we should not either for any reason since his life and actions should be our model is "Should we likewise believe that just because Christ never condemned the adulteress we should allow Christians to be adulterers?").

In an even more aggressive move, Sepúlveda accused those intellectuals who had influenced the students of not only misunderstanding Church doctrine but of essentially providing aid and comfort to the enemy:

> Y sé que no sólo consideras sospechosos de impiedad, sino odiosos y nefastos a esos hombres a quienes oigo propalar rumores encubiertos con falso color de cristianismo, según los cuales no es propio de la tolerancia cristiana el oponerse con la espada y las armas a la violencia de los turcos, a los que califican de azote de Dios, y dicen que los cristianos deben vencerlos no con violencia, sino con paciencia; voces éstas que estoy seguro no proceden, como otras opiniones heréticas, de error de la mente, de depravación de pensamiento o de ambición, sino del crimen e insidioso sacrilegio de quienes, corrompidos por los turcos con dones y promesas, tienden nefandas asechanzas a la libertad de los cristianos. (quoted in Losada 10)

> (I know that you consider them to be not only prone to impiety but hateful and evil those men whom I have heard spreading ideas deceptively wrapped in Christianity claiming that to take up the sword and arms against the Turks, whom they call a punishment from God, runs counter to Christian tolerance. They say that Christians should defeat the Turks not with violence but with patience. I am sure these voices, like other heretical opinions, do not originate from mental errors or defective thinking or ambition but rather from the criminal and insidious sacrilege of those who have been corrupted with gifts and promises from the Turks and therefore put the freedom of Christians in danger.)

Although the specific criticism in this passage most likely was directed at Luther, the implication was that anyone who questioned the policy of armed response was guilty of appeasement. Such accusations had a chilling effect on the entire debate about the possible incompatibility between military and Catholic values. By the time Sepúlveda began to circulate his "Demócrates Primero o de la compatibilidad entre la milicia y la religión cristiana" (1535) (The First Democrates or the Compatibility between Military Action and Christianity), he had constructed a systematic rebuttal of the students' arguments and by extension the teachings of Luther, Erasmus, and other heterodox intellectuals.

In the prologue to the "Demócrates Primero," Sepúlveda recalled the concerns the students in Bologna had articulated: "Pero ninguna cosa preocupaba más a aquellos jóvenes como el temor, que profesaban, de que un valeroso militar no pudiese a la vez dedicarse a su profesión y cumplir con los preceptos de la Religión cristiana" (134) (But nothing worried those young people more than their professed fear that a brave military man could not devote himself to his profession and still comply with the precepts of the Christian religion). In his textual elaboration of the issue, Sepúlveda juxtaposed the character of the old soldier Alfonso Guevara to the character of Demócrates the wise Greek philosopher. It is in the voice of Alfonso that we detect the basis for the students' doubts: "Me parece que la valentía y honor del caballero o soldado en asuntos que muchas veces nada tienen que ver con la guerra movida por autoridad pública, no concuerdan con la estrechez de las leyes cristianas" (180) (I believe the bravery and honor of a knight or soldier with regard to matters that many times have nothing to do with the war instigated by public authorities do not conform to the narrowness of Christian law). Demócrates quickly points out that such thinking is erroneous and marshals evidence from sources ranging from Aristotle's *Ethics* to a multitude of classical and biblical authorities. On the ground, the student movement was unable to extend its influence, but the debate about the use of military force in a Christian "civilizing" project had been reignited, and Sepúlveda had become one of the most influential spokesmen for the "military solution."

From Turks to Indians: Preemptive War and the Evildoers

In a climate of fear where acts of terror were thought to be imminent, the ability of the political and intellectual classes to manipulate opinion within the governing elites increased. Given the malleable nature of ideologies based on ethnic and religious stereotypes, it became relatively easy for some ideologues to transfer discursive fields related to the construction of "the enemy" from one group to another. For Sepúlveda, this act of transference extended from the Islamic threat in Europe directly to Amerindian societies in the colonies.[6]

Precisely because native peoples were subject to unacceptable moral values and tyrannical forms of government, Sepúlveda argued, it was the obligation of the Christian nations to apply force in order to facilitate their conversion out of barbarism and into civilization and spiritual salvation. In his *Demócrates II* also known as the *Demócrates Alter: On the Just Causes of War Against the Indians* (1550), he outlined his complete rationale for colonization, a series of arguments to which Las Casas would respond at Valladolid. But already in an earlier text directed to Felipe II, Sepúlveda had summarized his basic position:

> Así, pues, la razón de acabar con tan criminales monstruosidades y de liberar a personas inocentes de actos injuriosos contra ellas, podía por sí sola concederos el derecho, ya otorgado por Dios y la naturaleza, de someter a vuestro dominio a los bárbaros... A esto se añade el facilitar a los bárbaros muchas cosas utilísimas y muy necesarias... Aportados, pues, tantos bienes, suprimidas tantas monstruosidades pasmosas por su impiedad, por el esfuerzo, trabajo y valor de nuestra gente, introducida allí la Religión cristiana y óptimas leyes, ¿con qué comportamiento, con qué obsequios pagarán aquellas gentes tan grandes, tan variados y tan inmortales beneficios? (quoted in Losada 36)

> (And so the goal of putting an end to such criminal and monstrous deeds and of liberating innocent people from the injurious acts committed against them would be sufficient reason for you to assume the right, as God and nature have granted it, to subject the barbarians to your rule... To this we may add the fact that the barbarians are granted many useful and necessary things... and once so much good is accomplished and our people's efforts, hard work, and valor suppress so many acts that are frightening and monstrous in their impiety, and the Christian religion and its supreme laws are introduced there, how will those people ever repay us for such great and varied and immortal gifts?)

In this view, the civilizing mission brought only positive changes to the colonized who would be forever at a loss as to how to repay the colonizer's beneficence. The authority to use force, therefore, resided in the colonizer's superior system of values and form of government. Put another way, civilization was not Spain's gift to the world but God's gift to mankind. Spain was simply a vehicle for God's work.[7] As Sepúlveda wrote to his friend Francisco de Argote shortly after his debate with Las Casas:

El Derecho natural, pues, da la razón a aquellos pueblos que, por simples motivos de generosidad, se lanzan a implantar su dominio en pueblos bárbaros, no con el fin de sacar un provecho material, tratarlos injustamente y reducirlos a esclavitud, sino más bien para cumplir un deber de humanidad, al intentar desarraigar sus costumbres tan contrarias al Derecho natural, hacerlos cambiar de vida y adoptar por lo menos las obligaciones de dicho Derecho natural; con ello se consigue un doble beneficio al establecerse, además, un intercambio de favores entre la nación dominadora y los pueblos sometidos. ("Carta 53" 193–94)

(Natural law, therefore, authorizes those nations that venture forth to impose their control over barbarous nations, not for material gain or to treat them unjustly or to enslave them but simply because of that nation's generosity and desire to fulfil their debt to humanity by uprooting those customs that are so contrary to natural law and make them change their way of life and at least adopt the obligations of natural law. With that a dual benefit is achieved as well as an exchange of favors between the dominating nation and those who are made its subjects.)

In spite of the powerful attraction for many of this early variant of "manifest destiny," there continued to be intense policy debates about Spanish actions in the Americas. In April of 1550 the Consejo de Indias called for the suspension of all acts of conquest until key issues could be deliberated and ruled upon. In theory, there was to be a comprehensive ceasefire while the proponents of competing strategies, policymakers, and a panel of jurists attended a *Junta sobre Conquistas y Esclavitud* (Council of Conquest and Slavery).[8]

It is at this point that Sepúlveda faced his most formidable rival on the most public of stages. In 1547 Las Casas had returned to Spain from Mexico armed with what were essentially legal briefs on every important topic related to the colonizing project. Not only was he well prepared with documentation, he had spent the previous decades (especially the period between 1535 and 1546) actively engaged in a series of similar *juntas* held in Mexico City. Moreover, Las Casas brought a radical militancy to the event that already had begun to anger those in power, especially those who were aware of various *memoriales* such as the "La exención o la damnación" (1546) in which he essentially threatened the Spanish prince (the future Felipe II) regarding any attempt on the part of the monarchy to preempt or challenge ecclesiastical authority in the colonies.[9]

Whereas in its earliest stages the student antiwar movement had drawn tentatively upon an antimilitarist strain within Church writings and their Erasmian-inflected interpretations, it now found a powerful ally who was both an insider with access to imperial policymakers and a vocal critic of claims with regard to the legitimacy of global empire. Las Casas's rivals had argued that as the elected leader of the Holy Roman empire Carlos V was the legitimate sovereign of the entire world. But for Las Casas this position was the height of arrogance. While Carlos V most assuredly could claim sovereignty over all Christian nations, Las Casas argued that he exercised no authority whatsoever over non-Christian peoples: "Ahora bien, decir que el Emperador Romano es legítimo señor de todo el mundo es un total disparate, un modo de engañar con adulación a los emperadores y una ocasión para que el mundo se vea envuelto en discordias" (Las Casas, *Apología* 303) (Now to say that the Roman Emperor is the legitimate lord of the whole world is foolish and simply a way to deceive emperors with flattery and a way to involve the world in greater discord).

Not only were some of the ideologues linked to the court misguided in their understanding of imperial jurisdiction, according to Las Casas, but others were plotting to invoke imperial authority in order to reap personal gain. Under the cover of the Catholic missionary project and the stated objective of removing despots who persecuted their own people, these purported agents of God's will in reality pursued a program of economic exploitation and the brutalization of indigenous peoples. Las Casas cited the twelfth-century Italian legal scholar Graciano as his authority: "Cuando algunas personas se sienten movidas, por un oculto instinto, a perseguir a los malvados [pero] su intencion no es castigar los pecados de los delincuentes, sino apoderarse de sus bienes y someterlos bajo su jurisdiccion, no estan libres de crimen" (quoted in Las Casas 597) (Those people who feel motivated, by a mysterious impulse, to pursue the evil ones with the intention of appropriating their riches and subjecting them to their authority rather than punishing the criminals' sins are themselves engaged in criminal behavior). Las Casas then offered the following gloss:

> Aunque tales personas en cierto modo sirvan a Dios, sin embargo, pecan mortalmente puesto que mueven guerra no con la intencion de servir a Dios sino con la intencion de conseguir un botin y de extender su poder ... [Estos] propios tiranos (de quienes Dios se sirve) no tienen la intención de hacer aquello hacia lo que Dios los mueve, ni quieren lo que Dios quiere, sino que solamente dirigen su depravado corazón a despojar de sus bienes a las gentes y someterlas a su imperio ... Tales tiranos, al obrar asi, por gusto de dominio y no por amor de la virtud, cometen un gravísimo pecado mortal, y, al fin de su vida, serán atormentados en el fuego del infierno. (*Apología* 597–99)

> (Although such people serve God in some sense they nevertheless commit mortal sins because they pursue war with the intention of acquiring riches and extending their power rather than serving God ... [These] same tyrants [whom God uses]

have no intention of doing God's work nor do they want what God wants. Their depraved heart moves them only to rob people of their wealth and subject them to their empire . . . By doing this, such tyrants, in their thirst for power and their lack of love for virtue, commit a grave mortal sin and at the end of their lives will be tormented in the fires of hell.)

As Marcel Bataillon has taught us, the Spanish *erasmistas* were on the run by the early 1540s, and the few who remained in positions of influence opted to remain silent rather than to challenge Sepúlveda and the proponents of force.[10] Carlos V himself had grown impatient with the ongoing criticisms of colonial policy, and even influential thinkers like Francisco de Vitoria had begun to waver in their public statements. Vitoria, for example, wrote to his friend Fray Miguel de los Arcos that in the heated partisan environment of the court, anyone who raised questions ran the risk of being considered disloyal to the emperor.[11]

Nevertheless, it is important to note that some of the most influential ecclesiastical authorities with direct access to Carlos V shared several of the positions outlined by Las Casas. Domingo Soto, the emperor's Dominican confessor and one of the judges at the Valladolid *junta*, for example, would make similar arguments in his *De iustitia et iure* (1556). Far from being marginalized critics of imperial policy, for a brief period lasting into the 1550s the proponents of the system that Las Casas and others had struggled to construct out of biblical and classical traditions exerted considerable influence at the very center of royal power even if they did little to mitigate the situation in the colonies.[12]

The Debate over the Proper Use of Military Force

> Cuando yo hablo de la fuerza de las
> armas, hablo del mayor de todos los males.
> —Las Casas, *Apología*

> (When I speak about military force,
> I speak about the worst of all evils.)

For obvious reasons scholars have studied the debate at Valladolid primarily in order to understand European attitudes toward colonized populations. Las Casas's defense of native peoples is well documented and need not be summarized here. More important for my purpose are his criticisms of and strict limitations placed on military solutions and his implicit construction of an ethical system for the Spanish colonial project. Military action, he argued, carried with it a number of dangers that potentially could undermine the success of the ideological project of conversion and salvation. Moreover, those who participated in the use of force were themselves in danger of committing crimes against humanity and thereby losing their eternal soul.

If war were inevitable, strict guidelines should govern its prosecution. On the issue of civilian casualties, Las Casas wrote: "En consecuencia, los soldados deben abstenerse de hacer violencia a aquellas personas que llevan por delante la marca de inocentes. Los jefes del ejército deben amonestar sobre esto exacta y severamente a los soldados, si no quieren incurrir en el mismo pecado y daño" (*Apología* 1988, 385) (Soldiers should abstain, therefore, from committing violence against those people who appear to be innocent. Military commanders must be aggressive about making this policy clear if they themselves do not wish to fall into the same sin and harm). In this view, the highest levels of the military command are responsible for the actions of soldiers on the ground, and even their claim of ignorance will not release them from their "sins" or what would become in a much later stage of modern jurisprudence those acts classified as "war crimes." As for the soldiers themselves, Las Casas, in typically uncompromising fashion, refused to exempt them from the tremendous responsibility of choosing between their religious values and immoral orders or even those spontaneous decisions caused by the confusion of the battlefield: "Habiendo sido adoctrinados tales soldados en las enseñanzas de Cristo, no deben ignorar que no debe hacerse daño a las personas inocentes. Luego ellos no disciernen rectamente [y] son reos de un crimen gravísimo ante Dios y dignos de eterna condenación" (*Apología* 393) (Such soldiers who have been indoctrinated with Christ's teachings cannot claim they were unaware of the prohibition against harming innocent people. Those who make such a claim are ill-advised and guilty before God of a very grave crime and deserve eternal condemnation).

Las Casas's views did not coincide with that of a properly pacifist position, and he adhered to a belief in just wars in which civilian deaths might be unavoidable collateral damage ("los inocentes serían matados accidentalmente y no intencionadamente"). In his rebuttal of Sepúlveda's presentation, however, he outlined a coherent defense of non-combatants and a strong argument against the offensive or preemptive use of force:

> Pongamos otro ejemplo: Mujeres, niños, ancianos y otras inocentes personas se han refugiado en una fortaleza. Si no es de absoluta necesidad atacar esta fortaleza para el resultado favorable de toda la guerra, sería un pecado gravísimo destruir tal fortaleza mediante fuego o minas ... Esto sería matar inocentes deliberadamente ... Esto se prueba por el hecho de que la guerra no es lícita sino cuando es

necesaria y así de ninguna manera puede ser excusada. La guerra es peste y atroz calamidad para el género humano. (Las Casas, *Apología* 387)

(Let us take another example: Women, children, the elderly, and other innocent people take refuge in a fortress. If attacking the fortress is not absolutely necessary for the favorable result of the entire war, it would be a very grave sin to destroy the fortress with artillery fire or mines ... This would be the deliberate killing of innocents ... which is proved by the fact that war is only permissible when it is necessary and therefore cannot be avoided. War is a plague and a horrible calamity for the human race.)

Even in those cases in which military power is deployed to correct what is considered to be an intolerable situation for an oppressed minority, there must be meticulous planning to ensure that, as Las Casas put it, the remedy is not worse than the cure:

Dado que no debemos exponer al peligro a un gran número de inocentes, para liberar a unos pocos que también son inocentes, se sigue que ni la Iglesia, ni ningún príncipe o miembro de ésta, deben mover una tal guerra, si la hacen no bajo el pretexto de defender sus reinos que están muy alejados de los reinos de los infieles, sino solamente bajo pretexto de liberar personas inocentes, cuando en realidad, bajo este pretexto, perecería una infinita multitud de inocentes. (Apología 397)

(Given that we should not endanger large numbers of innocent people in order to liberate a few who are also innocent, it follows that neither the Church nor any prince nor member of the Church should instigate such a war. This is especially true if they go to war not to defend their kingdoms that are far from those of the infidels but rather with the pretext of liberating innocent people when in reality, using this pretext, a vast number of innocent people will perish.)

As we have already seen, the use of force in order to remove a tyrannical leader from power in and of itself was not sufficient cause for placing the civilian population in danger: "Y así, si bien es verdad que el hecho de matar a un tirano, que es peste de la república, es una buena y meritoria acción, tal no es el caso si su asesinato da origen a una rebelión o a un serio tumulto que duplica los males dentro de la república" (Las Casas, *Apología*, 415) (And so, although it is true that killing a tyrant who is a plague on the republic is a good and meritorious action, it is not true in a case where the tyrant's removal causes a rebellion or a serious disturbance that doubles the number of ills within the republic).

Armed intervention loses its moral legitimacy, therefore, whenever the destruction it wreaks surpasses the "evil" against which it was deployed. Over time, the realization of the ideological program designed to follow the use of force becomes impossible due to the heightened sense of outrage felt by the colonized or occupied population. According to Las Casas, the use of "compulsión corporal" can only undermine the conversion process:

> ¿Cómo podrá amarnos aquella gente y hacer amistad con nosotros (condición necesaria para recibir nuestra fe), cuando los hijos se ven huérfanos de los padres, las esposas privadas de los maridos, los padres privados de los hijos y amigos; cuando ven a los seres amados heridos, hechos prisioneros, despojados de sus bienes, y de la innumerable multitud que eran, reducidos a unos pocos? (*Apología* 79)

> (How can those people love us and develop friendships with us (a necessary condition for receiving the faith) if children see themselves orphaned, wives lose their husbands, fathers lose their children and friends; if they see their loved ones wounded, held captive, stripped of their possessions, and the entire population reduced to a few where before they were a countless multitude?)

By assuming that military force could accomplish anything other than the desolation of the ideological ground in which Christianity was expected to flourish, Sepúlveda and his followers had misread the entire history of the evangelical mission from its inception: "¡Cítenos Sepúlveda un solo pasaje en el que Cristo o los Santos Padres nos hayan enseñado que los paganos deben ser subyugados mediante la guerra antes de que se les predique el evangelio!" (Las Casas, *Apología* 545)[13] (Let Sepúlveda show us one passage where Christ or the Holy Fathers teach us that pagans should be subjugated through war before they can be taught the gospel!).

On Persuasion as the Ethical Alternative to Force

> Además, cuando Cristo envió a sus discípulos a predicar
> el evangelio, ¿con qué espadas y bombardas los armó?
> —Las Casas, *Apología*

> (Besides, when Christ sent his disciples to preach
> the gospel, did he arm them with swords and mortars?)

One of the central points of contention during the debate at Valladolid hinged on the interpretation of the parable of the banquet. In Luke 14, Jesus tells the story of a man whose invitations to a banquet do not yield a sufficient number of guests. The man orders his servants to scour the city for "the poor and maimed and blind and lame," but even then the banquet hall is not full. The man then tells his servants: "Go out to the highways and hedges, and compel people to come in, that my house may be filled."[14] For Sepúlveda, who followed the interpretation offered by no less an authority than St. Augustine, "compel" (*compelle intrare*) must be read literally, thereby justifying the use of force in the colonies "para preparar así el camino a la propagación de la religión cristiana" (quoted in Las Casas, *Apología* 556) (in order to thereby prepare the path for the propagation of the Christian religion). Las Casas would have to draw upon all his rhetorical skills to convince the judges that "to compel" could only be understood to mean to convince by persuasion.

Las Casas countered with a variety of authorities ranging from San Juan Crisóstomo to the twelfth-century Pope Innocent III. Although Pope Innocent's writings were related to the medieval debate over the forced conversion of Muslims, their authoritative and succinct admonitions were among the few interpretations of the banquet parable that served Las Casas's purposes:

> Y así, nadie debe ser forzado a hacerse cristiano. Y no se opone a esto el hecho de que, en la parábola del banquete nupcial, se diga al siervo que fuerce a los invitados a dicho banquete a que entren. En efecto, se trata aquí de una coacción que se realiza mediante la acción de la razón, no mediante la severidad de la espada material o de la violencia temporal, dado que el Señor prohibe al siervo, esto es, al cuerpo de predicadores o a los apóstoles en la persona de Pedro, que hagan uso de la espada. (quoted in Las Casas, *Apología* 557)

> [And so no one should be forced to become a Christian. And this is not negated by the fact that in the parable of the wedding banquet the servant is told to force the guests to enter. Indeed, what is being described here is an act that is accomplished with the use of reason and not with the severity of the physical sword or earthly violence. Because the Lord prohibits the servant, that is the body of preachers or the apostles in the figure of Peter, from using the sword.]

In fact, Sepúlveda had not argued for forced conversion but for the use of force as a preparatory stage before conversion could take place. Nevertheless, Las Casas made use of such passages in order to support his assertion that any offensive military action whatsoever negated the fundamental message of the Christianizing mission. In his gloss of Pope Innocent's text, he added: "Por lo cual, el siervo que invita a la boda, esto es, el predicador del evangelio, debe anunciar éste, no armado de bombardas, como el lobo que trata de matar y robar las ovejas, sino equipado con una santa conducta y la palabra de Dios" (Las Casas, *Apología* 557) (Therefore the servant who invites people to the wedding, that is, the preacher of the gospel, must announce the gospel equipped with saintly behavior and the word of God and not armed with mortars like the wolf who tries to kill and steal the sheep).

Persuasion, then, was to be the only weapon in the Christian's arsenal because the application of force for any reason could only negate the power of the "good news." Unlike Sepúlveda for whom the possession of "Truth" authorized the deployment of total power in order to level the foundation of colonized societies and reshape them, Las Casas argued that the truth of Christianity must be allowed to speak for itself. The agent of the gospel in this context is not a conquering subject but a teaching subject, and the application of force can produce only terror as a prelude to exploitation and greed. Using the same prophetic tone he had used in his *memorial* to the young Felipe II, he warned of serious consequences for those who contradicted Christ's message of peace in their approach to potential converts: "El remedio más eficaz para ellos es que vean que en nuestra conducta brilla la vida cristiana. Pero imponer el evangelio por el poder de las armas no es un ejemplo cristiano, sino un pretexto para robar las propiedades de otros y para subyugar sus provincias . . . . Teman, pues, a Dios, vengador de las perversas maquinaciones, aquellos que, bajo pretexto de propagar la fe, con la fuerza de las armas invaden posesiones ajenas, las saquean y se apoderan de ellas" (Las Casas, *Apología* 349–51) (The most effective solution for them is that they see how our behavior reflects the Christian life. To impose the gospel with force of arms is not a Christian example but rather a pretext to steal other people's property and subjugate their lands . . . . Let those who invade, sack, and take control of foreign lands with military force under the pretext of spreading the faith fear God for he is the avenger of perverse machinations).

Las Casas argues on two fronts in this passage. On the one hand, he calls to account those who would disguise their economic motives behind the screen of Christianity. The extraction of wealth and labor power in the Americas must not be disguised in the trappings of saving souls or bringing civilization to the barbarians. More important, he reasserts the absolute contradiction between Christian values and the application of preemptive military force. The conversion process can only succeed where the message of Christ is performed as a model to be imitated. The use of coercion in the name of an absolute truth can only expose the perverse nature of those who claim to represent that truth. Moreover, violence once unleashed cannot be contained and can only turn back on its perpetrators in a kind of brutal feedback model of divine retribution.

The Perils of Divine Blowback or "El que a hierro mata ... "

> Porque el nombre de Cristo ya despide mal olor por todas estas naciones.
> Huele con cierto mal olor inaudito y abominable.
> —Las Casas, *Sobre la destrucción de los indios* (ca. 1546)
>
> (Because the name of Christ now spreads like a bad odor across all these nations. It emits a certain unusual and repulsive stench.)

Contemporary commentators have called Las Casas "modern" for a variety of reasons ranging from his recognition of "the Other" to his pivotal role as a founding voice of human rights discourse. But insofar as "modernity" (in itself an empty abstraction susceptible to multiple constructed meanings) traditionally has signified a high degree of secularism we cannot enlist Las Casas in its ranks. Not only did he accept the idea of Catholicism's redemptive mission, he dedicated himself to facilitating its success by arguing that priests were simply soldiers in a different kind of *milicia*, that is, the "soldados de Cristo" or "la milicia celestial."[15]

It is worth remembering, however, that in his attempts to limit the use of military force and prescribe a set of ethical norms to be strictly followed in time of war, he followed in the ideological wake of Erasmus and others who viewed war as an evil to which the powerful should resort only in the direst of circumstances. If rulers adopted a policy of "war of choice" based on questionable motives, they jeopardized the ideological mission in which they claimed to believe, thereby producing, as the above epigraph clearly states, a situation in which potential converts would react to the name of Christ with disgust. The surprisingly "modern" spirit of this position is inescapable.

At the same time, Las Casas stated that rulers and their advisors who resort too quickly to violent solutions run the risk of incurring the wrath of God and endangering their own nation. In the section of the *Apología* titled "Cuatro argumento de Sepúlveda: Facilitar la predicación del cristianismo y abrir las puertas a los predicadores del evangelio," Las Casas launches one of his most pointed rebuttals: "En realidad, Sepúlveda trata con todas sus fuerzas de aumentar estos crímenes, hasta que la última nación de todo aquel [Nuevo] Mundo sea finalmente destruida; entonces Dios recto y justo, provocado por estas acciones, exhalará la furia de su ira y arremeterá contra España entera, tal vez antes de que lo hubiese decretado" (501) (In reality, Sepúlveda tries with all his might to multiply those crimes until the last nation of that New World finally is destroyed; then God who is righteous and just, provoked by these acts, will unleash the fury of his wrath and take action against all of Spain, perhaps sooner than he originally had planned).

Contemporary definitions of "blowback" guarantee that acts of violence will be directed against any nation whose foreign policy, particularly its use of military force, provokes retaliation.[16] At the early modern moment of this concept's long genealogy, because retaliatory strikes by colonized peoples against the colonizing power were logistically difficult, the right to inflict blowback resided in God's hands alone. At the risk of overly simplifying the mechanisms of international power, the complex consequences of military intervention, and the historical distance that separates us from the sixteenth century, I would argue that one of the links that connects our own time to that of Las Casas is the idea of blowback. Simply put, the fundamental principle of Las Casas's ethical stance in the *Apología* is that all empires must necessarily reap what they have sown.

Notes

1. The contemporary subtext for my essay is the foreign policy instituted during the administration of George W. Bush following the atrocities committed on September 11, 2001, especially the U.S. invasion and occupation of Iraq in 2003. The neoconservative project of preemptive military strikes as a prelude to "exporting democracy" and nation-building in Afghanistan and Iraq continues to sit in an uneasy relationship to international law and the putative democratic principles of the United States itself. The relevancy of Las Casas's writings on war and colonialism has been refunctioned consistently at least since the nineteenth century. During the American war in Southeast Asia, Hans Magnus Enzensberger invoked Las Casas to critique the U.S. war effort, and more recently Mexican author Pablo González Casanova recuperated Las Casas to describe indigenous resistance to the imposition of neoliberal regimes throughout Latin America at the beginning of the twenty-first century. In literary studies, Barbara Simerka has connected her highly original study of Las Casas' influence on early modern Spanish "counter-epics" to the period between the first U.S. Persian Gulf War in 1991 and the invasion of Iraq twelve years later. See her *Discourses of Empire: Counter-Epic Literature in Early Modern Spain* (University Park, PA: Penn State University Press, 2003).
2. Apparently, Suleiman's plan was to tunnel beneath one of the main entrances of the city, blow up the twin towers at the gate, and deploy ground forces through the opening. The city resisted, however, and by October the Turks withdrew only to return in 1532 when they were defeated by Carlos V and 80,000 imperial troops. See Andre Clot, *Suleiman the Magnificent: The Man, His Life, His Epoch* (London: Saqi Books, 2004).

3. On the North African context, see María Antonia Garcés, *Cervantes in Algiers: A Captive's Tale* (Nashville, TN: Vanderbilt University Press, 2002).
4. By 1529, Luther had shifted his position and moved closer to that of Erasmus. In the days after the terrorist atrocities of September 11, 2001, two of the most prominent Christian evangelists in the United States opined that the attacks were a punishment from God designed to correct the nation's "moral decay." Jerry Falwell stated: "What we saw on Tuesday, as terrible as it is, could be miniscule if, in fact, God continues to lift the curtain and allow the enemies of America to give us probably what we deserve." He apologized for the statement the next day. Partial transcript of the conversation between Falwell and Pat Robertson accessed on December 28, 2004 at http://www.truthorfiction.com/rumors/f/falwell-robertson-wtc.htm.
5. In this passage as in many others, Erasmus provides the discursive repertoire for Las Casas:
If the war is inspired by such motives as the lust for power, ambition, private grievances, or the desire for revenge, it is clearly not a war, but mere brigandage. What is more, although it is primarily the function of the Christian princes themselves to carry on wars, they must not resort to this most dangerous of expedients without the consent of their citizens and of the whole country. Finally, if absolute necessity dictates that a war must be fought, Christian clemency demands that every effort be made to confine the numbers involved to the minimum and to end the war, with the least possible bloodshed, as quickly as may be. (320)
Although history will judge whether or not the Bush administration's stated reasons for the invasion and occupation of Iraq were justifiable, it is worth noting that many who opposed the war argued that it did not meet any of the ethical guidelines outlined here.
6. In a not dissimilar act of transference in a totally different context, neoconservatives in the United States collapsed the threat of radical Islamists with undocumented Mexican workers after the attacks of 2001. Harvard professor Samuel Huntington drew upon such (il)logic when he shifted from his "clash of civilizations" thesis (Islam vs. the West) to the notion that Mexican immigration was the greatest danger to U.S. culture in the twenty-first century. See his *Who Are We?: The Challenges to America's National Identity* (New York: Simon and Schuster, 2004).
7. For the most recent recuperation of this ideological trick, see George W. Bush, "State of the Union Address" (2003): "Americans are a free people, who know that freedom is the right of every person and the future of every nation. The liberty we prize is not America's gift to the world; it is God's gift to humanity."
8. Las Casas had been seeking such a meeting for at least seven years. On the political background to the Junta de Valladolid and Sepúlveda's possible role as spokesman for economic interests seeking to repeal the "Nuevas Leyes de Indias" (among them Hernán Cortés), see Parish and Weidman; Angel Losada's "Introducción" to Las Casas, Apología; and Lewis Hanke, *All Mankind Is One: A Study of the Disputation Between Bartolome De Las Casas and Juan Gines De Sepulveda in 1550 on the*

Intellectual and Religious Capacity of the American Indians (DeKalb, IL: Northern Illinois University Press, 1994).

9. Las Casas's *memorial* "La exención o la damnación" ("De exemptione sive damnatione"), which remained unpublished until 1992, raised eyebrows in the court with passages such as the following:
   ¡Tenga, pues, cuidado el Príncipe Católico—si desea la ayuda del Señor para ganar victorias—que no quiera usurpar por sí o por sus jueces la autoridad y jurisdicción que pertenecen al sacerdocio y la dignidad eclesiástica o potestad espiritual. De otro modo, debe ser arrojado del templo, matado por la espada del anatema, y además herido por la destestable lepra del pecado mortal—quedando apartado de la gracia de Dios y al fin de la gloria celestial para toda la eternidad. (Parish and Weidman 230)
   (Let the Catholic Prince make sure—if he wants the Lord's help in winning victories—that he does not usurp for himself or for his judges either the authority and jurisdiction that belongs to the clergy or its dignity or spiritual power. For if he does, he will be thrown out of the temple, slain by the sword of exile, and wounded by the detestable illness of mortal sin thereby losing for all eternity the grace of God and ultimately the glory of heaven.)

10. "Lo que hay que consignar es la ausencia del erasmismo español, después de la muerte de Alfonso de Valdés, en los grandes debates sobre la guerra y la paz" (Bataillon 633) (After the death of Alonso de Valdes, what is striking is the absence of Spanish Erasmianism in the great debates about war and peace).

11. Luciano Pereña has argued that Vitoria's shifting positions on the use of force in the Americas and the treatment of native peoples were a direct result of his fear of appearing too "radical" and facing reprisals from those in power. See "Derechos civiles y políticos en el pensamiento de Bartolomé de las Casas" in *En el quinto centenario de Bartolomé de las Casas* (Madrid: Ediciones Cultura Hispánica: Instituto de Cooperación Iberoamericana, 1986), 109–124.

12. According to Las Casas scholars, those royal advisors who were critical of imperial overreach, especially the unwarranted use of military force, had left the court by the time Felipe II ascended to the throne in 1556. Political pressure from those who were making substantial economic gains in the colonies together with the financial hardships suffered by the monarchy were the deciding factors for policymakers. See Benjamin Keen, *Essays in the Intellectual History of Colonial Latin America* (Boulder, CO: Westview Press, 1998).

13. According to Las Casas, the use of force as a prelude to religious conversion was a tactic more compatible with the doctrinal teachings of Islam. As early as 1535 in a letter written to a member of Carlos V's court, he had called attention to what he considered to be Muslim practices: "No es este, señor, el camino de Cristo; no la manera de predicar su Evangelio; no el modo e costumbre de convertir las almas, sino propria la vía que tomó Mahoma, y aun peor que Mahoma, que decía haber venido in vi armorum; porque, a los que por armas sojuzgaba y su secta creían, daba la vida" (Las Casas, *Cartas* 1995, 97) (Sir, this is not the way of Christ, not the way to preach the

gospel, and not the traditional way of converting souls. Rather, it is the way of Mohammed and even worse than Mohammed who was said to come fully armed because he allowed those he subjugated by force to live and join his sect). At several points during the Valladolid debate he reiterated the same point: "Atraer a alguien a la fe con mortandades y terrores es propio de los mahometanos, pues Mahoma decía que había sido enviado en el terror de la espada y en la fuerza de las armas"(Apología 551) (To attract someone to the faith with massacres and terror is typical of Muslims, for Mohammed said he had been sent by the terror of the sword and the force of arms). Las Casas could not be more unambiguous—conquest, or exporting religion in the barrel of a gun, was what the enemy did and thus was unacceptable as part of any ideological project connected to Christian doctrine. On the relationship between Spanish and Islamic conversion practices, see Patricia Seed, *Ceremonies of Possession in Europe's Conquest of the New World, 1492–1640* (Cambridge: Cambridge University Press, 1995).
14. In a related parable in Matthew 22, Jesus tells the story of a king rebuffed by local dignitaries (who even murder some of the king's messengers) when he invites them to his son's wedding. After executing the guilty parties and destroying their cities, the king orders his staff to bring in anyone they can find to attend the wedding banquet. Church exegetes often collapsed this unusually violent parable with the banquet story from Luke 15. Both parables must have provided rhetorical ammunition for Sepúlveda during his debate with Las Casas.
15. At the conclusion of his "De exemptione sive damnatione," Las Casas refers the reader to the following gloss: "Así pues, los clérigos se pueden llamar 'soldados' . . . como los que abogan a favor de causas se dicen 'luchar'" ("Ergo clerici milites dicantur . . . similiter et patroni causarum dicantur militare") (quoted in Parish and Weidman 245, n. 256) (And so clergy may be called soldiers just as those who advocate for a cause are said to fight).
16. The most concise statement on the problem of blowback in the contemporary context is Chalmers Johnson, *Blowback: The Costs and Consequences of American Empire* (New York: Metropolitan Books, 2000).

Works Cited

Bataillon, Marcel. *Erasmo y España: Estudios sobre la historia espiritual del siglo XVI.* Mexico City: Fondo De Cultura Económica, 1950.
Clot, Andre. *Suleiman the Magnificent: The Man, His Life, His Epoch.* London: Saqi Books, 2004.
Erasmus, Desiderius. "De bello turcico" ("On the War against the Turks"). *The Erasmus Reader.* Ed. Erika Rummel. Toronto: University of Toronto Press, 1996.
Falwell, Jerry. http://www.truthorfiction.com/rumors/L/falwell-robertson-wtc.htm.

Garcés, María Antonia. *Cervantes in Algiers: A Captive's Tale*. Nashville: Vanderbilt University Press, 2002.

Hanke, Lewis. *All Mankind is One: A Study of the Disputation Between Bartolome de Las Casas and Juan Gines de Sepulveda in 1550 on the Intellectual and Religious Capacity of the American Indians*. Dekalb: Northern Illinois University Press, 1994.

Huntington, Samuel. *Who are We? The Challenges to America's National Identity*. New York: Simon and Schuster, 2004.

Johnson, Chalmers. *Blowback: The Costs and Consequences of American Empire*. New York: Metropolitan Books, 2000.

Keen, Benjamin. *Essays in the Intellectual History of Colonial Latin America*. Boulder: Westview Press, 1998.

Las Casas, Bartolomé de. *Apología*. Ed. Angel Losada. Vol. 13, *Obras completas*. Madrid: Alianza, 1988.

_____. *Cartas y Memoriales*. Ed. Paulino Castañeda, Carlos de Rueda, Carmen Godínez, and Inmaculada de La Corte. Vol. 13, *Obras completas*. Madrid: Alianza, 1995.

Losada, Angel, ed. and trans. *Tratados políticos de Juan Ginés de Sepúlveda*. Biblioteca española de escritores políticos. Madrid: Instituto de Estudios Políticos, 1963.

Parish, Helen-Rand, and Harold E. Weidman. *Las Casas en México: Historia y obra desconocidas*. Mexico City: Fondo de Cultura Económica, 1992.

Pereña, Luciano. "Derechos civiles y politicos en el pensamiento de Bartolomé de Las Casas." *En el Quinto Centenario de Bartolomé de Las Casas*. Madrid: Ediciones Cultura Hispánica. Instituto de Cooperación Iberoamericana, 1986. 109–124.

Seed, Patricia. *Ceremonies of Possession in Europe's Conquest of the New World, 1492–1640*. Cambridge: Cambridge University Press, 1995.

Sepúlveda, Juan Ginés de. "Demócrates Primero o de la compatibilidad entre la milicia y la religión cristiana." In Losada.

_____. "Exhortación al Emperador Carlos V para que hecha la paz con los príncipes cristianos haga la guerra contra los turcos."

_____. "Carta 53." *Epistolario de Juan Ginés de Sepúlveda*. Ed. Angel Losada. Madrid: Ediciones Cultural Hispánica, 1966.

Simerka, Barbara. *Discourses of Empire: Counter-Epic Literature in Early Modern Spain*. University Park, PA: Penn State University Press, 2003.

State of the Union Address. *Public Papers of the President of the United States* (2003).

◆ 14

Imperialism and Anthropophagy in Early Modern Spanish Tragedy: The Unthought Known

Margaret Greer

"Anthropophagy": the mere pronunciation of the word produces a shiver, together with a morbid fascination that captures the attention of an audience, something today's journalists and filmmakers know as well as did ancient chroniclers. To classify a people as anthropophagous is to mark them with the most radical sign of alterity and barbarity, as creatures alien to reason and civil society, closer to cannibalistic species of animals than to ethical human community. At the same time, their gastronomic violence is one of several practices that are (with apologies to Lévi-Strauss), "good to think with," useful to societies in contact with very different cultures, as they shape or reshape their own self-image for internal and external consumption, differentiating their own use of supposedly civilizing violence from that practiced by a "savage" enemy. While some anthropologists and ethnologists who study anthropophagy organize their work around the questions who eats whom, when, and why (Petrinovich 3–4), others judge that the important issue is not the practice of cannibalism, but analysis of the cultural use of its representation, which is the pathway I follow in this essay.[1] Rather than a deliberate and conscious thought process, I will argue that the figuration of anthropophagy in two early modern Spanish tragedies reveals its operation on cultural equivalent of the level of what Christopher Bollas calls an "unthought known": a type of primary yet intersubjective repression, a knowledge that a child develops somatically, ahead of conceptual capacity to express it verbally; hence, known, but unthought (3–4).

Tragedy, as Raymond Williams said, "attracts the fundamental beliefs and tensions of a period" (45), and in its tragic theory, the fundamental shape of a culture is realized. One of the primary tensions of early modern Spain was that of negotiating the incorporation of an enormous territory populated by peoples of very different cultures and assimilating it in the collective Imaginary as well as in its political, socioeconomic, and religious institutions. Among the authors of the relatively small number of tragedies in the vast corpus of early modern Spanish drama, the two who had a direct, lived experience of imperialism and the consequent clash of cultures were Miguel de Cervantes in his five years of captivity in Algeria and Tirso de Molina, sent to Santo Domingo from 1616 to 1618 to assist with evangelization and to teach theology. Both dramatize anthropophagy in tragedies that unsettle the civilization/barbarism binary.

Reports of the existence of anthropophagi are as old as narrative history itself and are, from those reports forward, regularly intertwined with the history of imperial expansion. Herodotus (fifth century B.C.) in the opening preface to *The Histories* wrote "so the human achievements may not become forgotten in time, and great and marvelous deeds—some displayed by Greeks, some by barbarians—may not be without their glory; and especially to show why the two peoples fought with each other" (3). As François Hartog argues, Herodotus constructs the Scythians as the principal model of alterity that served his audience as an inverted mirror of Greek society (13, 30–33). Scythians are for Herodotus distinguished from the Greeks by their youth as a nation, their nomadic life, their position at the outer limit of known global settlement (Hartog 241–42), and the ferocity that included occasional cannibalism, as revenge or bizarre funeral practices (33, 260). In war, reports Herodotus, "the Scythian custom is for every man to drink the blood of the first man he kills" (*Herodotus* 260). He first mentions the Scythians as nomadic invaders of Asia, an escapade that would provide the pretext for the Persian king Darius to invade their territory. When the Scythians are faced with the massive army Darius raised, as Herodotus narrates their search for defensive allies, he introduces us to the Androphagi, a yet more savage, doubly marginal people, the outer northern limit of an outer limit. Beyond the Androphagi, there is only true desert. "The Androphagi," says Herodotus, "are the most savage of men, and have no notion of either law or justice. They are herdsmen without fixed dwellings; their dress is Scythian, their language peculiar to themselves, and they are the only people in this part of the world to eat human flesh (*Herodotus* 275–76). Pliny follows

Herodotus's location and description of the Scythian Androphagi in his equally influential *Natural History*:

> Some Scythian tribes, and in fact a good many, feed on human bodies—a statement that perhaps may seem incredible if we do not reflect that races of this portentous character have existed in the central regions of the world . . . and that quite recently the tribes of the parts beyond the Alps habitually practiced human sacrifice, which is not far removed from eating human flesh. . . . The . . . cannibal tribes . . . to the north, ten days journey beyond the river Dnieper, drink out of human skulls and use the scalps with the hair on as napkins hung round their necks. (513, 515)

Aristotle in the *Nichomachean Ethics* included examples of cannibalism in his discussion of the distinction between wicked human behavior and bestiality:

> Bestial characters [are] like . . . certain savage tribes on the coasts of the Black Sea, who are alleged to delight in raw meat or in human flesh, and others among whom each in turn provides a child for the common banquet. . . . Other unnatural propensities are due to disease, and sometimes to insanity, as in the case of the madman that offered up his mother to the gods and partook of the sacrifice. (401, 403)

Bestiality and vice caused by morbidity are more horrible, according to Aristotle, but less evil, because they are not due to the corruption of man's highest faculty, his intellect, rather than to its lack in bestial characters (411).

Aestheticized representations of anthropophagy, particularly those of Ovid and Seneca that were again widely circulated in the Renaissance, also figured as significant contributors to the Imaginary order of early modern Europe. Ovid's most influential story of anthropophagy was that of Tereus, the king of Thrace who fed his horses with human flesh, and his wife Procne, who cooked and served him their children after learning of his rape of her sister Philomela (Baraz 156).[2] Seneca's violent tragedies were an important model for early modern tragedy in Spain and in Italy, and his *Thyestes* ends with a similar scene of children served to their father.[3]

Together with ancient descriptions of the barbaric Other, these classical images of anthropophagy played a continuing role in European narratives of cruelty. According to Daniel Baraz, the perception of cruelty in the late middle ages and early modern period shifted from attacks on clergy and church property to accounts of sexual violence and cannibalism. European reports of the destruction wreaked by Mongol invasions of medieval Europe repeatedly wrote of cannibalism as well as rape and wholesale massacres; Muslim sources, in contrast, without the Latin tradition, did not mention cannibalism in their more matter-of-fact accounts of Mongol destruction (95–121). The Renaissance scholar Sebastian Münster, on the other hand, used the same drawing in his *Cosmographia* (1544) to represent the habitat of the Mongols and the Scythians, thus linking these two barbaric "Others" visually, adding as well a drawing of a Mongol roasting a headless man on a spit and describing at length their cannibalism and the pleasure such cruelty afforded them (Baraz 150–52).

Albeit without charges of cannibalism, the issue of purported Muslim cruelty played a role in the recruitment and conduct of the Crusades, figuring as an incentive in some Crusade propaganda (*Baraz* 76). But it was Christians, not Muslims, who resorted to cannibalism on one and possibly two occasions during the first Crusade. On sacking the city of Ma'arra an-Naman, in northern Syria in 1098, after a long siege, the famished Christian forces cooked and ate the bodies of the Muslims and Jews they had killed on taking the city. The episode was related with various degrees of horror in three chronicles written shortly after the event. Apparently there was another episode of cannibalism by Christian soldiers earlier, during the siege of Antioquia, but the published sources are more reticent in labeling it (Heng 21–24).

Given this insistently intertwined portrayal of the invading or invaded other as anthropophagous, it is not surprising that this practice should have been attributed, accurately or fancifully, to various indigenous peoples of America, beginning with the first letters of Columbus. From his "Carta a los Reyes" of March 4, 1493, he speaks of an island called "Caribo": "[donde] están aquellos pueblos, de que están todos los restantes de las otras islas de Yndia[s] temerosos; éstos comen carne humana, son grandes frecheros, tienen muchas canoas, ... con las cuales corren todas las islas de Yndia[s], y son tan temidos que no han par ni evento" (Zamora 188, 196) (Here are found those people which all of the other islands of the Indies fear; they eat human flesh, are great bowman, have many canoes, ... in which they travel all over the islands of the Indies, and they are so feared that they have no equal). He extends his report on anthropophagous Indians in the *Diario del Primer Viaje,* transmitted in the copy made by Bartolomé de las Casas.[4] In the ensuing debate over the legality of the Spanish conquest in the Americas and of forced conversion to Christianity, Francisco de Vitoria, in his 1534–35 lecture *On the Evangelization of Unbelievers,* cited cannibalism as the only legitimizing factor:

> There are some sins against nature which are harmful to our neighbours, such as cannibalism or euthanasia of the old and senile, which is practiced in Terra Firma,

and since the defence of our neighbours is the rightful concern of each of us, even for private persons and even if it involves shedding blood, it is beyond doubt that any Christian prince can compel them not to do these things. By this title alone the emperor is empowered to coerce the Caribbean Indians. (347)

Covarrubias, defining "antropófago" at the beginning of the seventeenth century, as "el que come carne humana" (he who eats human flesh) recognizes the Greek origin of the word, but situates its use above all in the New World: "Notoria cosa es que los indios, antes de ser conquistados por los españoles, comían carne humana, y la nuestra les sabía mejor que otra, como cuentan las historias de las Indias; éstos lo hacían por vicio, pero algunos lo han hecho por necesidad de hambre, y aun comiéndose sus propios hijos; cosa de gran horror" (125) (It is well known that the Indians, before being conquered by Spaniards, ate human flesh, and ours tasted better to them than others, as the histories of the Indies relate; these people do it as a bad habit, but some have done it because of hunger, even eating their own children, a great horror). The next century, the succinct definition given in the *Diccionario de Autoridades* points to the American Other now considered a cannibal by antonomasia: "El Caribe que come carne humana" (307) (the Carib who eats human flesh).

Cervantes, however, does not evoke the specter of anthropophagy in an American context contemporaneous with him but rather in the legendary historical struggle in which it is peoples of the Iberian peninsula who confront Roman imperial ambitions. In the tragedy *La destrucción de Numancia* (ca. 1581–87), he dramatizes the heroic resistance of Celiberian Numantia against imperial Roman troops commanded by Scipio Aemilianus in 133 B.C.

The Roman conquest of Iberia began in 218 B.C., and by 133, the Romans had conquered most of the peninsula. Nevertheless, they had failed to take Numantia numerous times, even with an army led by ten elephants around 153 B.C., and with 20,000 troops assigned to the conquest in 137. Scipio finally succeeded in conquering the city, not with a direct attack, but by means of an eight-month siege, starving the population to death. Descriptions of the siege by historians of the day Polybius and Livy did not survive, but the history of the campaign written by Appian of Alexandria in the second century AC is based on Polybius, who was with Scipio during the siege. According to Appian, before their ultimate surrender, the Numantines had resorted to cannibalism, first consuming their dead, then the sick, and finally the weakest members of their community. This is the type of anthropophagy that anthropologists today classify as "survival cannibalism," and as endo-anthropophagy, the consumption of members of one's own group (Petrinovich 6). Appian said that many of the Numantines elected to commit suicide before surrendering, that Scipio took fifty Numantines to display in his triumph in Rome, sold the rest as slaves, destroyed the Town and distributed its territory among neighboring tribes. An alternate history also emerged in the second century according to which not a single inhabitant survived the siege, and Scipio was therefore denied a triumphal celebration and reward for his victory. Numantia came to symbolize the independence of Iberian spirit, and many of the ingredients Cervantes employs in his tragedy circulated in ballads. For the humanist Ambrosio de Morales, whose *Corónica general de España* appears to have been Cervantes' principal source, the defense of Numantia was "una de las cosas más señaladas que en España, y aun en mucha parte del universo han sucedido" (f. 122) (one of the most exceptional things that has taken place in Spain, or even in the greater part of the universe).

Cervantes dramatized the conflict in four acts with an episodic structure that alternates between the Roman forces and the besieged Numantines, beginning with Scipio's disciplinary harangue to the Roman troops for devoting themselves not to war but to the pleasures of Bacchus and Venus. Scipio concludes his exhortation to defeat these "rebellious, barbarous Spaniards" with the prophetic assertion that: "Cada cual se fabrica su destino. / No tiene allí fortuna alguna parte. / La pereza fortuna baja cría; / la diligencia, imperio y monarquía" (63–64) (Everyone makes his own destiny. / Fortune plays no part in it. / Laziness breeds ill fortune; / diligence, empire and monarchy). He curtly dismisses a Numantine request for a peace accord, as he would later scorn their proposal to decide the conflict by single combat between the best Roman and Numantine fighter, calling them caged beasts whom he will tame without losing a single Roman soldier. The Numantine women dissuade their desperate men from a suicidal plan to break through the Roman fortifications and die fighting, leaving their wives and children prey to Roman rape and slavery. Vowing to leave nothing from which the Romans might profit, the Numantines then elect to burn all their goods and to die at each other's hands.

Before this collective suicide is carried out, however, Cervantes performs a double sublimation of the memory of Numantine cannibalism. First, he converts the historic endo-anthropophagy into an exo-anthropopaghy. Teógenes, the town's leading citizen, presents it as a weapon of battle turned against the enemy and carried out as a humanitarian act that nourishes the community in an egalitarian fashion:

> Para entretener por algún hora / la hambre que ya roe nuestros güesos, / haréis descuartizar luego a la hora / esos tristes romanos que están presos, y sin del chico

al grande hacer mejora, / repártase entre todos, que con esos / será nuestra comida celebrada / por España, cruel, necesitada. (116)

(To stave off for a time / the hunger that now gnaws our bones, / quarter right away / those dismal Romans who are our prisoners, and let them be distributed among all, / without distinction between the small and the great, / for with them will our repast be celebrated / by cruel, needy Spain.)

Secondly, Cervantes turns it into a lover's sacrifice that prefigures the celebration of that of Christ in the Catholic mass (an association with the symbolic cannibalism of the mass itself already suggested by Teógenes reference to "celebrating a repast," as Barbara Simerka points out) (123).[5] The young Marandro vows he will die before allowing his fiancée Lira to die of hunger, jumps the Roman walls to steal their bread, and returns with a basketful drenched with his own blood to die in Lira's arms. At the same time, Marandro and his friend Leoncio earn Roman acclaim for their valor and put the lie to Scipio's vow not to shed a drop of Roman blood, as they kill six guards to get the bread.

The transformation of the memory of a society reduced to the extreme of cannibalism to one characterized by heroic sacrifice for the good of the community is further underlined in the final scene. One young man, here named Bariato after the most famous individual hero of the Celtiberian resistance, hides in a tower as the Numantines turn their swords on one another, but when the Romans discover the carnage and destruction within the suddenly quiet city, rejecting Scipio's offer of pardon and riches, he jumps to his death to deny Scipio his triumph over the Numantia he loves.

In this sublimation and other aspects of *Numantia*, I read a striking validation of Timothy Reiss's concept of tragedy in *Tragedy and Truth* as the discourse that in periods of profound political and social change serves to grasp the inexpressible, to fill in the absence of meaningfulness in the transition from one dominant discourse to another, to enclose that hole of unmeaning in an ordered discourse that creates a new signified and contributes to the consolidation of a new episteme (2–38, 283–84). "Tragedy," says Reiss, "is the discourse that at once produces and absorbs that absence called the tragic" (3); it affords the spectator the knowing position that the tragic characters cannot possess, and "at once the fear of a lack of all order and the pleasure in seeing such a lack overcome" (27). Surely if there is a prospect of disorder, an unthought known that excites that fear, it is the image of cannibalism, here twice sublimated and redeemed by heroic sacrifice.

Geraldine Heng analyzes an analogous instance of narrative sublimation in medieval England of the painful memory of the cannibalism that took place during the first Crusade. Two decades later, between 1130–39, Geoffrey de Monmouth wrote the first formulation of the legend of King Arthur of England in the *Historia Regum Britanniae*, a chronicle full of novelesque episodes. The crusaders' cannibalism is transformed into a fable of King Arthur's battles with two anthropophagous giants, two monstrous invaders of Europe. The tale says explicitly that one of them is from Hispania; an Hispanic origin is implied for the other giant as well. Hispania, according to Heng, constituted a kind of double inscription of Islam, matching Muslim Spain with Syria to distance the memory of cannibalism from England and from Christian forces. In subsequent medieval Arthurian chronicles, cannibalism is converted into an explicit metaphor for imperial conquest and colonization (Heng 68). Heng argues that these Arthurian chronicles, in their combination of history and fantasy, served three functions: 1) dealing with medieval Europe's first transnational imperial project and the anxiety regarding identity that it produced; 2) giving shape to a concept of the English nation; and 3) establishing "the emerging grammars of racial classification and hierarchy that appear in the process of national formation" (5).

The Sixteenth and Seventeenth centuries were for Spain a period of profound political and socioeconomic change, from a semi-feudal society periodically fighting to complete the reconquest of the peninsula from Arab control to an imperial power enmeshed in multiple wars to maintain its extended dominions. The theme of imperialism was very much present when Cervantes wrote *Numantia* in the 1580s. After a decade dedicated to defeating rebellions—in the Low Countries and that of the *moriscos* in the Alpujarras—and combating Turkish aggression in the Mediterranean, Philip II chose to renew the policy of active imperialism initiated by Charles V. In 1579–80, he incorporated Portugal to the Spanish monarchy when the throne was left vacant by the death of the young Portuguese king Sebastian in a disastrous campaign against Islamic forces in Africa. This action drew substantial criticism even within Spain.

Alfredo Hermenegildo (Cervantes 11) argues that Cervantes meant to associate Spain *both* with the besieging Roman forces and with their victims, akin in his day to the *moriscos*, the Dutch rebels, the Portuguese, and the indigenous civilizations of America. Willard King connects his drama with Alonso de Ercilla's epic, *La Araucana*, and asserts the following:

> Two epochs of Spain, it may be said, fight against each other in *Numancia*—a primitive, idealized Spain waging a just war in defense of liberty against Cervantes' contemporary imperial Spain (disguised behind the figures of Scipio and the Roman army), fighting less easily justifiable wars of aggression in the New World

and of repression in Flanders, and failing to remember the necessity for combining strength and moral rectitude . . . with clemency and tolerance in dealing with colonies and subjugated peoples. (216)

Cervantes put on stage a number of allegorical figures (Spain, the Duero River, War, Sickness, Hunger, and Fame) to make sense for his audience of this tragic history and the moral ambiguity the action posed for imperial Spain. The figure Spain laments her continual history of invasions, from the Phoenicians and Greeks to the menacing Romans. The Duero then foresees the Roman Empire crumbling under the invading Goths and Huns, the 1527 invasion of Rome by the troops of Charles V, papal baptism of Spain's monarchs as "Catholic Kings . . . insignia of Gothic union," and the "blessed" imperial rule of Philip II who will unite all Spain's realms, including the "Portuguese strip" and bring a thousand foreign nations under her flag and sword (Cervantes 77–78). Nowhere in the play do these allegorical prophets allude to the Arab conquest, however, or the seven centuries of Arab rule in Iberia, equal in duration to the Roman presence. This is despite the fact that Cervantes himself had just returned from five years of captivity in Algiers and drew on that experience for other works he wrote in the same period. Rather, in the sense-making discourse of this tragedy, the Arab invasion is repressed and in Spain's lament, its proximate cause— division among the Visigoths and the resentment of their rule by the more urban Roman Hispanic and Jewish peoples of the Peninsula—is transferred back in time to the Celtiberians.[6] Anthropologists say that one of the purposes of ritual cannibalism of the enemy is that of incorporating the physical and spiritual force of the enemy through ingestion of their flesh; if consuming the prisoners effected the incorporation of Roman strengths to the Celtiberians, the Duero's speech works the symbolic merger of the Goths with the ancestral Iberian peoples in the dramatic prophecy of *translatio imperii* from Rome to Spain.

The tragic ambiguity of a Spain both imperial victim and victimizer is thus both performed and contained within the work. Debates over the identity of the tragic hero of the work underline that ambiguity. Critics who look for the presence of an Aristotelian *hamartia* and *anagnorisis* consider Scipio the tragic hero; as he surveys the ashes and blood that are all that remains of Numantia, he acknowledges his arrogance and lack of pity, asking himself: "Estaba, por ventura, el pecho mío / de bárbara arrogancia y muertes lleno / y de piedad justísima vacío"? (Cevantes 152) (Was my breast perchance full of barbarous arrogance and death, / and barren of most just pity?) He accords the glory of victory to Bariato: "lleva la ganancia / y la gloria que el cielo te prepara / por haber, derribándote, vencido / al que, subiendo, queda más caído" (157) (take the profit / and glory that heaven prepares for you / who, throwing yourself down, / has triumphed over he who, through rising, has fallen). Other readers argue for considering the population of Numantia a collective tragic hero, synecdochically present in the body of Bariato, carried off at the end of the play to the acclaim of white-robed Fame. Most contemporary critics conclude that the ultimate ambiguity is deliberate,[7] a conclusion strongly supported by David Lupher's study of ambivalence in sixteenth-century Spain toward the Romans as both positive and negative imperial models. Alongside the identification with Roman emperors and pride in the yet greater feat of Spanish conquerors, Lupher demonstrates a widespread "anti-Romanism," identification with the Celtiberians as the original Spaniards, viewed as suffering at Roman hands an unjustified conquest and enslavement parallel to that of the Indians by contemporary Spain.[8] In Lupher's view, Cervantes play and Ambrosio de Morales' historical account were the two works central to crafting a tale of two parallel conquests, the Spanish in America and the Roman in Iberia, which was "both product and producer of a strong sense of *hispanidad*, a consciousness of long-term ethnic unity and continuity in the Iberian Peninsula" (189); as in the Arthurian chronicles, they shaped a proto-national identity while dealing with the ethical issues raised by imperial conquests.

One of the defects that purist critics of tragedy have located in *Numantia* is that it is in some senses more epic theater than tragedy, a critique that also applies to a later tragedy dealing with imperial conquest: *Las Amazonas*, one part of Tirso de Molina's trilogy on the history of the Pizarros in Spain and Peru. *Las Amazonas* is a highly partial meaning-making discourse; with the other two parts of the trilogy, it constitutes an apology for the four Pizarros—Francisco, Gonzalo, Hernando, and Juan—and their part in the civil wars in Peru. Tirso wrote the plays between 1626 and 1631, during and shortly after his residence in Trujillo, the home of the Pizarros, as *Comendador* of the Mercedarian convent there, a convent founded in 1594 by the mestiza Francisca Pizarro, daughter of Francisco and an Inca princess and widow of Hernando (Rostworoski). Tirso also includes her as a character in *Las Amazonas*. He was probably commissioned to write the plays by Francisca and Hernando's grandson, Juan Fernando Pizarro, who was seeking restitution of the title of Marquis with 20,000 vassals that Charles V granted to Francisco, but which the family lost as a result of Gonzalo's rebellion against the viceroy Blasco Nuñez Vela, sent out to enforce the 1642 New Laws that had been dictated by Charles V in response to Bartolomé de Las Casas's campaign in favor of the natives—abolishing slavery, and forced labor of Indians in mines, and eliminating the hereditary nature of encomiendas (Zugasti 13–14).

How to redeem Gonzalo for his action in Peru? Tirso does so by painting the rival Almagros, father and son, and the viceroy Nuñez Vela in the worst possible light—including the kidnapping of Francisca Pizarro—and shows Gonzalo choosing to accept execution by the soldiers who demand he declare himself king rather than to rebel against Charles V. Furthermore, both at the beginning and the ending of *Las Amazonas*, he shares the spotlight. Virtually all *comedias*, comic, tragicomic, or tragic, include a love interest to forge a sympathetic bond with the protagonists. Lope de Vega invented "indigenous" women in his American *comedias*, including amorous trysts between two of Columbus's men and indigenous women in *El nuevo mundo descubierto por Cristóbal Colón*. Tirso, with an American experience Lope did not possess (albeit with no more contact with indigenous Americans),[9] takes a different tack.

Tirso creates two love interests for Gonzalo, one with a substantial basis in historical records, the other in the myth of the Amazons that, like the image of anthropophagy, was a regular player in the European imperial Imaginary from Herodotus, Homer, and Virgil to the Spanish *conquistadores*. In the early years in Peru, with no European women present, Tirso opens and closes his tragedy with the nearest equivalent, a beautiful Amazon queen, familiar in European myth yet exotic, who shortly abandons her man-hating custom to fall in love with Gonzalo and invite him to stay and rule with her. Tirso opens the drama with a battle between hatchet-armed "Amazons" and Spanish soldiers. Gonzalo and his field marshal, Francisco de Carvajal, meet Menalipe and her sister Martesia on a voyage into the interior of Peru in search of cinnamon trees, a harrowing trip down the Marañon river that he in fact did make. He later shows him proposing marriage to his niece Francisca, granddaughter of the Inca emperor Huayna Cápac and daughter of his sister the princess Inés Huayllas Yupanqui (Rostworoski 84–88), a royal genealogy that she rehearses in accepting his proposal. Publicly emphasizing intermarriage with Inca royalty was in fact a practice used in establishing prestige in colonial Peru.[10] Thus, Tirso shows us Gonzalo "conquering" a doubled image of America as a compliant woman of highest rank, both an Inca princess and an Amazonian queen.

Strikingly, however, Tirso adds to the mythic plot the idea that the Amazon tradition is also anthropophagic. Menalipe asks herself, "Pues si . . . a los hombres nos comemos, / ¿cómo los querremos bien? / Carne humana es el manjar / que alimenta nuestra vida" (Molina 27) (If . . . we eat men, / how can we love them? / Human flesh is the food / that nourishes our life). This "fact" is reiterated in each of the two following acts; in the third, his comic servant reports having narrowly escaped the fate of being made into meatballs. Nevertheless, Menalipe repeatedly tries to protect Gonzalo against the betrayal and death she foresees awaiting him among his kind, returns to see him despite his "betrayal" with Francisca, wants to commit suicide after seeing him executed, and is swallowed up by a mountain as she returns to her own kingdom, vowing not to accept another man from a society so treacherous to its own heroes.

From Columbus's first letters on, as we have seen, reports circulated of cannibalistic peoples in America, in the next island over, among the most feared enemies, or in the primitive society conquered by the Incas. Tirso would certainly have heard of them, during his residence in Santo Domingo if not before, because the pre-Columbian Tainos had regularly been subject to raids by the Caribs on the eastern end of Hispaniola (Maya Pons 2–3). He would also have read such reports in the sources he used for his Pizarro trilogy, Agustín de Zárate's *Historia del descubrimiento y conquista del Perú* (1555) (History of the Discovery and Conquest of Peru), the Inca Garcilaso's *Historia general del Perú* (General History of Peru), and Fernando del Pizarro y Orellana's *Varones ilustres del Nuevo Mundo: Descubridores, conquistadores y pacificadores del opulento, dilatado y poderoso imperio de las Indias Occidentales* (1639) (Illustrious Men of the New World: Discoveries, Conquerers, and Pacifiers of the opulent, vast, and powerful empire of the West Indies). References to warrior women also abounded. Columbus in his *Carta a los Reyes* situated them on the island of Matenino, today Martinique. He also associates the Amazons with the Caribs, as Herodotus had linked them with the Scythians, and in his *Diario*, lamented not being able to take some back to his sovereigns. One of the instructions that the governor of Cuba, Diego Velázquez, gave to Cortés on sending him on an expedition to Yucatan in 1518 was that of finding the Amazons whom the Indians said were in that area (Lupher 9). Closer to Tirso's art was Lope de Vega's 1621 comedy, *Las mujeres sin hombres*, from which he probably drew the name Menalipe, as well as other elements of the legend. But prior to Tirso's *Las Amazonas*, anthropophagy had not been attributed to Amazonian women, in European myth, or in chronicles of New World discovery. Tirso transforms the primitive anthropophagous enemy into two beautiful women who leave off hating men when they encounter the Spanish leaders; nevertheless, she cannot save them from the threat of their European compatriots.

In part, this attribution of cannibalistic mores to the Amazonian beauties may have served Tirso, as it did Cervantes, as a fictional sublimation of an historical record he could not totally erase. Pizarro y Orellana's account of the expedition Gonzalo and Carvajal led down the Marañon in search of cinnamon twice mentions their desperate recourse to survival cannibalism after Francisco de Orellana, a companion whom they had trusted with the boat they had fabricated, left for Spain without waiting for them at the agreed meeting place, in order to claim their rich discoveries for himself. The first time, the phrasing leads one to presume that it was the nameless Indians who accompanied them who partook: "y murieron de hambre mas de dos mil Indios de los que avian quedado, aviendose comido sus cavallos, y muchos a sus compañeros muertos" (Pizarro y Orellana 353) (and more than two thousand of the Indians whom they had left died, having eaten their horses, and many of them their dead companions as well). The report that Gonzalo delivers to interim governor, Cristobal Vaca de Castro, however, suggests that the Spaniards participated as well: "los [trabajos] que mas le hizieron salir de su entereza y natural al buen Vaca de Castro, fueron los que en la jornada de la Canela avia padecido Gonzalo Pizarro, y sus compañeros; particularmente quando oyó que se sustentavan de carne humana" (354) (the sufferings that most made the good Vaca y Castro lose his natural serenity were those that Gonzalo Pizarro and his companions had undergone on the search for cinnamon, particularly when he heard that they had sustained themselves on human flesh). Rather than confronting head-on the unthought known of the recourse to survival cannibalism by members of his own society, Tirso, like Geoffrey of Monmouth in the King Arthur legend, projects the practice on a mythical other.

At the same time, Tirso's addition of the image of cannibalism to this work suggests metonymically that imperialism is the consumption of one society by another, and in the case of the civil wars in Peru, a political cannibalism between rival factions of the conquering Spaniards. The threatening anthropophagous beauties who opened the play close it as well, vowing to defend their natural riches against other greedy adventurers from a nation so ungrateful to its heroes. Tirso's own experience of political factionalism in the courts of Philip III and Philip IV, which had led to his exile in 1625 and the order that he cease writing plays, gave him a visceral comprehension of the effects of such infighting. His earlier experience in a Santo Domingo radically depopulated and impoverished due to the wrong-headed policies applied by officials dispatched from Madrid (see note 9) had provided him with a dark view of Spanish imperialism in operation in the New World.

Peter Hulme in *Cannibalism and the Colonial World* argues that study of anthropophagy today should change its directions and direct its gaze:

> from elsewhere to here, from the sense that cannibalism is practiced over the seas and beyond the hills to the inkling that we need to look within to understand why

the cannibal scene means so much to us. . . . to the self-reflective analysis of imperialism as itself a form of cannibalism. (5)

What Reiss calls "the sense-making discourse" of tragedy, its capacity to give meaning to the inexpressible, is in Tirso's case very partial, an apology for the Pizarros. But it is also the ultimate truth in its association of imperialism and anthropophagy—at least as a metaphor for the slaughter and consumption of one society for another. It is significant that Tirso has Gonzalo meet Menalipe in his search for cinnamon, a spice of great value on the European market, as his *gracioso* says. There is, we know today, an intimate relationship between imperialism and the primitive accumulation that financed the development of European capitalism, a second type of metaphorical cannibalism of the wealth of other peoples. Tirso does not, in fact, demonstrate empathy with the conquered indigenous population in *Las Amazonas*. Aside from the noble *mestiza* Francisca Pizarro and the Amazonas, Indians in his play are nameless and faceless. Rather, in Carvajal's long account of the voyage down the Marañón, Tirso makes the explorers victims of the rigors of terrain and climate, ferocious animals, vicious insects, and warrior women. And in the end, victims of the treachery are their own men, hungry not for human flesh but for power and wealth to be wrung from the conquered land. Whereas Cervantes' *Numantia* performed the tragic ambiguity of a Spain both imperial victim and victimizer, the unthought known figured in Tirso's play is that of an imperial Spain that devours their own along with its nameless indigenous victims in Peru.

Notes

1. See Francis Barker, Peter Hulme, and Margaret Iverson, *Cannibalism and the Colonial World* (Cambridge: Cambridge University Press, 1998).
2. In Francisco de Rojas Zorrilla's version of the Procne story, the sisters murder Terens rather than serving him his children; that banquet is replaced by some awkward comedy with two *graciosos*, one with an insatiable appetite for sweets, the other for money.
3. The Senecan model in general and *Thyestes* in particular are important to understanding the unconscious logic of Cueva's portrayal of the internecine self-destruction of family rivalries and the treatment of *moriscos* and *conversos* in sixteenth-century Spain. See Margaret R. Greer, "Woman and the Tragic Family of Man in Juan De La Cueva's *Los Siete Infantes De Lara*," *Hispania* 82 (1999).
4. See Christopher Columbus, *Textos Y Documentos Completos: Relaciones De Viajes, Cartas Y Memoriales*, ed. Consuelo Varela, 2nd ed. (Madrid: Alianza, 1984), 115–16.

5. See also De Armas, 47, 83, and Whitby. Along with Numantine necromancy and suicide, Simerka argues that it balanced the civilizing elements of Cervantes's portrayal of the Numantines with a barbarism and savagery that would have been repellant to his audience.
6. In fact, the fragmentation of Iberia into tribal societies that had to be conquered one by one was a perverse source of strength against the Roman campaign, slowing its advance.
7. See De Armas, Lupher, and Simerka. De Armas's central interest in the play is what he sees as Cervantes' conscious and explicit imitation therein of a wide variety of classical authors to create a foundation myth for imperial Spain enriched by resonances and critiques of those authors and their handling of the issue of power, its uses and abuses. Simerka argues that the juxtaposition of multiple genres and contradictory ideologies within this and other early modern Spanish history plays helped formulate and communicate potential opposition to imperial policies.
8. Lupher documents these views in a wide range of writers, including Gonzalo Fernández de Oviedo, Carlos V's Franciscan chaplain, Antonio de Guevara, Melchor Cano, and Bartolomé de Las Casas, who linked Numantine to Cuban cannibalism.
9. The Tainos of Hispaniola had been exterminated long before Tirso arrived in 1616. Brutal treatment, forced labor, and epidemics had reduced the perhaps 400,000 residents at the time of Columbus's arrival to 60,000 by 1508 and a mere 3,000 by 1519. Black slaves were imported to replace their labor beginning in 1518. The period of Tirso's residence in Santo Domingo was one of poverty and hunger due to a disastrous policy of forced resettlement to the southeast of the island of people and cattle from the North and West, who had been carrying on a lively contraband trade in cattle hides and other goods with Dutch, French, and English ships, which were also bringing in religious and political ideas seen to pose a threat to Spanish authority. See Frank Maya Pons, *Manual De Historia Dominicana*, 7th ed. (Santiago, República Dominicana: Universidad Católica Madre y Maestra, 1983), 26–29. 51–65.
10. See Timberlake, 584–85.

Works Cited

Aristotle. *The Nicomachean Ethics*. Vol. 19, *Aristotle in Twenty-Three Volumes. The Loeb Classical Library*. Cambridge, MA: Harvard University Press, 1968.

Baraz, Daniel. *Medieval Cruelty: Changing Perceptions, Late Antiquity to the Early Modern Period*. Ithaca, NY: Cornell University Press, 2003.

Barker, Francis, Peter Hulme, and Margaret Iverson. *Cannibalism and the Colonial World*. Cambridge: Cambridge University Press, 1998.

Bollas, Christopher. *The Shadow of the Object: Psychoanalysis of the Unthought Known*. New York: Columbia University Press, 1987.

Cervantes Saavedra, Miguel de. *La Destrucción de Numancia*. Ed. Alfredo Hermenegildo. Madrid: Clásicos Castalia, 1994.

Columbus, Christopher. *Textos Y Documentos Completos: Relaciones De Viajes, Cartas Y Memoriales*. Ed.Consuelo Varela. 2nd ed. Madrid: Alianza, 1984.

Covarrubias, Sebastian de. *Tesoro de la lengua castellana o española*. Madrid: Ediciones Turner, 1976.

De Armas, Frederick A. *Cervantes, Raphael and the Classics*. Cambridge: Cambridge University Press, 1998.

Greer, Margaret R. "Woman and the Tragic Family of Man in Juan De La Cueva's *Los Siete Infantes De Lara*." *Hispania* 82 (1999): 472–80.

Hartog, François. *The Mirror of Herodotus: The Representation of the Other in the Writing of History*. Trans. Janet Lloyd. Berkeley: University of California Press, 1988.

Heng, Geraldine. *Empire of Magic: Medieval Romance and the Politics of Cultural Fantasy*. New York: Columbia University Press, 2003.

Herodotus. *The Histories*. Trans.Audrey de Sélincourt and John Marincola. New York: Penguin Books, 2003.

Hulme, Peter. "Introduction: The Cannibal Scene." *Cannibalism and the Colonial World*. Ed. Francis et al Barker. Cambridge: Cambridge University Press, 1998. 1–38.

King, Willard F. "Cervantes, *Numancia* and Imperial Spain." *Modern Language Notes* 94 (1979): 200–21.

Lupher, David A. *Romans in a New World: Classical Models in Sixteenth-Century Spanish America*. Ann Arbor, MI: University of Michigan Press, 2003.

Maya Pons, Frank. *Manual De Historia Dominicana*. 7th ed. Santiago, República Dominicana: Universidad Católica Madre y Maestra, 1983.

Molina, Tirso de. *Amazonas En Las Indias*. Ed. Miguel Zugasti. Vol. 3, *Trilogia De Los Pizarros*. Kassel: Edition Reichenberger, 1993.

Morales, Ambrosio de, and Florián de Ocampo. *Corónica General de España*. Vol. 3. Alcalá de Henares: Iuan Yñiguez de Lequerica, 1578.

Petrinovich, Lewis F. *The Cannibal Within*. New York: Aldine de Gruyter, 2000.

Pizarro y Orellana, Fernando. *Varones ilustres del Nuevo Mundo*. Madrid: Diego Díaz de la Carrera, 1639.

Pliny. *Natural History*. Trans. H. Rackham. Vol. 2, *The Loeb Classical Library*. Cambridge, MA: Harvard University Press, 1961.

Real Academia Española. *Diccionario de autoridades*. 3 vols. Madrid: Gredos, 1979.

Reiss, Timothy J. *Tragedy and Truth: Studies in the Development of a Renaissance and Neoclassical Discourse*. New Haven, CT: Yale University Press, 1980.

Rostworoski, María. *Doña Francisca Pizarro, Una Ilustre Mestiza 1535–1598*. 3rd ed. Lima: Instituto de Estudios Peruanos, 2003.

Simerka, Barbara. *Discourses of Empire: Counter-Epic Literature in Early Modern Spain*. University Park, PA: The Pennsylvania State University Press, 2003.

Timberlake, Marie. "The Painted Colonial Image: Jesuit and Andean Fabrication of His-

tory in *Matrimonio De García De Loyola Con Ñusta Beatriz*." *Journal of Medieval and Early Modern Studies* 29, no. 3 (1999): 563–98.
Vitoria, Francisco de. *Political Writings*. Ed. Anthony Pagden and Jeremy Lawrance. Cambridge: Cambridge University Press, 1991.
Whitby, W. "The Sacrifice Theme in Cervantes *Numancia*." *Hispania* 45 (1962): 205–10.
Williams, Raymond. *Modern Tragedy*. Stanford, CA: Stanford University Press, 1966.
Zamora, Margarita. *Reading Columbus*. Berkeley: University of California Press, 1993.
Zugasti, Miguel. *Trilogía De Los Pizarros: Estudio Crítico*. Vol. 1. Kassel: Edition Reichenberger, 1993.

15

Reason and Utopia at the Imperial Borders: Modernity/Coloniality in the Jesuits' Reducciones in Paraguay

Fernando Ordóñez

The study of cultural phenomena from a geographical perspective requires an analysis of the complex interdependencies that have always existed, in one form or another, between different contexts and social groups. Given the hegemonic role that different European societies, and Europe as a whole, have had in the creation of a world system, European studies require the study of the relationships established in a particular historical moment between Europeans and the "others." In this sense, Enrique Dussel suggests that Europe invents itself in relationship to America, while I propose that Europe also sees itself in the diverse experiences of colonial expansion. Consequently, modernity and coloniality implicate each other; one cannot be studied without considering the other.

These assertions are more important when we refer to situations experienced during the baroque period, a time when a series of factors coincide to determine what we now call modernity/coloniality. The following situations developed concurrently: the consolidation of the colonial system in America and other African and Asian enclaves; the implementation of the Counter-Reformation as action and reaction on the part of the Catholic Church to the Protestant Reform movement; and the transition to the mercantilist system as economic paradigm.

In the same vein, another level of this discussion is philosophical and gnoseological, given that it is during this period that new systems to understand reality are developed; that analytical criteria become secularized, and thinkers look for a way to control—instrumentalize—nature by attempting to measure and predict.

For these reasons, I propose to show in this essay that in the baroque context, characterized by a cultural tension between freedom and containment, European utopian reason—which unfolded during the Renaissance—migrated to the margins of the Spanish Empire, where control imposed by the monarchical-seignorial system was challenged by other powers at the Empire's edge. In these cultural processes, new and complex actors are perfecting their performance, in order to optimize the freedoms offered by the context in which they live, while containing the restrictions that reined throughout the Empire. Of these new actors, I will focus on the Company of Jesus, given the influence the Jesuits have during this period in Europe as well as in the rest of the world. Hence, the main source that I have analyzed is the writings of Antonio Ruiz de Montoya. His texts serve as an example of the utopian thinking found in the borderlands of the empire, and, as I see it, describe attempts to create an "other" modernity, one that is still Catholic, but which, seen from a historical perspective, may be designated as a "failed modernity."

I intend to reinterpret Father Montoya's proposal from a postcolonial perspective and present a discussion of the Jesuits' missionary models, which I understand as attempts to create an alternate imperial administration—one that, in addition to be more efficient, is also respectful of otherness. This would mean an "other" modernity/coloniality.

Pertinent to this discussion is a brief examination of several concepts. It is necessary to point out that in the European philosophical tradition, beginning in the first part of the modern period, what is really a form of local history (that of Europe) is designated as being universal. As Enrique Dussel has suggested, European modernity is constituted as such in a dialectical relationship between Europe and the non-European world. This modernity originates with the dominion over the Atlantic at the end of the fifteenth century, when Europe defines the colonial world, placing itself at the center in relation to a periphery (*The Invention* 29).

The supposed universality of European thought has been emphasized in different ways and is expressed most clearly in Hegelian philosophy, which positions Europe as center and culmination of history. Europe marks the most evolved phase in the development of universal spirit; "Universal history goes from East to West. Europe is absolutely the end of history" (Dussel, *The Invention* 30). Therefore, the idea of historical development, going from East to West, as well as the linear categorization of history with its tacit idea of progress, are ideological constructs produced by Eurocentric thinking. Therefore, from a historical perspective, we can assert that Europe's centrality emerged only recently, in 1492 with the discovery of America and its incorporation as periphery.

Following this line of logic, modernity arises from the confrontation with the "other," when the conquest of American territory gives Spain more power over the Arab world, India, and China. Before the conquest, Europe cannot be considered the center; it is a periphery in relation to the "more developed cultures" located in what are now Turkey and Egypt: "never the center and during most of its history the periphery, Europe rises to ascendancy when it finds itself blocked on the east by Islam and embarks upon the Atlantic in a history that began in Genoa (Italy)" (Dussel, *The Invention* 35). In this process, geopolitics and gnoseology are connected, inasmuch as the conquest of new territories supposes a domination which is geographic, economic, linguistic, and especially cultural, and within this cultural domination, mastery also over the form and content in which reality is expressed.

In the development of this global economic system, the emergence of the Americas was fundamental, as Quijano and Wallerstein have established:

> The modern World-system was born in the long sixteenth century. The Americas as a geosocial construct were born in the long sixteenth century. The creation of this geosocial entity, the Americas, was the constitutive act of the modern world system. The Americas were not incorporated into already existing capitalist world-economy. There could not have been a capitalist world-economy without the Americas. (quoted by Mignolo 53)

From our contemporary perspective, to assume colonial difference supposes a critique of the myths of European modernity. In this context, Dussel classifies the concept of European modernity as Eurocentric. Within this vision the key historical events would be the Italian Renaissance, the Reformation, the Enlightenment, the French Revolution, and later the Industrial Revolution. This implies that modernity is seen as a process of emancipation, of overcoming "immaturity," a process that results from the application of reason. To challenge this vision, Enrique Dussel proposes a "world" vision, considering that modernity is thought to have begun when Europe succeeds in defining itself as the center of "world history" in relationship to a peripheral space. Modernity, therefore, does not originate in Europe, but in Europe's relationship to the colonial world, and only while Europe's emancipation depends on colonial exclusion.

During the long history from 1492 to 1992, "the Latin American people, the block of the oppressed, have struggled to create their own culture. Any attempt at modernization which ignores this history is doomed to fail, since it will be overlooking its own other face" (Dussel, *The Invention* 131). The myth of modernity to which Dussel refers consists in the suppression of the "dark side" in hegemonic narrative, of coloniality, the other side of modernity. Hence, Dussel's proposal that modern reason should be transcended not as a negation of reason itself, but of the violent, Eurocentric, hegemonic reason. (132) For Dussel, a project that genuinely liberates would require passing from modernity to transmodernity. This transmodernity supposes transcending European modernity, as a worldwide project of liberating the negated "other." Reason, from this perspective, loses its universality and can now be seen as the violent legitimation of a local history.

This constructive process of modernity/coloniality supposed the creation of the world system. As Taylor has established, "the formal political control of parts of the periphery has been a feature of the World-economy since its inception. From early Spanish and Portuguese Empires through to the attempt by Italy in the 1930s to forge an African empire, formal imperialism has been a common strategy of core domination over periphery" (74). This supposes a systemic organization of international relations where nation-states perform a function and exchange commodities. Thus, we can analyze the ideas that have created the world system—the operating logic during the period we are discussing being mercantilism, which presumed that a nation's wealth was determined by its gold and silver reserves. Given the scarcity of these materials in Europe, this system prompted the incorporation of new territories as colonies and reoriented colonial production to serve the needs of the metropolis. Consequently, an uneven exchange was required, where Spaniards monopolized colonial trade, through a combination of isolation and important naval forces. The metropolis also needed to maintain control through local elites, who differed from the natives in education, religion, and customs, creating dialectics of civilized vs. barbarians, integrated vs. marginal. These colonial spaces were a social laboratory where new classes began to emerge and confront each other. This established a complex cultural and symbolic exchange that required the joining of very different cultures; syncretism and the Baroque were the means to these ends.

Among the mechanisms that Europeans used to impose their visions of the world as universal, Walter Mignolo remarks that in the sixteenth century, Spanish missionaries judged and categorized human intelligence and civilization based on the possession (or lack) of alphabetic writing (3). This fact became crucial to "colonial difference" and the construction of an Atlantic imaginary, which later would become the colonial-modern world imaginary. Within this plan, translation was the special tool which absorbed the previously established colonial difference (3). In this context, border thinking fought for the restitution of the colonial differences that had been erased by colonial translations. In the sixteenth century, colonial difference was conceived of in spatial terms, but the Enlightenment changed this conception: history would be the measure of colonial difference. Colonized communities would be communities without a history, and historians from the communities with a history should write that of the others. According to Mignolo, an "anticolonial fight" is needed, in terms of an epistemology that permits the liberation of "other" ways of knowing located in the borderlands of the modern-colonial world system (4).

What Mignolo proposes is to recuperate the gnosis and gnoseology—as opposed to the epistemology and hermeneutics—that include the doxa and the episteme from a subaltern perspective. This is a way of knowing constructed from the outer edges, which analyzes the interstices where the ways of knowing of modern colonialism meet those generated from the colonized spaces of Asia, Africa, and Latin and Caribbean America.

This perspective opens up new possibilities in the analysis of the Jesuit *Reducciones* as a space where knowledge was specially developed, on the borders, but in an attempt to recognize and celebrate the differences between the present actors. It is clear that the Jesuits' aspiration was the evangelization of the Guaranies, but in contrast to the rest of the Catholic religious orders, they searched for a way that did not require the invalidation of the other. On the contrary, they sought to recognize the value of the other.

Within the frame of the "historic baroque," we see how different cultural experiences develop in America, experiences that are characterized by an attempt to integrate or merge different realities and cultural concepts, so that they fit in the dominant culture.

Contemplating the dynamics of subaltern groups and of individuals, one could describe the baroque culture as dialectic between freedom and containment, accentuating those spaces of liberty that allow for proposed alternatives to the hegemonic discourse. In America, these free spaces would have permitted the emergence of a Creole subjectivity—considering the Baroque to have functioned as a kind of social glue—which established a colonial monumentality, an expression of the benefiting classes' lack of faith in the colonial system. It is important to remember that this is a spatial reasoning which was articulated geopolitically throughout a complex system of central and secondary cities that administered a fundamentally extractive economic force. The colonial city is a space of social relationships where different processes are produced—a space of the geopolitics of power, from which point the laboring population was subjugated and exploited, and also the site of imperial rituals and where, later on, Americanist social and economic interests battle metropolitan interests (Vidal 91). To further this analysis, it is necessary to critique the evangelistic models that were employed in the colony.

As Subirats has argued in his text *El Continente Vacío*, the Christian Salvationist universalism that is the foundation for colonial expansion and its forms of domination allows us to assert that the reasoning behind colonization was a true theology of colonization. It is interesting to note the nuances or heterodoxies that are also present in the evangelizing process, considering that this process was especially complex and presented different paradigms. This effort is central to the Jesuit case, as Axtell points out: "while the Jesuits were morally and doctrinally unbending, their anthropology in the field was flexible and, to a point, culturally relative" (157). In a theocratic world, ideological disputes are processed in a religious way; therefore the Church as an institution can also be seen as contradictory, despite the homogenizing efforts of the majority of the ecclesiastic sectors.

According to Floristán, a theocratic state is one of the fundamental requirements of the colonial mission (24). It is necessary to remember that the theocratic system supposes that the monarch's authority had as its foundation divine right, which means that even the Church itself was subject to royal authority. These divine rights were consecrated in the Patronato of 1508, bringing the ecclesiastic mission in America under the crown's protection. As Dussel maintains, this system is an absolutely novel one: "This was the first time in history that the Papacy gave to a nation twofold authority to colonize and evangelize, that is, temporal and eternal, political and ecclesiastical, economic and evangelistic authority" (*A History* 38).

Therefore, the object of the conquest came to have a dual function: to incorporate new territories in the Spanish Empire while increasing the number of Christian faithful; as well as continuing the religious politics of the crown, which sought to "mantener la unidad religiosa en cada estado y para ello considera vía inevitable la nacionalización y estatización de la Iglesia" (Maravall, *Estado moderno* 236) (maintain religious unity in each state and considered the nationalization of the Church inevitable). Thus, the framework of this relationship between the crown and the Church was never free from the multiple conflicts that occurred throughout Europe's long historical process. In reference to this moment in Spanish history, Maravall has established that:

> Relaciones de este tipo, de los reyes con Iglesia en tanto que organización político-económica, fueron decisivas en el proceso de formación de los Estados, en el doble aspecto de un centro de poder con el que tenían que contar en su actuación respecto de otros Estados y con el que tenían que enfrentarse en relación al gobierno de sus súbditos. En los dos aspectos es importante la consecuencia, de modo que sin tomarla en cuenta no se acaba de entender el Estado Moderno. En el primer aspecto, se dio lugar a que las nuevas unidades cerradas de tipo estatal se mantuvieran como miembros de un conjunto universal; en el segundo aspecto, se fomentó la ininterrumpida elaboración doctrinal sobre el sentido y alcance de los derechos de superioridad del poder del Estado. (*Estado moderno* 219)

> (This kind of relationship between the crown and the Church as pertaining to political and economic organization was decisive in the process of state formation, in the dual aspect of a center of power that a state had to count on in its dealings with other states and that it had to confront as a subject in relation to its government. In both aspects the consequence is important; ignoring this consequence, one cannot understand the Modern State. In the first aspect, new, closed states became members of a universal group; the second aspect fostered the uninterrupted elaboration of doctrine about the meaning and reach of the superior rights of the State.)

This venture, however, was not free from the religious debates of the period, especially the confrontation between Erasmians and the Scholastics. It is my understanding that the Jesuit model should be thought of in terms of a continuity of the humanist model, although the humanist program had failed by the time the Jesuits started their missions.

Aware of the system in place in the American colonial city, the Jesuits propose another structure for the *Reducciones*. These *Reducciones* were located at the margins of the empire and directed toward communities that were not part of the *Encomienda* system. Therefore, the restructuring must take place in the methods of administration by the empire, in terms of military, economic, and pastoral efficiency.

Another distinct element of these evangelizing models is related to the relationship they had with certain Millennarian discourses in the Sixteenth and Seventeenth centuries. According to Jean Delumeau, Millennialism is a large part of Occidental cosmovisions; the ideas of Millennialism, utopia, and the ideology of progress are interrelated (1). Delumeau conceives Millennialism not as an "ideology awaiting a series of catastrophes that will announce the coming of a kingdom beyond death, but an ideology that waits hopefully for one thousand years of happiness on Earth" (1). José A. Maravall makes a useful distinction between Millennialism and utopia. According to Maravall, in a utopia, man plays at being God, while in Millennialist ideology, man dreams of a divine world that can be reached only through divine intervention (*Utopía* 48).

"Utopia" is a paradigmatic mental construct that responds to a sociopolitical image in an effort to influence society. In this sense, utopia is a product of modernity. These processes, that begin to develop during the Renaissance, emerge from a consciousness of the human capacity to create a second nature. However, these utopian processes were always viewed as controlled social models that sought to restrict liberty (*Utopía* 50). According to Maravall, Millennialism is a space of social fury, but ineffective in transforming society.

The distinction that Maravall presents is an interesting way of understanding the phenomenon but proves inadequate to analyze Jesuitism as a missionary experience. The Jesuits offer a series of metaphors and tropes specific to Millennialism—the arrival of a new era, a community of salvation, a chosen people, etc.—along with other elements that are specific to utopias: they predict and fight for a different earthly society that will bring into being eschatological expectations.

The Millennialist perspective was always very much present in the conquest. Christopher Columbus himself had perceived of his venture within an apocalyptic context. Similarly, Franciscans, Augustinians, and Dominicans all conceived of the "New World" as a paradise on Earth or as the appropriate space where an earthly paradise could be constructed.[1] The Jesuits, however, systematically organized their Millennialist expectations in such a way that they would be operative in reality. They believed that the time was coming, but that they, as Christ's militia, were responsible for gathering and guiding a pious congregation that would make the advent of the kingdom of God possible. What is surprising is that this process included attention to the economic and cultural dynamics that would make viable the spiritual enterprise. Particularly, the Jesuits presented a vision of reality that incorporated geopolitical and economic information in their understanding of the world. Consequently, the *Reducciones* experience should be analyzed in conjunction with the initiatives that the Company of Jesus developed on a global level. Following the ideas proposed by Walter Mignolo, it is possible to assert that the Jesuits in the missions were developing a series of local histories within a global design.

It should be pointed out that the Company of Jesus was founded between 1538 and 1541, during a time of profound religious changes, particularly the Protestant Reformation and, within Catholicism, the growing Observance movement. In addition, those who followed the teachings of Erasmus were accused of heterodoxy and persecuted, and the Catholic hierarchy itself thought more and more necessary the convocation of the General Council, which would occur the following decade in the city of Trent. In this context, and under the guidance of Ignacio López de Loyola, Jesuitism emerged as one of the most vigorous religious movements of the Renaissance.

With the papal seal *Regimini militantes ecclesias,* Pope Paul III gave official recognition to the new religious order, whose constitution included a series of elements that were clearly different from the constitutions of the other orders of the period. The Company was characterized by its absolute obedience to the pope, which became known as the "fourth vow." Similarly, they adapted the monastic model to the requirements of an evangelizing mission in a world of constant change. Several noteworthy elements characterized Jesuitism: the vindication of the individual; the emphasis of mental prayer over ritual worship; the cultural and educational level of its members, etc. It is clear that the first two elements are similar to Protestant practice, but within a framework of Catholic doctrine.

During the early years, the Company did not have a concrete ministry, which allowed the Jesuits to devote themselves to any type of mission, given that the work was toward "the higher glory of God." Later, they defined their education and mission *ad gentes* to the service of the Pope, central to their mission.

The Jesuits' missionary work constituted a large part of the Company's identity. The most transcendental missions were the famous Guaraní *Reducciones,* which led to the myth of the Jesuit State or Republic. These missions were carried out in an extensive area that included what are now Paraguay, Uruguay, Brazil, and Argentina. The Company settled in this area in 1550–1551, but the first foundation is dated 1609. The figure who stands out among the first missionaries is Antonio Ruiz de Montoya.

The sedentary lifestyle of the Guaranis made it easier to "reduce" them, as did their monotheistic belief system. Caraman has established that: "Monotheists, believing in a Father God without offering him any worship, they had a natural aptitude for Christian experiment" (41). In this sense, Ruiz de Montoya appears to recognize in the language of the Guaranis a theology similar to that of the Old Testament: "[The Guaraní] knew that God existed, and to certain extent his being One, and from the name they gave him, tupán, the first word, *tú,* signifies admiration; the second *pan* is interrogation, and thus corresponds to the Hebrew vocabulary manhunt, quid est hoc, in the singular" (quoted by Beebee 318).

In 1611, the Spanish king awarded royal protection to these missions. They had a large degree of autonomy, although with the condition that a representative of the king be present. The Jesuits respected the Amerindians' familial organization, although they did fight their practice of polygamy. Further, the Jesuits respected the chiefs, who had access to the *cabildo*. Each *cabildo* included one Jesuit; there was also a *corregidor*, appointed by the Council of Indies. The relationship between the *Reducciones* was similar to that of a confederation.

According to Caraman, with respect to land ownership, "alongside the private *hacienda* there was the communal land called tupambaé or God's property" (118). God's property included the best land, and all of the Amerindians farmed it. The profits from this land went toward the construction and maintenance of the temple, hospital, and school. The Amerindians held individual property which allowed them to feed their families and, if they grew more than they needed, the extra production was given to the community. It is worth noting that: "none of this property belonged to the Jesuits. Like the church, the houses, the estancia buildings, it was tupambaé. The priests claimed only the 250 pesos which was the royal grant to all serving in the reductions" (Caraman 123). Moreover, as Caraman points out, "any fish, eggs, vegetables or meat taken by priests from the common fund had to be paid for, usually with salt, knives, shears, fish hooks, medals, pins and other objects sent from headquarters in Candelaria" (123).

Also interesting is the fact that the missions were, in practice, a cooperative system, which succeeded in creating a welfare state long before the concept came about in Europe (Caraman 119). The Jesuits proposed a six-hour work day, which, although it was shorter than that of the *encomiendas*, achieved a higher level of production.

In ecclesiastical terms, the Jesuits also enjoyed certain privileges, as Dussel has mentioned:

> There also developed within the Portuguese and Spanish endeavors a fundamental ambiguity between colonizing and evangelizing. Only the Jesuits were able to constitute as *territorium nullius Diocesis* the newly discovered lands under direct protection of the Holy See, and for a long time this Order enjoyed a greater freedom than other churchmen in Latin America. (*A History* 38)

These benefits afforded them a place of privilege but also meant constant conflict with the civil and ecclesiastical authorities in America, who saw the Jesuits as a threat to their interests.

In this sense, the Jesuits enjoyed some degree of independence from the monarchy's ambitions because their fourth vow made them subject only to papal authority. As Dussel has remarked:

Because of their fourth vow and the strength and possibly the universal vision of Ignatius Loyola, the Jesuits regarded themselves as under the exclusive authority of the Pope and therefore not under the kings. The struggle between the representatives of the Company of Jesus and those of the *Patronato* was intense and without respite. (*A History* 58)

Another element which is central to the *Reducciones* is their condition of existing in the periphery of the empire. The implementation of the Treaty of Tordesillas had been difficult in general but even more so in areas that were hard to access. The Portuguese continued moving west in search of slaves, and the Spanish had very little control over this territory. The Portuguese incursions into the missions, carried out by "*bandeirantes*," would be one of the reasons Ruiz de Montoya would travel to Madrid, as well as a reason for the texts he wrote, especially his *Conquista Espiritual*.

The writings of Antonio Ruiz de Montoya (1583–1653), a Jesuit from Lima, Peru, and one of the most important and prolific Jesuits working in Paraguay, are essential to an understanding of the *Reducciones* processes, in which Millennium, utopia, and modernity/coloniality converge. His *Conquista espiritual del Paraguay* is a crucial text that nevertheless—according to what I've gathered from its Millennialist references—has all but been ignored by historical as well as cultural critics.

Antonio Ruiz de Montoya enters the Company of Jesus in Lima in 1606 and immediately expresses his desire to work in the recently formed province of Paraguay. With this goal in mind, he studies in Cordova, is ordained in Santiago de Estero in 1611, and by 1612 is a part of the mission among the Guaranis in Guayrá, Paraguay. When he arrived, the *Reducciones* system was only starting, and a heroic mysticism stimulated the missionaries, as Ruiz de Montoya remarks: the priests are "pobrísimos, pero ricos en entusiasmo. Los remiendos de sus vestidos no daban distinción de la materia principal, tenían zapatos remendados con pedazos de paño que cortaban de la orilla de sus sotanas" (12) (extremely poor, but rich in enthusiasm. Their clothing had been mended so many times that the original material was indistinguishable; their shoes were patched with pieces of cloth that they had cut from the edges of their cassocks).

Ruiz de Montoya worked as a missionary in this region between 1612 and 1622. He was head of the Guayrá missions between 1622 and 1634, before occupying the position of head of all of the *Reducciones* in 1637 (Maeder 12).

During this time, the greatest challenge to the missions' expansion was the *bandeirante* invasions. Given the gravity of the problem, the Jesuits resolve to send representatives to Rome and Madrid to defend the missions' cause in both courts. Thus, while Father Díaz Tano is in Rome, Ruiz de Montoya goes to Madrid in 1637, where he stays until 1643.

The problem afflicting the missions was associated with a larger one for the crown as the conflict between the Spanish and the Portuguese over the royal succession in Portugal was also being played out in America. In any case, Ruiz de Montoya was able to meet with King Phillip IV, who became sufficiently interested in the crisis that in 1639 the Council of Indies proposed a series of measures in order to prevent the attacks and educate local authorities about their responsibility to defend the missions and the Amerindians. Information about the penalties for these invasions was even disseminated within Brazil, until the entire process came to an end in 1640 with the uprising that ended Phillip's rein over Portugal. The uprising also required Ruiz de Montoya to stay in Spain to modify the work he had been doing (Maeder 15).

It is in this context, that Ruiz de Montoya publishes in Madrid *La Conquista espiritual del Paraguay hecha por los religiosos de la Compañía de Jesús en las provincias del Paraguay, Paraná, Uruguay y Tape* (1639), *Tesoro de la Lengua Guaraní* (1639), *Arte y Vocabulario* (1640), and a catechism. He wrote these works at the request of the bishop of Puebla de los Ángeles, when the latter was *oidor* of the Indies.

In both content and style, the *Conquista espiritual* seems to be more an allegation than a chronicle. This becomes apparent when the word "relación" is removed from the author's proposed title by an editor at the time of printing (Maeder 23). In terms of style and genre, the work is mixed—hybrid—in that it integrates different elements: chronicle, report, testimony. Furthermore, it can be argued that the text expresses a way of knowing from the very borderlands of the system, where different traditions that are forced to be resynthesized and rewritten become integrated. Thus, the author finds his ability to express Guarani ideas and concepts limited by the Spanish language, which establishes the need for translation.

Given the objectives of the text, it includes scarce documentation, which turns it into a kind of testimonial to the extent that the author and narrator are blurred in a narration that does not attempt to be objective and has an imprecise chronology and multiple digressions. The testimonial style may be due to Ruiz de Montoya's urgency to produce the text, although it also tends to give the narration authority in so far as it is written by a witness to events that are being narrated. In order to reaffirm his authority, Ruiz de Montoya includes entire discourses of chiefs and sorcerers, showing the oratory function of the Guaranis (relating theirs to classical civilizations).

Another stylistic element worth noting is the incorporation of colloquial language, including expressions such as "de quien ya dije" and "con razón." This mechanism emulates a dialogue in which the narrator seeks to connect with the reader in an attempt to partially control the text's reception.

The appearance of the natural and supernatural worlds reaffirm the dual task that the Jesuits carried out in the missions. There are constant references to the devil as instigator of all evil and as the greatest obstacle to the conversion of the Guaranis. As Beebee has established: "Satan comes in three forms: in that of the traditional Guarani karai or prophets, in illusory shapes and personages often of priests; and in the shape of the Portuguese who invades and destroy the reductions" (320).

In representational terms, the Jesuits are part of the followers of the Archangel Saint Michael, "prince of the heavenly militia," who at the same time plays a central role in the final battles against the devil in the book of Revelations, which represents the Company as part of a specially chosen group that will participate in the definitive battle between good and evil.

As previously mentioned, the author writes in the style of a testimonial, although this does not prevent him from referring to the *Cartas Anuas*—that is, to internal communications from the Jesuits to their superiors in which they discussed the community's activities and included relevant documentation. In *Conquista espiritual*, Ruiz de Montoya references a letter written by Father Diego de Boroa, dated Cordova, 1637. The author also includes biblical and magisterial quotes and a reference to the chroniclers, but these serve a function that is more rhetorical than erudite.

Ruiz de Montoya's effort to include the Guaranis among the world's civilizations is clear in the text. He often presents them as capable and rational, even showing them to adapt better to the colonial context than the Spaniards and creoles—an obvious criticism of the latter groups. In many instances, he juxtaposes the ability to adapt that the Guaranis have with the poverty in which the Spaniards in the region were living. In this sense, the text constructs a type of anti-epic: all of the heroes are Amerindians, and never do they seem to be expressing the empire's greatness.

Ruiz de Montoya's most surprising line of argumentation is related to a tradition that recognized Saint Thomas the apostle as having preached in America. Ruiz de Montoya not only accepts this tradition, but also explicitly promotes it and recognizes signs in several places in Paraguay that reveal the apostolic teachings. For example, there are the Amerindians' respect for the cross, the importance of the priest, etc. that according to Ruiz de Montoya were clear signs that the Guaranis have the right to obtain salvation. As Ruiz de Montoya maintained: "Fama constante es en todo el Brasil entre los moradores portugueses y entre los naturales que habitan toda la Tierra Firme, que el santo Apóstol empezó a caminar por tierra desde la isla de Santos, sita al sur, en que hoy se ven rastros que manifiestan este principio de camino o rastro, en las huellas que el santo Apóstol dejó impresas" (115) (It is well known by the Portuguese and the natives throughout Brazil that the holy Apostle began walking through the land on the island of Santos, in the south, where there are still traces of the beginning of that journey, the footprints left by the holy Apostle). This fact is interesting because the inclusion of this part of the world in the apostolic teachings indicated that these civilizations were equal to that of Spain, which had also been subject to the apostolic teachings of Santiago, according to tradition. Hence, this claim operates as a defense of the Amerindians, at the same time as it incorporates an element which seeks to surprise and amaze readers, typical of baroque discourse. In any case, the entire discourse about Saint Thomas implies an effort of translation and the Jesuits' ability to transculturate (suture) indigenous traditions and cultures, rather than suppress them (Beebee 319). Finally, this story about Saint Thomas would complement the belief that the Church itself held about its founders, a belief that, from a local perspective, completes the very story of the "universal church."

Ruiz de Montoya's defense of the Amerindians is present throughout the text; what is innovative about his approach is that, while this defense is founded on theory, it is also explained in practical terms. He constantly refers to the Spanish anti-testimonial, which becomes an element of the indigenous resistance to conversion. In Ruiz de Montoya's words: "En muchas provincias hemos oído a los gentiles este argumento, y visto retirarse de nuestra predicación, infamada por malos cristianos" (68) (In many provinces we have heard this argument from the pagans, and seen them leave our preaching, made infamous by bad Christians . . .). He goes on to demonstrate how the European and Creole practices not only complicated the work of the missionaries, but also prevented the pacification of the region, by implementing an effective system of production insofar as the majority of the resources were used to provide security and maintenance of the lands. In Ruiz de Montoya's view, the failure of the evangelization project was an example of the empire's state of ruin, not only in religious terms, but also in historical terms. He states:

> Y si en la provincia del Uruguay, donde el Evangelio entró desnudo de armas, derramaron su sangre cinco sacerdotes de la Compañía con insignes martirios, no es flaqueza del Evangelio sino fortaleza suya y riesgo para su crecimiento, y no es deshonor de España, sino honra suya y aumento de la Real Corona, pues tan

dichoso riego ha producido copiosísimo de veinticinco poblaciones o reducciones que la Compañía tiene hoy firmes en la fe y la obediencia de Su Majestad, a quien como yo en su nombre he propuesto en mis memoriales, ofrecen el tributo que Su Majestad fuere servido de imponerles. (71)

(And if in the province of Uruguay, where the Gospel entered stripped of weapons, the blood of five priests of the Company was spilled in famed martyrdom, it is not the weakness of the Gospel but its strength and risk for its growth, and it is not Spain's dishonor but its honor and expansion of the Royal Crown, as such joyful care has produced a copious twenty-five settlements or *Reducciones* that the Company has firmly in their faith and obedience to His Majesty, to whom, as I have petitioned in his name, they offer the tribute that His Majesty is served to require of them.)

This passage demonstrates Ruiz de Montoya's strategies for persuading his reader, as well as a clear vision of the geopolitical implications of the *Reducciones*.

The exercise and distribution of power in the mission are another significant and distinctive component of the image of the Guaranis that the Jesuits had. It is interesting to observe that Antonio Ruiz de Montoya does not question the chiefs' nobility. If he does indeed recognize that the Guaranis lack a monumentalized form of government, he obscures the deficiency by referring to their system of lords and vassals, terms consistent with conditions found in Europe. Actually this vision was put into practice in the missions: the chiefs' status was recognized and in this capacity they participated in the missions' *cabildo*, or high council. Conceding this power allowed the Jesuits to focus their efforts on education and conversion in the mission. As Caraman explains:

> With the aim of delegating as much responsibility as possible to Indians, the Jesuits established schools in all Reductions. During the later period the teaching was done by Indians themselves. Here boys, principally the sons of caciques and more prominent Indians, could learn to read, write and add. In this respect the Jesuits' townships were in advance of the Spanish. Boys who were particularly gifted received instruction in Latin. (156)

The use of the Guarani language is noteworthy—let us recall that Ruiz de Montoya knows the language well enough to write its first grammar—especially the functions it serves in the *Reducciones*. Significantly, Guarani continues to be used today in Paraguay, where it is recognized as an official language along with Spanish, and also recognized in northeast Argentina. Another aspect to consider is how the use of language in the mission allowed for the creation of new identities. Ashcroft has established that the juncture of language and space always leads to conflict in the creation of a colony (138). What may be the most radical consequence of Ruiz de Montoya's work was related to his grammar and to his general work in education: teaching the Guaranis how to write in their own language to minimize their dependence on Spanish. In fact, written Guarani becomes a significant means of resistance, as well as an expression of colonial difference. But language was not their only weapon: the Guaranis had access to firearms and formed militias that played an important role during the fight for independence. These two geopolitical elements meant that the *Reducciones* experience was significantly different within the colonial context.

The instrumental logic of modernity is present in these texts and can be demonstrated through his treatment of the herb *mate*. According to Ruiz de Montoya, *mate* was associated with witches and the devil, but rather than condemning it, he explains that it is used to stay alert while working and that it is in great demand in the region. He also points out that the Spaniards have learned (from the Amerindians) the herb's medicinal functions. However, what Ruiz de Montoya emphasizes are the economic and monetary factors, and concludes by comparing *mate*'s varied prices throughout the region, which stretches from La Plata to Potosí (67). Therefore, one could argue that Ruiz de Montoya overcomes possible superstition to provide a brief economic study of the product.

It is rather disconcerting that, as Ruiz de Montoya points out, the Jesuits achieved all this without the use of weapons. As Caraman has commented, "Yet the Jesuits were unusual soldiers in that they were strictly forbidden to carry weapons of any kind; even the General could be cashiered for the 'inflection of a wound.' Their armaments were of a different sort: weapons of will, intellect, and persuasion rather than arquebuses and Toledo swords" (156).

According to Thomas Beebee, several Millennialist elements are present in this text. Among them are references to the devil in the form of priests, which according to tradition, is one of the signs of the Antichrist. The fact that Ruiz de Montoya describes the Portuguese incursions as the "final judgment" implies that the Portuguese are connected to the Antichrist. Ruiz de Montoya states:

> No es cosa inusitada el dar Dios señas y demostraciones en cosas graves y portentosas. . . . Y Cristo nuestro Señor en su Evangelio da las señales del Ante-

Cristo, y dice de la perdida de muchos. ... [L]a prevención que mas de veinte anios antes la Majestad de Dios de enviar a la provincia de Guaira sujetos para que recogiesen los predestinados, antes que el Ante- Cristo les turbase ... Los demonios que en el par. 16 dije, lo significaron mostrando ser en el habito semejantes a estos de San Pablo y costa del Brasil, mostrándose es su figura con sus escopetas y armas, y aun dijeron que eran sus amigos. (quoted in Beebee 322)

(It is not unheard of for God to give signs and demonstrations in grave and prodigious things. ... And Christ our Lord in his Gospel gives the signs of the Antichrist, and speaks of the loss of many. ... [T]he prediction that more than twenty years before the Kingdom of God of sending to the Guaira province subjects to gather the chosen ones, before the Antichrist disturbed them ... The demons that I mentioned in paragraph 16 signified this showing them wearing habits similar to those of San Pablo and the Brazilian coast, showing their figure with its rifles and weapons, and they still said they were their friends.)

In conclusion, using Ruiz de Montoya's texts we can problematize Subirats's assertions that through historical narration of the conquest of America it is possible to "reconstruir la racionalidad del proceso civilizador moderno, inherente tanto a sus efectos devastadores sobre formas de vida y de conocimiento, y la organización de civilizaciones enteras, cuanto a su trabajo constructivo e instaurador de nuevas identidades y sistemas de dominación" (Subirats 499) (reconstruct the rationality of the modern civilizing process, as inherent to its devastating effects on ways of life and of knowing, and the organization of entire civilizations, as it is to its work constructing and establishing new identities and systems of domination). Therefore, the analysis of coloniality allows us to consider possible continuities from the past to the present, which could help to clarify the relationships between that particular conquest and the modern ones that have come in the forms of technology, science, and democracy. Furthermore, we may conclude by focusing on the milestones that characterize the "infamy" committed on this *empty continent*: the emptying of the American continent; the imposition of a single, absolute identity, violent and transcendent; and the establishment of this colonial order in the name of universal progress brought by technology and science and "la salvación apocalíptica, incluida la cancelación mediática de la historia, en nombre de una universal mercantilización de todos los aspectos imaginables de la existencia individual y colectiva" (499) (the apocalyptic salvation, including the mediated cancellation of history, in the name of a universal commercialization of all imaginable aspects of individual and collective existence).

The Jesuit experience, however, requires more precision; in the midst of the American genocide, a group of men appears to be proposing an alternate model. As Rupert de Ventos has argued, "lo que caracteriza a los jesuitas no es tanto su papel en la idealización-defensa del indio como su conciencia de que para superar su postración de los indígenas había que 'desarrollar' su sistema socioeconómico" (66) (what characterizes the Jesuits is not so much their role in the idealization-defense of the Indian as their consciousness that to overcome the prostration of the indigenous people, it was necessary to "develop" their socioeconomic system). This will involve technical and scientific development within Amerindian communities without imposing a foreign cultural model, and teaching them modern technology without corrupting them with instrumental reason (Rupert de Ventos 66). The Jesuit teachings were conscious of Anglo-Saxon colonization, and in a global context they adapted to the new requirements of an emerging capitalism. Based on their Millennialist and utopian hopes, as well as comprehension of the processes initiated by money and the world market, the Jesuits were finding a way to live and create a community that could achieve a level of political and economic development without paying the price of a theology of inequality that was unfolding in the Protestant sphere. As Gómez maintains, the utopian proposals of this period always involve the creation of regulated societies, in which rules and self-sufficiency stand out (93). It is clear that although the *Reducciones* were a regulated space, given the vicissitudes of their time, they were a favorable space for the Amerindians, evidenced by the fact that they were given firearms that they used only against external enemies, never against the Jesuits. Therefore, in the colonial borderlands between two empires, the Jesuits implemented a different kind of modernity/coloniality which was one of the only utopian experiences during the Baroque and early Enlightenment periods. Despite its failure, it allows us to recognize that even in early modernity those in the borderlands were fighting for the possibility of a different world.

Note

1. It is important to point out that this very perspective is also found among the "Founding Fathers," who sought to found in North America a new land free of the evil and sin that was destroying true faith in Europe.

Works Cited

Ashcroft, Bill, et al. *The Empire Writes Back: Theorya and Practice in Post-Colonial Literatures*. London and New York: Routledge, 1989.

Axtell, James. *Beyond 1492: Encounters in Colonial North America*. New York: Oxford University Press, 1992.

Beebee, Thomas. *They Built Millennium: Jesuits and Guarani, 1610–1768*. Vol. 5. Zeitsprunge: Forschungen zur Fruhen Neuzeit, 2001.

Caraman, Philip. *The Lost Paradise: An Account of the Jesuits in Paraguay, 1607–1768*. London: Sidgwick and Jackson, 1975.

Delumeau, Jean. *Historia del milenarismo en Occidente*. Historia Critica 23. Santiago: Universidad de los Andes, 2002.

Durston, Alan. *El Proceso Reduccional en el Sur Andino: Confrontación y Síntesis de Sistemas Espaciales*. Revista de Historia Indígena N°4. Santiago: Departamento de Ciencias Históricas Universidad de Chile, 2001.

Dussel, Enrique. *El Episcopado Hispanoamericano: el Episcopado Hispanoamericano, Institución Misionera en Defensa del Indio, 1504–1620*. Cuernavaca: Centro Intercultural de Documentación, 1969–1970.

———. *Europa, Modernidad y Eurocentrismo*. Buenos Aires: CLACSO http://168.96.200.17/ar/libros/dussel/artics/europa.pdf, January 2005.

———. *A History of the Church in Latin America: ColonialismtTo Liberation (1492–1979)*. Trans. and ed. Alan Neely. Grand Rapids, MI: Eerdmans, 1981.

———. *The Invention of the Americas: Eclipse of "The Other" and the Myth of Modernity*. Trans. Michael D. Barber. New York: Continuum, 1995.

Floristán, Casiano. *Para Comprender la Evangelización*. Pamplona: Ed. Verbo Divino, 1993.

Gómez, Fernando. *Jesuit Proposal for Regulated Societies: The Cases of Antonio Ruiz de Montoya y Antonio Vieira*. Mester 27. Los Angeles: Department of Spanish and Portuguese Studies UCLA, 1998.

Maravall, José A. *La Cultura del Barroco*. Barcelona: Ariel, 1980.

———. *Estado Moderno y Mentalidad Social (siglos XV a XVII)*. Madrid, Revista de Occidente: 1972.

———. *Utopía y Reformismo en la España de los Austrias*. Madrid: Siglo XXI, 1982.

Mignolo, Walter. *Local Histories/Global Designs: Coloniality, Subaltern Knowledges, and Border Thinking*. Princeton, N.J: Princeton University Press, 2000.

Ruiz de Montoya, Antonio. *Conquista espiritual del Paraguay hecha por los Religiosos de la Compañía de Jesús en la [sic] Provincias de Paraguay, Paraná, Uruguay y Tape*. Estudio preliminar y notas, Ernesto J. A. Maeder. Asunción: El Lector, 1996.

Rupert de Ventos, Xavier. *El Laberinto de la Hispanidad*. Barcelona: Ed. Anagrama, 1999.

Subirats, Eduardo. *El Continente Vacío: La Conquista del Nuevo Mundo y la Conciencia Moderna*. Madrid: ANAYA & Mario Muchnik, 1994.

Taylor, Peter J. *Political Geography: World-Economy, Nation-State, and Locality*. Harlow, Essex and New York: Longman Scientific & Technical Wiley, 1993.

Vidal, Hernán. *Socio-historia de la literatura colonial hispanoamericana: tres lecturas orgánicas*. Minneapolis, MN: Institute for the Study of Ideologies and Literature, 1985.

Zwartjes, Otto. "Modo, Tiempo y Aspecto en las Gramáticas de las Lenguas Mapuche, Millcayac, y Guaraní de Luís de Valdivia y Antonio Ruiz de Montoya." In Otto Zwartjes (Ed.). *"Las Grámaticas Misioneras de la Tradición Hispánica" (Siglos XVI–XVII)*. Amsterdam: Radopi, 2000.

◆ 16

Universal History: The New Science between Antiquarians and Ethnographers

Giuseppe Mazzotta

In the Third Section of the *New Science* Vico seeks to establish the general "Principles" (a term that figures in his title page). The aim of this section consists in giving legitimacy to the "principles" on which his new knowledge is founded. The "principles" are in fact origins, beginnings, foundations, causes, or true criteria of the historical science, as Vico's self-reflection makes clear (330–37).[1] He argues that his vision of universal history—ideal eternal history—rests on three shared "principles" or human customs: burial of the dead; solemn contraction of marriages; and observance of religion. What makes universal history intelligible, furthermore, is that, although divine Providence rescues it from disaster, it is created by man. The difference between Vico's conception and, say, Bossuet's version of *Discours sur l'Histoire Universelle (*in which history is viewed as shaped by a *Providence particulière* [particular Providence] rather than Malebranche's general laws) is immediately plain. At any rate, the intelligibility of Vico's "ideal eternal history," of which he now begins to discuss the "principles," resides neither in the investigations conducted by antiquarians nor in the conceptualizations by the philosophers of nature (331). The criteria shaping and underlying our knowledge of the historical world or the "world of nations," in short, cannot be settled abstractedly or by deciphering the confused, uncertain, and obscure traces of past civilizations.

In order to have knowledge of the historical world, this knowledge must be located, Vico says, "within the modifications of the human mind" (331). He also says that all historical epochs—those distantly ancient and those modern; the barbarous and the civilized—bear witness to the "universal and eternal principles" of Vico's own science (332). These principles, as stated above, make themselves manifest in three universal institutions or customs on which all nations are founded: observance of religion, contraction of solemn marriages, and burial of the dead (333). As a frame of reference for probing these universalizing claims and customs, Vico focuses on the discovery of the "new world" (334). It is as if for him the discovery of America imaginatively parallels the very paradigm of his own original discoveries. Not for anything does he obliquely allude to the conviction that he, like Descartes or Columbus, must begin his theoretical investigation on the "Principles" of the *New Science* with the assumption that the problem he faces is new, that no books existed in the world to avail him (330).

There are, however, books that he relies on for his theories. The attention that he pays to the discovery of the new world finds a discrete counterpart in the analysis of antiquarian practices. To be sure, only a brief but clear reference to the antiquarians occurs in this Third Section of his text. The antiquarians' investigations about "the principles in any field of pagan antiquity" are mentioned alongside "misplaced memories" (330). Nonetheless, a critique of antiquarianism's conceits (which are contained under the larger rubric of the "conceits of scholars") runs through the *New Science*, and elsewhere I have highlighted the cracks Vico perceives in antiquarianism's scientific claims of objectivity and certainty.[2] Antiquarians' genuine concerns hinge on the myth of origins and their political implications. From this point of view, let me add here, one antiquarian is steadily subjected to a radical critical scrutiny: Varro, a polymath and the librarian of Caesar, and "the most learned of the Romans" (*New Science* 6); (cf. St. Augustine III, 4).[3]

Varro's juridical philosophy of nature as the script of the law is acknowledged and favorably cited in Vico's *De uno*. In the *New Science*, however, his *Antiquitates rerum divinarum et humanarum*, of which only fragments are extant, is treated with considerable ambiguity. It is generally cast as a model of true wisdom. Its exemplary value is singled out by Vico because it directs human institutions toward the highest goods (364). Yet, not all of Varro's opinions are accepted as authentic or authoritative. For instance, Vico relegates into the "museum of imposture" (and among the "counterfeiters of medals") Varro's view that Hesiod had conquered over Homer in song. The ambivalent, nuanced judgment of Varro's intellectual project touches other and more substantial questions, which have ultimately to do with his myth and conception of universal history.

Vico frequently attributes to Varro the formulation of the tripartite division of history inherited, so Vico insists, from the Egyptians (*New Science* 6; 25; 40; 52). In his reconstruction of the remote and obscure origins of history, Varro comes forth as the radical thinker who liquidates the myth of the sacredness of origins. His erudition goes unchallenged when Vico finds remarkable his diligent collection of the 30,000 names of the gods (*New Science* 175). By the same token, the excellence of his scholarship shines as he is credited with numbering the "false religions" worshipping various Jupiters. Among these, Vico mentions—as a case of antiquarianism's complacent, false claim of primacy and originality—the Egyptian belief that Jupiter Ammon is the most ancient of all (62).

The recognition of the value of the historical fragment surviving from the Egyptian antiquity (i.e., the tripartite division of world's history as well as the three languages spoken by the Egyptians) stands firm in the *New Science*. Rhetorically, however, such recognition heightens Vico's sense of Varro's self-contradictions. Thus, he points out that Varro tried to locate Roman institutions within a specific, pure Latin origin. And he stresses how skeptical Varro was about the myth of the Romans' taking the Law of the Twelve Tables from the Athenians (52). This theory of the self-origination of Roman law is followed up by the opinion (which Vico says he gleans from St. Augustine's *De Civitate Dei* [City of God] about Rome's modest extensions at the time of the Kings) (88).

The ambiguous assessment of Varro depends on the fact that Vico interprets his intellectual role from the standpoint of St. Augustine's critical account in the De Civitate Dei [City of God]. As is known, St. Augustine devotes in his treatise considerable attention to Varro's secular, Roman ideology of history. *De Civitate Dei* (VI, 2–6) both recapitulates and dismantles Varro's cultural project for a universal Roman empire. Varro's 41 books of antiquities, which constitute a veritable encyclopedia of "human matters" and "divine matters," appear to St. Augustine as an eloquent rationale for Roman *potestas* (VI, 3). His polemic against the Roman theorist, however, comes to a focus in his discussion of the division of theology "into 'mythical,' 'natural,' and 'civil'" (VI, 5). Varro, who is pursuing the idea of a universal, reliable, and certain knowledge, arbitrarily excludes mythical or fabulous theology from the orbit of acceptable knowledge. In his effort to forge links between philosophy and politics, and to articulate a secular version of political theology, Varro makes manifest his prejudicial hostility to theology. Vico follows closely the outline of St. Augustine's own critique of Varro:

We must, then, distinguish three kinds of theology: 1) poetic theology, which was proper to the theological poets, and was the civil theology of all the pagan nations; 2) natural theology, which is proper to the metaphysicians; and 3) our Christian theology, which combines civil and natural theology with the highest revealed theology. (This division is truer than the one proposed by Varro, who regarded poetic theology as the third kind. In fact, the poetic theology of the pagans was the same as their civil theology. But since Varro was misled by the common error that the myths contained profound mysteries of sublime philosophy, he thought that poetic theology combined both the civil and natural kinds.) All three kinds of theology are connected by their contemplation of divine providence directed toward human institutions so that the poetic and natural theology prepared the nations for revealed theology. For poetic theology governed them through certain sensible signs, which they believed to be divine counsels, sent by the gods to humankind; while natural theology demonstrates Providence by eternal and insensible arguments. Hence these two disposed the nations to accept revealed theology by virtue of a supernatural faith, which is superior not only to our senses but to human reason itself. (*New Science* 366)

Vico's reflection explicitly revises Varro's distinctions as they are reconstructed and recorded by St. Augustine. According to the reconstruction, Varro, who asserts the spiritual originality of Rome against the encroachments of outside powers, calls for a national approach to and understanding of culture. More importantly, for Varro philosophy is never dangerous to the state in so far as it rests on the granite of reason. Poetic theology, on the contrary, totters on the quicksands of magic, edges toward superstition, and disseminates God's essence in a fantastical, false proliferation of names. On the basis of Varro's theories that aim at erasing mythical theology in favor of the philosophical and political theologies, St. Augustine concludes that Varro wishes to place Roman history on an authentically earthly foundation. The gods are introduced into the city by poets, philosophers, and politicians (*De Civitate Dei* IV, 27). But only by the rational science of the philosophers can the engine of the Roman Empire be fueled.

In the wake of St. Augustine, Vico dismisses Varro's tripartite division of theology. Unlike Varro, he links together poetic and political theology. And, against Varro, he introduces Christian theology as the experience capable of joining together all forms of theology and culture. Clearly, Vico reads Varro from the standpoint of the Augustinian two cities. The whole *De Civitate Dei* presents the two cities, Jerusalem and Babylon, as two rigidly parallel configurations without any possible synthesis between them. They are woven together in the fabric of history, but their radical dissociation can never be concealed: politics and theology are necessarily kept apart from each other.

From the shared standpoint of both St. Augustine and Vico, Varro shows himself incapable of formulating a universal principle for his intellectual project. In his subdivision of theology, he discards poetic or mythical theology as a deceptive play of vain phantasms and superstitions. He invests natural theology with intellectual rigor and asks that it be kept away from the public square or the forum. The reason for this willed self-separation is evident. The multitudes love fictions and show no tolerance for philosophical debates. In order to preserve philosophy's speculative purity, it must be confined to the schools. Finally, Varro's political theology—so does St. Augustine argue—is compatible with philosophy. Because of this presumed compatibility, Augustine inveighs against Varro's arbitrary exclusion of the theatrical/poetic fictions from the perimeter of valid knowledge. For such an exclusion, which is tantamount to an exclusion of the many, violates the principle of a totalizing encyclopedia. Furthermore, it shows that Varro manipulates knowledge in order to ensure the survival of the universalizing pretensions of the Roman elites.

Varro's cultural-aristocratic project, thus, appears as a mere sacralization or idolatry of the earthly city. Against Varro's political idolatry (or his sense of the alliance between philosophy and politics), St. Augustine announces the end of political history; secular history, for him, leads to a dead end, and the only way out of it lies within the theological horizons opened up by the new Christian epoch. Consistent with this premise, the *City of God* counters Varro's version of history and is shaped by a central conviction: world history is preparing itself for the messianic advent which will usher in the creation of a new heaven and a new earth (Isa. 65:17). Thus, it dramatizes a vision of universal history that is modeled on Eusebius's account of the six ages as well as on Jewish apocalyptic history.

Although Vico follows closely St. Augustine's polemic with Varro, he takes his distance from both. He acknowledges that Varro is correct in pursuing a vision of knowledge that unifies human things and divine things (*New Science* 284). In the wake of St. Augustine, Vico also points out Varro's self-contradictory stance. His ideal pursuit of a unified knowledge turns out in reality to be a separation of various forms of knowledge and an arbitrary discarding of what he deems unworthy of reflection. And like St. Augustine, Vico grasps Varro's failure to universalize his historiographic plan.

At the same time, however, Vico understands that the Augustinian universal history of the two eschatological cities, although it is radically juxtaposed to Varro's secular dogmatism, resembles it as if it were its secular image. In effect, St. Augustine, who is sharply critical of the paradigms of the classical world, cannot escape Varro's classical dualism. For Varro, politics is an absolute. Any idea of transcendence is a vain imagining. For St. Augustine, salvation-history, which is poised at the threshold of its apocalyptic conclusion, leaves no room for politics as the stage for the drama of the earthly city. His own universalizing design, crystallized in the eschatology of *De Civitate Dei*, suppresses the contingent, political realities of history.

The inadequacy of St. Augustine's theology of history was recently discussed by Eric Voegelin, who also argues that Vico's *New Science* seeks to fill the lacuna left open by *De Civitate Dei*.[4] Vico, in effect, writes the history not just of Rome but of the earthly city in its multiple historical metamorphoses. It should be clear, however, that Vico, unlike Varro, never elevates the earthly city to an absolute. He circumscribes its history within a providential scheme and, unlike St. Augustine, frees it from any sense of apocalyptic closure. Even so, Voegelin finds Vico's rejection of a dualistic historical conception too inadequate for a genuine representation of universal history. He argues that Vico produces a false universality and points out its empirical omissions: his historiographic representation leaves out, for instance, China's particular history.

No doubt, Vico's model of universal history is marked by lacunae and omissions. Yet Voegelin misses two crucial facts in Vico's work. The first concerns his articulation of the so-called *universali fantastici*: the view, that is, that the principle of unification of all history and all knowledge, indeed the medium of construction of an interconnected world of knowledge, lies in the modifications of the mind and in the poetic imagination. This "poetic" aspect of universality, which can never be dissociated from a sense of the singularity of poetry, lies at the heart of Vico's discussion of the "Discovery of Homer" in the *New Science*. Such an insight into the *universali fantastici*, in short, provides the paradigm for the inclusion of all possible myths and fables, even if they are *de facto* left out of Vico's representation. The second fact, which Voegelin ignores and to which the rest of this paper is devoted, concerns Vico's lucid awareness that the universal "Principles" of his science have to be tested against cultures that lie outside the limited parameters of European history. The discovery of America, which is treated in the Third Section of the "Principles," serves this purpose.

Vico refers often throughout his text, even if on occasion he does so quickly, to the discovery of the new world. He recalls, for instance, the "grotesque savages whom travelers at the foot of South America say they found in Patagonia, the land named for these *Patacones*, or Big Feet" (*New Science* 170; 338). Such a legend leads him to dismiss as groundless the "philosophers" suppositions on giants and primitives. More than that, the reference to the accounts by "travelers" is striking because of its vagueness. It leaves it unclear whether Vico had any notion of Columbus's *Letters to the Spanish Crown* (1498), Vespucci's *De novo orbe* (1505), or Pietro Martire's *Decades de orbe novo* (which contains letters and reports from the new world sent to Pope Leo X).[5]

The vagueness in Vico's reference to travelers suggests that he intends to take his distance from the whole rhetorical genre of *relaciones* or *recits de voyage*. In the section on "Principles" he refocuses, with a hint of irony, on "present-day travelers," who "relate that tribes of Brazil, the Kaffir of Africa, and other people of the New World live in society without any knowledge of God" (*New Science* 334). And he is merciless about the claims made by travel narratives: "these are tales told by travelers who hope that such exotica will help them peddle their books" (334). Such fabulous travel books are deceptive in that they equate the "new" with the "monstrous" for the sake of titillating the readers' curiosity and fascination/fear with the unknown. More fundamentally, they are also deceptive in that they posit a universality of reason: like Antoine Arnauld and, in his wake, Pierre Bayle and Andreas Rudiger, they make the "new" a mere mirror image of Europe. They judge the "new" from the perspective of European rationality and, in the process, they obliterate any idea of genuine difference between the Old World and the New World.

If the rhetorical tradition of *recits de voyage* appears false, there is one science to which Vico makes recourse: ethnography. This science is practiced in Naples (cf. *La universal fabrica del mondo* by Giovanni Lorenzo Anania [1573 and 1582]), but Vico never refers to it. Nonetheless, ethnography emerges in the economy of the *New Science* as the counterpart to antiquarianism. The indigenous people of the new world stand to the Europeans the way the ancients do to the moderns. More importantly, ethnography is a peculiar form of history-writing. As such, they deployed through the mediation of the *historias* written by the theologians/missionaries (or philosophical travelers), who approach the indigenous, "primitive" cultures of the Americas in order to place them within the eternal, universal economy of Christian revelation.[6]

Two are the authors of ethnographic *historias* who dramatically reflect on the essentials of the culture of the Amerindios: Oviedo and his successor Acosta. Vico cites as his ethnographic sources both the *Historia natural y moral de las Indias* (1590) by Acosta (*New Science* 337) and the *Historia general de las Indias* (1535) by Oviedo (517). Acosta is credited with providing evidence that the people of Peru and Mexico believe in the immortality of the souls and bury their dead. Oviedo, on his part, recounts the sacrificial cannibalism among the American Indians, a ritual that offends the modern criteria of western rationality. There figure in the *New Science* other allusions to the Latin edition of these texts (such as the recall of feathers with which the nobles adorn themselves in the West Indies) (488). One can also find references to the ethnographic writings by other Jesuits up to Lafiteau's *Moeurs des sauvages ameriquains compares aux moeurs des premieres temps* (1726) (Morals of the savages Americans compared to the morals of the primitive times) as well as Martini's mission to China.

Why are both Oviedo and Acosta so conspicuously singled out? To answer this question we must go back to the text where Vico seeks to establish the "scientific" principles of his own work:

> Ora, per fare sperienza se le proposizioni noverate finora per elementi . . . preghiamo il leggitore che rifletta a quanto s'e' scritto d'intorno a' principi di qualunque material di tutto lo scibile divino ed umano della gentilità. (*New Science* 330)

> (Let us make experience of the propositions enumerated as elements of my New Science, and see whether they can give form to the matter outlined in the chronological table. I ask the reader to review what others have written about the principles in any field of pagan antiquity, whether human or divine.)

The passage begins by drawing attention to the "experience"—a term, which, from Leonardo to Bacon and Galileo, establishes the validity of a science. The word, from the Latin *experientia* (etymologically from ex-per-ire), implies a passage and a going-beyond, as if on an itinerary or crossing of new spaces. In this sense, the term foreshadows and shapes the language of discovery and travel punctuating this whole section of the text. More to the point, "experience" translates the Greek *empeiria*, which Aristotle posits as the offshoot of memory and *techne* (*Met.* I, 1, 981a). It is linked to *peira* in the sense of an experiment or proof. Since Vico is skeptical about the knowledge drawn from travel literature, he must burden his sense of "experience" with a peculiar significance, and we must probe its implications. He speaks of "making" experience. The verb stresses the concreteness of his idea of knowing and alludes to the reality of discoveries and journeys that manage to bring to light what exotic narratives fail to do. Such an empirical point of departure in the investigation of "principles" (a term that, as stated at the outset, figures prominently on the title page of Vico's own text) leads to a brief but pithy discussion of the possible objectivity of experience.

To test the validity of his propositions, Vico appeals to the reader and asks him to reflect on and confirm his textual procedure (*New Science* 330). By this rhetorical move, the understanding of "experience" cannot be dismissed as a simple modality of a scientific, external knowledge. It casts "experience" also as an inner reflection or an inner knowledge. More than that, the text presents

Vico carrying out his probing through the scholastic language of "form" and "matter." Such a specialized lexicon, which Bacon criticizes, Hobbes neglects, and Locke rejects as completely unintelligible, is replaced in Descartes by the correlation between *res cogitans* and *res extensa*. Yet, Francisco Suarez revives and valorizes once again in his age this seeming fossil from scholastic terminology in his *Disputationes Metaphysicae* (XIV–XVI).

Even in its antiquarian flavor and deliberate anachronism (made more dramatic by the textual thrust toward the conceptualization of new principles and new discoveries), this neo-scholastic terminology seeks to place the quest for principles within a context that is not merely empirical. Empiricism installs us in the universe of things and, consequently, degrades or contracts the idea of knowledge by its bracketing the possibility of an intuitive or speculative knowledge. From this standpoint, the neo-scholastic terminology (as well as the appeal to the reader's knowledge) lays bare the need to impose on the observed phenomena an intellectual framework that makes it intelligible.

The antiquarian account of origins, which Vico links with Bacon's empiricism, is a fiction to be discarded. With renewed critical energy, Vico groups together in his criticism both philosophers of history and philologists. They share a common error. They cast a blinding light on the sense of experience. They both observe the history of barbarians from the standpoint of natural scientists: from their privileged perspective the barbarians are viewed as objects by the observers/scientists. In their effort to transform historical knowledge into an exact science (". . . they have so earnestly pursued a knowledge 'scienza' of the world of nature"), the philosophers lapse into error: in their conceits they make up false genealogies and teleologies because they employ criteria of judgment that are external to the facts they perceive. By the same token, the philologists, who posit a chain of causality among disparate events in order to get rid of confusions, lapse into a skepticism stemming from the absence of a value perspective. Against all of them Vico insistently asserts that historical origins are wrapped in confused memory and are ". . . tutte immagini di mal regolata fantasia" (*New Science* 330). The principle he upholds is recapitulated in the proposition that the civil world is a human creation and its principle must be discovered in the modification of the human mind. Experience, in short, concerns objective historical-symbolic productions (i.e., religious practices, burials, and marriage institutions), and their significance is inseparable from an examination of the history of the inner workings, operations, and shifts of the mind.

Vico's discussion of the three universal customs he singles out as vestiges of all history takes place through the deployment of a language of moral philosophy and natural law. He refers to "execrable abominations of the lawless world," "brutish and abominable error," "law of nature," "advanced decadence" (*New Science* 336). This ethical rhetoric echoes the representation of man's fallen condition. Vico's "principles" are formulated within this understanding of the universal history of man's fall. They are providentially intended to preserve mankind from anarchy and chaos and to upkeep the laws of difference within the original promiscuity of things. These principles and their finalities are suggested to him by the ethnography of the New World (334). In point of fact, Vico articulates his principles by binding together ethics, experiences, and discoveries, and he probes the relation connecting them.

As shown earlier, the text unleashes a brief but harsh critique of the narratives by "present-day travelers" (334) to Brazil and South Africa. These narratives (the metaphor recalls Herodotus's view of history as a journey narrative) hinder any genuine knowledge of the "other." They play up to the whims of the marketplace and, to this end, they falsify reality. Even if trivial, moreover, they are shaped by an enlightened and rational tradition (Bayle, Rudiger, and the university professors at Geneva) that ultimately erases any sense of constitutive difference among cultures in the persuasion of a universal rationality common to all or emergent for all. It turns out that these analyses end up as fabulous and fantastic descriptions that keep an eye on how a book becomes a bestseller. Finally, they falsify reality not just because they assimilate any objective difference to one's superior view. They ignore the religious origins of culture. This fundamental critique leads Vico to undertake the road traced by Oviedo and Acosta (whose value is confirmed by the findings of Hariot and Schouten) (*New Science* 337).

A wide gap separates the fantastic "nouvelle" from their *historias*. Oviedo and Acosta witness the enigma of the American Indians. They give evidence of their heterogeneity, safeguard their singularity, and set up a reliable, objective comparison between European culture and American native culture without reducing one to the other. These concerns figure prominently in the body of American-Indian *relaciones* Vico cites (*De indicis* and *De historia indica*) (*New Science* 337; 517). Let me add in passing that the grand Roman fresco by the Jesuit painter, Andrea Pozzo, in the church of St. Ignatius on the universal mission of the Jesuits recapitulates the theological substance in the sinews of the *relaciones*. Further, this theological/ethnographic tradition finds its extension in a variety of texts, such as those by Bartolomé de Las Casas (*Historia de las Indias*) (1527) and *De Thesauris in Peru* (1566); by Francisco de Victoria (*Relectio "De Indis"*); by Melchor Cano (*De dominio indorum*); and by

Francisco Suarez (*De bello et de Indis*) (1584), in which the colonization of the New World is either fiercely attacked or justified only as a means to Christian missions. More than that, Suarez, who is credited to have founded, along with Grotius, the discipline of international law, affirms the equal moral worth of the European and the American Indians. In their systematic critique of the practices of the Spanish empire (which, nonetheless, they serve and whose role they uphold), these writers all draw inspiration from the Dominican theology of the so-called "School of Salamanca." The *historias* by Acosta and Oviedo are shaped by the belief in the moral order of the world. This notion lies at the heart of the Neo-Thomism or *Barockscholastik* of Tommaso di Vio, Francisco Suarez, and Luis de Molina.[7]

Vico's relation with Neo-Scholasticism continues to draw the interest of scholars. At any rate, it is well to recall that Vico's own process of intellectual maturity is marked by a conspicuous pedagogical drama. In his *Autobiography* he records the transition, which took place under the guidance of the Jesuit Giuseppe Ricci, from "scotism" to the *Disputationes Metaphysicae* of Suarez. It can never be sufficiently stressed that, after the recognition of St. Thomas Aquinas as a doctor of the Church in 1576, St. Ignatius organizes his *ratio studiorum* (which was formalized in 1586) on an Aristotelian and Thomistic basis.

Suarez's *Disputationes* embrace these rich Dominican and Jesuit strains of thought. And they play a central role in the philosophical programs at places such as La Fleche and Naples in the eighteenth century. Vico's *Autobiography* attributes to the *Disputationes* the intention of organizing all the sciences in a coherent whole. It also records how the protagonist/apprentice is led to Suarez's metaphysics by his legal studies, or, which amounts to the same thing, ethics and the "science of right" need for Vico the metaphysical perspective of Suarez. In much the same way, at the point where the *New Science* confronts the radical otherness of the American Indians and discovers the falseness of the drastic juxtaposition between old and new, the self-same neo-scholastic solutions articulated by Suarez reemerge, for they undergird Acosta's *Historia natural y moral de las Indias* (Natural and Mineral History of the Indies).

Translated into Italian in 1596, Acosta's treatise exercised considerable influence on Botero, Grotius, and Vossius. The Europeans—this is the burden of Acosta's text—cannot simply absorb within the paradigm of their culture the alien rituals and traditions of the American Indians. They do not belong to Europe nor can they merely be interpreted from Europe's standpoint. They constitute an authentic civil society that is totally divergent from and irreducible to Europeans' history of reason or self-interest. As a matter of fact, the Europeans, from Aristotle to Lactantius, have misunderstood the origins of this different culture: their theories of the "fabled" antipodes (which also St. Augustine ridicules in *De Civitate Dei* XVI, 9) prove it. It follows that the American Indians must be studied in their historical differences, even if this difference is bound to appear a scandal to the rationalist, homogenizing European impulses. Only a moral relation based on the doctrine of natural law and of nature as the common foundation of the moral order of the world can be forged between Europeans and Amerindios.

This relation between the two spatially separate cultures is understood by Acosta as a variant of the temporal relation between ancients and moderns. Like the ancients, the Amerindios belong to a particular time of universal history. Even terms such as "savage" and "barbarian" connote peculiar meanings. They were introduced by the Europeans either to idealize the Amerindios or to legitimize their own pretensions of superiority over the natives.[8] Paradoxically, these terms circulate at the very moment when traditional forms of understanding are unsettled and upset by the traumatic irruption into modernity by human beings who are still caught in the archaic stage of their history. Further, these terms are deployed as if they designated unequivocal scientific categories. At best, they serve as signs of an alibi for European imperial, hegemonic designs.

Clearly, for Vico, the essential teaching of Acosta, Oviedo, and Suarez (and one might add the names of di Vio, De Soto, and Las Casas) consists in their power to weave together historical and moral perspectives. The scientific findings by Acosta enable Vico to reflect on the possibility of a "scientific" history-writing. Further, from their theological perspective, every journey leading beyond the borders of the known world and of Europe ends up leading back to the heart of Europe, to its very interiority. As it does so, it completely reverses the European standpoint of historical knowledge. Thus Acosta faces the culture of the Amerindios, describes with scientific diligence the natural phenomena of the land, and never discards his scientific, detached viewpoint even when he keeps under his gaze the *historia moral* of the American Indians. From the scientific study of natural phenomena Acosta descends to the theory of natural law as well as the moral/theological principles underlying those phenomena.

The rhetorical-conceptual organization of the Third Section of the *New Science* forces us to insert Vico's thought within the framework of historical/moral issues to which the text obliquely and yet firmly alludes. Acosta's ethnography, which binds together the experience of a journey, contingent scientific description, and transcendent moral judgments, opens up a new dimension within Vico's sense of history and sense of science. He has discovered the possibility of writing a universal history that is made of singularities. In his understanding, history unfolds like a plot in which the new and concrete encounters occur between bearers of the Christian revelation and the people who, like the ancients of the gentile world, have not yet been exposed to it. Yet, exactly like the ancients and the moderns, what these two cultures, remote and different from each other, deeply share is the universal, eternal moral law providentially inscribed in the heart of history.

This moral law alone can make intelligible to the Old World the historical lineaments and reality of the New World. It alone can unveil their common humanity, a word that Vico memorably links to burial grounds. And it is this shared moral law that, by correlating all distinct cultural experiences, can also unveil, from the perspective of the New World, the limitations, complacencies, and self-delusions of the Old World.

It is possible to see—indeed it is inevitable that we see in such an understanding of a universality made of historical singularities and local differences—an extension of Vico's *generi fantastici* or *universali intelligibili* or imaginative universals (*New Science* 34). Even his reflections on the simultaneous origin of the natural law of nations, the customs of the nations, which conform to a human common sense (311), both stem from and confirm Vico's insight into universality as a necessary mode of thinking. The imaginative universals he calls the master key of his science. As is known, imaginative universals designate the poetic character or, in the rational age, the poetic character of a species reduced to a universal. In this sense, they are always forms of a "concrete universal," a paradoxical term that gathers together and individualizes all entities sharing a common quality: the Achille's story exemplifies and stands for all these heroes sharing the common quality of valor.

With admirable consistency, the theology and science of the ethnographers turn into an instrument of discovery of the laws binding together mankind, which, though dispersed all over the globe in myriad local entities, shares in a common providential destiny. Finally, these philosophical-poetic principles Vico forges are never kept at the level of intellectual abstractions. Quite to the contrary, as this paper has argued, they are rooted in the concreteness of Roman history, and they adumbrate the idea of Rome and its unique role in world history.

Its history encompasses a political universality, whose rationale was justified by an antiquarian such as Varro, by a poet such as Virgil, and, in modern times, by ethnographers such as Acosta and Oviedo, whose science, to put it in the terms Bacon deployed for the desired alliance he meant to forge between science and the English empire, ushers in the Spanish empire. It encompasses a theological universality, which was tested by the ethnographers traveling to the New World. Both modes are rooted in the Ciceronian principles of the universality of the natural law. And all three of them—politics, theology, and poetics—are validated, shaped, and expressed by the mind's production of *universali fantastici*.

Notes

1. All quotations from the *Scienza nuova* are taken from Giambattista Vico, *Opere*, ed. Andrea Battistini (Milan: Mondadori, 1990். The English translation is taken from Giambattista Vico, *New Science*, trans. David Marsh (London: Penguin Books, 1999).
2. Giuseppe Mazzotta, *The New Map of the World: The Poetic Philosophy of Giambattista Vico* (Princeton, NJ: Princeton University Press, 1999), 103–105.
3. I am paraphrasing some ideas put forth by me in "Varrone, sant'Agostino e Vico," in *Il Mondo di Vico/Vico nel mondo*, ed. Franco Ratto (Perugia: Edizioni Guerra, 2000), 157–63.
4. Eric Voegelin, *"Scienza nuova nella storia del pensiero politico,"* (Naples: Guida, 1996).
5. On Columbus see Djelal Kadir, *Columbus and the Ends of the Earth: Europe's Prophetic Rhetoric as Conquering Ideology* (Berkeley: University of California Press, 1992).
6. For a detailed description of the development of ethnography among the American Indians see Anthony Pagden, *The Fall of Natural Man: The American Indian and the Origins of Comparative Ethnology* (Cambridge: Cambridge University Press, 1982). See also his *Facing Each Other: The World's Perception of Europe and Europe's Perception of the World* (Burlington, VT: Ashgate Variorum, 2000).
7. On the relationship between Vico and the Scholastic tradition, see Elio Gianturco, "Suarez e Vico," *Harvard Theological Review* XVII (1934): 207–10; and see Cesare Vasoli, "Vico, Tommaso d'Aquino e il tomismo," *Bollettino del Centro di Studi Vichiani* IV (1974): 5–35. Noteworthy are the two volumes by John Milbank, *The Religious Dimension in the Thought of Giambattista Vico 1699–1744*, (Lewiston, NY: Mellen Press, 1991–92). See also Claudio M. Burgaleto, "The Jesuit Theological Humanism of José de Acosta (1540–1600): A Study in the History of Theology" (PhD Dissertation, Boston College, 1996).
8. See R. de Mattei, "Sul concetto di barbaro e barbarie nel medioevo," *Studi di storia e diritto in onore di Enrico Besta* 4 (1939): 485–98. And, for the tendency to idealize the "savages," see José Antonio Maravall, *Antiguos y modernos* (Madrid, 1966).

Works Cited

Anania, Giovanni Lorenzo. *La Universal Fabrica del Mondo.* Napoli: Giuseppe Cacchij dell'Aquila, 1573.
Aristotle, *The Metaphysics.* Oxford; New York: Oxford University Press for Sandpiper Books, 1997.
Augustine, Saint. *De Civitate Dei.* New York: Modern Library, 2000.
Burgaleto, Claudio M. "The Jesuit Theological Humanism of José de Acosta (1540–1600): A Study in the History of Theology." PhD dissertation, Boston College, 1996.
De Mattei, R. "Sul concetto di barbaro e barbarie nel medioevo." *Studi di storia e diritto in onore di Enrico Besta* 4 (1939): 485–98.
Gianturco, Elio. "Suarez e Vico." *Harvard Theological Review* XVII (1934): 207–10.
The Holy Bible, King James Version. Grand Rapids, Mich,: Zondervan Bible Publishers, 1984.
Kadir, Djelal. *Columbus and the Ends of the Earth: Europe's Prophetic Rhetoric as Conquering Ideology.* Berkeley: University of California Press, 1992.
Maravall, José Antonio. *Antiguos y modernos.* Madrid, 1966.
Mazzotta, Giuseppe. *The New Map of the World: The Poetic Philosophy of Giambattista Vico.* Princeton, NJ: Princeton University Press, 1999. 103–105.
_____. "Varrone, Sant'Agostino e Vico." *Il Mondo di Vico/Vico nel mondo.* Ed. Franco Ratto. Perugia: Edizione Guerra, 2000. 157–63.
Milbank, John. *The Religious Dimensions in the Thought of Giambattista Vico 1699–1744.* Lewiston, NY: Mellen Press, 1991–92.
Pagden, Anthony (Ed.). *Facing Each Other: The World's Perception of Europe and Europe's Perception of the World.* Burlington, VT: Ashgate Variorum, 2000.
_____. *The Fall of Natural Man: The American Indian and the Origins of Comparative Ethnology.* Cambridge: Cambridge University Press, 1982.
Suárez, Francisco. *Disputationes metaphysicae.* Hildeseim: G. Olms, 1965.
Vasoli, Cesare. "Vico, Tommaso d'Aquino e il tomismo." *Bollettino del Centro di Studi Vichiani* IV (1974): 5–35.
Vico, Giambattista. *New Science.* Trans. David Marsh. London: Penguin Books, 1999.
_____. *Opere.* Ed. Andrea Battistini. Milan: Mondadori, 1990.
Voegelin, Eric. *Scienza nuova nella storia del pensiero politico.* Naples: Guida, 1996.

◆ **Afterword
Reasoning the Other**

Luis Martín-Estudillo and Nicholas Spadaccini

Reason and its relationship to otherness have been a topic of reflection from the early modern period to contemporary times. Since Descartes first enunciated his famous first principle of philosophy (*cogito ergo sum*), the raising of cautionary flags was not far behind, as illustrated in Blaise Pascal's famous phrase that there are "two excesses: to exclude reason; to admit nothing but reason." Pascal postulates that the apprehension of truth comes not only through reason but also through the heart, "a faculty for obtaining knowledge of the principal truths which are the basis of reasoning" (quoted by Marías 229).

The twentieth century in particular has seen extraordinary challenges to the ideals of the Enlightenment as reason became associated with coercion, violence, and genocide. One can point to the critical theorists of the Frankfurt School, Max Horkheimer and Theodor Adorno; to postmodernist philosophers such as Jean-François Lyotard, Richard Rorty, and Gianni Vattimo; and to Enrique Dussel, a Latin American philosopher of liberation, who proposes another kind of reason—what he calls "reason of the other" or "postcolonial reason" which, according to Walter Mignolo in *Global History/Local Designs*, is identified "as a different locus of enunciation" (117). Mignolo himself, influenced by the work of Dussel, among others, talks about "subaltern reason" and the possibilities that it offers to contest modernity (96), pointing to the early colonial period and to people such as Guamán Poma de Ayala, in order to argue that different loci of enunciation were already present in the beginning of colonial expansion. Interestingly, the editors of the present volume contend that a look at the Southern European cultures of the early modern period, specifically those of Spain and Italy, as illustrated through the essays in this collection, "provide ample opportunities to reexamine the legacy of Western rationality from a Southern perspective." This kind of reexamination is in line with Dussel's questioning of Hegel's notion of a modernity created in Western Northern Europe, especially Germany (*The Invention of the Americas*), and the idea that one cannot dismiss from this discussion 1492 and its aftermath, meaning that one cannot properly speak of modernity without considering the protagonism of those other entities in the heart of Europe.

In reading the present volume one is struck by the extraordinary range of discussion undertaken in the essays, both in conceptual terms and geographical scope. Some of the issues raised activate a reflection on developments that had precipitated a New World Order following 1492 and on the myriad of symbolic manifestations that accompanied and shaped the sociopolitical tensions of the early modern period. Moreover, the scope of the essays is often expanded to touch on contemporary issues whose broader understanding requires a constant "check" with the past, just as the past can be productively reexamined through an analysis of current phenomena, practicing what Mieke Bal calls a "preposterous history" (Quoting *Caravaggio*).

A concept that is silently, but somewhat pervasively, present in this volume is that of the "modern" nation-state, especially in reference to Spain, with its extensive, centralized bureaucracy, and expansion in both Europe and the New World. Italy, in the meantime, while lacking political unity and centralization (it was then home to some two hundred independent territories), was also in the heart of Europe if one considers other factors traditionally associated with modernity. One can point to a highly developed humanistic thought in the Fifteenth and Sixteenth centuries, especially at the court of Cosimo de' Medici in Florence, and the productive forces that were unleashed through humanist personalities, some of whom attempted to synthesize ideas stemming from Christianity, Platonism, Aristotelianism, and the Jewish Cabbala, as Castillo and Lollini point out in reference to Pico della Mirandola (1463–94). Then, there were theoreticians of politics and State of various persuasion, from Niccolò Machiavelli (1469–1527), whose State is not contingent upon a religious and moral authority, to Tommaso Campanella's (1568–1639) utopia and the proposition of a universal monarchy subordinated to papal authority. This sort of effervescence could also be seen with extraordinary figures such as Leonardo da Vinci (1452–1519) in the arts, Bernardino Telesio (1508–88) in the study of natural sciences, and Galileo Galilei (1564–1642) in mathematical physics, which, as Battistini argues in this volume, unleashed a "fear of open spaces" when the Earth was deprived of its centrality in the cosmos. Thus, despite Hegel's kind of chauvinism, their ideas, together with those of other "actors" in the Southern European arenas, would also become a substantial part of the imaginary of modernity, even if those Southern European entities (with Portugal among them) have been perceived for centuries by their northern neighbors, and by groups of different political affiliations within themselves, as backward and in need of guidance through the "universal principles" of reason. It is also well known that those entities have been accompanied in this exclusion by a growing periphery of regions around the world which, from a northern-based Eurocentric point of view, were constructed as ex-centric and pre-modern.

Paradoxically, this same standpoint and modernity itself are linked to the conquest and colonization of Amerindia, mostly an Iberian enterprise that counted with the action of major Italian players. This thesis, which has been forcefully espoused by Dussel, contests the Hegelian idea of a modernity created in a North which looked down upon a South, excluding it from the culmination of history. Hegel highlighted the notion that "the principle of the free Spirit has made itself [...] the flag of the world, and from it universal principles of reason have developed" (Hegel in Dussel 23). This particular conception of reason is attached to the violence of a center, which sought to impose its "universal principles" upon the periphery; it is a center which negates the idea of a "reason of the other."

The Hegelian ideas discussed above were so prevalent well into the twentieth century that even a Southern intellectual, the philosopher Benedetto Croce, while recognizing the political relevance of the Spanish empire during the Sixteenth and Seventeenth centuries, downplayed Spain's role in the "formation of the modern spirit," which he considered an achievement of Italy, France, England, and Germany (388), even if he later was to go on to link modernity with "the ideas of extreme Protestantism and rationalism" (385). (Interestingly, even in the seventeenth century there was an anxiety about Italy's centrality within the European imaginary as seen in Francesco Negri's *Viaggio Settentrionale* [see Nathalie Hester in this volume].) A few years prior to Croce's observations, Max Weber (*The Protestant Ethic and the Spirit of Capitalism*) had famously related the cultural origins of modernity and the instrumental rationality of capitalism to the customs and religious discipline of the Protestant north, although he was to point out that those origins "lay not in a rational world view, but, in the deeply irrational impulse of salvation within the terrifying theology of Calvin" (Turner 18).

Critics of the alliance between capitalism and reason tell us that this association is fundamentally irrational, since it unleashes destructive dynamics which jeopardize the conditions of human existence. Also, as a form of exploitation and domination, this alliance ignores the principles of ethics and solidarity which make that very existence "human," thus producing alienated or disturbed individuals. This perception has stimulated the discussion of alternative models of modernity and reason.

One of the concepts that has gained currency during the last several decades has been that of the Baroque, which Walter Benjamin understood as a key notion for a revaluation of the origins of modernity. In *The Origins of German Tragic Drama*, Benjamin was to argue for an "archeology of modernity" which explored its pre-Enlightenment roots and, through an interpretation of some landmarks of baroque symbolism, pointed to the dubious rationality of historical processes and the impossibility of epistemic absolutes. Benjamin's ideas have resonated recently in the work of Christine Buci-Glucksmann, who has approached the Baroque as a period that can inspire a suggestive way of looking at contemporary culture, insofar as it can offer a model for overcoming the dualities that structure Western thinking. According to Buci-Glucksmann, the Baroque "is a moment within Christianity, and even within the counter reformation, which will introduce the double and will hybridize the low into the high and the high into the low" (26–27). If the rationalistic mind perceives dualities as troublesome discordances to be annulled, those same dualities are celebrated and reaffirmed by the powers of oxymora and metaphors, those pillars of baroque writing which find a strong resonance in postmodernist aesthetic and intellectual proposals. These proposals have found the symbolic production of early modern Southern Europe and the New World to be such a rich source of insight that concepts such as "Ultrabaroque" and, more importantly, "Neobaroque" have become necessary for an adequate discussion of many contemporary cultural issues (see Spadaccini and Martín-Estudillo).

Let us recall that the Baroque is a powerful concept that appeals to a broad spectrum of European and Latin American intellectuals, among them, historians, philosophers, literary and cultural theorists, and creative writers. In the cases of Spain and Latin America, there are those who were interested in historically oriented interpretations focusing on the Baroque's containment side (Maravall is perhaps the most notable exponent of this tendency in conjunction with the dominant culture of seventeenth-century Spain), while others highlight its transgressive or liberating aspects as evidenced by many Latin American voices on this subject (José Lezama Lima and Severo Sarduy, to mention two prominent examples). Yet, even in those instances in which the Baroque as a category of analysis was used to focus on questions of alterity and difference, it might be seen less as being opposed to rationality than as a way of dealing with the many paradoxes and problematic elements that are ignored by reason in order to achieve its desired coherence. Those elements are highlighted as part of an encompassing worldview that is not troubled by the bizarre, the contradictory, and the obscure; they are elements which are everywhere to be seen in moments of radical spiritual and epistemic crises such as those of Early and Late Modernity.

In conjunction with the Baroque of the Spanish seventeenth century, especially the poetic practice of Francisco de Quevedo and Luis de Góngora, it has been argued that it was anticipated by the theoretical writings of Juan de Herrera insofar as their poetic subjects were not solid, unified entities. Thus, the self-contained package that was the renaissance sonnet of Juan Boscán explodes into ludic linguistic practices which would eventually evolve to evoke the precarious ontology of a time obsessed with the degeneration of all things human. (See Leah Middlebrook in this volume.) Similarly, the modern subject would arise "from a moment of absolute negativity and madness," which makes one question the notion of a clear break between baroque and rationalist approaches to subject construction, as shown in the case of Baltasar Gracián whose orthodox treatment of *desengaño* is said to underlie a nihilism that belies the official doctrine of the post-Tridentine Church (see Bradley Nelson in this volume).

The heterogeneity that is present within the Baroque—and that has been emphasized by contemporary thinkers and artists—cannot be naively understood as the reflection of an unproblematic acceptance of otherness in early modern cultures. If indeed the Hegelian construct of modernity mentioned earlier ignored a great part of the world, it is also true that the dynamics of exclusion were operative in those same regions, meaning that the South of Europe did not lag behind in the creation of its own "souths" of alienation: for centuries, Moors, Jews, *moriscos*, women, heretics, Amerindians, and other groups suffered the repression of institutional systems eager to suppress "unreasonable" differences in order to build unified communities, as *Reason and Its Others* shows. Thus, it was often the case that dominant social discourses during the period in question showed a reliance on rumor—as demonstrated by the Inquisition's *libros de testificaciones*—which is seen as being antithetical to debates based on rationality (see Childers in this volume.) This same line of argumentation is extended to various historical and geographical contexts to explore the work of various women authors in order to recover common traces that contest normative sexual representations (see Dugaw and Powell in this volume.)

This volume finds an appealing middle ground between the need to anchor its topics in precise geographical contexts and the urge to contest the national models which have traditionally dominated the writing of cultural history. Those models have often ignored the linguistic and ethnic diversity present within national boundaries (see Moraña, *Ideologies of Hispanism*), thus reproducing and/or feeding the states' centralistic strategies of suppression of troublesome disparities or "impurities" which could potentially undermine their project of unification and homogenization.

In *Reason and Its Others* there is an emphasis on difference, which the contributors have found mostly within discourses already established as "central" to an understanding of the cultures that are being studied. Thus, with few exceptions, the contrapunctual voices heard in many of the essays belong to authors who might be called "dissidents" from the system to which they were initially ascribed (for example, las Casas was initially an *encomendero* and later a bishop; Cervantes, a soldier and a tax collector). Las Casas's critique of imperialism (see Mariscal in this volume), Galileo's defense of autonomy of thought (see Battistini in this volume), or Cervantes' antiauthoritarian writing and the emphasis in many of his texts on the interplay between the rational and the irrational (see respectively Baena and Egginton in this volume) which extends to the treatment of imperialism through the topic of anthropophagi (see Greer in this volume) are examples of a contestatory practice which today finds special resonance within the academy, as master narratives have come increasingly into question and the notions of "difference" and "otherness" are brought into ever greater relief.

In his discussion of the importance of Cervantes as a novelist, Milan Kundera was to observe that there exist two separate, distinct, and counterbalancing traditions in Western writing: one characterized by Cervantes' "wisdom of uncertainty," which uses a language of "relativity and ambiguity"; another involving Descartes' philosophical discourse of certainty which privileges intellectual abstraction and a reduction of experience (Wihl 102). For the rationalist Descartes, astonishment or an excess of wonder needed to be restrained by reason, as Cascardi reminds us in this volume. Yet, many of the texts discussed in *Reason and Its Others* offer an understanding of the limits of reason and demonstrate awareness on the part of thinkers and artists of the need to expand its boundaries by making them permeable to other voices. Giambattista Vico is said to have distinguished between the "certainties of physics" and the "uncertainty of morality," and unlike Descartes' followers, who related imagination to "obscure impulses of the body," he revindicated its role in the social and political spheres (see Contarini in this volume). The importance of Vico in this discussion is also highlighted in this volume by Giuseppe Mazzotta, who focuses on how the universal principles of the New Science needed to be validated through an analysis of environments that are outside the bounds of European history. To antiquarians (philosophers of history and philologists) and travel writers who wrote to sell books, Vico is said to have preferred the ethnographic/theological tradition that stressed the heterogeneity and singularity of Amerindian and European cultures rather than a narrative that privileged a universalist, rational, and homogeneous approach to self-knowledge and knowledge of the other.

There are many other attempts to expand the bounds of European reason, and one might say that Spanish colonial expansion both in the New World and in Europe also offered practical responses to abstract rationalizations. For example, one might point to the utopian project of the Jesuits among the Amerindians, especially the Guaraní, as they sought to create an "other" modernity, one that "could achieve a level of political and economic development without paying the price of a theology of inequality that was unfolding in the Protestant sphere" (see Ordóñez in this volume); or, one might focus on a less benign rhetoric of otherness that was to dominate baroque anthropology, one that displaces the alternative model of Las Casas and his egalitarian message in favor of seeing the Amerindians as false and treacherous people (see R. de la Flor in this volume).

Moving away from the conventional orientation toward national mappings of cultural phenomena, the volume explores the convergences and confrontations of forces and ideas that have a presence beyond political borders. This becomes especially important when dealing with a time period, Early Modernity, when the expansion of European powers such as Spain was a prominent factor, making an understanding of essential issues very difficult without taking into account tensions at the regional (i.e., Mediterranean) and global levels. Such processes are illustrated by the essays that deal with the Spanish colonial enterprises in America but also in Italy, a presence that has not received much attention from Hispanists. The Treaty of Cateau-Cambrésis (1559) recognized Spanish hegemony over Italy and marked the official beginning of several centuries of direct political influences and cultural exchanges, which operated in both directions. Giulio Cesare Capaccio's *Il Forastiero* (1634), an anti-Machiavellian treatise on good government which defends the established sociopolitical and religious order in Naples under the Spanish crown, is a case in point. Capaccio writes against a background of violence within Neapolitan society, and his narrative voice is clearly on the side of a Spanish elite threatened by unruly commoners who were soon to rebel against aristocratic colonial rule (Maraniello revolt, 1647) only to see their hopes dashed through even greater repression (see Marino in this volume).

Reason and Its Others challenges us to question the certainties of reason and the instrumentalization to which it often leads. This challenge is made even more urgent by the events of the twentieth century—a time of unprecedented technological and scientific growth as well as unparalleled violence and genocide—and the need to analyze its origins and dynamics. People such as Dussel and Mignolo have argued for alternative epistemic constructions, pointing variously to a "reason of the other," "postcolonial reason" (Dussel), or "subaltern reason" and the possibilities that it offers to contest modernity (Mignolo 96). One can thus focus on different loci of enunciation present, for example, in the beginning of colonial expansion by figures such as Guamán Poma de Ayala (Mignolo) as well as within alternative spaces of thought within the European contexts, as those represented, for example, by Vico, Cervantes, and other "dissidents" of reason discussed in many of the essays that constitute this volume.

Works Cited

Bal, Mieke. *Quoting Caravaggio: Contemporary Art, Preposterous History*. Chicago: University of Chicago Press, 1999.

Benjamin, Walter. *The Origin of German Tragic Drama*. Trans. John Osborne. London and New York: Verso, 1998.

Buci-Glucksmann, Christine. *Orlan, triomphe du baroque*. Marseille: Images en Manoeuvres, 2000.

Croce, Benedetto. "Spanish Culture in Italy in the Seventeenth Century." *Hispania*. Vol. 10, No. 6. (December 1927): 383–88.

Dussel, Enrique. *The Invention of the Americas: Eclipse of "the Other" and the Myth of Modernity*. Trans. Michael D. Barber. New York: Continuum, 1995.

Kundera, Milan."The Depreciated Legacy of Cervantes." *The Art of the Novel*. Trans. Linda Asher. New York: Harper and Row, 1988. 3–20.

Maravall, José Antonio. *Culture of the Baroque*. Trans. Terry Cochran. Minneapolis: University of Minnesota Press, 1986.

Marías, Julián. *History of Philosophy*. New York: Dover Publications, 1967.

Mignolo, Walter. *Global History/Local Designs: Coloniality, Subaltern Knowledges, and Border Thinking*. Princeton, NJ: Princeton University Press, 2000.

Moraña, Mabel, ed. *Ideologies of Hispanism*. Hispanic Issues 30. Nashville, TN: Vanderbilt University Press, 2005.

Spadaccini, Nicholas, and Luis Martín-Estudillo. "The Baroque and the Cultures of Crises." *Hispanic Baroques: Reading Cultures in Context*. Ed. Nicholas Spadaccini and Luis Martín-Estudillo. Hispanic Issues 31. Nashville, TN: Vanderbilt University Press, 2005. ix–xxxvi.

Turner, Bryan S. "Introduction." In *Baroque Reason: The Aesthetics of Modernity*, by Christine Buci-Glucksmann, 3–36. London: Sage, 1994.

Weber, Max. *The Protestant Ethic and the Spirit of Capitalism*. New York: Scribner, 1976.

Wihl, Gary. "Novels as Theories in a Liberal Society." *Constructive Criticism: The Human Sciences in the Age of Theory*. Ed. Martin Kreiswirth and Thomas Carmichael. Toronto: University of Toronto Press, 1995. 101–13.

◆ Contributors

Julio Baena is Associate Professor of Spanish at the University of Colorado, Boulder. The focus of his work has been the double issue of critical theory implied by the emergence of the modern novel and the modern praxis of poetic language in Spain's late Sixteenth/early Seventeenth centuries. He is the author of *El Poemario de Fray Luis de León* (1989); *El círculo y la flecha: principio y fin, triunfo y fracaso del Persiles* (1996); and *Discordancias cervantinas* (2003). He has also published two books of poetry.

Andrea Battistini is Professor of Italian Literature at the University of Bologna. He has edited the *Works of Giambattista Vico* and *Galileo Galilei's Sidereus Nuncius*. His books include *La degnita' della retorica*; *Lo specchio di Dedalo: Autobiografia e biografia*; *Il barocco: cultura, miti, immagini*; *Galileo e i gesuiti: Miti letterari e retorica della scienza*; *Sondaggi sul Novecento*, and *Vico tra antichi e moderni*.

Anthony J. Cascardi is Interim Dean of Arts and Humanities at the University of California, is the Margaret and Sidney Ancker Professor in the Departments of Comparative Literature, Spanish, and rhetoric, and Director of the Consortium for the Arts and the Art Research Center. He is the general editor of the Penn State series in literature and Philosophy and author and editor of numerous books and articles, including *The Limits of Illusion: A Critical Study of Calderón*, *The Bounds of Reason: Cervantes, Dostoevsky, Flaubert, Literature and the Question of Philosophy*, *The Subject of Modernity*, *Ideologies of History in the Spanish Golden Age*, *Consequences of Enlightenment: Aesthetics as Critique*, and *The Cambridge Companion to Cervantes*.

David R. Castillo is Associate Professor of Romance Languages and Literatures at the State University of New York at Buffalo. He is the author of *(A)wry Views: Anamorphosis, Cervantes and the Early Picaresque*. He has published articles on Cervantes, Gracián, the picaresque, the Comedia, and other aspects of Spanish Golden Age culture. At present he is working on a book tentatively titled *Baroque Gallery of Horrors and Curiosities: Dark Fantasies in the Spanish Golden Age*.

William Childers is Associate Professor of Spanish at Brooklyn College, CUNY. University of Toronto Press will publish his first book, *Transnational Cervantes*, in 2006. His current research combines literary and archival sources to reconstruct relations between Moriscos and other social groups in early modern Spain.

Silvia Contarini is Researcher of Italian Literature at the University of Udine. Her research focuses primarily on eighteenth-century aesthetics, travel literature and medicine. She is the author of *"Il mistero della macchina sensibile." Teorie delle passioni da Descartes e Alfieri*. She has edited the Italian version of *Premier voyage dans l'intérieur de l'Afrique* by François Levaillant and *Discorso sull'indole del piacere e del dolore* by Pietro Verri.

Dianne Dugaw is Professor of English at the University of Oregon. Her books include *"Deep Play"—John Gay & the Invention of Modernity*; *The Anglo-American Ballad*, editor; and *Warrior Women and Popular Balladry, 1650–1850* for which she has recorded a CD, *Dangerous Examples—Fighting & Sailing Women in Song* (see http://www.cdbaby.com/dugaw). She has written articles on eighteenth-century literature and culture, Anglo-American folklore, and women's and gender studies. Her current book project is a study of baroque culture in seventeenth-century Britain, emphasizing links to Spain and Catholicism.

William Egginton is Associate Professor of Romance Languages and Literatures and Comparative Literature at the State University of New York at Buffalo. He is the author of *How The World Became a Stage: Presence, Theatricality, and the Question of Modernity*, *Perversity and Ethics*, and *A Wrinkle in History: Essays in Literature and Philosophy* (forthcoming).

Margaret R. Greer is Professor of Spanish and Chair of the Department of Romance Studies, Duke University. Her publications include: *María de Zayas Tells Baroque Tales of Love and the Cruelty of Men*; *The Play of Power: Mythological Court Dramas of Pedro Calderón de la Barca*; editions of two Calderón de la Barca plays; and a special issue of the *Journal of Medieval and Modern Studies, Decolonizing the Middle Ages*, edited with John Dagenais. Current books projects include *Approaches to Teaching Early Modern Spanish Drama* (with Laura Bass), a book on early modern Spanish tragedy, and a book on hunting.

Nathalie Hester is Assistant Professor of Italian and French in the Department of Romance languages at the University of Oregon. Her scholarly interests include early modern travel literature, historiography, theater, and women's writing. She has published articles in *Bibliotheque d'Humanisme et Renaissance*, *Modern Philology*, *Annali d'Italianistica*, and *Romance Languages Annual*. She is currently completing a book on seventeenth-century Italian travel writing.

Massimo Lollini is Hatzantonis Distinguished Fellow in Italian and Romance Languages at the University of Oregon. He has written widely on seventeenth- and eighteenth-century literature. He is the author of *Le muse, le maschere e il sublime: Giambattista Vico e la poesia nell'età della "ragione spiegata"* and *Il vuoto della forma: Scrittura, testimonianza e verità*, which includes essays on Dante, Petrarch, Galileo Galilei, Renato Serra, Antonio Gramsci, Italo Calvino, Primo Levi, and Paul Celan. He is presently working on a manuscript on the European idea of autobiography.

John A. Marino is Professor of Early Modern European History at the University of California, San Diego. He is the author of *Pastoral Economics in the Kingdom of Naples*, and editor or co-editor of *Good Government in Spanish Naples*; *Early Modern History and the Social Sciences: Testing the Limits of Braudel's Mediterranean*; *Early Modern Italy 1550–1796*; *A Renaissance of Conflicts: Visions and Revisions of Law and Society in Italy and Spain*; and *Spain in Early Modern Italy: Politics, Society and Religion* (forthcoming).

George Mariscal is Professor of Spanish and Chicano Cultures at the University of California, San Diego. He is currently director of the Chicano/a~Latino/a Arts and Humanities Program and co-director of the California Cultures in Comparative Perspective Program. He is an active member of Project YANO, a counter-recruitment and antimilitarism organization in San Diego. His most recent book is *Brown-eyed Children of the Sun: Lessons from the Chicano Movement, 1965–1975*. He is also the author of *Contradictory Subjects: Quevedo, Cervantes, and Seventeenth-Century Spanish Culture*.

Luis Martín-Estudillo is Assistant Professor of Spanish and Cultural Studies at the University of Iowa. He has published several articles on Spanish literature and cultural history in American and European journals and is co-author of the book *Libertad y límites. El Barroco hispánico* and co-editor of *Hispanic Baroques: Reading Cultures in Context* . His research interests include the relationships between early modern and contemporary aesthetics and epistemologies. He is co-director of *Ex Libris, Revista de Poesía*.

Giuseppe Mazzotta is the Sterling Professor of Humanities for Italian at Yale University. He has written a number of essays about every century of Italian literary history. His books include *Dante, Poet of the Desert: History and Allegory in the Divine Comedy*; *The World at Play in Boccaccio's Decameron*; *Dante's Vision and the Circle of Knowledge*; *The Worlds of Petrarch*; *The New Map of the World: the Poetic Philosophy of Giambattista Vico*; and *Cosmopoiesis: The Renaissance Experiment*.

Leah Middlebrook is Assistant Professor of Comparative Literature and Romance Languages at the University of Oregon. She has published articles on Petrarchism, on poetics and body politics, and on comparative issues in Spanish and French theater. She is currently completing work on her first book, *Imperial Lyric: The Politics of Form in Early Modern Spain*.

Bradley J. Nelson is Associate Professor and Chair of Classics, Modern Languages and Linguistics at Concordia University in Montreal. His work has appeared in the *Bulletin of the Comediantes, Cervantes, Gestos* and several volumes of the series Hispanic Issues. He has recently completed a manuscript on emblematic and allegorical modes of discourse in early modern Spain entitled *The Persistence of Presence: Emblem and Ritual in Early Modern Spain*.

Fernando Ordóñez is Graduate Instructor at the University of Minnesota, where he specializes in early modern Spain and colonial Latin America. He has taught in Uruguay and has held research fellowships in Italy. He is co-author of *Estudios socio-religiosos en el Uruguay* and has participated in many research projects dealing with social and cultural issues in Spain and Latin America. He is the former executive director of the OBSUR social science research center in Montevideo, Uruguay.

Amanda Powell is Senior Instructor of Spanish/Latin American literature and literary translation at the University of Oregon. Her translations of poetry and prose appear in *Untold Sisters: Hispanic Nuns in Their Own Works*. She has edited and translated *The Answer/La Respuesta by Juana Inés de la Cruz* (with Electa Arenal); *A Wild Country Out in the Garden: The Spiritual Journals of a Colonial Mexican Nun* (with Kathleen A. Myers); and *Book for the Hour of Recreation, a "Protofeminist" Defense of Teresa of Avila by María Salazar* (with Alison Weber). She has written on sixteenth and seventeenth century Spanish and Colonial Latin American women writers, convent writings, and sapphic lyric.

Fernando Rodríguez de la Flor is Professor of Spanish literature at the Universidad de Salamanca and member of the San Fernando Royal Academy of the Arts (Real Academia de Bellas Artes de San Fernando). He has written on different aspects of the Hispanic Baroque. He is the author of *Emblemas. Lecturas de la imagen simbólica; Política y fiesta en el barroco*; *La peninsula metafísica: arte, literatura y pensamiento en la España de la contrarreforma*; and *Barroco: Representación e ideología en el mundo hispánico*. His current work includes two books in press: *La era melancólica, figuras del ordenamiento barroco* and *Pasiones frías: Disimulación y secreto en el barroco hispano*.

Nicholas Spadaccini is Professor of Spanish and Comparative Literature at the University of Minnesota. He has published books, editions, and collective volumes, with an emphasis on early modern Spain and Latin America. His most recent studies include *Libertad y límites. El Barroco hispánico* (co-authored) and *Hispanic Baroques: Reading Cultures in Context* (co-edited). He is currently completing a book on Cervantes and the culture of crisis of baroque Spain. He is editor-in-chief of the Hispanic Issues series.

Index

Compiled by Nicole M. Schiro

Adorno, Theodor, 204, 213-218, 331
aesthetics, 24, 82, 96, 120, 128, 204, 222-224, 227-230, 232, 234, 237-238
Alciato, Andrea, 97, 156, 162
Aligheri, Dante. 77
Alonso, Carlos, 91, 99, 174, 182-183, 286
Amiel, Charles, 182-183
Andreadis, Harriette, 139
Ariosto, Lodovico, 28, 49, 58, 158
Aristotle, 9, 11, 17, 20, 24, 30, 43, 51, 105, 114, 118, 121, 138, 226-227, 229, 237, 263, 281, 293, 323, 327
Arriaga, Pablo Joseph de, 245, 256
Ashcroft, Bill, 311, 314
Ashfield, Andrew, 237-238
Augustine, Saint, 43, 47, 51, 138, 247, 254, 271, 317-321, 327, 330
Avellaneda, Alonso, F. de, 205, 218
Avilés, Luis F., 202
Axtell, James, 314
Ayala, Jorge M., 79, 98, 248, 332, 338

Bacco, Henrico, 159, 162
Baena, Julio, 188-189, 199-202, 218, 336
Baffetti, G., 10, 35
Baglioni, Tommaso, 7, 36
Bailey, J.O., 28, 35

Bakhtin, Mikhail Mikhailovich, 89, 98
Bal, Mieke, 332, 338
Baldwin, Anna, 128, 139-141
Banfi, A., 7, 35
Barash, Carol, 138-139
Baraz, Daniel, 281-282, 293
Barker, Francis, 293-294
baroque, 6, 8, 11, 17, 24, 79-81, 84-85, 92-93, 95, 123, 128, 135, 137, 139, 145, 151-152, 186-190, 192, 195, 197-199, 206, 208, 212, 222-225, 227-230, 232, 237-238, 251, 299-300, 334-335, 337-338
Barthes, Roland, 209, 216, 218, 220
Bartra, Roger, 244, 256
Basile, G., 20, 35
Bataillon, Marcel, 267, 277
Batllori, Miguel, 79, 98
Battistini, Andrea, 3, 46, 58, 60, 329-330, 333, 336
Baudrillard, Jean, 208, 218
Baumgärtel, Bettina, 138, 140
Beebee, Thomas, 304, 308-309, 311-312, 314
Behn, Aphra, 125-127, 134-137, 139-140
Bell, Catherine, 80-81, 83-85, 88-89, 93-94, 98, 122
Bellone, E., 34-35

Benjamin, Walter, 276, 334, 338
Bentley, Jerry H., 159, 162
Benvenga, Michele, 160, 163
Bergmann, Emilie, 139, 140
Bernardo Ares, José Manuel de, 168, 183
Bernat Vistarini, Antonio, 98
Biagioli, Marco, 111-112, 120
Blumenberg, H., 35
Bollas, Christopher, 279, 294
Bonet, Juan Pablo, 249, 256
Bontempelli, M., 21, 34-35
Borja, Juan de, 92, 98
Boscán Almogaver, Juan, 77
Bourdieu, Pierre, 87, 98, 170, 214
Bouza, Fernando, 167, 183
Boyce, Elizabeth S., 137, 139, 141
Brecht, B. B., 10, 25, 35
Bruno, Giordano, 11, 20-21
Buci-Glucksmann, Christine, 334, 338-339
Burgaleto, Claudio M., 329-330
Burke, E., 24, 35, 221, 23-8
Burke, Peter, 24, 183, 221
Butler, Judith, 75-77

Cabanelas, Darío, 182-183
Cachey, Theodore, Jr., 117, 121
Calderón de la Barca, Pedro, 121, 238
Caloprese, Gregorio, 41, 43, 46-58
Calvino, I., 8, 18, 28, 35
Camporesi, P., 27, 34-35
Cantillo, Clementina, 57-58
Capacco, Giulio Cesare, 158, 162
capitalism, 292, 312, 333-334
Caraman, Philip, 304-305, 310-311, 314
Caravita, Gregorio, 116, 121
Cardillac, Louis, 244, 256
Casalduero, Joaquín, 200, 202

Cascardi, Anthony, 65, 68, 77, 79, 81, 85, 90, 98, 215, 218, 221, 336
Casini, P., 15, 27, 36
Castelli, B., 8, 10, 14, 25, 29, 36
Castillo, David R., 77, 86-87, 96, 98, 188-189, 200, 202, 207, 209, 218, 332
Castro, Américo, 78, 200, 202, 215, 217-218, 246, 256, 291
Castro, Diego de, 78, 200, 215, 217, 246, 256, 291
Catholicism, 106, 109, 117-118, 124, 134, 138, 147, 153, 175, 233, 259-261, 263, 266, 273, 276, 285, 287, 296-297, 300, 303-304
Cavaillé, J.P., 21, 36
Certeau, Michel de, 202, 208
Cervantes Saavedra, Miguel de, 294
Cervantes, Miguel de, 99, 186, 188-203, 205, 208-209, 213-214, 216-219, 222, 226, 231-232, 235-238, 275, 280, 283-288, 290, 292, 294-295, 336, 338
Checa, Jorge, 90, 99
Chevalley, C., 7, 36
Chiodo, Carmine, 116, 121
Christianity, 30, 49-50, 55, 65, 68, 100, 106, 128, 138, 142, 150, 153, 156, 171, 174, 176-178, 180, 185, 205, 211, 244-247, 250, 252-254, 260-264, 266, 270-272, 275, 277, 282-283, 286, 301, 304, 319-320, 322, 326, 328, 332, 334
Cioni, A., 7, 36
Cirillo, Niccolò, 41, 42, 58
Clamurro, William H., 200, 202
classical, 114, 126, 128, 131, 136-137, 139, 150, 159, 223, 228, 247, 263, 267, 281, 308, 321

Cochrane, Eric, 159-163
Colapietra, Raffaele, 159, 162
Collard, Andrée, 237-238
Collenuccio, Pandolfo, 147-148, 152, 159, 162-163
Colombardo, Gernando, 140
colonization, 29, 250-251, 253, 264, 286, 301, 312, 326, 333
Columbus, Christopher, 29, 105, 140, 259, 282, 289-290, 294-295, 303, 317, 322, 329-330
Congilio, Giuseppe, 159, 163
Conley, Tom, 99, 118, 121
Contardi, B., 21, 36
Contarini, Silvia, 39, 46, 52, 58, 337
Conti, Vittorio, 57-58
Contreras, Jaime, 182-183, 256
Corominas, Joan, 133, 140, 237
Correa Calderón, E., 79, 99
Cortázar, Julio, 219
Costo, Tommaso, 145, 147-150, 152, 158-160, 163
Cottingham, John, 46, 58
Counter Reformation, 79, 81-82, 96
Cozzi, Gaetano, 4, 30, 36
Croce, Benedetto, 57, 60, 333, 338
Cruz, Anne, 77-78, 126, 140, 182, 184, 206, 219
Cruz, San Juan de la, 77-78, 126, 140, 182, 184, 206, 219

Daly, Peter M., 99
Damasio, Antonio R., 82, 99
Darst, David, 76-78
De Armas, Frederick A., 294
de Bolla, Peter, 237
De Liguori, Girolamo, 42, 58
De Maio, Romeo, 42, 58
De Rentiis, Dina, 201-202

Dedieu, Jean-Pierre, 182-183
Deleuze, Gilles, 87, 99, 187, 189-190, 201-202, 204, 214, 218-219
Della Casa, Giovanni, 52-53, 57, 59
Derrida, Jacques, 184, 187, 196, 201-203, 205, 207, 214, 219
Descartes, René, 16, 36, 39-54, 58-60, 82, 95, 99, 102, 235-236, 238, 317, 324, 331, 336
Deumeau, Jean, 314
Di Capua, Leonardo, 39, 42, 46, 59
Díaz Esteban, Francisco, 256
Dini, Alessandro, 59
Dixon, Annette, 138, 140, 142
Doiron, Normand, 102, 113, 115, 117, 120-121
Donne, John, 22, 34, 36, 132-133, 140-141
D'Ors, Eugenio, 238
Dover, Kenneth, 129, 140, 338
Dudley, Edward, 209, 219
Dugaw, Dianne, 123, 138-140, 336
Durston, Alan, 314
Dussel, Enrique, 253, 256, 296-299, 301, 305, 314, 331-333, 338

Echeverría, Bolívar, 82, 99
Edwards, John, 183-184
Egginton, William, 75, 78, 80-81, 83, 93, 96, 99, 169-170, 184, 186, 217, 336
El Saffar, Ruth, 200-202
empire, 128, 150, 243, 260, 266-267, 284, 297, 299, 302, 306, 308-309, 318, 326, 329, 333
Enlightenment, 55, 61, 83, 90, 142, 165, 169, 181, 214, 216, 228, 298, 300, 313, 325, 331
Epalza, Mikel de, 184

Erasmus, Desiderius, 97, 246, 261-263, 273, 275, 277, 303
Escobar, Matías de, 250, 256
Espinosa Medrano, Juan, 252, 256
Ettinghausen, Henry, 182, 184
evangelization, 254, 280, 300, 309

Fish, Max H., 59
Florencia, Francisco de, 251, 256
Floristán, Casiano, 301, 314
Forcione, Alban, 92, 99, 200-201, 203, 208, 219
Foucault, Michel, 11, 36, 89, 181, 184, 205, 206, 216, 219
Fox, Christopher, 140, 152
Fraser, Nancy, 181, 184
Freccero, John, 75, 78
Freud, Sigmund, 141, 190, 193, 203
Friedman, Edward H., 201, 203
Fuchs, Barbara, 197, 199, 202, 203

Gadamer, Hans-Georg, 79, 81, 90, 99
Galilei, Galileo, 3, 34, 36-38, 333
Gallego-Morell, Antonio, 78
Galluzzi, Paolo, 36-37, 120-121
Garau, Francisco, 244, 256
García Arenal, Mercedes, 179, 184
García Calvo, Agustín, 205, 213, 217, 219
García Cárcel, Ricardo, 255-256
García de Enterría, María Cruz, 182, 184
García Icazbalceta, Joaquín, 256
Garin, E., 34, 36, 57
Gebhardt, Jürgen, 59
Gemelli Careri, Giovanni Francesco, 117, 121
Gentile, Giovanni, 150
Gerli, E. Michael, 207, 209, 217, 219
Gianturco, Elio, 329-330
Ginzburg, Carlo, 255-256

Giovio, P., 17, 36
Giovo, Niccolò, 49, 53-55, 57, 59
Gitlitz, D.M., 256
Gitlitz, David Martín, 256
Gjertsen, D., 36
Godoy Alcántara, José, 182, 184
Gómez, Fernando, 312, 314
Gracián, Baltasar, 79-100, 169, 184, 233, 235-236, 238, 245, 335
Green, Roland A., 63, 75, 77-78
Greenblatt, Stephen, 105, 121
Greer, Margaret R., 294, 336
Grimaldi, Costantino, 42-43, 59
Gronda, Giovanna, 52, 59
Gruzinski, Sergei, 249, 256
Guaragnella, P., 31, 36
Guattari, Félix, 187, 201, 204, 218-219
Guerrini, Luigi, 59
Guglielminetti, Marziano, 120-121
Guha, Ranajit, 172, 184
Gumbrecht, Hans Ulrich, 80, 99
Guzmán, Juan de, 141, 234, 238

Habermas, Jürgen, 165-166, 170-171, 181, 184
Hagarty, Miguel José, 182, 184
Hägglund, Martin, 199, 203
Hammond, Paul, 136, 140
Hanke, Louis, 255-256, 275
Harbison, Robert, 228, 231, 238
Hartog, François, 280, 294
Hauser, Arnold, 208, 212-213, 217, 219
Heng, Geraldine, 282, 286, 294
Heraclitus, 205-206, 213, 217, 219
Hernández, Máximo, 178-179, 183, 255-256
Herodotus, 280-281, 289-290, 294, 325
Horkheimer, Max, 204, 213-217, 331
Horozco y Covarrubias, Juan de, 99
Howe, Elizabeth Teresa, 201, 203

Huarte de San Juan, Juan, 91, 99, 206, 215, 226, 238
Huergo, Humberto, 207, 219
Hughes, Aaron, 128-129, 138, 140
Hulme, Peter, 291, 293-294
Humanism, 62, 64- 67, 74, 109, 147, 157, 284, 329-330, 332
Hume, David, 236-237, 239
Hutton, Sarah, 128, 140-141

Ioly Zorratini, Pier Cesare, 257
Iverson, Margaret, 293

Jaffe, Irma, 137, 140
Jiménez Montserrín, Miguel, 182, 184
José A, Walter, 37, 80, 96, 99, 169, 184, 219, 302, 314, 330, 338

Kadir, Djelal, 329-330
Kagan, Richard L., 168, 184
Kant, Immanuel, 21, 169, 221-222, 224-225, 228, 237, 239
Kaplan, Caren, 61-62, 64, 71, 75, 78
Kepler, J., 7-9, 16, 20, 23, 26, 28-29, 33, 35-36
Killigrew, Anne, 125, 137, 140
King, Willard F., 101-102, 132, 140, 153, 209, 286, 291, 294, 307
Koyré, A., 11, 15, 36
Kraye, Jill, 129, 140
Kristeva, Julia, 219
Kundera, Milan, 336, 338
Kuznecov, Boris G, 9, 35, 36

Lachterman, David, 59
Laqueur, Thomas, 123, 141
Las Casas, Bartolomé de, 259-261, 264-278, 289, 326-327, 336
Lempriere, John, 136, 141
León Pinelo, Antonio de, 255, 257

Leone, Giuseppe, 214
Leopardi, G., 12, 28, 33, 37
Lettere, Vera, 33, 35, 38, 42, 53-54, 57, 60, 122, 160, 163
Lévi-Strauss, Claude, 212, 219
Levy, Evonne, 233, 239
Lojacono, Ettore, 41, 43, 59
Lollini, Massimo, 56, 59, 332
Longinus, 223, 226-227, 237, 239
López García, José Tomás, 255, 257
López Pinciano, Alonzo, 234, 239
López, Gregorio, 100, 178, 219-220, 234, 239, 255, 257, 304
Losada, Angel, 258, 261-264, 275, 278
Lovejoy, A.O., 20, 37
Loyola, S. Ignacio de, 99, 138, 206, 220, 231, 239, 295, 304, 306
Lupher, David A., 288, 290, 294

Macksey, Richard, 223, 237, 239
Maczak, Antoni, 117, 121
Magalotti, Lorenzo, 111, 113, 117, 122
mannerism, 206-209, 212-213, 215-217, 229
Maravall, José Antonio, 9, 37, 80-82, 84-85, 91-93, 96, 99, 169, 184, 199, 203, 211-212, 217, 219, 222, 301-303, 314, 329-330, 334, 338
Marías, Julián, 331, 338
Martín de Nicolás, Juan, 183, 185
Martín-Estudillo, Luis, 331, 338-339
Martínez-San Miguel, Yolanda, 141
Masi, Giorgio, 159, 163
Mattei, R. de, 329, 330
Maya Pons, Frank, 290, 294
Mazzella, Scipione, 149, 150, 152, 160, 163
Mazzola, Roberto, 46, 59
Mazzotta, Giuseppe, 316, 329, 330, 337
Medcalf, Stephen, 138, 141

352 INDEX

Meijjer, Maaike, 141
Mendieta, Jerónimo de, 249, 252, 254, 257
Menocal, Maria, 77-78
Middlebrook, Leah, 61, 116, 139-140, 335
Middleton, William Edgar Knowles, 120, 122
Mignolo, Walter, 298-300, 303, 314, 331, 338
Milbank, John, 329-330
Milhou, Alain, 255, 257
modernity, 26, 61-63, 65, 69, 71-72, 74-75, 80, 83, 85, 87, 95-96, 102-103, 110, 114, 117-118, 120, 123-125, 128, 136, 155, 165, 167-168, 170-172, 176, 181-183, 186, 188, 221, 223-224, 226, 273-274, 279-281, 296-299, 303, 306, 311, 313,-314, 327, 331-335, 337-338
Molho, Maurice, 96, 99, 200, 203
Molina, Tirso de, 225, 280, 288, 290, 294, 326
Monk, Samuel, 228, 239
Morales, Ambrosio de, 284, 288, 294
Moraña, Isabel, 255, 257, 338
Morreale de Castro, Margherita, 78
Mújica Pinilla, Ramón, 246, 255, 257
Mut, Vicente, 255, 257

Nancy, Jean-Luc, 92, 99, 181, 184
Navarrete, Ignacio, 73, 76, 78
Negri, Francesco, 101-122, 333
Neubauer, Hans-Joachim, 171-172, 185
Nicolson, M.H., 22, 33-35, 37
Nigro, Salvatore, 160, 163
Novellino, Pasquale, 158, 160-161, 163
Nussbaum, Martha C., 51, 59
Nuzzo, Enrico, 43, 47, 59

Ocampo, Florián de, 294
Olivares, Julián, 137, 139, 141, 151
Orgel, Stephen, 138, 141
Osbat, Luciano, 42, 60

Paden, William D., 141
Pagden, Anthony, 122, 255, 257, 295, 329-330
Paleotti, Gabriele, 233, 239
Parish, Helen-Rand, 275-278
Pastor, beatriz, 255, 257
Pelegrin, Benito, 79, 99
Peralta, Ceferino, 215-216
Percas de Ponseti, Helena, 200-203
Petrinovich, Lewis F., 279, 284, 294
Philips, Katherine, 131-133, 139, 141
Piazza, G., 35, 37
Picinelli, F., 19, 34, 37
Pico della Mirandola, Giovanni, 12, 332
Pirandello, L., 22-23, 37
Pizarro y Orellana, Fernando, 290-291, 294
Plato, 43, 123, 128-129, 138, 140, 226
Pliny, 106, 118, 122, 280, 294
Pliny the Elder, 122
Pontano, Giovanni Gioviano, 147-148, 159, 164
Porzio, Lucantonio, 42, 44-46, 48, 59-60
Powell, Amanda, 123, 133, 139, 140-141, 336
Prosperi, Adriano, 119, 122
public sphere, 55, 165-172, 176-178, 180-181

Quevedo, Francisco de, 74, 205-206, 220, 237, 335
Quint, D., 37, 78
Quiroga, Pedro de, 255, 257
Quondam, Amedeo, 59, 160, 164

R. de la Flor, Fernando, 85, 100, 243, 246, 255, 257
Raimondi, E., 13-14, 16, 33-34, 37
Rak, Michele, 42, 52, 60
Rama, Ángel, 246, 257
Ramírez Prado, Lorenzo, 257
Rappaport, Roy A., 94, 99
Read, Malcolm, 81-82, 87, 92, 98, 100
reason, 5, 7, 17, 19, 21, 24, 27, 30, 47, 48, 50, 52-53, 55-56, 62-63, 66, 70, 73, 75, 79, 82, 102-103, 110, 114, 123, 127, 129, 134, 137, 145, 156, 165, 169, 186, 187-189, 194, 196, 198-200, 204-208, 210-213, 215-216, 221-222, 226-227, 232, 235- 236, 238, 249, 252-253, 262, 264, 271-272, 279, 297-299, 306, 312, 319-320, 322, 327, 331, 333-338
Recuperati, Giuseppe, 42, 60
Redondi, P., 13, 37
Redondo, Augustín, 182, 185
Reeves, E., 17, 37
Reiger, Angelica, 139, 141
Reiss, Timothy J., 224, 239, 285, 292, 294
Renaissance, 38, 78, 96, 103, 118, 122, 128-129, 138, 140-141, 145-147, 158-159, 161, 164, 215, 229, 281-282, 294, 297-298, 303-304
Rey López, María, 220
Rey, Roselyne, 48, 60, 210, 217, 220
Ribadeneira, Pedro de, 247, 257
Ribadeneyra, Pedro de, 231, 239
Ricci, Virgilio, 116, 122, 326
Riccio, Monica, 46, 60
Righini, 15, 34, 37
Rivadeneira, Pedro de, 206, 220
Rivero Rodríguez, Manuel, 159, 164
Robb, Nesca, 138, 141

Rodríguez, Juan Carlos, 81-82, 85, 87, 96, 100, 159, 164
Roe, John, 138, 141
Rossi. P., 11, 12, 28, 34, 35, 37, 60
Rostworoski. María, 288-289, 294
Rubiés, Joan-Pau, 118, 120, 122
Ruibal García, A., 251, 257
Ruiz de Montoya, Antonio, 297, 304, 306-307, 314-315
Rupert de Ventos, Xavier, 312, 314

Saavedra Fajardo, Diego de, 19, 92, 100
Sacerdoti, G., 33, 37
Salecl, Renata, 97, 100
San José Palau, Félix, 183, 185
Sánchez Ferlosio, Rafael, 205, 207, 216, 220
Sánchez, Francisco, 81-82, 100, 205, 207, 216, 220, 257
Sarpi, P., 4-5, 30, 32, 35-36, 38
Sautman, Francesca Canadé, 139, 141
Savvedra Fajardo, D., 19, 38
science, 4-5, 7, 10, 12-13, 15-18, 20-28, 30-31, 34-35, 39, 42-44, 46, 50, 55-57, 80, 83, 104-105, 111, 113, 115-118, 120, 199, 215, 236, 312, 316-317, 319, 321-324, 326-328, 338
Sepúlveda, Juan Ginés de, 259-268, 270-273, 275, 277-278
Serrapica, Salvatore, 41, 57, 60
Sheingorn, Pamela, 139, 141
Sicardo, José, 254, 257
Silva, Jamie Theodoro de, 231-232, 255, 257
Simerka, Barbara, 274, 285, 294
Slaniceanu, Adriana, 201, 203
Slawinski, M., 10, 38
Smith, Paul Julian, 36, 74, 78, 209, 220
Snyder, Jon R., 158, 164

Sosio, L., 30, 38
Spadaccini, Nicholas, 81, 84, 87, 90, 99-100, 184, 203, 219, 331, 338-339
Spiller, Michael R. G., 78
Stagl, Justin, 121-122
Stanton, Domna, 137, 141
Starr-LeBeau, Gretchen D., 182, 185
Steele, Timothy, 77-78
Stewart, Susan, 66, 78
Strong, Roy, 138, 141
Subirats, Eduardo, 249, 258, 301, 312, 315
subjectivity, 6, 12, 14-17, 25, 45, 54, 57, 61-66, 69-71, 73, 75-76, 79-80, 82, 85-87, 89-97, 103, 105, 107, 114-115, 124-125, 131-132, 145, 160, 166, 169, 172-173, 176, 181, 187-188, 199, 201, 204-207, 218, 221-222, 225, 231-232, 249, 251-252, 254, 264, 267, 272, 279, 290, 300-302, 305, 309, 321, 325, 335
sublime, 24, 49, 53, 56, 59, 151-152, 221-231, 236-238, 251, 319
Summonte, Gio, 150, 152, 160, 164
Suppa, Silvio, 43, 57, 60

Tabarroni, G., 15, 29, 34, 36, 38
Talens, Jenaro, 81, 84, 87, 90, 99, 100, 184
Tasso, Torquato, 22, 48-52, 58, 60, 146, 148, 150-152, 158-159, 164
Tassoni, A., 27, 35, 38
Taylor, Peter James, 299, 315
Teresa de Jesús, 220
Tesauro, E., 17-19, 34, 37-38
Théo, Giambattista, 60
Thomas, Patrick, 51, 60, 131, 138, 141, 172, 308-309, 311, 314, 326, 339
Thorpe, Clarence DeWitt, 237, 239
Timberlake, Marie, 295, 313

Tooley, Marian J., 120, 122
Torrini, Maurizio, 42, 57-58, 60
Tozzi, Luca, 40-41, 60
Tullia d'Aragona, 138, 142
Turner, Bryan S., 83, 85, 89, 97, 100, 334, 339
Turner, Victor, 83, 85, 89, 97, 100, 334, 339
Tuzet, Hélène, 6, 38

Vaccalluzzo, N., 34, 38
Valencia, Pedro de, 248, 258
Valéry, P., 21, 34, 38
Valtierra, Angel, 255, 258
van Gemert, Lia, 137, 142
Vasoli, Cesare, 329-330
Verbeek, Théo, 40, 60
Vico, Giambattista, 41, 45-48, 55-60, 316-330, 336-338
Vidal, Hernán, 301, 315
Villamediana, Juan de Tassis, Conde de, 208-209, 220
Villari, Rosario, 34, 38, 160-161, 163-164, 255, 258
Villava, Francisco, 244, 258
Viola, Paolo, 119, 122
Violante del Cielo/do Ceu, 142
Virgil, 136, 158, 230, 236, 239, 289, 328
Viroli, Maurizio, 161, 164
Vitoria, Francisco de, 267, 276, 282, 295
Vives, Juan Luis, 214, 220
Voegelin, Eric, 321, 329, 330

Wahl, Elizabeth, 139, 142
Wallace, William A, 4, 31, 38
Weber, Max, 333, 339
Weidman, Harold E., 275-278
Weisbach, Werner, 230, 239
Welles, Marcia L., 203

Whitby, W., 295
White, Hayden, 118-119, 122
Wiener. Philip, 138, 142
Wiesner-Hanks, Merry, 138, 142
Wihl, Gary, 336, 339
Wilcox, Donald J., 160, 164
Williams, Raymond, 280, 295
Williamson, Edwin, 200, 203
Wis Murena, Cristina, 118, 122
Wollstonecraft, Mary, 124-125, 127, 131, 137-138, 142

Ximénez Patón, Bartolomé, 244, 258

Zamora, Margarita, 219, 282, 295
Zappullo, Michele, 150, 160, 164
Zayas, María de, 96
Žižek, Slavoj, 80, 83-85, 90, 92, 95, 100
Zugasti, Miguel, 289, 294-295
Zwartjes, Otto, 315

VOLUMES IN THE HISPANIC ISSUES SERIES

32 *Reason and Its Others: Italy, Spain, and the New World*,
    edited by David Castillo and Massimo Lollini
31 *Hispanic Baroques: Reading Cultures in Context*,
    edited by Nicholas Spadaccini and Luis Martín-Estudillo
30 *Ideologies of Hispanism*, edited by Mabel Moraña
29 *The State of Latino Theater in the United States: Hybridity,
    Transculturation, and Identity*, edited by Luis A. Ramos-García
28 *Latin America Writes Back. Postmodernity in the Periphery
    (An Interdisciplinary Perspective)*, edited by Emil Volek
27 *Women's Narrative and Film in Twentieth-Century Spain:
    A World of Difference(s)*, edited by Ofelia Ferrán and Kathleen M. Glenn
26 *Marriage and Sexuality in Medieval and Early Modern Iberia*,
    edited by Eukene Lacarra Lanz
25 *Pablo Neruda and the U.S. Culture Industry*, edited by Teresa Longo
24 *Iberian Cities*, edited by Joan Ramon Resina
23 *National Identities and Sociopolitical Changes in Latin America*,
    edited by Mercedes F. Durán-Cogan and Antonio Gómez-Moriana
22 *Latin American Literature and Mass Media*,
    edited by Edmundo Paz-Soldán and Debra A. Castillo
21 *Charting Memory: Recalling Medieval Spain*, edited by Stacy N. Beckwith
20 *Culture and the State in Spain: 1550–1850*,
    edited by Tom Lewis and Francisco J. Sánchez
19 *Modernism and its Margins: Reinscribing Cultural Modernity from Spain
    and Latin America*, edited by Anthony L. Geist and José B. Monleón
18 *A Revisionary History of Portuguese Literature*,
    edited by Miguel Tamen and Helena C. Buescu
17 *Cervantes and his Postmodern Constituencies*,
    edited by Anne Cruz and Carroll B. Johnson
16 *Modes of Representation in Spanish Cinema*,
    edited by Jenaro Talens and Santos Zunzunegui
15 *Framing Latin American Cinema: Contemporary Critical Perspectives*,
    edited by Ann Marie Stock
14 *Rhetoric and Politics: Baltasar Gracián and the New World Order*,
    edited by Nicholas Spadaccini and Jenaro Talens

13 *Bodies and Biases: Sexualities in Hispanic Cultures and Literatures*,
    edited by David W. Foster and Roberto Reis
12 *The Picaresque: Tradition and Displacement*, edited by Giancarlo Maiorino
11 *Critical Practices in Post-Franco Spain*,
    edited by Silvia L. López, Jenaro Talens, and Dario Villanueva
10 *Latin American Identity and Constructions of Difference*,
    edited by Amaryll Chanady
 9 *Amerindian Images and the Legacy of Columbus*,
    edited by René Jara and Nicholas Spadaccini
 8 *The Politics of Editing*, edited by Nicholas Spadaccini and Jenaro Talens
 7 *Culture and Control in Counter-Reformation Spain*,
    edited by Anne J. Cruz and Mary Elizabeth Perry
 6 *Cervantes's Exemplary Novels and the Adventure of Writing*,
    edited by Michael Nerlich and Nicholas Spadaccini
 5 *Ortega y Gasset and the Question of Modernity*, edited by Patrick H. Dust
 4 *1492-1992: Re/Discovering Colonial Writing*,
    edited by René Jara and Nicholas Spadaccini
 3 *The Crisis of Institutionalized Literature in Spain*,
    edited by Wlad Godzich and Nicholas Spadaccini
 2 *Autobiography in Early Modern Spain*,
    edited by Nicholas Spadaccini and Jenaro Talens
 1 *The Institutionalization of Literature in Spain*,
    edited by Wlad Godzich and Nicholas Spadaccini

www.ingramcontent.com/pod-product-compliance
Lightning Source LLC
Chambersburg PA
CBHW030105010526
44116CB00005B/98